CONTEMPORARY ECONOMIC PROBLEMS 1979

American Enterprise Institute

CONTEMPORARY ECONOMIC PROBLEMS 1979

William Fellner, Project Director

American Enterprise Institute for Public Policy Research
Washington, D.C.

ISBN 0-8447-1334-1

ISSN 0149-9130

Printed in the United States of America

CONTRIBUTORS

William Fellner—*Project Director*

Sterling professor of economics emeritus at Yale University, former member of the Council of Economic Advisers, and past president of the American Economic Association. Resident scholar with the American Enterprise Institute.

Phillip Cagan

Professor of economics at Columbia University, research staff of the National Bureau of Economic Research, and former senior staff economist for the Council of Economic Advisers. Adjunct scholar with the American Enterprise Institute.

Barry R. Chiswick

Research professor, department of economics and Survey Research Laboratory, University of Illinois at Chicago Circle, and former senior staff economist for the Council of Economic Advisers. Adjunct scholar with the American Enterprise Institute.

Edward F. Denison

Associate director for national economic accounts for the Bureau of Economic Analysis, U.S. Department of Commerce, senior fellow emeritus of the Brookings Institution, and former associate director of research of the Committee for Economic Development.

Gottfried Haberler

Galen L. Stone professor of international trade emeritus at Harvard University, and past president of the American Economic Association and International Economic Association. Resident scholar with the American Enterprise Institute.

CONTENTS

PART TWO

THE INFLATIONARY ENVIRONMENT

PART THREE
SPECIAL PROBLEMS

PREFACE

This is the fourth annual volume of a series of studies developing from an ongoing project of the American Enterprise Institute. The studies deal with problems many of which have all along belonged among the main topics of economic analysis, and all of which are relevant to a discussion of contemporary policy. The volume has resulted from the work of economists who have discussed their research with each other on several occasions during this year, as they have in previous years. In the prefaces to the preceding volumes of *Contemporary Economic Problems*, the jointness of our interest in a basic set of problems confronting the American economy was described, and this need not be repeated on the present occasion. The titles of the sections will rightly suggest to the reader that the studies have to do with difficulties that have developed in an inflationary era and with the relationship between the macro- and the microeconomic aspects of these, as well as with issues of economic policy that need to be faced in the effort to overcome the difficulties.

W. F.

Part One

The American Productivity Trends

The Declining Growth of American Productivity: An Introductory Note

William Fellner

(1) *The problem.* The pronounced reduction of productivity growth in the United States has become one of the most intriguing adverse developments on the economic scene. From 1948 to 1969, the average yearly increase in output per worker's hour in the private business sector was about 3 percent, and the increase was well in excess of 2 percent during any reasonably chosen subperiod during that span. The yearly increase was 2.3 percent even during the subsequent four years, 1969 to 1973. For 1973–1977 the yearly increase dropped to 1.0 percent; and a similar increase from 1977 to 1978 held the average for the five-year period 1973–1978 at about the same level. In light of the supply behavior of the inputs, an attribution of this low rate of productivity increase to a fall in the output level below the "potential" in the terminal year of the period would be unconvincing. Although this paper concerns the private business sector as a whole,[1] it is worth noting that for manufacturing viewed separately, the trend in output per worker's hour weakened from an annual rate of 2.8 percent for 1948–1973 to 1.8 percent for 1973–1977 and to 1.6 percent for 1973–1978.

The present note is followed by Herbert Stein's brief analysis of the remarkable fact that so far the significant slackening of our productivity trend has been accompanied not by a slackening but by a steepening of the trend in per capita disposable income and consumption. Stein's explanation of this divergence of trends was included in his contribution to the June 1979 issue of the *AEI Economist* and is

---

[1] Including the government would lower all these rates of productivity increase. The data are based on statistics published by the U.S. Bureau of Labor Statistics. Worker's hours used for estimation are "hours paid." These used to be called "manhours" but, in view of female participation in the labor force, the BLS now calls them "hours of all persons." I shall use the briefer term "worker's hours."

reproduced here. His analysis helps to place in focus a broader complex of problems of which the productivity problem is an essential part. The three papers following Stein's relate specifically to the significant weakening of our productivity growth. The study by John Kendrick, which was prepared for this series, is followed by a reprint of an article by Edward Denison from *Basis Point*, a periodical published by the Equitable Assurance Society of the United States. That article is accompanied by a brief introductory comment by Denison. The section on productivity concludes with an appraisal by Mark Perlman of issues in the current debate.

Both Kendrick and Denison have developed general analytical frameworks for appraising productivity trends. Their systems are similar in some essential respects, but different in others. Those who are interested in these problems should hope that the two authors will continue to explore the results that can be obtained on consistently maintained sets of assumptions. Those who use the results in their own work have reason to be eclectic in choosing among the assumptions Denison and Kendrick make; but it would be a loss to the profession here and abroad if specialists in this area adopted this kind of eclecticism instead of remaining within their frameworks. A case can be made for flexibility, but it is the reader who should have it.

The present context calls for such flexibility on the reader's part. Thinking his way through the contributions of Denison and Kendrick, a reader will ask whether, directly or indirectly, they do not suggest that the weakening of the productivity trend is attributable in part to changes in the social-political environment that are of recent origin or that have gradually accumulated to a "critical mass." When the environment changes, it is particularly important to keep an open mind about specific features of explanatory frameworks that were designed to perform well on the past record.

(2) *Policy-related "suspects."* Some of the recent difficulties are apt to be related directly to the political process. The list of such "suspects" includes uncertainties and distortions created by inflationary policies; tax disincentives reducing the amount of investment in productive activities that are risky for the individual investor; and the specific uncertainties, reduction of competition, and burden of paper work caused by administrative controls and regulations. Another suspect is a legal-institutional setting conducive to a lessened emphasis on competence and work effort, though nothing identifiable as legal or institutional is a necessary condition of changes in attitudes in this regard. Several items on this list have the unwelcome property

of being self-reinforcing. By way of illustration, in an economy in which, partly as a result of inflationary policies, the increase in output per worker's hour in the private business sector has dropped to less than 1 percent annually, the money wage trend compatible with non-inflationary conditions is very moderate, and the adjustment period for restoring noninflationary conditions is therefore likely to be lengthened.

In the spirit of long-wave hypotheses of economic development it may be tempting to speculate also about a slower pace of new inventions for industrial innovations. Such speculations relate to an area that merely *overlaps* the list of policy-related suspects, but an overlap does exist because speculations about long waves are hard to distinguish from arguments suggesting insufficiency of market incentives for innovative activity in a risky environment. All these factors have to do with the political subordination of long-run economic efficiency to other objectives, and thus raise the question of what price the nation wishes to pay for attempts to achieve these other objectives.

Institutional arrangements reflecting the subordination of long-run economic efficiency to other objectives have often been introduced in the name of equity, as interpreted in the political process. Some of these do express consciously and widely held value judgments, but by no means do all. Even with respect to policies that do reflect widely held value judgments there exists a significant question of trade-offs, because only a very limited number of objectives is held with little regard to economic cost. One may hope that the near-collapse of the productivity trend will direct attention to the problem of trade-offs—all the more because the conviction is spreading that the objectives receiving priority over long-run economic efficiency have often been poorly served. Inflationary policies have clearly not served any reasonable objective successfully, nor have several of the other measures included in the list of suspects.

Denison's comparison of the period 1973–1976 with 1948–1969 suggests that the 1973–1976 average yearly productivity trend has been reduced by nearly 2 percentage points by factors he regards as unexplained, even after allowance for the adverse productivity consequences of the sharp increase in energy prices.[2] This part of the reduction between the two periods may well have resulted, at least in large part, from factors falling in the suspect area. Kendrick's results suggest that, 0.9 percentage point of the weakening of the an-

---

[2] Without allowance for energy, Denison obtains an unexplained component slightly exceeding 2 percentage points.

nual increases between the periods 1948–1966 and 1973–1978 is attributable to two factors alone: the reduced contribution of the advancement of knowledge and government regulations. The conclusions of the two authors overlap in some respects, but they are not identical. Nor are their approaches or the periods they chose for comparison identical. While I will try to cut across these differences, an understanding of the present state of productivity analysis demands a careful study of these authors in the original.

As I see it, the main problem at this stage of the debate is whether a reasonable interpretation of this weakening in the productivity trend can avoid including some of the policy-related factors that reflect the subordination of long-run economic efficiency to other purposes. I believe that by now the change is very difficult to explain without allowances for factors of that kind. This suggestion will be supported by a piece of analysis that remains noncommittal concerning many specific assumptions that Denison and Kendrick need to make to construct their comprehensive systems of growth accounting. But it will be argued that this is exceedingly unlikely to weaken the conclusions here.

(3) *How much can be explained without allowance for the policy-related suspects?* In suggesting an answer to this question I will compare 1973–1977 with 1948–1973, although other plausible choices of periods for comparison show an even steeper decline of productivity growth. Underlying the reasoning in this paper is that that part of the weakening in the productivity trend that is *not* explained in Table 1 is very likely due to the political-institutional suspects described in the preceding section. The table is intended to explain that part of the weakening of the trend which it is reasonable to attribute to factors *not* falling in that area (see lines 2 through 5).

The items included in the table call for explanation.

(1) Lines 2 and 3 (age-sex composition and farm-nonfarm transfer) express generally accepted assumptions of productivity experts, and line 4 (energy) contains an upward adjustment of an estimate by Denison based on George Perry's work. As concerns the future, the new difficulties in the area of energy supply could call for further raising the allowance in line 4.

(2) Line 5 (safety-health, environment, and crime) includes one-half of Denison's 0.4 percentage point estimate of the cost of these items. This inclusion is viewed as proper, since expenditures on these forms of protection promote long-run economic efficiency, and hence the whole amount does not represent a diversion to other goals.

TABLE 1

Weakening of the Productivity Trend from 1948–1973 to 1973–1977: Derivation of the Component Falling in the Suspect Area

	(1) 1948–1973	(2) 1973–1977	(3) Difference (1 minus 2)	(4) Reduction of Difference from Preceding Line
(1) Average yearly rate of increase in output per worker's hour in private business sector.	2.9	1.0	1.9	0
(2) Same if age-sex composition of work force had remained unchanged.	3.1	1.3	1.8	0.1
(3) Same if also no transfer of resources had occurred from farm to nonfarm sector.	2.7	1.3	1.4	0.4
(4) Same if also no shift had recently occurred from energy-intensive to capital and labor-intensive methods.	2.7	1.6	1.1	0.3
(5) Same with further modification that *proportion* of resources representing costs of protecting safety and health and the physical environment, and costs of crime against property, is assumed to have risen recently only *half as much* as it has.[a]	2.7	1.8	0.9	0.2
(6) Residual component falling in the suspect area.[b]	—	—	0.9	—

[a] Other half of costs included in line 6.

[b] Same as line 5, column 3. Obtained by deducting the sum of the entries in column 4 from the first entry in column 3.

The other half of these estimated costs does, however, belong among the suspects. In the first place, the arbitrary design of the present health-safety and environmental regulations pays very little attention to achieving the yield at costs that are commensurate with the benefits. Second, the rapidly rising costs of crime against property are also included in Denison's estimate, and presumption is strong that more efficient law enforcement could accomplish better results at lower cost.

(3) The table takes no account of the increase between the two periods in the level of education of workers. If it did, the "unexplained" component of the productivity weakening, pointing to the suspect area, would be larger by several decimal points. Education was not considered, partly because in analyzing an elusive complex of problems it is preferable to understate rather than overstate an argument, and partly because I am reluctant to postulate that the relationship between formal education and productivity can be projected from the earlier to the later period.

(4) Because the table treats as a residual (line 6) any slackening in the productivity trend related to the suspect area, it relegates to the residual the reduction of the rate of increase of the capital-labor ratio, which according to some estimates fell from a 2.3 percent annual rate for 1948–1973 to 1.9 percent for 1973–1977.[3] The capital-labor ratio relates the capital stock to unweighted worker hours (our measure of labor input), and the decline by 0.4 percentage point between the two periods turns out to result from the declining growth rate of the capital stock with practically no change of the growth rate of the labor input. It is this negative effect of the reduction in capital growth on the increase in output per worker's hour that is viewed here as belonging in the area of the policy-related suspects. Some may object that savings and thus capital formation are limited by the "given" behavioral functions of the public and are largely uninfluenced by the suspect policies. But such objections are unconvincing, first, because in the recent period the personal saving ratio *rose* somewhat, and it is the clearly policy-related corporate saving rate that declined to a low level by past standards; and second, be-

---

[3] The 0.4 percentage point reduction of the yearly increase of the capital-labor ratio is based on estimates of the so-called gross capital stock in the private business sector, not on the so-called net stock. In other words, discards rather than straight-line depreciation allowances are deducted from the gross investment flow. During most of the three decades considered here, the net stock grew faster than the gross stock, but the contrary is true of recent years; the result is that the difference between the 1948-1973 and 1973-1977 rates of increase would be greater if the net rather than the gross capital stock were under consideration.

cause the savings available for capital formation are obtained by deducting the equally clearly policy-related government deficits from the private savings. Thus whatever the magnitude of any given reduction of the rate of increase of the capital-labor ratio on the trend in output per worker's hour, that factor does not belong in the table.[4]

(5) The analysis fails to make a number of specific attributions to causes that Denison and Kendrick, in different ways, do take into account. But our failure to make these further attributions to causes is very unlikely to be responsible for our inability to explain the weakening of the productivity trend without reference to the suspects. In fact, we have seen that for differently chosen periods Denison suggests a much larger unexplained component, and in Kendrick's framework almost 1 percent per annum shows merely as a result of a lesser contribution of the advancement of knowledge and of additional government regulations.

As for causes omitted from the table, changing trends in the output mix other than the practical ending of the farm-nonfarm transfer do not seem to have contributed to the explanation of the slackening of the overall trend. Nor was the proportion of new workers, presumably still low-productivity trainees, greater in the later than in the earlier period *except* to the extent that this is taken care of in the table under the heading of the work force's changing age-sex composition. Once allowance is made for this change (as it is in line 2 of the table), an increased inexperienced-worker effect would have to originate in a higher annual rate of increase in the

---

[4] The customary methods, including that used by Denison, would impute no more than a 0.1 to 0.2 percentage point weakening of the trend in output per hour to the reduction of the increase in the capital-labor ratio from 1948-1973 to 1973-1977. This small attribution disregards the possible complementarity between the growth of the capital stock and the introduction of new technological methods due to improved knowledge. Denison argues rightly that the relation between technological advance and the *use of new types of capital goods* does not carry over in any simple fashion into a relation between technological advance and the *growth of the capital stock*, because stepping up the rate of technological advance becomes associated *also* with a higher rate of scrapping of old capital goods. On the other hand, it seems unclear how complete this offset is, since the most advanced technological methods often coexist with less advanced ones over a considerable period. At a different analytical level, essentially the same question—that relating to the proportion of the output increment attributable to the growth of the capital stock—has given rise to controversies about how to *measure* the increase in the stock. All these are controversial methodological problems, and it would be possible to raise the estimated contribution of the slackening of the capital growth beyond the 0.2 percentage point referred to in this note. Although the problem is significant for productivity analysis in general, we can circumvent it here. We have good reasons for placing the item in the policy-related suspect area rather than listing it in the table.

unweighted labor input, which in reality was just about the same from 1973 to 1977 as from 1948 to 1973.

It is sometimes suggested that the lowering of the utilization rate of the labor force and of industrial capacities from 1973 to 1977 contributes to explaining the reduction of the productivity trend, and thus partly "exonerates" the "suspects." In the present context that suggestion is unconvincing because it itself reaches deep down into the area of our policy-related suspects. Given the inflationary antecedents and various other policy-determined factors, it would be highly unrealistic to assume that the American economy was operating under capacity in 1978, and the 1973–1978 productivity trend was even weaker than the 1973–1977 one.

Even the 0.9 percentage point estimate of the unexplained component falling in the suspect area ignores the downward bias of that estimate involved in the choice of periods. The analysis therefore suggests that the causes of at least 1 percentage point annual slackening of the trend in output worker's hour can be found among the suspects. Eliminating a shortfall of this size would double the actual 1.0 percent productivity increase observed from 1973 to 1977. In thirty years, when today's teenagers will still be in middle age, a 1 percent annual shortfall will have cumulated to a 26 percent reduction below the annual output that would otherwise have been achievable at that time. The problem is not de minimis by any acceptable interpretation.

I see no reason to modify the conclusion that, without the policy-related suspects, about 1 percentage point of the recent worsening of the productivity trend is exceedingly difficult to explain. This conclusion implies merely a modest manipulation of the crude data— those summarized in the table. Yet on general grounds skepticism is justified concerning all steps involving attributions to causes. I will therefore end by taking another look at the crude data.

(4) *Returning to the crude data.* These data show a very large reduction of the postwar trend in output per worker's hour for the private business sector. The average annual rate of increase has fallen from roughly 3 percent in 1948–1973 to about 1 percent in 1973–1977. At present we cannot make a reasonable guess of the further worsening that the complications of energy supply might cause. Aside from this, we would conclude that in due—but unpredictable and distant—time nearly 1 percentage point of this 2 point difference would be apt to disappear even without a determined attack on the policy problems posed by the precipitous decline. This is because *in due time* the shift in the age-sex composition of the work force

toward lower-productivity workers would presumably stop anyhow, and so would the rise of the proportion of resources absorbed by the protection of health, safety, and the physical environment—and, we may hope, by crime.[5] Further, the presumptive decline of the growth rate of the labor force would raise the rate of increase of the capital-labor ratio even at unchanging rates of increase of the capital stock, which in itself would act to raise labor productivity.[6]

Indeed, other things equal, a small fraction of the 1 percentage point improvement might materialize soon because of the impending reduction of the labor-force weight of teenagers. But if the policy aspects of the problem are ignored, a substantial proportion of the recent worsening would be apt to remain, even if the deterioration in the conditions of energy supply fails to materialize. Moreover, quite aside from any automatic resumption of part of the earlier good performance, the neglect of the policy-related suspects appears to be very costly.

Whatever one's reservations, it seems clear that not all of the precipitous reduction in the productivity trend can reasonably be attributed to immutable factors. It seems clear also that promotion of long-run economic efficiency deserves increased emphasis among the policy objectives when there are strong indications that the costs of subordinating it, or of simply neglecting it, are greater than most people expected, and when doubt is spreading about the achievement of competing objectives. The main suspects are inflationary policies, a tax structure that creates disincentives, inefficiencies caused by controls and regulations, and hiring and job-organization practices that place too little emphasis on competence and work effort. Civilized people will, to be sure, deny to pure economic efficiency the highest rank among their values. Yet it would be a mistake to believe that a modern industrial country and its civilization can be maintained in a healthy state if a productivity record such as that now shaping up

---

[5] In terms of the table, this would mean that, other things equal, the 0.3 point augmentation in column 2 (moving from line 1 to line 2) and *twice* the 0.2 point augmentation in the same column (moving from line 4 to line 5) would come about "automatically" (*twice* in the latter case because the line 5 estimate includes only half of the cost for those items; the other half is included among the suspects of line 6). This explains an "automatic" improvement by 0.7 percentage points. The next sentence in the text raises the 0.7 to roughly 1 percentage point.

[6] This latter effect—in contrast to those explained in note 5—is not identifiable in the table. The reason is that we interpret the reduction of the rate of increase of the capital-labor ratio from 1948-1973 to 1973-1977 as a policy-related suspect (not as belonging in the table), because the rate of increase in unweighted worker hours was unchanged between those two periods: it was the growth rate of the capital stock that declined.

is accepted "hands down." This to me seems the essential point to be kept in mind. A lasting deterioration of our economic productivity trend would far more likely be associated with a weakening than with a strengthening of our performance in other areas.

Why Did Consumption
Not Reflect the Slackening
of the Productivity Trend?

Herbert Stein

Two basic measures of the welfare of individuals improved more rapidly in the decade 1969 to 1979 than on the average of the two decades 1949 to 1969 (see Table 1). Real disposable personal income (DPI, personal income after taxes) per capita rose at the annual rates of 2.64 percent in the more recent period and of 2.25 percent in the earlier period. Real personal consumption expenditures (PCE) per capita rose at an annual rate of 2.59 percent in the more recent period and 2.07 percent in the earlier period. (These results would be as strong if the last year were compared with the earlier decades. The results do not conceal any deterioration in the past year.)

This improvement of per capita living standards occurred despite a marked worsening in the growth rate of output per worker. In the past decade real gross national product (GNP) per employee rose at a rate of only 0.82 percent a year, whereas in the period 1949 to 1969 it rose at a rate of 2.42 percent a year.

How did the standard of living, as measured by per capita disposable income or consumption, rise faster while output per employee rose much more slowly? There are two explanations.

First, the number of workers per hundred people in the population was steady in the first two decades, but in the past decades the number rose substantially, from about 40 per hundred to about 45 per hundred. So we offset a good deal of the slowdown of output per employee by working more.

Second, in the earlier period, from 1949 to 1969, we increased the proportion of the GNP devoted to defense, from 6.44 percent to 8.84 percent. In the past ten years, however, the share going to defense fell to 4.55 percent. As a result, the output available for private

TABLE 1
Developments in the American Economy

	1949	1969	% Change Annual Rate 1949–69	First Quarter 1969	First Quarter 1979	% Change Annual Rate 1969:1 to 1979:1
Population (millions)	149.2	202.7	1.54	202.0	219.6	0.84
Employees (millions)	60.3	82.1	1.55	81.3	98.7	1.95
Employees per capita	.404	.405	0.01	.402	.449	1.11
Real GNP[a]	490.7	1,078.8	4.02	1,074.8	1,416.3	2.80
Real GNP per employee[b]	8,138	13,147	2.42	13,221	14,351	0.82
Real GNP per capita[b]	3,289	5,322	2.44	5,321	6,449	1.94
Real PCE[a]	320.0	655.4	3.65	649.9	912.4	3.45
Real PCE per capita[b]	2,145	3,233	2.07	3,217	4,155	2.59
Real defense expenditures[a]	31.6	95.4	5.68	96.0	64.4	−3.91
Defense as % of GNP	6.44	8.84	1.60	8.93	4.55	−6.52
Real DPI[a]	336.1	712.3	3.83	701.8	990.2	3.50
Real DPI per capita[b]	2,253	3,514	2.25	3,474	4,509	2.64

NOTE: GNP = gross national product; PCE = personal consumption expenditures; DPI = disposable personal income.
[a] In billions of 1972 dollars.
[b] In 1972 dollars.

consumption rose less than GNP in the first period and more than GNP in the second period.

We have speeded up the increase of per capita consumption, in spite of producing less per worker, by putting in more work and reducing the share of our national output going to defense. Certainly, we would have been better off if output per worker had continued to rise as rapidly as it did in the first two decades. But whether, when all things are considered, our condition improved as rapidly in the past decade as in the two previous ones depends on the answers to some hard questions, including:

• Have conditions in the world changed so that our security can be adequately maintained with a much lower share of our GNP, or have we been weakening the nation and endangering our security so we could consume more?

• Is the additional input of labor, mainly the additional work of married women, to be considered a net loss, especially because of possible damage to traditional family values, or should it be considered a net gain, representing the reduction of previous inhibitions, which liberated women from dependence and drudgery?

• How should we evaluate the risk of living in an inflationary world? Incomes on the average have kept pace with inflation, and this has probably been true for a large majority of all individuals. But inflation has increased the risk of falling behind. People are conscious of this risk and may have an exaggerated perception of it. This is certainly one reason for the prevailing degree of unhappiness about the economy.

Productivity Trends and the Recent Slowdown: Historical Perspective, Causal Factors, and Policy Options

John W. Kendrick

Summary

The pace of growth in the U.S. business economy has averaged close to 4 percent a year since 1800. Increases in total factor productivity (TFP), reflecting chiefly cost-reducing innovations in production technology, have gradually accelerated from 0.3 percent a year throughout most of the nineteenth century to 2.4 percent after World War II. This has offset the gradual deceleration in the growth of labor, capital, and natural resource inputs and doubled the rate of increase in real product per capita to over 2 percent a year in this century.

Since 1966 there has been a disturbing deceleration in the growth of TFP down to 1.6 percent a year through 1973 and only 0.8 percent in 1973–1978. On the basis of Denison's growth accounting framework, the chief causes of the slowdown appear to have been significant reductions in the contribution of advances in applied productive knowledge, changes in labor quality (chiefly because of shifts in the age-sex composition of employment), and volume-related factors. Diminishing returns to domestic natural resources and a negative impact of government intervention in the business economy had a lesser but still significant influence.

Looking ahead to the 1980–1990 decade, the U.S. Department of Labor projects a growth of real business product of about 3.4 percent a year, assuming no major new policies to promote productivity. Its projection implies that TFP growth will accelerate modestly to 1.6 percent a year, up from the 0.8 percent of 1973–1978 but still well below the 2.8 percent average for the 1948–1966 subperiod. Behind the improvement will be favorable shifts in the age-sex mix of employment and in volume-related factors, on the assumption of a high rate of *employment in 1990. However, continued declines in the average quality of natural resources, negative effects of interindustry shifts of factor inputs, and a leveling of advances in technology will prevent a significant resurgence of TFP growth.*

The deceleration in growth of real product per hour was greater than in TFP because growth of capital per unit of labor input decelerated as the growth of the labor force and hours worked accelerated substantially after 1966. In the 1980 decade the projected retardation in rate of growth of the labor force and hours worked and the acceleration in growth of capital per hour will cause the growth of labor productivity to improve somewhat more than that in TFP. Even so, the Bureau of Labor Statistics (BLS) is projecting an average increase in real product per hour of only 2.1 percent a year for 1980–1990, compared with 3.5 percent for 1948–1966.

In my view, a positive program to release the dynamic forces of the private economy could raise the rate of growth of TFP close to the 2.8 percent a year experienced in the two decades prior to 1966 and raise the rate of increase in real business product to 4.8 percent. The centerpiece of the program would be the pursuit of macroeconomic policies, including significant reductions in business income tax rates, that would raise the rate of return on investment by about 2 percentage points (closer to that of the mid-1960s) and increase the proportion of income saved and invested about 1.5 percentage points. This would not remove the biases against saving and investment now present in the U.S. tax system, but it would reduce the biases sufficiently to have a marked stimulative effect. Together with measures to reduce the incentives for early retirement of workers, the increase of total factor input would be raised by about 0.5 percentage point.

The increase in rates of return and in tangible investment, embodying new technology, would also help speed up creation and application of advances in knowledge. In view of the high social rate of return on research and development (R&D), however, I recommend an investment tax credit or other subsidy for privately financed R&D and a substantial increase in government R&D outlays in selected areas, including basic research. These measures could increase the contribution of technological progress to productivity by 0.5 percentage point—almost back to the rate prior to the mid-1960s, before the ratio of R&D to GNP began to decline sharply.

There are other policy options available to promote education and training, health, factor mobility, and economic efficiency and to improve the net effect of governmental activities on unit real costs of business. The impact of these measures will be reenforced by wider opportunities for economies of scale and a more stable economic growth rate.

An economic growth rate in excess of 4.5 percent is not the most probable outcome for the decade ahead and will not be achieved without broad public and official understanding of the requisite measures and their benefits. If it is attained real income per capita will increase at a rate of almost 3.5 percent a year in the 1980s. The accelerated growth of productivity would also help reduce the impact of money wage-rate increases on unit costs, contributing to reduced inflation and increased international competitiveness of U.S. products.

Introduction

One of the notable achievements of the U.S. economy has been a relatively strong secular rate of economic growth for the almost two centuries since 1800 for which reasonably reliable estimates of national income and product are available. More significant as an indicator of economic progress, real income per capita has grown at accelerating rates from the late nineteenth century until the mid-1960s, reflecting acceleration in the rate of productivity growth offsetting deceleration in the rate of growth of population and factor inputs.

Although in recent years the economic growth associated with increasing population has been widely questioned, it would appear from the behavior of most members of our society that they still aspire to increase real income per person. Further, the increases in total tangible factor productivity that make this income increase possible reflect reductions in requirements for human and nonhuman resources per unit of output. The resources themselves have desirable alternative uses—leisure in the case of labor; consumption in the case of capital formation; and recreational use or conservation for future use in the case of natural resources. Investments should be made in productivity-enhancing activities up to the point at which the expected rate of return from cost-reductions equals the marginal cost of the funds.

The retardation in growth of productivity and real income per capita that began in the mid-1960s has been a source of some concern. Not only are the positive material benefits of economic progress reduced, but also social conflict over income distribution is sharpened. The slowing of real income growth per capita also contributes to the acceleration of wage demands as workers try to regain former rates of increase in real income. This exacerbates inflationary tendencies when not accompanied by a similar acceleration in productivity. In those industries particularly affected by the decline in productivity advance, international competitiveness of American producers has been reduced. Further, slower growth of real income unaccompanied by rising saving rates has raised the specter of "capital shortages" in the years ahead in a normative sense. That is, the capital formation projected to be required to meet social as well as private goals exceeds the prospective saving of the community unless real rates of interest are allowed to rise significantly.

The disadvantageous aspects of a slowing productivity trend have naturally raised questions as to what changes in government policies could facilitate or promote a stronger rate of advance in the future. Those of us with a liberal economic philosophy address the question with full recognition that the proper province of government is not to mandate a target rate of growth of real product or productivity—nor is it within the power of government to do so. To a major degree in our modern type of predominantly private enterprise market economy, the rate of growth does and should reflect the composite decisions of myriad households with respect to work and leisure, saving and expenditures, and allocation of expenditures particularly between current consumption and investments, including investments in self. It should also reflect the decisions of enterprises with respect to allocation of net income between disbursement to owners and saving, and decisions to invest in various types of tangible and intangible capital required to expand output- and income-producing capacity. In this process financial markets are relied upon to equilibrate the supply with the demand for loanable funds, and thus the rate of time discount of individuals with the expected rate of return on investments. Similarly, product markets are relied upon to reallocate resources through time to reflect changes in conditions of supply and demand attendant on changes in technology, resources, preferences, institutions, and other dynamic forces.

A major force behind technological advance is the pressure of competition as firms seek to widen or preserve profit margins by cost-reducing or market-expanding innovations. Barring monopolistic control over price, above-average profit margins tend to be competed away as other firms imitate the innovators. The only way above-average margins can be maintained is by a firm's continuing to stay technologically ahead of the pack. Thus, competitive markets are a mighty engine of progress, with abnormal profits under competition recognized to be socially desirable as both incentive and reward for superior performance.

This is not to minimize the inevitably important role of government in economic growth and change. First and foremost, government (federal, state, and local) is responsible for developing, enforcing, and modifying—as circumstances dictate—the framework of laws and regulations within which the private economy operates. Laws and regulations, both those which are general and those which are sector or industry specific, have different impacts on costs and incentives and affect rates and directions of growth as well as resource allocation in given periods.

Second, government budgets affect the economic factors: types and rates of taxation affect disposable incomes and investment incentives; types and levels of expenditures, particularly the allocation of outlays among public consumption and investment objectives, affect growth both directly and, by their impact on the private sector, indirectly.

Third, governmental conduct of fiscal and monetary policies and its operation of other control levers influence both the rate and the degree of stability of economic growth, which are themselves interrelated.

Fourth, the proportion of resources commanded by government and changes in productivity in the use of those resources affect the national growth rate. More generally, the efficiency and finesse with which government performs its functions affect attitudes and expectations of private actors and thus the rate of economic progress generally.

It is appropriate, then, to set forth various policy options available to government to accelerate rates of growth of productivity and real income per capita within the constraints of economic rationality. The objective is confined to economic progress, not total economic growth, since the latter involves growth of population and labor force, which are generally not appropriate direct policy targets— although to the extent that government policies are not neutral in these areas, changes might be in order.

The initial section of this paper consists of a summary review of the historical record of growth of real product, aggregate and per head, and total tangible factor productivity in the U.S. business economy since 1800, by significant subperiods. In the second section I discuss the major causal factors behind productivity increase and apply the analytical framework to a quantitative analysis of the U.S. economic growth over the periods 1929–1948, 1948–1966, 1966–1973, and 1973–1978, with emphasis on the causes of the productivity slowdown since 1966. At the same time, I project the rates of growth of inputs, productivity, and real product in aggregate and per head from 1980 to 1990, assuming no change in major governmental policies. In the concluding section I offer a menu of policy options whereby the federal government could facilitate and promote economic progress subject to the usual economic constraints. An alternative projection of real product and productivity for the decade 1980–1990 quantifies the potential effects of a positive program for liberating the forces of progress in the U.S. economy.

The Historical Record of Growth

The analytical framework used to present the historical growth record is shown in Table 1. The table is confined to the U.S. private domestic business economy, for which independent estimates of outputs (real product) and tangible factor inputs are available. But since the business sector contributes about 85 percent of GNP in recent

TABLE 1

U.S. DOMESTIC BUSINESS ECONOMY:
REAL GROSS PRODUCT, FACTOR INPUTS, AND PRODUCTIVITY RATIOS FOR
SELECTED SUBPERIODS, 1800–1973
(average annual percentage rates of change)

	1800– 1855	1855– 1890	1889– 1919	1919– 1948	1948– 1973
Real gross product	4.2	4.0	3.9	3.0	3.8
Population	3.1	2.4	1.8	1.2	1.5
Real product per capita	1.1	1.6	2.1	1.8	2.3
Total tangible factor input	3.9	3.6	2.2	0.8	2.4
Labor	3.7	2.8	1.8	0.6	0.7
Capital	4.3	4.6	3.1	1.2	2.5
Total factor productivity ratio	0.3	0.3	1.7	2.2	2.4
Labor	0.5	1.1	2.0	2.4	3.1
Capital	−0.1	−0.6	0.7	1.6	1.3

NOTE: The weights for capital in each of the successive periods, beginning with 1800-1855, are as follows: 0.35, 0.45, 0.34, 0.26, 0.28. The weights for labor are 1.00 minus the weights of capital.

SOURCES: 1800-1890 based on Moses Abramovitz and Paul David, "Economic Growth in America: Historical Parables and Realities," Reprint no. 105, Center for Research in Economic Growth, Stanford University, 1973, tables 1 and 2; 1889-1973 from John W. Kendrick, *Productivity Trends in the United States* (Princeton, N.J.: Princeton University Press for the National Bureau of Economic Research, 1961); estimates from 1948 forward revised and extended by the author.

years, according to the official Commerce Department estimates, and more in earlier periods, the numbers are indicative of aggregate economic growth.

Real gross product is viewed as the product of tangible factor inputs and total factor productivity. Since the record is presented in terms of average annual percentage rates of change, which are relatively small numbers, the relationship can be viewed as additive for all practical purposes. Total tangible factor input is obtained as a weighted average of human inputs (labor hours) and nonhuman capital inputs assumed to move proportionately to the real gross stocks of structures, equipment, inventories, and land. Since industry or other internal weights are not used for each class of input, the effects of interindustry shifts of resources are reflected in the productivity ratios. And since the inputs are not adjusted for quality change, changes in quality also affect measured productivity, as do changes in rates of utilization of the measured inputs.

Three productivity ratios are presented. The most significant is total (tangible) factor productivity (TFP), the ratio of real product to total tangible factor input. This ratio indicates the net saving of factor inputs per unit of output achieved over time, primarily as a result of cost-reducing innovations in the ways and means of production. Such technological advance results to an important extent from intangible investments designed to enhance the quality and efficiency of the tangible factors, particularly investments in research and development (R&D) and education and training. But there are other non–investment-related sources of productivity growth discussed in the next section.

The two "partial productivity" measures, the ratios of real product to labor and to capital inputs, reflect not only changes in productive efficiency but also substitutions among factors. Thus, the larger increase in "labor productivity" in all subperiods is due to the increase in capital relative to labor input.

Real product per capita is presented as a crude indicator of economic progress. This variable may be viewed as the product (or sum of rates of change) of total factor productivity and total input per capita.

The Record for the Aggregate Business Economy.[1] As shown in Table 1 for successive subperiods since 1800, the rate of TFP advance

---

[1] Parts of this section have been drawn from an article by the author, "The Role of Productivity in U.S. Economic Development," prepared for the *Dictionary of American Economic History* (New York: Charles Scribner's Sons, in process).

accelerated from an average 0.3 percent a year during most of the nineteenth century to 1.7 percent 1889–1919, 2.2 percent 1919–1948, and 2.4 percent during the quarter century 1948–1973. Since 1966, however, there has been a slowing in productivity growth that may indicate a retardation of the long-term trend, as discussed later.

The estimated 0.3 percent a year rate of growth in TFP prevailed both in the 1800–1855 period and in the subsequent thirty-five years on average, although there were variations during shorter subperiods. Both real product and total factor input grew almost as fast in the 1855–1890 period as in the previous fifty-five years. But there was a significant deceleration in the rate of growth of labor input, virtually offset by an acceleration in the growth rate of real capital stocks and inputs reflecting significant increases in the proportions of gross income and product saved and invested during the nineteenth century.

The rate of growth of real product per hour accelerated from 0.5 percent a year in 1800–1855 to about 1.0 percent in 1855–1890. This reflects an increase in the rate of substitution of capital for labor (the difference between the growth rates of total factor input and labor input) from 0.2 to 0.8 percent a year. This means, of course, that capital productivity, the inverse of the capital coefficient, declined at the rate of 0.6 percent a year in 1855–1890, faster than the 0.1 percent average annual rate of the earlier period.

Real income per capita grew at an average annual rate of 1.1 percent in 1800–1855, accelerating to 1.6 percent in 1855–1890 as the rate of growth of population decelerated much more than that of real gross income and product. Since the contribution of the rate of growth of total factor productivity was the same 0.3 percentage point in both periods, it is plain that the difference was the acceleration in the average annual rate of growth of total factor input per capita from 0.8 percent to 1.2 percent. The relatively small contribution of total factor productivity to rising planes of living throughout most of the nineteenth century, and the still smaller contribution to aggregate economic growth, stand in contrast to subsequent developments. Although the average rate of productivity advance throughout much of the nineteenth century seems low compared with the subsequent record, it is virtually certain that this must have been the case. For if the much higher rates prevailing since World War I were extrapolated back, levels of productivity and real income per capita in colonial times would have been much lower than other evidence indicates.

Examination of the annual time series of TFP for the private domestic economy indicates that, following the initial speeding up around 1890, the next significant acceleration in the rate of growth actually began around 1916 rather than 1919. Also, the average annual rate of 2.2 percent shown in the table was pulled down by the effects of the Great Depression. From 1916 to 1929 the rate was 2.3 percent; and again 2.3 percent from 1936 to 1948, although at a lower level since the trend line shifted downward in the early 1930s, reflecting the loss of capital outlays which could not be fully made up.

So the trend rate of 2.4 percent a year shown for the subsequent quarter century 1948–1973 does not represent a further acceleration in TFP. But there was an acceleration in the growth of real product per hour, which averaged about 2.5 percent a year in 1919–1948 when the depression years 1930–1935 are omitted, and about 3.0 percent a year from 1948 through 1973. This was due to much more rapid growth of real capital per unit of labor input after 1948 than occurred during the 1919–1948 period, which was marked by severe depression and World War II. Since the war, the much steadier pace of growth of real product and capital outlays, interrupted by only mild economic contractions, was largely responsible for the more rapid growth of real capital stocks and input than of labor force, employment, and labor input.

Since the acceleration of TFP growth during World War I, it has accounted for all the increase in real product per capita and the consequent rise in planes of living. That is, total tangible inputs grew little faster than population after 1919, so that the growth rates of real product per capita and per unit of input were roughly parallel.

Within the wider periods shown in Table 1, there were variations in rates of change of real product and TFP during significant sub-periods as measured between business cycle peak years (or cycle averages). In fact, there is some degree of positive correlation between rates of change in output and in productivity. Numbers for the subperiods since the cycle peak of 1948 are shown in Table 3. Note particularly the sharp deceleration in productivity growth after 1966, more than would be expected from the rate of growth of real product, which was only moderately below average.

Cyclically, productivity advance tends to slow before peaks in output are reached and to accelerate in advance of troughs. This performance plays an important role in the explanations of economic fluctuations, as first explained by Wesley C. Mitchell (1913) and since

25

documented by Geoffrey Moore (1975).[2] Briefly, the deceleration in productivity gains before peaks is associated with an acceleration in factor prices and unit costs, which eventually exceed price increases, squeezing profits and reducing investment commitments. Conversely, the acceleration in productivity gains before the trough was associated with declines in factor prices prior to World War II and with deceleration of increases since then. This meant that unit costs fell relative to prices, and profit margins increased, leading to an upswing in economic activity. Monetary and other factors were, of course, involved, but the behavior of productivity and unit costs in relation to prices has been an important part of cyclical sequences.

Productivity Trends by Industry Groups. The rate of productivity change in the business economy is, in effect, a weighted average of the rates of change in the component industry groups. This section provides a quick review of productivity trends for different industries over several periods since 1889, with a more detailed look at shorter subperiods bounded by cycle peak years between 1948 and 1973, plus the subperiod 1973–1976 (although it now appears that the current cycle peak will not come until after 1978). Industry productivity estimates are important in helping explain different rates of change in unit costs, prices, production, and employment. Further, they provide an approach to assessing the relative importance of the various causal factors behind productivity change, discussed in the next section.

Among the broad Standard Industrial Classification groups in Table 2, TFP in farming showed much more of an acceleration over the three periods than TFP in the private domestic economy as a whole. Between 1889 and 1919 the 0.2 percent a year increase in farm TFP was much below average (and below the average agricultural rate for much of the nineteenth century); from 1919 to 1948 the growth was almost average—pronounced acceleration began only after 1937; while the 3.3 percent increase in the final quarter century was well above average. As a consequence the rates of increase in nonfarm TFP showed much less acceleration over the three periods than those for the entire business economy.

Within the nonfarm sector, mining TFP also showed a marked acceleration from 1.6 percent during the first period to 2.4 percent in the third, although by 1970 it began to decline. On the lower end of

---

[2] Wesley C. Mitchell, *Business Cycles* (Berkeley: University of California Press, 1913); and Geoffrey Moore, "Productivity, Costs and Prices: New Light from an Old Hypothesis," in National Bureau of Economic Research, *Explorations in Economic Research*, vol. 2, no. 1 (Winter 1975), pp. 1-17.

TABLE 2

U.S. DOMESTIC ECONOMY BY MAJOR INDUSTRY GROUPS: TOTAL TANGIBLE
FACTOR PRODUCTIVITY, FOR MAJOR SUBPERIODS, 1889–1973
(average annual percentage rates of change)

Industry Group	1889–1919	1919–1948	1948–1973
Private domestic economy	1.7	2.2	2.5
Farm	0.2	1.7	3.3
Nonfarm	1.5	1.9	2.1
Mining	1.6	2.3	2.4
Contract construction	N.A.	N.A.	0.9
Manufacturing	0.7	2.9	2.3
Transportation	2.4	4.0	2.6
Communications	2.2	1.7	4.2
Electric and gas utilities	3.8	4.6	3.9
Trade	0.8	1.5	2.3
Finance, insurance, real estate	—[a]	—[a]	2.0
Services	2.2	1.0	1.7

N.A.: Not available.

[a] Output per unit of labor for finance, insurance, and real estate is shown combined with that of services in the row below.

SOURCE: John W. Kendrick, *Productivity Trends in the United States*; estimates since 1948 revised and extended by the author.

the spectrum, TFP in contract construction increased by about 1 percent a year in 1948–1973 and apparently by a bit less during the earlier periods, to judge from the available output per hour series.

Manufacturing TFP showed less than 1 percent a year increase in the 1889–1919 period, reflecting in part a rapid build-up of capital; but in the subsequent period the 2.9 percent average annual gain was above average. The regulated groups—both rail and nonrail transportation, communications, and electric and gas utilities—generally showed above-average rates of growth of TFP during all three periods. In contrast, the rates of the services sector, comprising trade and finance, insurance and real estate, as well as private services, were generally below the private domestic economy average rates—although measurement problems may impart some downward bias to growth rates in this sector.

The greater industry detail for 1948–1973, shown in Table 3 by subperiod, exhibits even greater dispersion in rates of change. Within the manufacturing group, rates of change ranged from less than 1 percent a year for primary metals, on average, up to nearly 4 percent

TABLE 3

U.S. PRIVATE DOMESTIC BUSINESS ECONOMY BY MAJOR INDUSTRY SECTORS AND
GROUPS: TOTAL TANGIBLE FACTOR PRODUCTIVTY, BY SUBPERIODS, 1948–1976
(average annual percentage rates of change)

	1948-76	1948-53	1953-57	1957-60	1960-66	1966-69	1969-73	1973-76
Private domestic business	2.3	3.4	2.0	2.1	3.4	1.5	1.8	0.7
Farming	3.0	5.4	2.7	3.8	2.3	3.2	2.8	1.1
Manufacturing	2.1	2.9	1.0	1.1	3.9	0.9	2.7	0.1
Food	2.9	3.3	2.6	1.1	4.0	1.1	2.8	3.8
Tobacco	2.6	1.1	3.5	4.8	2.0	3.5	3.0	1.1
Textiles	3.0	0.8	3.6	1.9	8.2	0.1	2.7	0.7
Apparel	2.5	2.8	1.4	2.0	2.0	0.8	5.5	2.5
Lumber	2.9	0.4	5.8	1.5	7.2	1.6	4.9	-4.7
Furniture	1.8	2.2	2.7	0.1	2.7	2.0	1.0	0.8
Paper	2.0	3.7	-0.4	1.7	2.8	2.7	5.3	-3.5
Printing and publishing	1.5	2.2	2.8	0.6	3.1	0.2	0.7	-1.0
Chemicals	3.2	1.8	4.3	2.5	5.0	2.9	4.7	-0.9
Petroleum	2.1	1.8	0.6	5.4	4.1	0.8	2.3	-1.7
Rubber	1.8	2.1	-2.4	5.7	3.6	3.2	1.4	-1.5
Leather	1.1	-2.0	0.7	3.0	3.1	-0.3	2.1	1.2
Stone, clay, and glass	1.3	2.4	0.1	1.1	2.4	0.8	1.6	-0.9
Primary metals	0.1	3.2	-1.5	-4.1	3.3	-3.1	1.8	-3.9
Fabricated metals	1.2	1.4	0.3	2.0	2.6	1.5	0.9	-0.9
Machinery, nonelectrical	1.1	2.5	-1.1	1.1	2.6	-0.2	2.3	-0.5
Electrical machinery	3.7	4.4	2.0	2.6	6.2	2.9	3.7	1.6

Transportation equipment	2.7	3.2	1.5	3.3	4.2	−0.5	2.6	3.0
Instruments	2.2	4.6	0.6	3.0	3.5	3.1	−0.4	0
Miscellaneous	2.7	4.0	3.3	2.6	1.6	3.1	2.8	1.6
Nonfarm nonmanufacturing	2.0	2.5	2.1	2.2	2.8	1.3	1.1	0.8
Mining	1.7	4.1	2.2	0.6	4.6	1.7	−0.7	−4.6
Contract construction	1.0	2.6	1.8	4.2	2.0	−0.3	−5.0	1.8
Transportation	2.4	1.8	2.7	2.3	4.2	1.9	2.3	0.3
Communications	4.2	5.7	4.5	5.9	3.5	3.4	2.5	4.3
Electric and gas utilities	3.0	6.8	4.7	4.6	3.7	2.7	0.2	−3.8
Finance and insurance	0.1	1.2	1.7	−1.5	−0.2	0.9	−2.2	0.8
Real estate	2.8	4.4	2.9	3.8	2.6	1.3	1.2	3.0
Trade	2.0	2.1	1.6	1.8	3.6	1.0	2.9	0
Services	1.6	1.7	1.6	0.8	1.6	2.2	2.3	0.3

SOURCE: John W. Kendrick and Elliot Grossman, *Productivity Trends in the United States: Trends and Cycles* (Baltimore: Johns Hopkins University Press, 1979).

for electrical machinery. Within nonmanufacturing, average gains in TFP ranged from about 1 percent in contract construction to 4.2 percent in communications. Within agriculture, output per hour estimates from the U.S. Department of Agriculture for the 1950–1970 period show average annual rates of change from over 8 percent for poultry production and cotton down to between 2 and 3 percent for fruits and nuts and tobacco.

Variation in patterns of productivity change among industry groups over the subperiods bounded by cycle peak years, ending with the peak year 1973 (which was the most recent peak at the time of writing) are also shown in Table 3. As noted earlier, changes in TFP in the business economy are roughly associated with changes in real product, but some industries exhibit contrasting patterns. Thus, despite the severe deceleration in business economy TFP for 1966–1969, agriculture maintained its average performance. And in contrast to the partial recovery in the rate of TFP advance for 1969–1973 shared by manufacturing, transportation, trade, and the service industries, the other groups exhibited deceleration.

Relative rates of productivity change by industry have shown a significant degree of positive correlation with relative rates of change in output. This reflects the negative correlations between relative changes in productivity and in prices and between relative changes in prices and in sales or output. That is, industries with above-average increases in productivity have shown relative declines in unit costs and prices (reflecting the forces of competition or regulation), which have tended to stimulate sales and output—if demand is reasonably price elastic, and if the price effect were not offset by income elasticities working in the opposite direction, as in agriculture and services. The reverse sequence generally holds for industries with below-average productivity gains, but the relationship was to some degree reciprocal. That is, industries with above-average output gains enjoyed greater opportunities for economies of scale, which reenforced the superior productivity performance, and vice versa.

The positive relationship between changes in productivity and in output has been strong enough to offset the labor-saving aspect of productivity advance. That is, there is not a significant negative association between relative changes in productivity and in employment. A notable exception to this finding is extractive industry, however, where above-average productivity advances have been associated with relative and absolute declines in employment in recent decades because of low price and income elasticities of demand for food and raw materials.

Sources of Growth, 1948–1978, with Projections to 1990

In the previous section, the rate of growth in real gross business product was decomposed into the rates of growth of tangible factor inputs and of the total factor productivity (TFP) residual through the latest business cycle peak year, 1973, by major period. In this section, the analysis is carried further in two respects. First, the last period is broken down into two subperiods, 1948–1966 and 1966–1973, to show the retardation of growth in real product and in productivity, and there is discussion of estimates for the subperiod 1973–1978, which exhibits a further marked deceleration of growth. Although 1978 was not a peak year, unemployment was within one percentage point of the 5 percent rate, which is considered to represent reasonably full employment given the current age-sex mix of the labor force. In any case, the effect on the five-year growth rate of the 1978 ratio of actual to potential real GNP is indicated later.

Second, for all three subperiods, estimates of the contributions to TFP growth of all the major causal factors are presented and discussed. For this analysis, I employ a modified version of the growth accounting framework developed by Edward F. Denison.[3] The modifications are:

1. I attempt to explain statistically the growth rates of real gross product of the business sector rather than real national income of the nonresidential business sector. This means that my capital input estimates are based on real gross stocks of business capital, including residential rental real estate, whereas Denison used real net stocks excluding the latter category; and my capital weights are thus larger relative to weights for labor input since they include depreciation (less retirements) as well as net property income. I feel that gross capital income weights are appropriate, since labor compensation weights are also gross in that no deduction is made for depreciation of human capital. Also, I think that real gross capital stocks are a better measure of output-producing capacity than the combination of gross and net used by Denison. The difference in scope of the sector and of tangible factor input would have little effect on the movement and relative importance of the other explanatory variables, however.

2. Denison includes variables affecting the average quality of labor as part of labor input, whereas I count only labor hours as the tangible input and shift the variables affecting labor quality to the

---

[3] Edward F. Denison, *Accounting for United States Economic Growth, 1929-1969* (Washington, D.C.: Brookings Institution, 1974).

categories used to explain TFP. This would seem to be more consistent with Denison's treatment of capital input, which he does not adjust for quality change.

3. Denison's category, "advances in knowledge and n.e.c." (not elsewhere classified), was subdivided and several variables broken out that seemed both significant and at least roughly quantifiable. This results in a somewhat more comprehensive explanation of changes in TFP, although there still remains an n.e.c. category, which I interpret as comprising primarily changes in the ratio of actual to potential efficiency with given technology.

For the subperiod 1948–1966, I rely largely on Denison's estimates—as for the previous subperiod, 1929–1948, shown in Table 4 but not discussed. Denison has also published some estimates for the periods after 1966,[4] which I use, but I have prepared independent estimates for the majority of the causal factors for the last two subperiods. In particular, I have directly estimated the contribution of advances in knowledge in terms of its major components.

Finally, projections of economic growth for 1980–1990 are presented, based on the latest aggregate projections of the Bureau of Labor Statistics.[5] Since BLS projections of inputs and productivity seem reasonable, assuming no new policy initiatives to accelerate growth, I accept them and rationalize the projection of productivity in terms of the components of productivity advance. To economize space, after discussing the movements of each of the components in past subperiods, I go on to the projection of each. The "basic" projection serves as the basis for developing an alternative projection that assumes the adoption of policies to accelerate the growth of productivity and real product.

Factor Input and Productivity Ratios. Between 1948 and 1966, real gross business product grew at around the historical trend rate of nearly 4 percent per annum. The rate slowed somewhat to 3.5 percent in 1966–1973 and then more markedly to 2.4 percent in 1973–1978 (see Table 4). In 1978, however, according to estimates by the Council of Economic Advisers, the ratio of actual to potential real GNP was about 97.3 percent, assuming a benchmark unemployment

---

[4] See Statement by Edward F. Denison in *Special Study on Economic Change*, Hearings before the Joint Economic Committee of Congress, pt. 2, June 8, 9, 13, and 14, 1978 (Washington, D.C., 1978), pp. 487–93.

[5] See Norman C. Saunders, "The U.S. Economy to 1990: Two Projections for Growth," *Monthly Labor Review*, December 1978. I use the base projection; the high-employment projection assumes faster growth of the labor force and lower unemployment rates—and less productivity growth.

TABLE 4

Sources of Growth in Real Gross Product: U.S. Domestic Business Economy, for Selected Subperiods, 1929–1978

	1929–1948	1948–1966	1966–1973	1973–1978[a]	1980–1990 (projected)
Average annual percentage rates of change					
Real gross product	2.6	3.9	3.5	2.4	3.4
Total factor input	0.3	1.1	1.9	1.6	1.8
Labor	0.3	0.4	1.4	1.3	1.3
Capital	0.3	2.8	3.3	2.3	3.2
Real product per unit of labor	0.3	3.5	2.1	1.1	2.1
Capital/labor substitution	—	0.7	0.5	0.3	0.5
Total factor productivity	2.3	2.8	1.6	0.8	1.6
Sources of total factor productivity growth: Percentage point contribution					
Advances in knowledge	0.7	1.4	1.1	0.8	0.9
R&D stock	0.5	0.9	0.7	0.6	0.6
Informal	0.3	0.3	0.3	0.2	0.2
Rate of diffusion	−0.1	0.2	0.1	—	0.1
Changes in labor quality	0.8	0.6	0.4	0.7	1.0
Education and training	0.5	0.6	0.7	0.8	0.8
Health	0.3	0.1	0.1	0.1	0.1
Age/sex composition	—	−0.1	−0.4	−0.2	0.1
Changes in quality of land	—	—	−0.1	−0.2	−0.3

(Table 4 continues on the next page.)

33

TABLE 4 (continued)

	1929–1948	1948–1966	1966–1973	1973–1978[a]	1980–1990 (projected)
Resource reallocations	0.4	0.8	0.7	0.3	0.3
Labor	0.3	0.4	0.2	0.1	0.1
Capital	0.1	0.4	0.5	0.2	0.2
Volume changes	0.4	0.4	0.2	−0.1	0.4
Economies of scale	0.4	0.4	0.3	0.2	0.3
Intensity of demand	—	—	−0.1	−0.3	0.1
Net government impact	0.1	—	−0.1	−0.3	−0.2
Services to business	0.3	0.1	0.1	0.1	—
Regulations	−0.2	−0.1	−0.2	−0.4	−0.2
Actual/potential efficiency and n.e.c.[b]	−0.1	−0.4	−0.6	−0.4	−0.5

Dash (—): Zero or negligible.

[a] Preliminary.

[b] Not elsewhere classified.

SOURCE: John W. Kendrick, based in part on estimates by Edward F. Denison, *Accounting for United States Economic Growth, 1929-1969* (Washington, D.C.: Brookings Institution, 1974), and on his statement in *Special Study on Economic Change*, Hearings before the Joint Economic Committee of Congress, June 1978 (Washington, D.C., 1978).

rate of 5.1 percent.[6] On this basis, the growth rate of potential real GNP for 1973–1978 is estimated at around 3 percent a year, still a one percentage point deceleration from the pre-1966 situation.

The growth rate of factor input, however, accelerated sharply from little more than 1 percent a year, on average, from 1948 to 1966, up to nearly 2 percent in 1966–1973. The moderate sag to 1.6 percent in 1973–1978 largely reflects some underutilization of capacity in 1978. The acceleration was due chiefly to the more rapid growth after 1966 of labor hours, which accelerated from 0.4 percent a year in 1948–1966 to 1.4 percent in the subsequent subperiod, dropping negligibly in the final subperiod. The average annual rate of growth of real capital inputs (including land and inventories as well as fixed capital) accelerated from 2.8 percent to 3.3 percent between the first two periods—less than the acceleration in labor input—and then dropped by more, to around 2.3 percent in the final subperiod as a result of the recession of 1973–1975 and the sluggish recovery of real gross private domestic investment thereafter.

In terms of the conventional index of output per hour worked by all persons engaged in the business economy, productivity grew at an average annual rate of 3.5 percent in 1948–1966, decelerating by more than two-thirds to 1.1 percent in the final subperiod 1973–1978. Even if the benchmark unemployment rate of 5.1 percent had been reached in 1978, I estimate that labor productivity would have risen by only 1.4 percent, on average.

The deceleration in the average rate of increase in total tangible factor productivity was somewhat less (at a lower level), dropping from 2.8 percent in 1948–1966 to 0.8 percent in 1973–1978. The difference between the growth rates of real product per unit of labor and of TFP is accounted for by the rate of substitution of capital for labor. This is computed as the difference between the growth rates of total input and of labor input (or by the increase in capital per unit of labor, weighted by the share of capital compensation in gross national income, which is about 28 percent after adjustment for capital replacement costs). As shown in Table 4, the rate of substitution of capital for labor dropped from 0.7 percent in 1948–1966 to 0.3 percent in 1973–1978. The growth rate of the output/capital ratio (not shown in the table) fell from 1.1 percent to 0.1 percent between the first and third subperiods.

---

[6] See *Economic Report of the President*, transmitted to the Congress January 1979, together with the Annual Report of the Council of Economic Advisers (Washington, D.C., 1979), p. 75.

Looking ahead to the 1980–1990 decade, the BLS base projection contains or implies the following trends of real product, inputs, and productivity. Real gross private product is projected to grow at an average annual rate of 3.4 percent—an average of 3.6 percent in 1980–1985 and 3.2 percent in 1985–1990. The slowing of growth between the two halves of the decade reflects the projected deceleration in growth of the labor force—from 1.6 percent in 1980–1985 to 1.1 percent in 1985–1990. Total employment growth decelerates somewhat faster in the projection, since it is assumed that the decline in the unemployment rate slows—from 5.5 percent in 1980 to 4.7 percent in 1985 to 4.5 percent in 1990. Since public employment is projected to rise by significantly less than the labor force, private employment rises by more—by 2 percent in 1980–1985 and 1.3 percent in 1985–1990. Average hours worked per year are projected to continue to decline at the average annual rate of 0.3 percent throughout the decade. Thus, labor hours are projected to rise by 1.7 and 1.0 percent a year during the two halves of the decade—an average of over 1.3 percent for 1980–1990. Growth of real private product per hour is expected to improve over its record of the 1970s and accelerate somewhat to 1.9 percent a year in 1980–1985 and 2.2 percent in 1985–1990. I examine below what this implies for the various components of productivity growth.[7] To recapitulate, the 3.4 percent rate of growth of real gross private product for the decade is the result of a 1.3 percent rate of growth in labor hours and a 2.1 percent rate of growth in real product per hour.

The BLS projection of the gross private domestic investment component of real GNP implies a 3.6 percent average annual rate of increase in the real gross stock of nonresidential fixed capital.[8] Since the stocks of residences, inventories, and land would not increase by as much, I estimate the rate of increase of total capital input at about 3.2 percent a year.

When labor and capital inputs are weighted together, total input is projected to increase at a 1.8 percent average annual rate. This means that total factor productivity would grow by 1.6 percent, on average—the same as the 1966–1973 rate, well above the 1973–1978 rate but well below the 2.8 percent rate that prevailed between 1948 and 1966. The difference between the 2.1 percent rate of increase in real product per hour and the 1.6 percent in total factor produc-

---

[7] See Joint Economic Committee of Congress, *U.S. Economic Growth from 1976 to 1986: Prospects, Problems and Patterns*, vol. 1, *Productivity* (October 1, 1976), pp. 1, 2.

[8] *Monthly Labor Review*, December 1978, p. 41.

tivity is accounted for by a 0.5 rate of substitution of capital for labor—up a bit from the rate between 1973 and 1978.

The discussion now turns to the various sources of growth in total productivity, first noting the changes in the percentage point contributions of the causal forces between the subperiods 1948–1966 and 1973–1978 and then setting forth the likely contributions in the coming decade (see Table 4). A growth accounting framework is very useful for analyzing sources of past growth and projecting future growth of inputs, productivity, and real product. Properly specified, the model includes all the significant inputs and variables affecting productivity. The estimates indicate the relative importance of the various contributions, together with their net impact on growth. Even if the estimates in some cases are little more than informed judgments, the accounting framework ensures a systematic and comprehensive treatment of the significant variables in historical analysis and projections. Historical analysis is, of course, necessary to give perspective and proportion to the judgments and calculations required to assess future prospects.

Advances in Applied Productive Knowledge. In modern economies the most important force behind productivity growth is technological progress resulting from cost-reducing innovations in the ways and means of production. This is the factor that Denison calls "advances in knowledge," by which he means knowledge and know-how applied to productive processes. Denison estimates that advances in knowledge and n.e.c. (he considers the net effect of factors not elsewhere classified to be negligible) contributed 0.7 percentage point in 1929–1948 and 1.4 points in 1948–1966. This was the chief element in the acceleration in TFP between the two periods as well as earlier in the century as the industrial laboratory spread rapidly among larger firms. To extend and project this variable I break it down into three major components: (1) advances in knowledge stemming from formal R&D programs; (2) those resulting from informal inventive and innovative activities of individuals and groups not working in industrial laboratories or other formal programs included in the R&D statistics; and (3) changes in the rate of diffusion of new processes and producers' goods throughout the economy.

For the first component, my estimates of the real stocks formed by business R&D are directly relevant.[9] The stock estimates take

---

[9] See John W. Kendrick, *The Formation and Stocks of Total Capital* (New York: National Bureau of Economic Research, 1976), table B-26, extended to 1973 by the author.

account of the duration of research and development projects, the lags between completion of projects and commercial application, and the lengths of economic life of the process and product innovations. Thus, increases in the real stock would be closely related to advances in knowledge applied to production. My real R&D stock estimates for the business sector rose from $31.6 billion in 1948 to about $165 billion in 1966 and $235 billion in 1973, at average annual rates of increase of 9.6 and 5.2 percent during the two periods, with growth slowing further to less than 4 percent in 1973–1978. To estimate the effect on growth of real product, at least rough estimates of rates of return are necessary. Relevant studies summarized in a recent National Science Foundation colloquium suggest that, for the earlier period, private before-tax rates of return average around 25 percent and social rates at least twice as much. Accordingly, I use an average rate of return of 50 percent on the R&D stocks for 1948–1966.[10] Unfortunately, the studies have not yet been carried forward to more recent years. Since my estimates of the overall rate of return on total capital in high-level years declined by about 10 percent from 1948–1966 to 1966–1973 on average, I assume that the rate of return on R&D declined proportionately to a 45 percent average rate for the latter period, and to about 40 percent for 1973–1978.

To estimate the contribution of the growth of the real R&D stock for each period, I compute its mean absolute growth, apply the rate of return, and divide the contribution by the mean real gross product. The percentage point contributions were 0.85 in 1948–1966, 0.71 in 1966–1973, and about 0.6 in 1973–1978. The deceleration was much less than that in the growth of the real R&D stock, since the stock grew significantly in relation to real gross product in the successive periods. If it is assumed that R&D expenditures will level out at about 2 percent of GNP in the years ahead, as projected by the National Science Foundation, with a gross rate of return the same as in 1966–1973, the contribution of the growth of the real R&D stock would average around 0.6 percentage point in 1980–1990.

It is possible to get a handle on a significant aspect of the rate of diffusion of innovations in terms of the average age of fixed capital stocks in the business sector. A weighted average of Bureau of Economic Analysis estimates of the average ages of structures and equipment, after rising from 1929 to 1948, fell by three years

---

[10] See National Science Foundation, *Relationships between R&D and Economic Growth/Productivity* (November 9, 1977), p. A-7.

in 1948–1966, and by one year in 1966–1973, with little further net change by 1978. The earlier computation of the effect of advances in formal knowledge per year can be used to calculate that the increase in the rate of diffusion of new technology embodied in successive vintages of capital goods contributed about 0.25 percentage point in 1948–1966, a bit under 0.1 between 1966 and 1973, and nothing for 1973–1978. The fixed investment projections of BLS for 1980–1990 imply a renewed mild reduction in average age, with a 0.1 positive effect on growth.

If we accept Denison's estimate of 1.4 percentage points total contribution of advances in applied knowledge in 1948–1966, and subtract my estimates of the contribution of the two sources just covered, then 0.3 percent remains as the contribution of informal inventive and innovative activity. One would expect this source of advance to be significant, since many small improvements are made by the workers generally as they apply and adapt new processes and producers' goods in the production process. And the work of individual inventors whose value is not captured by the R&D statistics continues to be important. After all, technological advance and productivity growth was significant in nineteenth-century America (although much slower than in the twentieth century) before industrial laboratories became a commonplace, and the informal sources of cost-reducing innovation are still with us.

If it is assumed that informal contributions slowed in proportion to the deceleration in the formal R&D contributions, the total effect of advancing knowledge is seen to decline from 1.4 percent in 1948–1966 to 1.1 percent in 1966–1973 and 0.8 percent in 1973–1978. The deceleration across the three subperiods is substantial. Then there is a slight acceleration to 0.9 percent in 1980–1990, because of somewhat stronger performance of real fixed investment projected by BLS and the associated decline in the average age of capital goods.

Changes in Labor Quality. Next in importance are several factors, particularly education and training, affecting the average quality of labor inputs. The progress of education interacts with technological change, of course, not only in the production of scientists, engineers, managers, and others who make inventions and innovations, but also in meeting the rising skill requirements associated with an increasingly complex technology. On the basis of earnings differences among persons who had attained different educational levels (with differences in ability standardized), Denison estimated the contribution of increased average education to growth at about 0.5 percentage point for both 1929–1948 and 1948–1966. I have used a different approach, based on increases in real stocks of intangible capital resulting from outlays for both education and training.

The real stock of education and training embodied in the labor force employed in the business sector grew at an average annual rate of 3.6 percent in 1948–1966 and by 5.2 percent in 1966–1973.[11] With respect to the contribution to growth, however, it is the growth of the real stock in relation to labor input that is relevant. On that basis, the growth accelerated only from 3.2 percent a year in 1948–1966 to 3.75 percent in 1966–1973, since more of the growth in the stock in the latter period was needed to keep up with the accelerated increase in labor input.

Using the same methodology described for R&D, I calculated the contribution of increased education and training per unit of labor at 0.6 percentage point between 1948 and 1966 and 0.7 for 1966–1973. I used an average before-tax gross rate return of 12.5 percent for the earlier period and 12.0 percent for the later period, based on my estimates of returns on total human capital, of which education and training is more than half.[12] These rates of return are in line with other estimates, and they have the advantage of relating precisely to the periods under study. Presumably, gains because of increases in the content or quality of education and training are included under "advances in knowledge," since these are embodied in the labor force as well as in capital goods through investments. The estimates do not necessarily reflect changes in the efficacy of the learning process, however.

The estimate of 0.6 percentage point contribution of education for 1948–1966 compares with Denison's estimate of 0.5. But when it is taken into account that my estimate includes the effects of training (which contributed about 10 percent of the total stock over the period), whereas Denison's estimate does not, the estimates are quite consistent. This is gratifying in view of the differences in methodology used.

The growth of real educational and training capital has accelerated a bit further since 1973, and I estimate a 0.8 percentage point contribution for 1973–1978. The growth of these stocks per worker is expected to continue at recent rates during 1980–1990; consequently, the contribution is held at around 0.8 percentage point.

---

[11] Kendrick, *Total Capital*, Appendix C.
[12] Ibid., table C-8.

The second factor affecting labor quality is health, safety, and vitality. These factors have a positive effect on potential efficiency, just as their absence, reflected in increased time lost because of illness or accident, has a depressing effect on productivity. Denison considers the positive effect on vitality and potential efficiency of reductions in the average length of the workweek, but puts changes in other aspects of health, safety, and vitality into his n.e.c. compound.

My estimates of the real stocks of human capital created by outlays for health and safety provide a possible approach for estimating their contribution to growth. The growth of health capital per unit of labor input was 3.5 percent in both periods, 1948–1966 and 1966–1973,[13] and only slightly less in 1973–1978. Even if it is assumed that only half this capital has a productivity effect and that the rates of return are the same as on human capital generally, and if the contribution of shorter hours to efficiency is added in, the total contribution of the category still rounds off to 0.1 percentage point, as shown in Table 4. Given the prospect for a continued strong increase in real outlays for health and safety and the resulting stocks, I project a further positive effect of 0.1 percentage point for 1980–1990.

The effect on productivity of changing age-sex mix of the labor force was estimated by Denison as virtually nil for 1929–1948 and −0.1 for 1948–1966. It dropped to at least −0.4 in the 1966–1973 period, reflecting the accelerated influx of youth and women who earn less than the average of the ten groups in terms of which Denison estimates the effect on income of changing composition. I view this variable as capturing part of a broader causal force that might be called "learning by doing," since the experience factor is a major element in the differential incomes of the various age-sex groups.[14]

During the 1973–1978 subperiod, however, changes in age-sex mix became a less negative influence. The effect will become positive in 1980–1990, as the bulge of youthful entrants of the latter 1960s advances in age and moves into the higher-earning categories. Also, the rate of increase in female participation ratios will slow somewhat, according to BLS labor force projections, and the relative pay of females is expected to increase as their experience rises and equal employment opportunity laws are applied.

---

[13] Ibid., table B-24.

[14] See William Fellner, "Specific Interpretations of Learning by Doing," *Journal of Economic Theory*, vol. 1, no. 2 (August 1969).

Changes in Quality of Land. Another category I have added to Denison's is the effect of a declining average quality of natural resources used as production expands; that is, the tendency toward diminishing returns. In the past, this tendency has been much more than offset by technological advance, and mining as well as farming had above-average productivity gains. But since 1966 productivity in extractive industries has declined drastically relative to that for other industries. In mining, productivity has declined absolutely since 1970, in part because of the regulations of the Occupational Safety and Health Administration (OSHA) and the Environmental Protection Agency (EPA). But part of the relative decline in extractive sector productivity appears to reflect a declining average quality of natural resources; weighting by the sector's share of business product, I come up with a −0.1 percentage point effect for 1966–1973 and −0.2 for 1973–1978.

Further expansion of output and exploitation of domestic natural resources will have a larger negative effect on productivity in the future, particularly as efforts expand to decrease dependence on foreign sources of energy by using higher-cost domestic sources. I project a −0.3 percentage point impact for 1980–1990. Some observers expect a more drastic impact, but they overlook the relatively small percentage of extractive industry in GNP.[15]

Resource Reallocations. The reallocation of resources, sometimes referred to as changes in economic efficiency, occurs when labor or nonlabor resources move from uses, regions, or industries in which their remuneration is below a normal "equilibrium" level to areas in which their rates of remuneration are relatively higher. Real income and product are then raised. In the case of labor, this increase is over and above the effect of increased education and training, which equip workers for higher-pay occupations or professions. Inefficient allocation may be the result of impediments to mobility of various types, such as government regulations, restrictive practices of firms and unions, or the sheer cost of movement.

Denison has estimated the impact of two aspects of resource reallocations. One is the shift from self-employment in the private nonfarm sector to an employee status, which raises earnings and value added per person. Of negligible importance in 1929–1948, this shift contributed 0.1 percentage point to average annual growth in 1948–1966, and I estimate a similar effect in the subsequent sub-

15 See E. F. Renshaw, "Productivity," in Joint Economic Committee, *Productivity*, pp. 21-23 ff.

periods. Of greater importance has been the shift of persons engaged in farming to nonfarm pursuits, in which remuneration is distinctly higher. This contributed around 0.3 percentage point in both 1929–1948 and 1948–1966. Reflecting the declining relative importance of the farm labor force, the effect dropped to about 0.1 point in 1966–1973 and dwindled to negligible proportions thereafter.

To Denison's categories, I have added the effect of relative shifts of capital (including land) from uses with below-average rates of return to higher-value uses. Professors Jorgenson and Gollop, using real capital estimates for over fifty industry groups, found that reallocations added 0.4 percentage point to growth in 1948–1966 and somewhat more in 1966–1973.[16] Using estimates for thirty-one industry groups, I calculate that the contribution from this source declined in the final subperiod. The BLS projections for 1980–1990 suggest that there will be further modest gains from resource reallocations, as dynamic forces create profitable opportunities for changes in the composition of output and of inputs.

Volume Changes. The next three factors are related to the growth rate. Economies of scale were estimated by Denison to contribute 0.35 percentage point to growth in 1929–1943 and somewhat more to the higher 1948–1966 growth rate. But the progressively slowing growth rates of 1966–1973 and 1973–1978 reduce the contributions of scale economies to 0.3 and 0.2 percentage points, respectively. The mild acceleration in growth projected by BLS for 1980–1990 brings the scale contribution back to 0.3 percentage point for that decade, according to Denison's method of estimation.

Changes in intensity of demand, as measured by the ratio of actual to potential real gross business product, made slight positive contributions to productivity growth in 1929–1948 and 1948–1966. Denison's estimates also imply a negative contribution in 1966–1973 of −0.1. The lower ratio of actual to potential real GNP in 1978 than in 1973 implies a −0.3 effect of this source in the last subperiod. Conversely, the BLS projection for 1990 means that higher demand intensity than in 1980 will contribute 0.1 percentage point for the decade ahead.

Finally, many irregular factors affect outputs, inputs, and productivity—particularly changes in the weather and the impact

---

[16] Frank Gollop and Dale W. Jorgenson, "Productivity Growth by Industry, 1947-1973," in John W. Kendrick and Beatrice N. Vaccara, eds., *New Developments in Productivity Measurement and Analysis*, Studies in Income and Wealth, vol. 44 (Chicago: University of Chicago Press for the National Bureau of Economic Research, forthcoming).

of strikes. Denison has explicitly estimated these impacts and found them to be negligible over the past periods under consideration here. The same appears to be true of the impacts of civil disturbances and wars in the terminal years of the subperiods. Therefore, a separate line for erratic factors is not included in the table. A continued negligible impact of these factors is assumed for 1980 and 1990, although it is obvious that they are essentially unpredictable.

Net Government Impact. Since this paper deals with the business sector alone, the net impact on productivity of its transactions with government is relevant. On the one side, government provides services to business; some are direct but most are indirect, such as the provision of infrastructure and maintenance of the social fabric, which benefit business and households jointly. My estimates of the real total capital (human and nonhuman but excluding that already considered) employed by government (excluding military) rose by 3.5 percent a year more than that employed by business in 1929–1948, 0.9 percent more in 1948–1966, and by 0.8 percent in 1966–1978. Assuming that the rates of return are the same on public as on private capital, and that half of government services benefit business, I estimate that the relative increase in public services contributed 0.3 percentage point to growth in 1929–1948 and 0.1 percent in the subsequent subperiods. I project no positive contribution for 1980–1990 since BLS projects a small relative decrease in government employment.

On the other hand, business costs are increased by government requirements and regulations. In recent years the most pervasive of these are the environmental protection and occupational safety and health regulations. In a recent article, Denison estimates that these regulations reduced the measured growth rate of the business economy by approximately 0.2 percentage point a year from 1967 to 1973, whereas the impact was negligible prior to that time.[17] For the period 1973–1976 Denison's numbers indicate a −0.4 percentage point effect, which I use for the 1973–1978 subperiod as a whole. Since the EPA and OSHA programs are expected to level out by the end of the decade as a proportion of unit costs, we project little further negative impact in the 1980s.

Residual. The last category is a residual, reflecting the net effect of variables not elsewhere classified (n.e.c.), as well as the net effect of errors in the other estimates. Denison lumps his n.e.c. variables with "advances in knowledge," but since I attempt to estimate the

---

[17] *Survey of Current Business,* January 1978.

latter major category directly, I have a separate residual. It is conceptually narrower than Denison's, since I explicitly estimate several variables noted above which are in his n.e.c. compound. I interpret it as reflecting primarily a decline in the ratio of actual to potential labor efficiency, when technology and other variables are held constant. One measurable element in this decline has been the reduction in hours actually worked relative to hours paid for, since the latter concept underlies most of the hours data used for the labor input measure. This decline has proceeded at near a 0.1 percent average annual rate, reflecting increased time paid for but not worked. In addition, University of Michigan surveys indicate that unproductive time at work (for coffee breaks, personal business, and the like) has increased by about 0.2 percent a year, on average, at least since the mid-1960s.[18]

Beyond this, there is considerable speculation that the efficiency of hours actually worked may have declined relative to the kinds of standards or norms used in work measurement studies. Certainly, there are many instances of restrictive work rules and practices throughout industry, although it is difficult to ascertain whether their impact has increased. Some observers maintain that efficiency has been adversely affected during the past dozen years by negative social trends, such as growing drug use and crime, loosening of the work ethic, increased questioning of materialism and of many institutions, including business. Denison has adduced evidence to show that increasing crimes against property have reduced the growth rate perceptibly, but less than 0.1 percent a year on average, since 1960. Some of the negative tendencies seem to have reached their peak during the Vietnam War era. It is interesting that the negative residual was largest during the 1966–1973 period and then receded somewhat. But in view of the relative margins of error of the estimates, changes in the residual are not necessarily significant.

The residual also reflects changes in those aspects of the legal, institutional, and social environment within which business operates that affect unit real costs. A major example is the honesty of the public in general and of customers, employees, and suppliers in particular, which affects business costs via security outlays and losses from crime. In his recent article, Denison has estimated the productivity impact of this specific variable at −0.05 in 1966–1976.

---

[18] See Frank Stafford and Greg Duncan, "The Use of Time and Technology by Households in the United States" (Ann Arbor: University of Michigan, Department of Economics, July 1977).

In addition, various forces are reflected either not at all or only partially in the other identified variables. Examples are changes in competitive or other pressures on enterprises to minimize and reduce costs (which has a cyclical component) and changes in the average quality of management that are not wholly reflected in the labor quality variables. Further research may eventually succeed in measuring the impact of more of the residual variables. Table 4 indicates that their net impact has not changed much in the past, although this may be due to offsetting errors in the other estimates. In any case, the explicit projections imply only small changes in the net impact of the n.e.c. factors for the forecast subperiod.

Recapitulation. The previous discussion can be summarized first in terms of the forces accounting for the slowing in growth of real product and productivity between the first and third subperiods 1948–1966 and 1973–1978. Second, the forces accounting for the projected partial recovery in rates of growth between 1973–1978 and 1980–1990 will be summarized. The recapitulation is centered on Table 5.

The growth of real gross business product slowed by 1.5 percentage points between the first and third subperiods. This represents the difference between a 0.5 point faster increase of factor inputs and a 2.0 point retardation in total factor productivity. Labor input alone grew at a 0.9 percentage point faster rate in the third subperiod than in the first, so that the more familiar real product per labor hour measure showed a 2.4 percent retardation. The reconciliation between the two productivity ratios is provided by a 0.4 percentage point slowing of the rate of substitution of capital for labor.

Three-quarters of the 2.0 percentage point retardation in TFP advance between the two subperiods was explained in almost equal degree by smaller contributions of three forces: advances in knowledge, resource reallocations, and volume changes. The remaining retardation was due to deterioration in the quality of natural resources and the negative impact of governmental regulations.

In the 1980–1990 decade, real gross business product is projected by BLS to grow at a 1.0 percentage point faster rate than in the subperiod 1973–1978. This is the result of a 0.2 point faster increase of factor inputs, and a 0.8 point acceleration in TFP advance. Since labor input is expected to grow at the same rate in both subperiods, labor productivity will increase by 1.0 percentage point

TABLE 5

CHANGES IN RATES OF CHANGE IN REAL GROSS BUSINESS PRODUCT,
BY MAJOR SOURCES OF GROWTH

	1948–1966 to 1973–1978	1973–1978 to 1980–1990 (projected)
Average annual percentage rates of change		
Real gross product	−1.5	1.0
Total factor inputs	0.5	0.2
Labor	0.9	—
Capital	−0.5	0.9
Real product per labor hour	−2.4	1.0
Capital/labor substitution	−0.4	0.2
Total factor productivity	−2.0	0.8
Sources of productivity growth: Percentage point contribution		
Advances in knowledge	−0.6	0.1
Changes in labor quality	0.1	0.3
Changes in quality of land	−0.2	−0.1
Resource reallocations	−0.5	−0.1
Volume changes	−0.5	0.5
Net government impact	−0.3	0.1
Actual/potential efficiency and n.e.c.	—	—

Dash (—): Zero or negligible
SOURCE: Derived from Table 4.

faster than in the 1973–1978 subperiod. The reconciliation item is a 0.2 point higher rate of substitution of capital for labor.

Over half the 0.8 percentage point improvement in TFP growth is expected to come from volume—greater economies of scale and particularly a rising rather than a declining ratio of actual to potential real GNP. The rest of the improvement may be attributed to increasing quality of labor as the age-sex mix of the labor force shifts toward more experienced, better-paid groups. Small positive contributions from advances in knowledge and from government impact are offset by further deterioration in the quality of natural resources and a lessened positive contribution of resource reallocations. The net contribution of actual/potential efficiency and miscellaneous factors is expected to continue negative in the coming decade, but no more so than in the previous subperiods.

The anticipated acceleration of productivity advance in the 1980s is welcome but is scarcely of a magnitude worth cheering about. The 0.8 percentage point improvement will not help much in mitigating inflationary pressures or in adding to the growth of real income per capita. And the projected 1.6 percent average annual rate of TFP growth is still more than one full percentage point below the rate achieved prior to 1966. Most observers agree that we will not return to the old trend rate of advance without the adoption of effective policies toward that end.[19] In my view a 2.6 percent trend rate of growth in TFP could be achieved if the appropriate policy measures were adopted, and I therefore consider policy options in the final section of this paper.

Policy Options for Promoting Productivity and Economic Progress

This section sets forth various policy options for promoting productivity and economic progress, subject to the usual economic constraints, under the same headings used in the preceding section for discussion of causal factors and their impacts. Under each heading I indicate generally what the impact on real product per capita might be of adopting selected policy options summarized in the "high growth" projection for 1980–1990 shown in Table 6. The table indicates a total impact on TFP growth of 1.0 percent as compared with the standard projection and on real product per capita of nearly 1.5 percent. Additional gains of these magnitudes would obviously have a beneficial effect on economic developments in the decade ahead.

Population and Labor Input. In this section productivity and economic progress are defined as real product per capita since in a democracy citizens generally look askance at the idea of a population policy, and I agree that policies intended directly to affect the birth rate are not appropriate. Although various government policies that affect costs of rearing children, such as tax exemptions and deductions for child care, may have some indirect influence, decisions regarding family size are a very personal matter and should be left to individuals. They are influenced, of course, by social considerations, and public discussion of the economic and social effects of

---

[19] See Joint Economic Committee of Congress, *U.S. Long-term Economic Growth Prospects: Entering a New Era* (January 25, 1978), pt. 8, "The Decade Ahead," pp. 109-11.

TABLE 6

U.S. PRIVATE DOMESTIC BUSINESS ECONOMY: ALTERNATIVE PROJECTIONS
OF REAL PRODUCT AND PRODUCTIVITY, BY COMPONENTS, 1980–1990

	Basic	High Growth
Average annual rates of change		
Real gross product	3.4	4.8
Total factor input	1.8	2.2
Labor	1.3	1.4
Capital	3.2	4.5
Real product per labor hour	2.1	3.4
Capital/labor substitution	0.5	0.8
Total factor productivity	1.6	2.6
Sources of productivity growth: Percentage point contribution		
Advances in knowledge	0.9	1.3
R&D stock	0.6	0.8
Informal	0.2	0.3
Rate of diffusion	0.1	0.2
Changes in labor quality	1.0	1.1
Education and training	0.8	0.9
Health	0.1	0.1
Age/sex composition	0.1	0.1
Changes in quality of land	−0.3	−0.3
Resource reallocations	0.2	0.2
Labor	0.1	0.1
Capital	0.1	0.1
Volume changes	0.4	0.6
Economies of scale	0.3	0.5
Intensity of demand	0.1	0.1
Net government impact	−0.2	—
Services to business	—	0.1
Regulations	−0.2	−0.1
Actual/potential efficiency and n.e.c.	−0.4	−0.3

Dash (—): Zero or negligible.

rates of birth and population growth is desirable. Thus, the publicity given to unfavorable future consequences of the population explosion of the post–World War II period must have helped bring about the sharp decline in birth rates in the United States during the last twenty years. On the other hand, scant attention has been given to the possibly unfavorable future consequences of a declining population in the twenty-first century, given a continuation of recent birth rates which are below the replacement level.

Apart from birth rates, the growth of population and labor force are necessarily influenced by public policy in two ways. First, public programs designed to enhance health and safety affect longevity and length of working life. Second, immigration policy affects both. At a later time, if the probabilities of a leveling and eventual decline of the population and labor force become greater, thought should be given to possibly liberalizing immigration restrictions and increasing the volume of work permits issued to aliens.

More immediately, various measures could be adopted to slow the projected decline in labor force participation ratios, particularly among men over fifty years of age, and women aged sixty-five and over. Congress has recently raised the permissible mandatory retirement age from sixty-five to seventy. The question arises why there should be any blanket mandatory retirement age. Permitting individuals and their employers to make the retirement decision on an individual basis may create some administrative problems, but it gives greater scope to individual freedom of choice and conduces to higher income. Greater flexibility by firms and other organizations in providing more opportunities for part-time work and adjustable hours would help raise labor force participation generally as well as among older workers, who might choose reduced work schedules rather than complete retirement. The ban against discrimination in employment on account of age has helped in this regard. Finally, modification of the social security law to reduce the disincentives for continued employment beyond stipulated ages could slow the decline in participation ratios.

Measures of this sort would seem desirable in view of the prospective leveling of the dependency ratio (of nonworkers to workers) at about 111.5 by the mid-1980s and a substantial rise in the 1990s and beyond. The prospective rise not only slows the growth of real income per capita but also aggravates problems of funding social security and private pension plans. It is not too early to think now about ways of slowing the rise in the dependency ratio by slowing the decline in labor force participation ratios of older age groups.

In the BLS projections underlying Table 6 it was assumed that labor force participation of persons fifty-five years and over would drop from 38.6 percent in 1970 to 33.8 percent in 1980 and 30.0 percent in 1990. I estimate that measures such as those suggested above could slow the decline enough to produce a ratio of 32.5

percent in 1990. This would increase the projected labor force in 1990 from 113.8 million to 115.0, or about 1 percent. Other things equal, this would increase the growth of labor input in the 1980 decade by an average annual rate of 0.1 percent, which is reflected in the high growth projection in Table 6.

Tangible Investment.[20] Policies to promote tangible investment and thus the rate of growth of real stocks and inputs of structures, equipment, inventories, and developed natural resources would obviously accelerate the growth of real product per unit of labor input and per capita. Real product growth would be favorably affected by the faster rate of diffusion of new technology, reflected in a declining average age of the fixed capital stock. In addition, the acceleration in tangible capital formation would have a positive effect on R&D spending and other intangible investments that are part and parcel of the inventive-innovative process.

Earlier it was implied that policies to promote investments, both tangible and intangible, should be constrained by the usual criteria of economic rationality. That is, investments should not be pushed beyond the point at which the expected rate of return from the projected cost-savings or other additions to revenue exceed the interest rate paid or other marginal costs of funds.

The key policy lever for stimulating business investment is the after-tax rate of return on investment. Increases in this rate influence the expected rates of return favorably and enlarge internal sources of funds. During the most recent eight-year period, 1970–1977 inclusive, adjusted domestic after-tax profits of U.S. nonfinancial corporations averaged 4.25 percent of their gross domestic product, compared with a 7.75 percent average for 1947–1969. The estimated 1977 ratio is below 4 percent. In this calculation by George Terborgh based on Commerce Department data, the profits estimates were adjusted so that capital consumption and inventory were valued at current replacement costs rather than the costs charged for income tax purposes.[21] When adjusted profits are related to net worth (with tangible assets restated at replacement costs), the 1970–1977 average

---

[20] Parts of this and the following sections were drawn from the paper by Kendrick in National Science Foundation, *R&D and Economic Growth/Productivity*, pp. E-1–E-19.

[21] See George Terborgh, *Corporate Earning Power in the Seventies: A Disaster* (Washington, D.C.: Machinery and Allied Products Institute, August 1977), p. 5. In computing net worth, Terborgh did not take account of the decline in liabilities, chiefly long-term debt, associated with rising interest rates.

rate of return is 3.55 percent compared with 5.90 for the 1947–1969 period. There was a similar drop in the before-tax profit rates.

A basic cause of the decline in the profit rate, which began in 1966, was the accelerating pace of price inflation. For one thing, most corporate managements apparently did not adopt pricing policies (even if they had some discretion over prices) to reflect fully the impact of inflation on costs, particularly the replacement cost of fixed capital and inventories. More important, in my view, has been the use of macroeconomic policy to restrain inflation by holding price increases below the increase of unit costs, thus squeezing profit margins, in periods of high-level activity—particularly 1966, 1969, 1973, and currently, when rates of return again appear to be declining a bit. In addition, the wage-price freeze and subsequent controls from August 1971 to April 1974 not only limited profits growth but also distorted relative rates of return, which contributed to inadequate investment and capacity bottlenecks in 1973–1974 in some basic industries.

In expansions it is important that monetary, fiscal, and incomes policies permit profits to return to adequate rates, thereby increasing both saving and investment. A close relationship between profit rates and investment lies at the heart of both the neoclassical and flow-of-funds theories and appears to be substantiated by various empirical investigations. Some economists subscribe to an accelerator model of investment behavior, claiming that in other models profits are a proxy for sales or output. I would argue that the reverse is true, and that when the movements of profits and sales diverge the profit rate is the more influential variable. Thus, in the recent recovery since April 1975 the sluggishness in growth of private fixed investment reflects the relatively low real rates of return and uncertain prospects for the future.

The sluggish investment performance since 1975 has been all the more disturbing in view of various recent studies of capital requirements in the years ahead.[22] A study by the Bureau of Economic Analysis indicated that in order to meet the capital requirements of mandated social programs (for the environment, occupational safety and health, and greater energy independence) as well as to increase capital per worker at the rate of the previous decade, nonresidential structures and equipment outlays would have to rise to around 12 percent of GNP in the later 1970s compared with an

---

[22] See the summary by Henry Wallich, "A Near-Term Look at the Capital Shortage," *Journal of Financial and Quantitative Analysis*, November 1976.

average of 10.5 percent in the 1965–1975 decade.[23] Since that study was completed the ratio sagged to 9.5 percent in 1976, 9.8 percent in 1977, and about 10.5 percent for 1978. This suggests, other things equal, that policies to raise the ratio of saving and investment to GNP by at least 1.5 percentage points would be desirable to avoid increases in the real interest rate that would reduce the growth of capital and output per worker.

More broadly, the case for raising the proportion of income devoted to saving and investment rests on the view that the U.S. tax system is biased against capital formation—more so than is true of most other industrialized countries, which have significantly higher ratios of gross saving and investment to GNP. It is held that a neutral tax system, or one in which the biases are reduced by various measures itemized below, would result in higher rates of capital formation and growth.

The theoretical case for greater capital formation has been made most forcefully by Martin Feldstein, president of the National Bureau of Economic Research. He points out that personal and corporate income taxes put a wedge between the national rate of return on capital and the net rate received by savers. He estimates that the latter rate, and thus the rate of discount of future consumption, is less than half the corresponding pretax average rate of return on private investment in the United States. As he puts it, "If the amount of future consumption that individuals require to forgo a dollar's worth of present consumption is less than the rate at which investment produces future income from current capital investments, we should save more."[24] He also argues that the social security system reduces saving in the United States.

Ture and Sanden explain the bias against saving and investment in the present U.S. tax system somewhat differently, stating:

> For the most part, neither the part of income which is saved nor the return on such saving is excluded from the base of the income tax, the principal source of tax revenue. Since saving is the capitalized amount of the future income purchased by the saving, this characteristic of the income tax subjects the part of current income used to buy future

---

[23] A summary of the BEA capital requirements study is contained in *Economic Report of the President, 1977* (Washington, D.C., January 1977).

[24] Martin S. Feldstein, "National Saving in the United States," *Capital for Productivity and Jobs* (Englewood Cliffs, N.J.: Prentice-Hall, for the American Assembly, 1977).

income to a double tax, whereas the part of current income used to buy consumption goods is taxed only once.[25]

Another way to put it is that income taxes reduce disposable income and thus affect both consumption and saving; but since future income from the investments into which savings flow are also taxed, after-tax returns and thus the present values of investments are reduced, making saving and investment less attractive relative to consumption than would be the case with a neutral tax system.

To give a quick example, suppose that $1,000 were available in a tax-free environment to spend for current consumption or to invest in a security yielding $50 per annum. If a 50 percent income tax were imposed, pretax income of $2,000 would be required to devote $1,000 to consumption as before. But $4,000 would be necessary to acquire investment yielding $50 a year after tax since of the $4,000 half would go in taxes, and of the $100 return, half would also go, leaving the desired $50 return. Thus, saving and investment is subject to double taxation, increasing the cost of saving relative to consumption.

Capital recovery allowances—which are not the full equivalent of expensing capital outlays, particularly in an inflationary environment when depreciation allowances are at original cost—ameliorate but do not eliminate the disproportionate burden on savings. So do certain tax loopholes. On the other hand, some non-income taxes accentuate the antisaving bias. This is true of taxes on capital gains, which are basically capitalizations of expected increases in the earnings of assets. Since such earnings increases will be taxed as they accrue, taxing the capitalized value of such increases is a further layer of taxation on the same income stream. Estate, inheritance, and gift taxes are similar to capital gains taxes in their impact. Property taxes also add to the burden of saving, since they are the equivalent of income taxes on explicit or implicit income from the property. Further, the provision of the Tax Reform Act of 1969 limiting the maximum marginal rate on earned income to 50 percent in contrast to 70 percent on property income plainly serves to discourage investment.

In order to eliminate the antisaving bias of the U.S. tax system, Ture recommends two major measures: (1) The corporation income tax should be repealed, and corporate earnings should be attributed to shareholders for inclusion in their taxable income—which, inci-

---

[25] Norman B. Ture and B. Kenneth Sanden, *The Effects of Tax Policy on Capital Formation* (New York: Financial Executives Research Foundation, 1977), p. 71.

dentally, would remove the differential treatment of corporations and unincorporated enterprises. (2) Current saving should be excluded from the base of the individual income tax, while returns from investment plus repayments of principal should be fully taxed.[26] Revenue losses could be made up by increasing tax rates on personal income less net saving or by a value-added tax which is essentially neutral with respect to saving decisions.

It is quite unlikely, however, that such a radical reform of the tax system will be enacted, particularly the second measure, despite the evident need to devote a larger fraction of national income and product to saving and investment. But there are a number of more modest tax options for stimulating investment and saving and some nontax measures.

Before relatively full employment is reached, measures to promote private investment are more appropriate than measures to increase saving directly. That is, measures that reduce the effective corporate tax rate, together with those that improve before-tax earnings recovery, tend to increase corporate saving as well as to stimulate investment. Further, the increase of investment will have the usual multiplicative effect on total national income (other things equal), which will generate the total saving necessary to accommodate the investment growth. But once the full-employment range is attained, measures to increase saving are indicated to achieve a higher investment/GNP ratio if the inflationary route of forced saving is eschewed.

Some of the more prominent tax proposals for stimulating private investment and saving are:

1. Reducing effective corporate income tax rates by one or more of the following measures:

    a. Further acceleration of depreciation charges for tax purposes and/or indexation of depreciation to adjust from book depreciation of fixed assets at original cost to replacement costs based either on specific capital goods price indexes or general price indexes such as the private GNP deflator.

    b. Reduction of corporate income tax rates by decreasing the 22 percent normal tax, decreasing or graduating the present 24 percent surtax applicable to income above the $50,000 surtax exemption, increasing the surtax exemption, or by some combination of the alternatives. To encourage small business, an increase in the surtax ex-

---

[26] Ibid., p. 71.

emption and a graduation of rates for increments of net income would be helpful.

c. Elimination or reduction of the double taxation of corporate dividends. Here, too, there are alternative approaches, principally either to allow the corporation a deduction for its dividend distributions (as is done for interest payments) or to allow the shareholder a credit equivalent to the tax paid by the corporation with respect to the distributed earnings. The former approach is administratively simpler. As a third approach, the corporate and personal income taxes could be completely integrated, with the shareholder paying personal income taxes on both dividends and his share of undistributed profits.

d. Increase of the investment tax credit from 10 percent to, say, 15 percent and expansion of its coverage to expenditures for new plant as well as equipment. The advantage of the credit is that tax liabilities can be reduced by businesses, other things equal, only by increasing investment. Most studies indicate that the credit does increase investment by somewhat more than the revenue loss.

2. Adjustments of the personal income tax:

a. The Tax Reform Act of 1969 provided a 50 percent maximum marginal rate on earned income. Extension of the maximum rate to property or capital income as well would encourage investment.

b. Reducing personal income taxes generally, as revenue requirements permit, and reducing the steepness of graduation of marginal rates would also reduce antisavings bias. Changes in graduation would, however, have to be weighted against equity considerations.

c. Strengthening tax incentives for personal saving. A number of such incentives in existing law provide tax exemption or deferral for income from capital, such as provisions relating to pension, profit-sharing, and stock bonus plans. Others give tax deferral to income that is saved. As discussed in the recent report of the Joint Committee on Taxation, some of the existing provisions could be broadened or new provisions added.[27]

---

[27] See the Joint Committee on Taxation for the House Ways and Means Committee Task Force on Capital Formation, "Tax Policy and Capital Formation" (April 1977).

3. Revision of the capital gains tax: A "rollover" treatment of capital gains, similar to that for owner-occupied residences, could be accorded to all assets by deferring the tax on gains so long as the proceeds from the sale of the assets were reinvested fully. Also, capital gains tax rates could be reduced or an annual exemption of a specific amount provided. A more symmetrical treatment of capital gains and losses would also be desirable to encourage greater willingness to undertake risky innovations.

Several econometric studies have been undertaken to answer the question of the effectiveness of investment incentives involving a reduction in the corporate tax rate.[28] Various analyses, such as those by Jorgenson and Hall, Bischoff, and Coen showed significant stimulative effects on investment of past increases in the investment tax credit, in particular, and of accelerated depreciation and reduction of the corporate tax rate. The effect of the latter was reduced, of course, by the fact that it lessened the tax-reducing effect of the other incentives on the implicit rental cost of capital.

As Christensen pointed out, however, the models showing strong effects of incentives were prepared in a partial equilibrium context.[29] When the investment models are specified within a general equilibrium framework and tested in complete econometric models of the U.S. economy, the effects of the investment stimuli were found to be considerably less. Harberger has noted that when tax incentives are analyzed in a general equilibrium framework the effects attributed to them will vary significantly, depending on the complementary policies pursued—particularly fiscal policy in financing the tax expenditures and associated monetary policies—as well as on related structural relations in the model such as the interest sensitivity of saving. Also, as Lucas discovered, if it is assumed that tax changes are correctly anticipated by businessmen, the investment impact is substantially increased.[30]

One important lesson from this discussion is, I believe, that tax incentives for investment (including R&D, discussed below) can be

---

[28] For a review of these studies, and references to them, see Michael Visscher, *Tax Policies for R&D and Technological Innovation* (Pittsburgh: Graduate School of Industrial Administration, Carnegie-Mellon University; processed), ch. 2, "The Effect of Tax Incentives on Investment Behavior."

[29] Lauits Christensen, "Tax Policy and Investment Expenditures in a Model of General Equilibrium" (Madison: Social Systems Research Institute, University of Wisconsin, December 1969; processed).

[30] R. E. Lucas, Jr., "Econometric Policy Evaluation: A Critique," in K. Brunner and A. Meltzer, eds., *The Phillips Curve and Labor Markets* (Amsterdam: North-Holland, 1975).

effective as long as the complementary macroeconomic policies are expansive and not offsetting. As Harberger wrote:

> In the final analysis the long-run effects of investment incentives on output will stem from their influence on the amounts of basic resources (labor and capital) which are voluntarily supplied to the market. Ultimately it is how these tax stimuli affect the labor-leisure choice and the savings decision that will determine their effect upon output.[31]

Suppose for the purposes of the high projection that business investment is increased as a ratio to GNP by 1.5 percent, or about $35 billion at current levels of GNP. To stimulate this much additional investment, profits after tax would have to rise about $45 billion, or 2 percent of GNP,[32] which would bring them closer to their average percentage for the 1947–1966 period. Part of this increase might be achieved by a gradual rise in the before-tax rate of return. An acceleration in productivity gains would be the preferred way of reducing unit costs relative to prices in order to restore adequate profit margins, of course. But since accelerated productivity growth cannot be achieved quickly, most of the stimulus would have to be obtained by a combination of the tax-reducing measures specified above, which could be spread over several years. By my calculations, the higher investment would result in about a 1.3 percent a year faster growth in real capital stocks of the business sector. When weighted by the 28 percent share of property income in gross factor cost, this would directly contribute 0.4 percentage point additional growth to real business product in the 1980 decade, as reflected in Table 6. Although the growth of consumption would be reduced somewhat while the investment ratio was being raised, the stronger subsequent growth of real product (assuming appropriate aggregate demand policies) would clearly mean larger consumption by the latter part of the decade than would have obtained without the increase in the saving ratio over the next several years.

With respect to the role of government in the investment process, it is frequently advocated that once the full-employment zone is reached governments should run budget surpluses to supplement private saving in the financing of business investment. That is well and good, if private demand is strong enough to maintain full em-

---

[31] Arnold Harberger, "Tax Policy and Investment Expenditures: Discussion," in G. Fromm, ed., *Tax Incentives and Capital Spending* (Washington, D.C.: Brookings Institution, 1971).

[32] Based on relationship in Data Resources, Inc. (DRI) model.

TABLE 7

U.S. DOMESTIC ECONOMY, BY SECTOR: TOTAL GROSS INVESTMENT IN
RELATION TO GROSS PRODUCT AND SECTORAL DISPOSABLE INCOMES
FOR SELECTED PEAK YEARS, 1929–1973
(percent)

	1929	1948	1966	1973
Persons				
DI/GNP	78.8	70.4	63.0	68.8
GI/DI	33.2	35.2	41.9	38.5
GI/GNP	26.1	24.8	26.4	26.5
Business				
DI/GNP	10.0	10.2	12.5	9.3
GI/DI	124.4	123.8	102.4	128.0
GI/GNP	12.4	12.6	12.8	11.9
Governments				
DI/GNP	10.4	18.7	24.2	21.7
GI/DI	44.3	28.6	46.3	46.5
GI/GNP	4.6	5.2	11.2	10.1
Total economy				
GI/GNP	43.1	42.7	50.5	48.5

NOTE: DI = disposable income of each sector; GI = total sector gross investment, tangible plus intangible; GNP = gross national product, or sum of sectoral disposable incomes.
SOURCE: John W. Kendrick, *The Formation and Stocks of Total Capital* (New
York: National Bureau of Economic Research, 1976), pp. 236-37.

ployment. But even more important for productivity growth is the
appropriate allocation of government outlays between current services
and investments, including the intangibles—R&D, education, training,
health, safety, and mobility. As shown in Table 7, governments at all
levels have devoted close to half their revenues net of transfer payments to tangible and intangible investments. This is a higher fraction than is devoted to investments (including child rearing) by the
personal sector, which has averaged less than 40 percent in high-
income years. Thus the relative shift of national income since 1929
from the personal to the public sector is one reason for the upward
trend of the total investment ratio through 1966. But the business
sector has consistently devoted more than its entire disposable income
(gross cash flow) to investment. A major reason for the decline in the
ratio of total gross investment to GNP after 1966 was the drop in the
ratio of business cash flow to GNP in 1966–1969, a decline in the

public investment ratio in 1969–1973, and the relative shift of gross income to persons after 1966.

It is important that governments continue to allocate a major fraction of their net revenues to total investment. The minor part of such investments devoted to reducing unit real costs of government operations has an important payoff in making public money go further by raising productivity of the resources commanded by governments and thus reducing their draft on resources for current operations. The major portion of public outlays devoted to infrastructure and intangibles are important as long as their social rate of return is at least equal to the rate of return on private investment. An important part of the return on public investment is its contribution to raising the productivity of private industry, thus increasing rates of return of private investments and innovational activity.

Advances in Knowledge. The spearhead of advancing productive knowledge and know-how is R&D, particularly that performed in or for the business sector. As noted above, a significant increase in profit rates would undoubtedly stimulate business-financed R&D. Conversely, accelerating R&D outlays and the growth of the resulting stock would help to reenforce the rising rate of return and the sharper increase in tangible investment in which much of the advancing knowledge is embodied. R&D directed to improving processes and producers' goods obviously conduces to reduced unit real costs and thus increased productivity. Even the R&D directed toward creating new or improved goods for private or collective consumption also helps promote productivity advance through the learning-curve effect.

The case for special measures to stimulate R&D investment and reverse its declining ratio to GNP rests on its three prime characteristics: (1) inappropriability by the funding firm of all the benefits of its inventions because of externalities; (2) the uninsurable uncertainties of the outcomes of R&D; and (3) indivisibilities requiring R&D resources on an optimal scale larger than many firms can afford. To these may be added the point that governmentally mandated standards of recent years have diverted increased amounts of R&D, as well as of fixed investments, from profit-oriented objectives.

The theoretical arguments have been buttressed by research such as Mansfield's suggesting that social rates of return to R&D are higher than—possibly double—private rates of return.[33] To the extent that the special characteristics of R&D differ by industry, size of firm, and

---

[33] See National Science Foundation, *Relationships between R&D and Economic Growth/Productivity* (November 9, 1977), p. A-7.

type of project, a case can be made for selective grants or subsidies, as discussed below. Across-the-board incentives are obviously much more economical and convenient to administer, however, and involve less bureaucratic judgment.

Business R&D outlays already enjoy an advantage over tangible fixed investment in that since 1954 they may definitely be written off as an expense in the year in which they are incurred. The most frequently mentioned additional incentive is some form of a tax credit for business R&D outlays or equivalent cash payments to firms paying no tax. Probably the most feasible plan would be to extend the present 10 percent tax credit on equipment purchases to cover industrial R&D as defined by the Financial Accounting Standards Board or as specifically defined in legislation. An advantage of this approach is that there would be little or no interference by government with the private decision-making process. The tax purist would prefer to see a direct subsidy payment, which would have the same effect.

One objection to this approach is that public funds would tend to substitute in some degree for private. To judge from studies of the tangible investment tax credit, however, there would be a substantial positive effect. An alternative proposal, which would induce a larger increase in R&D outlays, would be to permit a larger tax credit on incremental R&D over and above the outlays of the previous year or an average of several prior years. Even a 50 percent incremental R&D tax credit would cost the Treasury about $1 billion, if a 10 percent increase in business R&D between 1979 and 1980 is assumed. This compares with an almost $2 billion revenue loss from a 10 percent average credit on the $20 billion or so that business may spend on R&D in 1979.

A variant of the R&D tax credit proposal, whether average or incremental, would be to graduate the credit inversely to the size of the firm's R&D program up to some point. The rationale for graduation lies in the fact that uncertainties, indivisibilities, and even externalities tend to have a lessened negative impact on private R&D programs as they increase in size up to some point.

Another variant of the tax credit, which I proposed in a paper several years ago, would be to allow a larger credit to producers of capital goods and possibly of intermediate producers' goods.[34] The rationale for this stems from a priori reasoning buttressed by Ter-

---

[34] See John W. Kendrick, "Productivity and Business," in Jules Backman, ed., *Labor, Technology, and Productivity* (New York: New York University Press, 1974).

leckyj's research findings[35] that productivity effects of indirect R&D performed by makers of producers' goods and purchased by user firms are even greater than the effects of their direct R&D outlays. Another justification for special incentives for capital goods producers is that to the extent their relative productivity rises through process R&D and the product R&D of the firms from which they buy, the relative price of capital goods will tend to fall, which will stimulate tangible investment.

A related proposal is to allow accelerated depreciation of R&D plant and equipment by business or possibly a complete write-off for tax purposes in the year in which the costs are incurred. Alternatively, a larger investment tax credit could be granted for R&D facilities. Such measures would help increase the productivity of resources devoted to private R&D. By the same token, government grants to help modernize R&D facilities of universities and private nonprofit organizations would help improve the effectiveness of R&D activities in those sectors.

There have been proposals for creating a federal center for industrial R&D, which would disburse funds for R&D projects that are in the public interest but that would not otherwise be undertaken because of major uncertainties or costs or because of the great fragmentation of particular industries that undertake little or no research. In the latter case, the grants could be made on a matching basis to industry associations. Such arrangements for cooperative R&D might require special exemptions from the antitrust laws, however. Governments of many other industrialized countries support such centers.

Governmental procurement policies can also be used to stimulate innovative activity by suppliers, as the Experimental Technology Incentives Program of the National Bureau of Standards has demonstrated. Further institutionalization of such experimental programs on a cooperative basis, particularly at the state and local levels, would be desirable.

During the past decade, federal government support for the gathering of domestic and foreign scientific and technological information has declined drastically. It is time to increase informational services, particularly to gather information from foreign countries whose R&D activities have increased relative to those in the United States. Special attention should be paid to gathering and disseminating information that would be of value to technologically lagging industries in this country.

---

[35] Nestor E. Terleckyj, *Effects of R&D on the Productivity Growth of Industries* (Washington, D.C.: National Planning Association, 1974).

Renewed support by the federal government to state technical service centers should be considered. These are of particular value to smaller firms. Evaluation of the National Science Foundation's Innovation Center experiment may indicate the desirability of expanding the number of centers.

There are various other proposals for aiding small technical enterprises and "lone wolf" inventors, as by government guarantees of loans by small business investment companies to such enterprises, or the creation of a national research and development corporation after the British model, or tax incentives for shareholders of private corporations that invest in new or existing small technology-based companies.

Space precludes the discussion or enumeration of other proposals that have been made to encourage R&D and innovative activity. A useful compilation is contained in *U.S. Technology Policy.*[36] Unfortunately, there has not been enough research on the impacts of the various policy options, although the policy studies that have been and are being supported by the National Science Foundation are helpful and should be continued.

It is highly important for scientific and technological progress that the federal government pursue a reasonably steady and predictable policy with respect to investment of public funds in support of R&D. The sharp cutback in the late 1960s and early 1970s of such support was the primary reason for the substantial drop in the ratio of R&D expenditures to GNP and the bulge in the unemployment rates of scientists and engineers. I would hope that the new science adviser to the president and his Office of Science and Technology Policy would promote gradual increases in federal funding of R&D at least in line with the growth of potential GNP, and possibly somewhat faster if the estimated benefits warrant it. A steady, predictable R&D funding policy is important in view of the long lead time required for planning the education of scientists and engineers. Particularly important is steady, adequate support for basic research to keep up the flow of new knowledge into educational channels and into applied research, raising the productivity of both.

For the purposes of the high projection, it is estimated that a combination of the policies outlined above would increase the proportion of total R&D to GNP from the 2.2 percent of 1977 to 2.8 percent in 1990. This would result in a contribution to advances in knowledge

---

[36] National Technical Information Service, *U.S. Technology Policy,* for the Office of the Assistant Secretary for Science and Technology, U.S. Department of Commerce (March 1977).

of 0.8 percent, instead of the 0.6 projected on the assumption of no relative increase. Further, a 0.1 percent larger contribution would be expected from informal inventive and innovative activity, stimulated by the larger number of major inventions and innovations emerging from formal R&D programs. In addition, the higher rate of tangible investment discussed in the previous section would accelerate the rate of diffusion of new embodied technology by another 0.1 percent. All together the positive program for economic progress discussed above could accelerate the rate of advance of productive knowledge by nearly half, from 0.9 to 1.3 percentage points (see Table 6).

Changes in Quality of Labor. Projected increases in outlays for education and training and the associated real stocks of human capital should be accelerated somewhat by accelerated increases in stocks of tangible capital and of productive knowledge and know-how. Advances in technology generally upgrade the structure of demand for labor, increasing the requirements for more highly educated and trained personnel. Acceleration of technological advance, therefore, would tend to raise the prospective rates of return on higher education (which had declined in the 1970s) and on training for skilled occupations, and thus tend to accelerate the growth of such investments by individuals and firms.

Various governmental initiatives are available to reenforce the trend toward higher levels of average education and training per worker. There have been bills before Congress to permit deduction from individual taxable income or to provide tax credits for some portion of tuition expenses. Expansion of loans or loan guarantees from public funds for college or technical school expenses has been advocated.[37] Expansion of subsidies to industry for training of youth and disadvantaged workers by the Employment and Training Administration of the U.S. Department of Labor would help increase employment as well as training. Expansion of continuing adult education programs is particularly important in view of accelerated technological advance and the gradual increase in the average age of the labor force projected for the decade ahead.

Finally, programs for further development and more rapid diffusion of educational technology would help increase the productivity of education and training. Major technological advances have been and are being made in the areas of computer-assisted instruction,

---

[37] See National Commission on Productivity, *Education and Economic Growth* (June 1971). In his 1978 *Economic Report* President Carter recommended loans and loan guarantees rather than tuition tax credits.

programmed materials, closed circuit TV, films, and other teaching aids. But diffusion has been slow in part because of the fragmented nature of the market. Possibly performance standards could be agreed on and centralized purchasing done through national associations of state and local governments and of educational institutions at various levels. It is hoped that the commissioner of education in the Department of Health, Education, and Welfare and the administrator of employment and training in the Labor Department are developing policies to enhance the productivity as well as expand the volume of resources devoted to education and training. In the high projection of Table 6 it is estimated that the tendencies noted in this section could result in a 0.1 percent larger contribution of education and training to growth in the 1980 decade.

With respect to health and vitality, the projection of a continued decline in the length of the average workweek and workyear suggests further minor gains from this source according to Denison's analysis. So does the projection of continued increases of real health and safety outlays per capita. The possibility of further gains from this source is not envisaged in the high projection since the projected increases are already considerable. I would suggest, however, that intensification of health education programs, particularly for youth, offers the cheapest avenue for additional gains.

Policies to affect the age composition of the labor force and employment have already been discussed and are not expected to have any immediate significant effect on productivity.

Changes in Quality of Land. Historically, the market system has effectively promoted the substitution of relatively more abundant and cheaper natural resources for those that were becoming relatively scarcer and therefore more expensive. Such substitutions have been further accelerated by price incentives (when allowed to operate) for search, discovery, and development of new resource supplies and for research and development of alternative sources. Further, a liberal international trade policy mitigates the effect on productivity of a declining average quality of domestic natural resources. I would recommend more complete reliance on market pricing of natural resources and further liberalization of foreign trade policy, including reduction of nontariff barriers except where national security considerations dictate greater reliance on domestic resources.

Possibly the effectiveness of the market-directed enterprise system could be enhanced by better projections of future requirements by firms and concerned government agencies, which would make possible more timely actions to prepare for substitutions to hold down unit real costs. Nevertheless, I do not envisage any major offsets to the negative impact on productivity of a decline in average resource quality, especially in view of the accelerated growth projected in this section and the assumption of policies to promote greater energy independence. It is always possible, of course, that major new natural resource discoveries will be made or that technological breakthroughs on new energy sources will come sooner than expected.

Resource Reallocations. Less than perfect competition and various lags in adjusting labor and capital resources to dynamic changes in demand and supply conditions result in discrepancies in factor remunerations in different uses and industries. Relative shifts of labor and capital have resulted in raising productivity in past periods and are projected to continue to do so to a minor extent in the future. The tendency might be speeded up somewhat if competition and labor and capital mobility were increased. Certainly more vigorous enforcement of antitrust laws would help. So, too, would actions to reduce restrictions on entry by certain labor unions, professional associations, and other organizations. Better business and economic data would facilitate planning of adjustments. Improvement of programs to help retrain, relocate, and place displaced workers under the Comprehensive Employment and Training Act of 1973 could speed up reallocations. Maintenance of high-level aggregate economic activity itself facilitates adjustments.

Although I support these kinds of policies, I do not project a larger contribution to growth in Table 6 under high growth than under basic assumptions. Some increase in resource mobility would be required just to keep up with the faster pace of technological progress projected in the high growth model, and a faster shift to services would have a negative weighting effect.

Volume-related Factors. Given the faster rate of economic growth in the high projection, economies of scale would obviously contribute more than in the standard projection—0.5 compared with 0.3 percentage point. I do not project a higher rate of utilization of the higher productive capacity in 1990 than in the official projection, which assumed a 4.7 percent civilian unemployment rate. Therefore, the gain from the reduction of the 5.5 percent unemployment rate of 1980 is the same in both projections.

The rate of productivity is affected not only by the volume factors just described but also by the variability of production during a given period.[38] It is therefore important that fluctuations in real GNP, if they occur in the 1980 decade, be held to the small average amplitude of the post–World War II era up to 1973. The more severe 1973–1975 contraction produced the first absolute decline in productivity in a quarter of a century, with unfavorable effects from which the economy has not yet fully recovered.

Net Government Impact. In the standard projection it was assumed by BLS that the relative increase in government employment would not continue. This assumption is not altered in the high projection, but I do project that a vigorous program to enhance productivity in government at all levels can add 0.1 percentage point to the growth impact of government services to business.

Since 1973 BLS has been preparing and publishing labor productivity indexes, by functional groupings, now covering outputs produced by 65 percent of federal government civilian employees in 245 organizational elements of 48 agencies. Just as important, the Joint Financial Management Improvement Program was established by the Office of Management and Budget to prepare annual reports analyzing the reasons for the productivity changes and to prepare recommendations and plans for future productivity programs. The plans involve rationalization of internal agency programs for capital outlays to reduce costs, as well as the creation of agency productivity committees to develop ideas for enhancing worker efficiency.

The National Center for Productivity strongly supported the federal productivity measurement and improvement programs and took steps to encourage similar programs at the state and local level. If the National Productivity Council, successor to the center, is strengthened as recommended below, it is not too much to expect some acceleration in government productivity growth in the decade ahead with benefits to business and consumers (assuming the government selects appropriate activities and outputs!).

With respect to increases in business costs imposed by governmental requirements and regulations—such as paperwork and conforming to standards—the basic projection already assumes some easing in the decade ahead. Further progress toward reducing paperwork, simplification of regulations, and application of strict cost-

---

[38] See Michael Mohr, "Labor Productivity and the Business Cycle," in *New Directions in Productivity Measurement and Analysis* (New York: National Bureau of Economic Research; in process).

benefit principles in revising old standards and promulgating new ones, if necessary, could further reduce the negative productivity impact of government-business relationships. The Regulatory Council in the executive branch could serve as the vehicle to promote this objective.

Actual/Potential Efficiency and n.e.c. The ratio of actual to potential labor efficiency (under given technology) can be improved mainly where there are restrictive work practices, union work rules, or just plain lack of motivation and concern. In these areas quality of working life programs, job redesign, company productivity improvement programs, labor-management productivity teams, productivity bargaining, incentive pay systems, and other programs to enhance worker cooperation and to cut unit real costs can play an important role.[39] In response to the productivity slowdown of recent years, there has been increased emphasis on such programs. The initial impetus came from the creation by executive order in 1970 of the National Commission on Productivity, reconstituted in 1975 by congressional act as the National Center for Productivity and Quality of Working Life. The center expired September 30, 1978, and its functions were taken over by the National Productivity Council.

I would recommend that the council be strengthened by additional staff so that it can continue to promote productivity advance by further programs of the type discussed in this paper. Already a number of quality of working life organizations have been formed in the private sector, and the American Productivity Center founded in Houston by C. Jackson Grayson in 1977 is promoting productivity measurement and improvement at the company level in a succession of industries. If these efforts are continued and broadened they should have a cumulative impact on labor efficiency in particular and on productivity in general in the decade ahead. Accordingly, I show a 0.1 percentage positive contribution to growth from an increase in the ratio of actual to potential labor efficiency in the high projection.

Since fear of unemployment is a major cause of restrictive work rules and practices, maintenance of relatively full employment and provisions for job security by firms and other organizations to the extent feasible would also help increase labor efficiency. More generally, increased understanding of the principles of a modern

---

[39] See John W. Kendrick, *Understanding Productivity: An Introduction to the Dynamics of Productivity Change* (Baltimore: Johns Hopkins University Press, 1977), ch. 11.

mixed economy by the public generally and government officials in particular should help bring about changes in laws, institutions, regulations, and other social variables that would conduce to a more efficient operation of the economy. The present volume and the work of the American Enterprise Institute and similar organizations help promote the required economic understanding. Education in civics and ethics to instill the social responsibility that must accompany the tremendous individual freedom offered by our system should be expanded to reverse some of the negative social tendencies that have been aggravated in the past decade. After all, the economy is only one aspect of the broader society, and the state of health of the society inevitably affects economic performance.

Under the Humphrey-Hawkins Full Employment and Balanced Growth Act of 1978, the Council of Economic Advisers should move vigorously to review the impact of existing policies on productivity and economic progress and to coordinate and provide leadership in developing a coherent set of policy proposals to promote these objectives. In the past, the council had been largely concerned with short-term policies to promote high-level income, employment, and purchasing power. Now, its mission is broadened and its funding should be increased accordingly to permit it to undertake the coordination and leadership recommended here. Much thought will have to be devoted to defining the council's function so that it would focus on promoting and facilitating the dynamic initiatives and adjustments of the enterprise sector and not substitute centralized direction of resource allocations.[40] But the legitimate role of government in areas affecting capital formation, manpower, natural resources, science and technology, health and safety, education and training, competition and regulation, and so on is so pervasive that a more effective formulation and coordination of policies in all these areas affecting economic progress could have a profound impact.

---

[40] See the discussion in Joint Economic Committee, *U.S. Long-term Economic Growth Prospects*, pt. 8, "The Need for a National Growth Policy," pp. 114-18.

Where Has Productivity Gone?

Edward F. Denison

Note

This short article, written in the autumn of 1977 for Basis Point, *was based on research for a book,* Accounting for Slower Economic Growth: The United States in the 1970's, *which is to be published by the Brookings Institution. Developments after 1976, the terminal year of the estimates used in the article, have not brightened the productivity picture. As total output expanded in 1977 and 1978, productivity did not increase enough to offset its poor 1973–1976 performance, as some had hoped. On the contrary, it failed even to approach its 1948–1969 growth rate and consequently fell still further below its old trend line. In 1978 real national income per person employed in nonresidential business was the same as it had been five years earlier. The numbers for individual growth sources in 1973–1978, if they were available, would differ from those for 1973– 1976 used in the article, but the picture of a dismal performance only partially explained by measured determinants would remain.*

Some of the materials used in the article were developed with the financial support of the National Science Foundation Grant 75-23131. Views expressed are the author's and should not be ascribed to the Brookings Institution, its trustees, or other members of its staff, or to the National Science Foundation.

The years 1974 and 1975 witnessed a sharp, and rare, decline in output per person employed. Although part of the decline is attributable to the recession with which it coincided, most is not. In 1976 output per worker increased, but not more than is usual in a cyclical recovery of the 1976 magnitude. As a result, output per worker is

71

now much lower than it would have been if the past trend had continued. To regain the old growth path would require a productivity jump far greater than can be anticipated from the remainder of the current cyclical recovery.

To quantify these statements we have only to measure output by national income in constant prices and confine the measure to the nonresidential business sector, which includes agriculture but excludes services provided by the existing housing stock. In evaluating this sector, we shall bring into play a somewhat wintry acronym—NIPPE (national income per person employed). This measure increased by an average of 2.4 percent a year from 1948 to 1973. It dropped 4.9 percent in 1974, and a further 0.7 percent in 1975. Even after the 1976 increase, NIPPE was still 1.6 percent lower than it had been three years before; its 1973–1976 growth rate was -0.5 percent.

This experience can be better interpreted by removing the effects on output per unit of input of three factors that affect it erratically, so as to obtain an adjusted NIPPE. Although the effects of two of these factors—weather and work stoppages—are rather minor, the third is often important. This is the effect of changes in the intensity with which employed labor and capital are utilized. These changes result from fluctuations in the pressure of demand and are related to the business cycle, but the cycle in productivity usually is substantially ahead of that in unemployment.

The cyclical position was less favorable for productivity in 1976 than in 1948 or in an average postwar year, but slightly more favorable than in 1973. With the effects of the three irregular factors eliminated, national income per person employed grew 2.6 percent a year from 1948 to 1973 and increased appreciably every single year. Drops in 1974 and 1975 in NIPPE so adjusted, which totaled 3.8 percent, thus were without postwar precedent. The 1973–1976 growth rate was -0.6 percent. Although not all effects of the business cycle are removed from this measure, the biggest ones are.

In 1976, national income per person employed in nonresidential business equaled $15,120. It would have been 2.5 percent higher if the three irregular factors (chiefly, the state of demand) had been as favorable as in the average year from 1948 through 1973. Though substantial, this amount is swamped by the 10.1 percent by which NIPPE in 1976 would have been higher if its *adjusted* growth rate from 1973 to 1976 had been the same as from 1948 to 1973. (NIPPE would have been $17,055, or 12.8 percent higher than the actual 1976 figure, if both conditions had been met.)

The dip in adjusted NIPPE has had a strongly adverse impact upon living standards, business costs, inflation, and government revenues. The dip has also clearly intensified the stagflation dilemma. These consequences could be elaborated, but it seems more important to explore causes.

Sources of NIPPE Growth

The sources of NIPPE growth in nonresidential business (adjusted) prior to the 1973–1976 dip are worth studying in this connection. Estimates are available for the 1948–1969 period from my 1973 book, *Accounting for United States Economic Growth, 1929–1969*. They are shown in condensed form in Table 1. The adjusted growth rate was 2.8 percent. This growth rate can be broken down by its determinants, as is done in the table.

Present space limitations prevent a full description of estimating methods. Instead, I can only suggest the meaning of each entry and caution that the numbers, like those already cited, are estimates. Also, I apologize because space limitations force me to write as if the

TABLE 1

SOURCES OF GROWTH OF ADJUSTED NATIONAL INCOME PER PERSON EMPLOYED, NONRESIDENTIAL BUSINESS SECTOR, 1948–1969

	Percentage points
Adjusted growth rate[a]	2.8
Changes in labor characteristics	
Hours at work	−0.2
Age-sex composition	−0.1
Education	0.5
Changes in capital and land per person employed	
Nonresidential structures and equipment	0.3
Inventories	0.1
Land	0.0
Improved allocation of resources	0.4
Economies of scale from larger markets	0.5
Advances in knowledge and not elsewhere classified	1.4

[a] Adjusted to exclude the effects of three irregular factors on output per unit of input. Detail does not equal total because of rounding.

SOURCE: Edward F. Denison, *Accounting for United States Economic Growth, 1929-1969* (Washington, D.C.: Brookings Institution, 1974), p. 114.

economy were far more mechanistic, and growth sources less inter-related, than is in fact the case.

The first three sources of growth are changes in hours of work and in characteristics of the people working. Hours changes subtracted 0.2 percentage point from NIPPE growth in 1948–1969, mainly because of rising part-time employment and minor reductions in the average hours of full-time, nonfarm wage and salary workers. The effect of changes in age-sex composition of labor was a negative 0.1 percentage point because the proportion of total hours worked by highly weighted groups, particularly males thirty-five to sixty-four years of age, declined. An individual's education decisively conditions both the types of work he is able to perform and his proficiency in any particular occupation. The educational distribution of employed persons moved steadily and strongly upward, which added an estimated 0.5 percentage points to the growth of NIPPE.

The contribution of capital is divided between structures and equipment, which amounted to a positive 0.3 percentage points, and inventories, 0.1 points. The estimates represent the contribution of increases in the capital stock of each type per person employed. Capital contributed more to the growth of total national income, but much of the increase in the capital stock was matched by increased employment. The land available per worker declined as employment increased so that its contribution was negative, but the figure rounds to zero.

The estimate that 0.4 percentage points were contributed by improved resource allocation covers gains from reducing the percentage of the labor in the business sector that was overallocated to farming or misallocated to self-employment and unpaid family labor in nonfarm enterprises too small for efficiency.

The gain from economies of scale, put at 0.5 percentage points, refers to the rise in output per unit of input that is made possible by changes in the size of markets that business serves. It covers the beneficial effects of increased specialization of all sorts.

Five of the growth sources enumerated so far contributed a positive 1.8 percentage points, while three made negative contributions totaling −0.4 points (based on unrounded data). Since the adjusted growth rate was 2.8 percent, other output determinants must have made a net positive contribution of 1.4 points. This residual is labeled "advances in knowledge and not elsewhere classified." The contribution of advances in knowledge includes gains in measured output that result from the incorporation into production of new knowledge of any type, regardless of the source of that knowledge, the way knowledge is transmitted to those who can use it, or the way it is incorporated into production. "Not elsewhere classified" refers to the effects of a large number of determinants that are thought to have been individually small and on average as likely to have been favorable as unfavorable.

Thus I believe that the residual estimate provides a reasonable approximation to the contribution made by the incorporation of advances in knowledge during the 1948–1969 period. My annual index for this series rose without interruption and at a rather steady rate from 1948 to 1969. The index continued to do so until 1973.

The adjusted growth rate in national income per person employed fell from 2.8 percent a year in 1948–1969 to − 0.6 percent in 1973–1976, a drop of 3.3 percentage points (based on unrounded data). My current research makes it possible to examine the sources of this change.

Why Has NIPPE Turned Negative?

A drop of 1.6 percentage points can be specifically allocated. Governmental controls have required the diversion of a growing share of the labor and capital employed by business to pollution abatement and to the protection of employee safety and health. Also, rising crime has forced business to divert resources to crime prevention, and thefts of merchandise have directly reduced measured output. These particular changes in the legal and human environment in which business operates are estimated to have retarded the 1973–1976 growth rate of NIPPE by 0.4 percentage points.

Another 1.2 percentage points of the drop in the growth rate of NIPPE is attributable to six determinants discussed earlier: 0.3 points to a steeper drop in working hours, 0.1 to an accelerated shift in the age-sex composition of employed labor, 0.1 to slower growth of fixed capital per worker, 0.1 to slower growth of inventories per worker, 0.4 to resource reallocation as the gain from this source completely disappeared, and 0.2 points to economies of scale as market growth slackened.

In contrast, the contribution of education increased by nearly 0.4 percentage points as the educational distribution of persons employed by business moved upward at an accelerated rate. Among the reasons for this were the facts that government stopped absorbing a disproportionate part of the increase in the highly educated, and the average age of adult workers declined. (Young adults have more education than older workers.)

Contributions in the 1973–1976 period would have been different if unemployment had been the same in 1976 as in 1973. Some determinants would have contributed more, but on balance the growth rate of NIPPE was even lower on a potential output basis than on an actual basis.

Some 2.1 percentage points out of the 3.3 point drop in the growth rate of NIPPE remain in the residual series for advances in knowledge and not elsewhere classified. Its contribution fell from a positive 1.4 points to a negative 0.7 points. After rising steadily until 1973, the series dropped sharply in 1974 and 1975; then in 1976 made a normal gain from the lower level.

Why the sudden change? Some suggest that advances in knowledge have contributed less to recent growth. There could be a delayed reaction to the end in the mid-1960s of the previous long rise in research and development spending. As a mere happenstance, important new developments may not have come along recently. Managerial talent ordinarily devoted to developing means of cutting costs may have been absorbed by the need to adapt to a flood of new controls over the conduct of business. Requirements for a variety of government approvals and permits could have delayed implementation of productivity-advancing decisions that were reached.

But we cannot answer the question of why the impact came suddenly in 1974, rather than gradually over an extended period. This fact persuades me that lack of advances in knowledge was probably not responsible for much of the drop. The same problem is encountered if one resorts to most popular explanations that would affect components of "not elsewhere classified"—such as the allegation that people "don't want to work anymore," that inflation has caused misallocation and uncertainty, or that the impact of a flood of paperwork and new regulations has boosted overhead costs.

One suggestion is that the sudden rise in energy prices and in government controls to conserve energy is responsible. This suggestion conforms nicely to the time pattern. Some estimates of this effect are large. One, presented by Rasche and Tatom in the *St. Louis Federal Reserve Bank Review*, implies that higher energy prices reduced the residual part of my index by 5.3 percent in 1976. This would explain most of the drop in my index of the residual, which was 6.2 percent lower than if its 1948–1973 growth rate had continued through 1976. Though higher energy prices were surely a factor, I believe Rasche and Tatom greatly overestimate their effect. George Perry of Brookings obtains only 0.2 percent, a result I consider much more reasonable.

What of the Future?

Whether NIPPE will regain its old growth path, resume something near its old rate of growth at a new lower level, or—disastrously—follow a new and much lower growth path is yet to be determined. But it behooves us to seek explanations, and to act if and when action seems appropriate.

I have sought to provide—for business, academic, and government audiences—a way to analyze the productivity problem by breaking that problem down into its component parts. This should help to pinpoint the difficulties involved and to indicate possible avenues of action.

One Man's Baedeker to Productivity Growth Discussions

Mark Perlman

Summary

The widely voiced current concern about the productivity situation in the United States centers on the decline in productivity growth rates since 1973 and the fears that they will not return to previous levels. The second section of this chapter provides U.S. productivity growth rates. Whether shifts in the industrial structure with its greater emphasis on the tertiary sector imply a continuing fall in private business economic productivity remains moot. The second section also presents international comparisons in manufacturing that indicate U.S. productivity has lagged behind all ten foreign countries used for comparison, except the United Kingdom. Although, in the very recent period, U.S. international competitiveness has increased, that "improvement" follows solely from the sharp fall in the dollar's exchange value.

Various explanations and remedies for this productivity decline have been offered. Crucial to the analysis of the policy steps to be taken is an understanding of the measures and determinants of productivity. The third section discusses the development of four canons or stages of productivity analysis from the original microanalytic approach to an "expanded" or "mensurable" macro concept. The first stage emphasized the output per unit of labor input. The second approach added capital inputs with some weighting for both labor and capital in a total factor productivity measure; it also moved to the general economy and identified the existence of a residual. In the third stage analysis of qualitative changes in the inputs was greatly extended, and the elements within the residual were further quantified. The fourth stage argues that growth in real factor inputs (adjusted for quality) should explain all productivity changes.

Productivity analysis has moved in the mainstream of macro-economics and has indirectly affected discussions of capital availability, fiscal and regulatory policies affecting profit levels, research and development, and the demographic characteristics of the labor force. Most of all, where we now are seems to have been the likely consequence of certain macroanalytical and sometimes contradictory public policy choices. The emergence of some characteristics of on-the-job training and management administration suggests compelling reasons to reexamine the productivity question. This examination should be from the microanalytic standpoint of the traditional managerial responsibility for production efficiency.

Introduction: Perceptions of the Problem

Admonitions about the recent decline in American productivity growth have become something of an academic and journalistic staple. For example:

> Productivity, as measured by output per hour of all persons in the private sector, grew at a rate of 3.0 percent per year from 1947 to 1973. However, this average reflects a much sharper rate of gain during the first 19 years than the last 7. From 1947 through 1966, the rate was 3.2 percent, but from 1967 to 1973 the rate has dropped to 1.7 percent per year—a very substantial decline. From 1967 to 1976, productivity growth averaged 1.6 percent annually. During this latter period, the economy experienced two recessions . . . so that, in part, the decline in productivity growth is attributable to cyclical fluctuations. However, longer term factors also were operative.[1]

Although referring specifically to the electric lamp industry, the following paragraph is typical of many current jeremiads:

> In the most recent period, 1970–77, productivity growth resumed with 1.7 percent average annual gains. Although output increases were below normal during this period—averaging only 1.5 percent a year—employment and hours dropped an average of 0.2 percent per year. During the 2 recession years of this period, 1974–75, industry hours decreased 20 percent, dipping below the 1970 level. In 1976, both output and hours increased over the depressed levels of

---

[1] Ronald E. Kutscher, Jerome A. Mark, and John R. Norsworthy, "The Productivity Slowdown and the Outlook to 1985," *Monthly Labor Review*, vol. 100 (May 1977), pp. 3-4.

the preceding year. *In 1977, however, output declined 2.7 percent, while employee hours showed a 1.7 percent increase, resulting in the largest single-year drop in productivity over the period.*[2]

This current set of what are predominantly jeremiads is certainly worthy of careful examination.[3] The thrust of this essay is to argue that although the frequently repeated generalizations indicate a growing pessimism, they reflect in large part the unanticipated results of consciously ordered but nonetheless essentially contradictory public policy choices. Also, much of what goes into these discussions belies a knowledge of the historic variations in productivity growth in different areas of the economy or the impressive impact of intersectoral changes such as the 0.4 percent shift from farms to nonfarms, 1947–1966. Some are unaware that what has occurred is probably the result of recent *temporary* demographic changes within the labor force, including no less than a 44 percent increase in total civilian supply since 1960, with the great bulk of this increase occurring since 1966 (the annual rate of increase in 1960–1966 was 1.4 percent; in 1966–1973, 2.3 percent; 1973–1978, 2.5 percent). Others, concerned with the flow of increments to the capital goods supply, may be missing an important aspect of the efficient use of these capital goods. But one begins not by describing views but by focusing on what the data seem to show. And this seemingly obvious first step is not all that simple.

To start, the productivity indexes best reflect what is happening in the private sector. Also within the private sector, data on productivity changes are truly reliable only for primary and secondary industry, excluding construction.[4] Yet these two sectors involve a decreasing and by now minor part of the rapidly expanded labor force. In 1970 agriculture, forestry, and fishing involved 4.5 percent of the labor force; in 1977 the relevant figure fell to 3.7 percent. In 1970 manufacturing involved 26.4 percent of the employed labor

---

[2] Richard B. Caines, "Productivity in the Electric Lamp Industry," *Monthly Labor Review*, vol. 101 (August 1978), p. 16; italics added. See also J. Edwin Henneberger, "Productivity Growth Below Average in the Household Furniture Industry," *Monthly Labor Review*, vol. 101 (November 1978), pp. 23-29.

[3] All is not gloomy, however; see, for instance, Arthur S. Herman, "Productivity Increased during 1977 in a Majority of Selected Industries," *Monthly Labor Review*, vol. 101 (November 1978), pp. 54-57; and John W. Kendrick seemed generally optimistic in "The Outlook for Productivity and Unit Labor Costs," *Business Economics*, vol. 13 (January 1978), pp. 56-57.

[4] "Statistics on productivity in [the construction and financial] . . . sectors (and those in the government sector) are notoriously bad [sic]" (Council of Economic Advisers, *Annual Report, 1979*, pp. 71-72).

force; in 1977 that portion amounted to 22.8 percent. And what about the augmented services sector (including transportation, trade, financial intermediaries, services, and public administration)? In 1970 it was 62.3 percent of the employed labor force; in 1977 that percentage had grown to 66.5. In just seven years the goods-producing part of the employed labor force (agriculture, fisheries, forestry, mining, construction, and manufacturing) fell from 37.7 percent to 33.5 percent. On its previously shrunken base this amounted to a 11.1 percent downward shift.

To put the historical comparisons in a longer but no less relevant frame of reference, in 1947, 11.9 percent of the gross national product in current prices originated in the primary industry (including mining), while in 1976 it was only 5.5 percent; in 1947 secondary industry (manufacturing and construction) accounted for 32.7 percent of the gross national product; in 1976 it was 28.0 percent. As for the obvious growth area, tertiary industry, in 1947 it was 55.3 percent, and in 1976 it was 66.5 percent; on a larger base it has increased 20.3 percent. The clear point is that ours is less and less a goods economy (in GNP terms falling in twenty-nine years from 44.7 to 33.5 percent) and more and more a services economy. Measurement of efficiency in the services portion is a more subtle exercise than in the product portions, for which reason most of the international comparisons rely principally on sectors that are easier to measure and in truth rely only on manufacturing in the private sector. Thus, while this essay is on recent productivity changes, its inferences are most stable when the data come from only a portion of the American economy—and an increasingly minor portion in terms of both the American labor force and the gross national product. What is going on in the tertiary sector is quite probably dismal, but the services sector seems always to have been absolutely low in productivity. If the effect of compositional labor force change is frightening to some, there is no way to evaluate these fears until the data improve.

Furthermore, several historical tendencies have clearly been accentuated in the recent decade—for instance, encouragement of a vast diffusion of employment; improvement of the immediate work environment and the general abatement of air, water, and sound pollution; and security rights of individual employment (including steps toward compensatory hiring of groups previously discriminated against). Each of these policy areas has a certain threshold effect, which increases production costs without compensating increases in product output. In some cases it can be reasonably hypothesized that over time the threshold impact will be reversed—that is, hiring without regard to race or sex may in the long haul result in greater worker efficiency, but in other cases the reasonable expectation is that these historical policies will do little, if anything, to increase worker productivity.

The American choice of these policies is shared by some but probably not by all of the nations with which we compete in the more usual product markets. For example, several Western European nations have not sought to diffuse employment opportunity as we have and have actually deported foreign workers when efficiency considerations suggested that longer hours rather than employment diffusion made political and economic sense. And while many nations have elected to pursue policies to reduce pollution of the workplace and general environment, they may not have achieved as much in the way of results as has the American manufacturing sector. We do have data on the American experience; we lack it for other countries. Whatever are the direct costs of cleanup and prophylaxis, the costs of the political policing of pollution control are more than minimal and are likely to rise at an accelerating rate as environmental consciousness spreads. Adam Smith has long been criticized for drawing a distinction between productive and nonproductive labor. I do not want to fall into the obvious trap of suggesting that governmental policing is either unnecessary or nonproductive, but I am prepared to suggest that at current civil servant pay scales these cleanup policies are expensive for the public purse and that most business establishments, which are required not only to comply but to monitor compliance continuously, have incurred vastly expanded private overhead costs in doing so.

There is also evidence that the waves of lawlessness that have swept over most industrialized countries have not been everywhere of equal force or depth. Again, while we have some analysis of the adverse effect of this lawlessness in America, we lack it for other countries. In the private sector prophylaxis is expensive and, as the data show, significantly increases unit labor costs.

In sum, then, while it borders on becoming a commonplace that what ails the American manufacturing economy is a lack of vitality in its productivity growth, the phenomena are somewhat more complex than the usual articulator of the commonplace suspects. And the interpretation of what the truth means leads to the baring of some important, if forgotten, fundamentals. Jacob Viner used to remind his listeners regularly of the dangers of "erudite trumpery" or, more euphemistically, of "sophisticated nonsense." "Too smart by half," was Clement Attlee's preferred phrase. American manufacturing industry truly does have a problem of productivity growth, and I have referred to many of its macro elements—environmental concerns, capital, demographic changes, crime, and employment policies. It seems to me, however, that insufficient attention has been given to the micro area—the firm, where basically management and labor skills matter.[5] That, however, is the end of my tale. First, let us look at the figures.

What Do the Figures Show?

In 1977 John W. Kendrick published an excellent, succinct primer in which the reason for the current jeremiads was made even more explicit; 1966 seems to have been a watershed.[6] A quick perusal of this work reveals that these productivity ratios have a history of both long-term and purely business-cycle fluctuations, that the growth trend was probably upward until 1966, and that the heydays of Kendrick's subperiods were 1948–1953 and 1960–1966.[7] One specific additional point: labor force growth vastly accelerated after 1966. On the whole, real product per man-hour fluctuations (adjusted for business-cycle activity) have shown a continued downward trend in recent years. That trend is undoubtedly the overall basis for the pessimism.

In its January 1979 *Annual Report*, the Council of Economic Advisers stressed its concern with the performance in "the nation's nonfarm, nonmanufacturing sector, where productivity actually declined 0.3 percent during 1978."[8] The Council concluded, however, that "productivity growth in manufacturing . . . was strong." Tables 1 and 2 give a good summary of the Council's view, which, although it is not a vintage jeremiad, is certainly nothing to be cheery about.

But that is not all. Since 1966 and particularly since 1970, while America has progressed slowly when it has progressed at all, our economic competitors have progressed mightily. The intensity of the gloom, the jeremiad *par excellence*, comes from the international comparisons.

---

[5] My emphasis on the microanalytical approach is only a relative choice.

[6] John W. Kendrick, *Understanding Productivity: An Introduction to the Dynamics of Productivity Change* (Baltimore: Johns Hopkins University Press, 1977), p. 31. Others, such as Edward F. Denison, seem to suggest that whatever had been happening before 1973 and what has occurred since then indicate that the watershed was not in 1966 but well after. See Denison's paper in this volume.

[7] See Table 3 of Kendrick's paper in this volume.

[8] Council of Economic Advisers, *Annual Report, 1979*, p. 67.

TABLE 1
Labor Productivity Growth, 1948–1978

Sector	Percent Change per Year				
	1948–1955	1955–1965	1965–1973	1973–1977	1977–1978[a]
Private business					
economy	3.4	3.1	2.3	1.0	0.4
Nonfarm	2.7	2.6	2.0	0.9	0.6
Manufacturing	3.3	2.9	2.4	1.5	2.5
Nonmanu-					
facturing	2.4	2.4	1.7	0.6	−0.3

Note: Data relate to output per hour paid for, for all persons.
[a] Preliminary.
Source: Council of Economic Advisers, *Annual Report, 1979*, p. 68.

Table 3, derived from an article by Keith Daly and Arthur Neef, compares recent U.S. *manufacturing* productivity and output with that of several other countries, using 1970 as the base rather than 1967. The change makes this statistical display slightly different from that of Daly and Neef, since the economic performances of the various countries considered were quite different during the 1967–1970 period. My outstanding conclusions are:

- *Output.* Over the 1970–1977 period the U.S. economy has grown faster than the German but not as fast as the French or the Japanese. The midperiod recession was more severe in the United States than in Germany, Japan, or France. In 1977 the American economy clearly grew the most.
- *Employment.* Germany with a corps of foreign workers has shown the greatest reduction in manufacturing employment. In France and Japan employment has stayed at about the 1970 level, although it has been falling since 1974 and 1975, respectively. In 1977 the United States led all countries, with the United Kingdom the only other expansionary economy in this respect.
- *Hours.* From 1970 to 1977 hours generally fell in every country except the United States.
- *Output per hour.* The United Kingdom and the United States have the lowest output per hour; the best performances are by the French and the Germans. Only the United Kingdom figures are less than the American.

TABLE 2

PRODUCTIVITY GROWTH BY INDUSTRY, 1950–1977

Industry	1977 Output Share (percent)[a]	Percent Change per Year		
		1950–1965	1965–1973	1973–1977
Agriculture	2.9	4.9	3.6	3.0
Mining	1.5	4.3	1.9	−6.1
Construction	4.3	3.4	−2.1	0.3
Manufacturing				
Nondurable	9.9	3.2	3.3	2.2
Durable	14.4	2.5	2.2	1.2
Transportation	3.9	3.0	2.9	1.0
Communication	3.2	5.3	4.6	6.7
Utilities	2.3	6.1	3.5	0.2
Trade				
Wholesale	7.3	2.6	3.4	−0.8
Retail	10.0	2.3	2.1	0.8
Finance, insurance, and real estate	15.4	1.6	0.2	2.3
Services	12.0	1.2	1.7	−0.3
Government	12.5	0.4	0.5	0.1
All industries				
Current weights	100.0	2.7	2.0	1.1
Fixed weight (1977 output weights)	—	2.6	1.9	1.1

NOTE: Growth data relate to output per hour worked for all persons.
[a] Detail may not add to 100 percent because of rounding.
SOURCE: Council of Economic Advisers, *Annual Report, 1979*, p. 71.

- *Unit labor costs in dollars.* The United States shows the smallest increase. In figures not shown but from which these labor costs were derived, the American performance (least growth 1970–1977) is the best. But the weakening of the dollar has been the greater explanation for the recently improved American international competitiveness.
- *General.* France and Germany, which had outstanding performances, pursued slightly different strategies. France expanded output and held up employment while decreasing hours; Germany did not expand output as much while decreasing both employment and hours. The United States chose to expand output while maintaining employment and hours; this choice seems to have led to only a modest increase in output per hour (labor productivity).

TABLE 3

INDEXES OF MANUFACTURING OUTPUT, EMPLOYMENT, HOURS, OUTPUT PER HOUR, AND UNIT LABOR COSTS, 1970–1977

Year	United States	Canada	Japan	France	Germany	United Kingdom	Ten Foreign Countries[a]
Output							
1970	100.0	100.0	100.0	100.0	100.0	100.0	100.0
1971	101.4	105.9	102.7	106.3	101.4	99.4	102.6
1972	110.8	113.5	110.3	113.0	104.2	102.0	107.7
1973	120.1	123.7	127.8	120.9	110.7	110.6	117.8
1974	112.0	127.9	122.8	124.0	111.1	108.9	118.4
1975	106.3	120.8	109.2	120.9	104.3	102.3	110.3
1976	116.3	127.3	121.5	130.6	111.9	103.3	118.7
1977	123.7	132.1	126.4	135.1	115.4	103.8	121.9
1977/1976 (percent change)	6.4	3.8	4.1	3.5	3.1	0.4	2.7
Employment							
1970	100.0	100.0	100.0	100.0	100.0	100.0	100.0
1971	96.1	99.4	101.3	101.6	99.3	97.5	99.9
1972	98.8	102.3	101.7	103.1	97.1	93.6	99.0
1973	104.0	106.8	106.3	105.6	97.7	95.5	101.4
1974	103.6	108.9	106.7	107.0	95.1	95.8	101.5
1975	94.9	106.3	101.4	104.1	88.7	93.4	97.6

(Table 3 continues on the next page.)

TABLE 3 (continued)

Year	United States	Canada	Japan	France	Germany	United Kingdom	Ten Foreign Countries[a]
1976	98.2	106.3	101.1	103.1	86.6	90.8	96.2
1977	101.6	106.4	99.4	102.3	86.6	91.7	95.8
1977/1976 (percent change)	3.5	0.0	−1.7	−0.8	0.0	1.0	−0.5
Hours							
1970	100.0	100.0	100.0	100.0	100.0	100.0	100.0
1971	100.1	99.3	98.3	99.3	97.7	98.0	98.1
1972	101.3	99.0	97.9	98.4	96.8	97.6	97.2
1973	101.8	98.9	97.2	97.4	96.3	99.5	96.7
1974	100.3	98.6	92.8	95.9	93.5	96.7	93.9
1975	99.3	97.8	90.4	93.7	90.7	95.7	91.4
1976	100.4	98.5	93.3	93.6	92.2	96.0	93.0
1977	100.8	97.4	93.5	92.7	91.3	97.0	92.9
1977/1976 (percent change)	0.4	−1.1	0.2	−1.0	−1.0	1.0	−0.1
Output per hour							
1970	100.0	100.0	100.0	100.0	100.0	100.0	100.0
1971	105.5	107.1	103.1	105.3	104.6	104.0	104.6
1972	110.8	112.0	110.8	111.5	110.9	111.6	111.8
1973	113.8	117.1	123.7	117.6	117.7	116.3	120.0

1974	107.9	119.1	124.0	120.9	124.9	117.5	124.0
1975	113.2	116.2	119.2	124.0	129.5	114.5	123.5
1976	117.8	121.5	128.8	135.3	140.2	118.5	132.4
1977	120.8	127.4	136.0	142.4	146.1	116.6	137.0
1977/1976 (percent change)	2.5	4.8	5.6	5.2	4.2	−1.6	3.5

Unit labor cost in U.S. dollars

1970	100.0	100.0	100.0	100.0	100.0	100.0	100.0
1971	100.9	103.9	115.5	106.4	113.6	111.4	111.6
1972	101.4	109.2	141.1	122.4	130.7	119.4	127.8
1973	105.8	113.7	172.4	151.1	168.4	125.3	154.5
1974	122.8	132.2	209.6	162.2	188.0	151.2	176.1
1975	130.8	149.1	251.6	209.6	214.8	187.9	212.0
1976	135.9	167.8	252.0	197.0	205.3	174.2	205.6
1977	144.5	164.5	288.4	208.8	233.4	188.4	228.4
1977/1976 (percent change)	6.3	−2.0	14.4	6.0	13.7	8.2	11.1

[a] Canada, Japan, Belgium, Denmark, France, Federal Republic of Germany, Italy, the Netherlands, Sweden, and the United Kingdom.
SOURCE: Keith Daly and Arthur Neef, "Productivity and Unit Labor Costs in 11 Industrialized Countries, 1977," *Monthly Labor Review*, vol. 101 (November 1978), pp. 11-17.

But there is more to the story. As indicated at the beginning of this essay, much of what has happened in American manufacturing is likely the result of policy choices. These choices stem in part from the rapid growth of American population from 1946 to 1960,[9] resulting in a natural increase in the size of the traditional labor force starting in about 1964,[10] and from changes in living styles that became apparent in the mid-1960s when women's participation in the labor force increased further.[11] This growth in the labor force created an American employment problem, the dominance of which swamped considerations of worker efficiency (as measured in unit labor costs).

The expansion of the American labor force may not have been economically logical, but it carried a certain political persuasiveness. Such political persuasiveness has not been uniformly applied, as can be seen in relation to the further investment of capital. The non-hiring of labor by agricultural firms stands in vivid contrast to the hiring of labor by some manufacturing firms. On the agricultural side, particularly in grain production, productivity considerations have been paramount, and intensification of capital inputs continues at a high rate. In some areas of manufacturing there is a paradox between public cries for expansion of the labor force and tax regulations favoring capital substitutions.[12] The same contradiction applies in the services sector. Eliminating racial barriers, a policy often adopted without reference to the consequent impact on unit labor costs, is another example. My purpose is not to fault these choices, and it seems likely that both policy makers and the American public would have made the same choices even if the probable loss of productivity growth had been anticipated (which in some instances it probably was).

---

[9] The increase was 27.34 percent, an annual increase of 1.62 percent.

[10] In fact, the labor force increased 59.11 percent from 1947 to 1976.

[11] The female contingent in the 1947 labor force was 28.1 percent (approximately 17 million workers), and it was 41 percent of the 1976 labor force (38 million workers). The female section of the labor force increased 124 percent, while the male contingent increased only 32.1 percent.

[12] "Law as well as custom now decrees that penalty rates, occasionally running as high as an incremental two hundred percent, must be paid when workers exceed some magically critical number of hours worked in a week or 7-day period. American law has specified that regressive taxes be put on payrolls in order to finance a growing set of social security benefits. Other tax laws, and particularly tax regulations, have been enacted or proclaimed, which offer the temptation of tax-exempt wage benefits like life insurance, health care insurance, unemployment benefits and, even for a time, sick leave payments. These serve to complicate the earlier simplicity of deciding when to increase the firm's payroll by hiring an $(n + 1)^{th}$ worker with concomitant fringe benefits payable in the future or merely to pay the nth worker overtime. Our tax regulations go

A Bird's-Eye View of Recent Canonical Interpretations

While measuring and studying productivity is not a recent innovation in America, my interest focuses on changes in interpretation in the decade or so after the end of World War II. These interpretations specify measures of productivity, the determinants of productivity, and what policy measures are being recommended. It is useful to start at something like the chronological beginning.

John W. Kendrick, who himself is a major contributor to the current discoveries about productivity trends, gives a nutshell summary of the historic development of the American measuring process in his 1977 monograph.[13] He reports that in America episodic research started under Carroll Davidson Wright in the old Bureau of Labor in the 1880s when a concern, invariably voiced in depressions, was again expressed that machinery was the laboring man's enemy. The National Bureau of Economic Research (NBER) began in the 1920s to systematize empirical measurement. The NBER names whose contributions are seminal include Frederick C. Mills, Harry Jerome, Solomon Fabricant, C. A. Bliss, Simon Kuznets, Harold Barger, J. M. Gould, Daniel B. Creamer, Thor Hultgren, Victor R. Fuchs, and of course Kendrick. The NBER contribution also attests to the enduring value of nongovernmental basic research in economics.

The federal government, particularly since World War I, has now gotten far into the act.[14] The Department of Labor has a variety of

---

even further and offer employers tax-saving write-off benefits for switching from employment of labor to machinery, even machinery leased on a unit-output charge basis.

"Succinctly put, it seems to me that any discussion of 'Discrepancies of Supply and Demand in the Labor Market: Sectoral, Regional, and Professional,' has to start from a recognition that the institutional constraints ought to gear the analysis very much to the cobweb of regulations and customs of a particular place and time, regulations that tilt micro-production functions towards the use of more capital and away from labor. This, then, is my first point—we live with a discrepancy of supply and demand for labor and in a world with almost everyone shouting, 'Hire people,' but with the laws persuasively whispering, 'Choose machines.' " (Mark Perlman, "Discrepancies of Supply and Demand in the Labor Market: Sectoral, Regional, and Professional—Causes and Cures" in Herbert Giersch, ed., *Capital Shortage and Unemployment in the World Economy: Symposium 1977* [Tübingen: J. C. B. Mohr (Paul Siebeck), 1978], pp. 159-60.)

[13] Kendrick, *Understanding Productivity*, pp. 19 ff. A more detailed historical survey appears in his *Productivity Trends in the United States*, National Bureau of Economic Research General Series 71 (Princeton, N.J.: Princeton University Press, 1969), pp. 3-56.

[14] See especially a set of studies financed by the federal government in the mid-1930s and published by the National Bureau of Economic Research (NBER): National Research Project on Reemployment Opportunities and Recent Changes in Industrial Technique, *Studies of Production and Employment in Selected Industries*, nos. 1 and 2 (Philadelphia, 1938–1939).

statistical series designed to reflect changes in the output-input relationship of labor, and the Department of Agriculture has series designed to reflect comparable changes in the agricultural sector.

Nonetheless, in the beginning productivity was an output/input index where the numerator was the physical output (measured in goods) and the labor input was agglomerated to levels of the firm and the industry. This early approach of the National Bureau of Economic Research I would call the *original canonical interpretation*.[15] Its predominant characteristic in my view is its focus on the microanalytical aspects of productivity, which is essentially related to labor inputs and these rather specifically to industry-group data.

The perceived difficulty with this original canonical index as thus simplistically developed was that worker input was clearly not the only powerful input. A new synthesis was then developed, which ultimately became a second canonical interpretation. Capital, natural resources (including intermediate goods), and management were no less necessary than labor. Nor were any of these elements really "abstract"; each had qualitative characteristics. Capital inputs including technological improvements (meaning substitution of capital for some hourly labor), improved natural resource input (meaning less wastage or less need for expensive preliminary processing), and better managerial planning also improved the output/input ratio. Labor became seemingly more educated, and therethrough less supervision was needed because instructions could be given in lieu of continuous monitoring. The scale of productive operations changed and could seemingly be ever increased because with a larger scale more efficient techniques could be afforded (classically called "lengthened round-aboutness of production") and because the units of output produced could be distributed more cheaply.[16] The net result gave credence to the expectation that labor productivity would continue to grow. In a classification of intellectual perceptions of the topic, Fabricant's, Abramovitz's, and Barger's NBER studies were, as I have just noted, essentially microanalytical in perception (with aggregation of industries being a normal next step).[17]

---

[15] I use "canonical" in the sense of "general law, rule, or principle."

[16] There are some who argue that the really important output efficiency variable is a larger scale of operations.

[17] Solomon Fabricant, *Basic Facts on Productivity Change*, Occasional Paper 63 (New York: NBER, 1959); Moses Abramovitz, *Resource and Output Trends in the United States since 1870*, Occasional Paper 52 (New York: NBER, 1956); Harold Barger and Hans H. Landsberg, *Output, Employment, and Productivity: A Study of American Agriculture, 1899–1939* (New York: NBER, 1942); Harold Barger and Sam H. Schurr, *The Mining Industries: A Study of Output, Employ-*

A problem appeared: changes in output were greater than changes in input. The whole seemed greater than its parts. That difference, called "the residual," had to be explained.[18] The point of initial departure was the realization that the traditional approach needed refinement so that the unexplained residual could be measured.

Certain conceptual and measuring modifications were incorporated. Principal among these was a new idea, *total factor productivity*. Kendrick, as early as 1956,[19] cites the work of Hiram S. Davis (itself published in 1946) as pioneer in this exploration; he also lists George Stigler (1947), G. T. Barton and M. R. Cooper (1948), and Jacob Schmookler (1952).[20] It is clear that Moses Abramovitz focused on the topic in 1956,[21] and although historians of economic thought will differ as to priorities, I believe most of them will agree that the major impact on the economics profession is associated with Robert M. Solow's 1957 article, "Technical Change and the Aggregate Production Function."[22] His treatment was expanded in a 1960 essay, "Investment and Technical Progress";[23] further developed in a 1962 paper, "Technical Progress, Capital Formation and Economic Growth";[24] and again assembled in a 1963 book, *Capital Theory and*

---

ment, and Productivity, 1899–1939 (New York: NBER, 1944); Harold Barger, *The Transportation Industries, 1889–1946: A Study of Output, Employment, and Productivity* (New York: NBER, 1951). Several other NBER General Series studies could be cited.

[18] "The source of the great increase in net product per head was not mainly an increase in labor input per head, not even an increase in capital per head, as these resource elements are conventionally conceived and measured. Its source must be sought principally in the complex of little understood forces which caused productivity, that is, output per unit of utilized resources, to rise." (Moses Abramovitz, "Resource and Output Trends in the United States since 1870," *American Economic Review*, vol. 46 [May 1956], p. 6.)

[19] John W. Kendrick, *Productivity Trends: Capital and Labor*, Occasional Paper 53 (New York: NBER, 1956), pp. 2–3. Laurits R. Christensen reports that "By 1947 U.S. Department of Agriculture economists were experimenting with the total factor productivity approach (Cooper, Barber, and Brodell)." See his "Concepts and Measurement of Agricultural Productivity," *American Journal of Agricultural Economics*, vol. 57 (1975), Proceedings Issue, p. 910.

[20] To these might be added many others; specifically there is D. Gale Johnson's "The Nature of the Supply Function for Agricultural Products," *American Economic Review*, vol. 40 (September 1950), pp. 559-60; and Solomon Fabricant has a pertinent section in his "Productivity Research," *Review of Income and Wealth*, vol. 20 (September 1974), pp. 235-49.

[21] Abramovitz, *Resource and Output Trends*, pp. 5-23.

[22] In *Review of Economics and Statistics*, vol. 29 (August 1957), pp. 312-20.

[23] In Kenneth J. Arrow, Samuel Karlin, and Patrick Suppes, eds., *Mathematical Methods in the Social Sciences* (Stanford, Calif.: Stanford University Press, 1960), pp. 89-104.

[24] In *American Economic Review*, vol. 52 (May 1962), pp. 76-86.

the Rate of Return.[25] Solow's work can be seen as a basic statement of the second testament or *second canonical approach*. It was part of the then new view that macroeconomics was something distinctly different from its purported microanalytical foundations.

Total factor productivity came to grips with explaining productivity changes by shifting analytical focus from productivity as being worker-connected, materials-connected, or capital-connected to productivity as both a macroanalytic and a holistic index. Attention was no longer on the firm or even on the industry. It was transferred to the aggregate national economy or to its principal components, the agricultural, the manufacturing, and certain portions of the services sectors. In other words, productivity measurement was graduated from its microanalytical constraints, however aggregated, to *Volkswirtschaftslehre* (political economy); from a concern with labor and the business cycle it moved to measurement of all the inputs and to a concern with the efficiency of the more usual macroeconomic policy tools. The change of emphasis assumed that productivity was holistic: neither worker motivation nor management efficiency was seen at the heart of productivity changes; instead, it was the labor force in combination with capital, with a changing scale of output, with new materials, and with a reformulation of the final demand for goods and services. The new concept took into account certain demographic changes in the labor force, including age and sex composition, educational composition, and such institutional or secular trends as those associated with the civil rights and women's rights movements.

The new approach also tried to grapple with comparable changes in the age composition of capital goods. The result was a publication explosion, or what is called the Cambridges controversy. The English Cambridge sought, in my view unsuccessfully, to get Solow and his Massachusetts colleagues to concretize the capital machinery component in their production function/productivity analyses, much as he and others had concretized the labor component. The Massachusetts Cambridge sought, in my view also unsuccessfully, to get Joan Robinson and her Cantabrigian colleagues to understand why capital goods should be handled as a lump or, better yet, as a mensurable lump. In the end each theorist went his or her way. The significant point, however, is that the American and the British intellectual elites were now confidently treating productivity as a macroeconomic phenomenon with regard to both the whole economy and all the factors of production (or so they thought).

---

[25] Amsterdam: North-Holland, 1963; see particularly pp. 44 ff.

The second canon discovered "a residual," which was not "explained" by the usual quantitative inputs. As I read the excellent material fleshing out this canon, it implies that macro monetary and tax tools could be used to adjust rates of productivity change by means of manipulating rates of capital substitution for labor and patterns of national appropriation for research and development.

The next critically important analysis—*a third canonical contribution*—was made by Edward F. Denison in three separate books: *The Sources of Economic Growth in the United States and the Alternatives before Us,*[26] *Why Growth Rates Differ: Postwar Experience in Nine Western Countries,*[27] and *Accounting for United States Economic Growth: 1929–1969.*[28] Most recently Denison has gone on to add to his interpretation in two articles; one is, "Effects of Selected Changes in the Institutional and Human Environment upon Output per Unit Input,"[29] and "Where Has Productivity Gone?"[30]

Denison's findings are appropriately complex. Though incorporating the macroanalytical approach (which I believe was principally introduced by the second approach), he went on to introduce the precise kind of long-term statistical series quantification usually identified with the National Bureau of Economic Research and the writers of the first school. His essential numéraire is change in output per employed worker, or, as he phrases it in his most recent work, NIPPE (national income per person employed).[31] Yet his analysis is clearly macroeconomic and does not focus at all narrowly on what was originally a microanalytic perception of labor efficiency. In the tradition of Solow and others, Denison accepted productivity increases as containing an inexplicable "hard core" residual, but he did much to assign changes in *qualitative* input as a means to reduce the "inexplicable" hard core. To quote Abramovitz in his perceptive review of Denison's 1962 book, Denison's estimates show:

> [a] large reduction in the apparent importance of the increase in output per unit of input to under half its former size. Three adjustments in labor input account for the bulk of the change. Two large adjustments . . . allow for the alleged

[26] Supplementary Paper 13 (New York: Committee for Economic Development, 1962).

[27] With Jean-Pierre Poullier (Washington, D.C.: Brookings Institution, 1967).

[28] Washington, D.C.: Brookings Institution, 1974.

[29] In *Survey of Current Business,* vol. 58 (January 1978), pp. 21-44.

[30] Reprinted in this volume.

[31] Work done in the Bureau of Labor Statistics of the U.S. Department of Labor and elsewhere uses as the numéraire not "person worked" but "hour paid for."

TABLE 4

SOURCES OF GROWTH OF NONRESIDENTIAL BUSINESS SECTOR: ACTUAL NATIONAL INCOME PER PERSON EMPLOYED AND POTENTIAL NATIONAL INCOME PER PERSON POTENTIALLY EMPLOYED, 1929–1969

Percentage Contribution to Sector Growth Rate

	Actual national income per person employed			Potential national income per person potentially employed		
	1929–1969	1929–1948	1948–1969	1929–1969	1929–1948	1948–1969
Sector national income	2.14	1.57	2.65	2.22	1.52	2.86
Total factor input	0.33	0.11	0.52	0.32	0.09	0.54
Labor	0.20	0.25	0.16	0.20	0.24	0.17
Hours	−0.23	−0.24	−0.22	−0.23	−0.23	−0.21
Average hours	−0.49	−0.60	−0.38	−0.48	−0.60	−0.36
Efficiency offset	0.16	0.27	0.05	0.15	0.27	0.04
Intergroup shift offset	0.10	0.09	0.11	0.10	0.10	0.11
Age-sex composition	−0.06	0.01	−0.12	−0.06	0.00	−0.12
Education	0.49	0.48	0.50	0.49	0.47	0.50
Capital	0.17	−0.08	0.40	0.17	−0.09	0.41
Inventories	0.06	0.01	0.10	0.06	0.01	0.10
Nonresidential structures and equipment	0.11	−0.09	0.30	0.11	−0.10	0.31
Land	−0.04	−0.06	−0.04	−0.05	−0.06	−0.04
Output per unit of input	1.81	1.46	2.13	1.90	1.43	2.32

Advances in knowledge and n.e.c.[a]	1.10	0.73	1.44	1.11	0.72	1.44
Improved resource allocation	0.35	0.34	0.36	0.36	0.36	0.37
Farm	0.30	0.32	0.28	0.31	0.33	0.29
Nonfarm self-employment	0.05	0.02	0.08	0.05	0.03	0.08
Economies of scale	0.43	0.34	0.51	0.43	0.34	0.52
Irregular factors	−0.07	0.05	−0.18	0.00	0.01	−0.01
Weather in farming	0.00	0.01	−0.01	0.00	0.01	−0.01
Labor disputes	0.00	0.00	0.00	0.00	0.00	0.00
Intensity of demand	−0.07	0.04	−0.17	—	—	—

[a] Not elsewhere classified.

SOURCE: Edward F. Denison, *Accounting for United States Economic Growth: 1929-1969* (Washington, D.C.: Brookings Institution, 1974), p. 114.

effects of shorter hours and of the rise in the level of education upon the quality of labor input per hour worked. A third, smaller, adjustment takes account of the fact that women in the labor force . . . typically . . . represent a more experienced group. . . . The residual, moreover, no longer seems just that. It has seven different parts . . . the two largest of which are "economies of scale" and "advance of knowledge."[32]

Denison's findings in his 1974 book are summarized in Table 4, with the figures having a negative prefix being detrimental to productivity growth. The "powerful" positive explanatory elements include improved technological knowledge, economies of scale,[33] improved formal educational attainment in the labor force, improved resource allocation, improved factory and business plant layout, and improved resource allocation. The negative explanatory elements were largely tied up with reductions in the number of hours worked and changes in the age-sex composition of the labor force.

In his January 1978 article, Denison estimated quantitatively the negative impact on American productivity of the relatively new national enthusiasm for improving the working and consuming environment (see Table 5). His considerations involved pollution abatement, worker safety and health, and dishonesty and crime. The total negative impact of the three steadily mounted until 1975, when they further reduced an already weakened productivity growth rate by 0.51 points (from 1973 to 1976 national income per person employed fell 0.6 percent). Denison's concluding paragraph identifies his concern with a change in our priorities from economic growth to protection of the environment and, as such, is worth careful reading:

Annual growth rates in 1948–69 were derived in *Accounting* for total output (measured by NI [national income]) in nonresidential business and for a number of related series. These rates included 3.7 percent for total output, 2.6 percent for output per person employed, 3.1 percent for output per hour worked, 2.1 percent for output per unit of input, and 1.4 percent for the index that measures the contribution of advances in knowledge and miscellaneous determinants to these growth rates. In the 1948–69 period, the reduction in all

---

[32] Moses Abramovitz, "Economic Growth in the United States: A Review Article," *American Economic Review*, vol. 52 (September 1962), p. 767.

[33] Some argue that the residual ultimately can be reduced to impact of economies of scale. Denison, however, focuses on explaining what he can, and apparently does not worry about what ultimately cannot be explained by quantitation or in qualitative converted to quantitative terms.

TABLE 5

The Effects of Changes in Three Aspects of the Institutional and Human Environment upon Output per Unit of Input in Nonresidential Business

Year	Indexes, 1972=100				Percentage Change in Indexes from Previous Year			
	Pollution abatement	Worker safety and health	Dishonesty and crime	Total	Pollution abatement	Worker safety and health	Dishonesty and crime	Total
1957	100.41	100.17	100.33	100.91	—	—	—	—
1958	100.41	100.17	100.27	100.85	—	—	−0.06	−0.06
1959	100.41	100.17	100.28	100.86	—	—	0.01	0.01
1960	100.41	100.17	100.22	100.80	—	—	−0.06	−0.06
1961	100.41	100.17	100.20	100.78	—	—	−0.02	−0.02
1962	100.41	100.17	100.20	100.78	—	—	0.00	0.00
1963	100.41	100.17	100.17	100.75	—	—	−0.03	−0.03
1964	100.41	100.17	100.15	100.73	—	—	−0.02	−0.02
1965	100.41	100.17	100.16	100.74	—	—	0.01	0.01
1966	100.41	100.17	100.14	100.72	—	—	−0.02	−0.02
1967	100.41	100.17	100.09	100.67	—	—	−0.05	−0.05
1968	100.37	100.17	100.04	100.58	−0.04	0.00	−0.05	−0.09
1969	100.31	100.14	99.98	100.43	−0.06	−0.03	−0.06	−0.15
1970	100.21	100.11	99.91	100.23	−0.10	−0.03	−0.07	−0.20
1971	100.10	100.05	99.89	100.04	−0.11	−0.06	−0.02	−0.19
1972	100.00	100.00	100.00	100.00	−0.10	−0.05	0.11	−0.04
1973	99.89	99.96	99.95	99.80	−0.11	−0.04	−0.05	−0.20
1974	99.67	99.87	99.83	99.37	−0.22	−0.09	−0.12	−0.43
1975	99.44	99.75	99.67	98.86	−0.23	−0.12	−0.16	−0.51

SOURCE: Edward F. Denison, "Effects of Selected Changes in the Institutional and Human Environment upon Output per Unit Input," *Survey of Current Business*, vol. 58 (January 1978), p. 41.

these rates that resulted from the effect on output per unit of input of changes in the three determinants examined in this article [general environmental improvement, workplace environmental improvement, and deterioration of law observance and enforcement] had been only 0.02 percentage points. The transition to a situation in which, by 1975, the same determinants were deducting 0.5 percentage points has been a large drag upon the recent growth rate of all these measures—large, that is to say, when compared with their growth rates in the past. Thus, costs arising from protection of the physical environment, protection of employee safety and health, and crime help to explain why all these rates have fallen in recent years. It is likely that costs imposed by other new governmental controls, including those intended to protect the health and pocketbooks of consumers and to minimize fuel imports, are responsible for an additional portion of the drop in growth rates, but estimates for these determinants are yet to be attempted.[34]

Recently Denison has prepared a comprehensive survey of his views, brought up to date as of late 1978; it is forthcoming from the Brookings Institution.[35] A list of its nine chapters gives some indication of the wealth of his approach: "Output and Income"; "Labor Input in Nonresidential Business"; "Capital, Land, and Total Input . . ."; "Output per Unit of Input . . ."; "Determinants of Output in the Smaller Sectors"; "The Sources of Growth . . ." (with a subsection on the "Sources of Decline in National Income per Person Employed"); "The Unexplained Portion of the Decline in Output per Unit of Input"; and "Sources of Growth and Potential Output in the Economy as a Whole." This book is somewhat more somber in its assessment of the present situation than were Kendrick's earlier views and also quite probably his current views.[36] Like the Council of Economic Advisers' view, however, Denison's medium-term outlook is quite clearly not what I would call a solid jeremiad. The wealth of the policy factors affecting the present and the future separate this third canon from the one to which I shall shortly turn. In Denison's analysis, which differs in certain measurement estimates from Kendrick's later works, there is a strong assertion that better measurements and the usual macroeconomic policy tools will not

---

[34] Denison, "Effects of Selected Changes," p. 42.
[35] I am indebted to Dr. Denison for an opportunity to read his work in manuscript form. It is accordingly not appropriate for me to identify precisely in advance of its publication his findings, but they are fascinating.
[36] Kendrick, in this volume.

explain or cure everything. Even reconsideration of productivity-losing policies such as general environmental depollution, increased workplace safety standards, and the elimination of crime would not explain what has gone wrong or why all changes have occurred.

What may well be considered a *fourth significant canonical contribution* may be found in the econometric work done largely but certainly not exclusively by Dale W. Jorgenson and a variety of collaborators. Where Abramovitz (and Kendrick) had originally suggested that the waves of annual productivity increases could not be fully explained by increased quantitative inputs (there being an unexplained residual) and where Denison had gone on to stress qualitative changes, which when quantified diminished greatly the size of that residual, Jorgenson and his associates certainly originally believed that *all* the output changes could be explained by increased factor inputs: "Our main substantive conclusion is that growth in real factor input rather than growth in total factor productivity is the predominant source of growth in real product."[37]

In a 1967 essay, Jorgenson and Griliches evaluated Denison's work and criticized it for inconsistencies and inaccuracies.[38] The latter, the two authors believed, gave rise to the "productivity residual"—something that did not exist except for Denison's computational and conceptual errors. Done correctly, everything could be explained by measurement of changes in inputs (quantitatively or qualitatively)—and they proposed to do it "right." In due course Denison replied to these criticisms and found errors in their work comparable to those attributed to him. While his reply is phrased as point-by-point refutation, his final observation is a reassertion that he (Denison) has geared his system to "matching growth sources with the reasons that [national] income changes."[39] Not unexpectedly, Jorgenson and Griliches wrote a rebuttal: "Although Denison's objectives and our objectives are similar, any attempt to integrate his approach . . . into national accounts . . . gives rise to serious difficulties."[40] They also took care, while acknowledging previous computational and even conceptual errors, to lay out their remaining

---

[37] Dale W. Jorgenson and Zvi Griliches, "Issues in Growth Accounting: A Reply to Edward F. Denison," *Survey of Current Business*, vol. 52 (May 1972), part 2, p. 65.

[38] Dale W. Jorgenson and Zvi Griliches, "The Explanation of Productivity Changes," *Review of Economic Studies*, vol. 34 (July 1967), pp. 249-83.

[39] "Some Major Issues in Productivity Analysis: An Examination of Estimates by Jorgenson and Griliches," *Survey of Current Business*, vol. 40 (May 1969), part 3, p. 27.

[40] "Issues in Growth Accounting: A Reply," p. 65.

differences with Denison. Denison then published a counterrebuttal, which stressed that Jorgenson and Griliches were less certain than they had been that the great growth of the American economy had been due to increased inputs rather than to a productivity residual.[41] Jorgenson and Griliches then composed "A Final Reply," appearing in 1972, which very briefly summarized where they still believed Denison's interpretation conceptually inadequate and noted what I think is the critical matter:

> Since at the aggregate level the idea of an input is at best rather vague while the idea of "productivity" does not hide anything more than the "residual" from all the other calculations, it has been our tendency to take out most of the measurable sources of growth (such as intersectoral shifts) from the wastebasket of the "residual" and include them perforce in our concept of input. We have no objection, however, to a more complex classification scheme.[42]

On the whole, Denison's work seems to me to have remained intact, and he yielded less than did Jorgenson and Griliches who wrote:

> While better data may decrease further the role of total factor productivity in accounting for the observed growth in output, they are unlikely to eliminate it entirely. *It is probably impossible to achieve our original program of accounting for all the sources of growth within the current conventions of national income accounting.* But this is no reason to accept the current estimates of total factor productivity as final. Their residual nature makes them intrinsically unsatisfactory for the understanding of actual growth processes and useless for policy purposes.[43]

---

[41] "Final Comments," *Survey of Current Business*, vol. 52 (1972), part 2, pp. 95-110.

[42] Jorgenson and Griliches, "A Final Reply," *Survey of Current Business*, vol. 52 (1972), part 2, p. 111. The issue at hand really pervades a great deal of economic theory, both past and present. How predictable can economic processes be? Frank Knight divided the predictable from the unpredictable by distinguishing between risk and uncertainty. Some modern scholars focus entirely on improving our capacity to predict and seem to assume that, given sufficient opportunity to improve the processes, we should be able to forecast virtually everything. Others like G. L. S. Shackle postulate that *ex ante* one can never be sure of predicting with anything like adequate certainty, and time is a never-ending kaleidoscope; the best one can hope for is a learned capacity to apply first aid quickly. Theodore W. Schultz spells this out in an article, "The Value of the Ability to Deal with Disequilibria," *Journal of Economic Literature* (September 1975), pp. 827-46.

[43] Jorgenson and Griliches, "Issues in Growth Accounting: A Reply," p. 89; italics added.

Both Denison and Jorgenson continued their research investigation and I, for one, see little evidence that their conceptual differences were resolved. The eminence of Jorgenson's reputation as an econometrician, both theoretical and applied, has quite naturally attracted much attention to his work.[44] In my view his distinct interpretation is characterized by a belief that, properly perceived, there is no residual and by a policy view, which I shall shortly elaborate, that the key to production success is to increase qualitatively capital inputs.

In Jorgenson's recent international comparative work, he offers juxtapositions containing some fascinating policy implications that put him in a camp where Denison does not belong. Jorgenson's conclusions require consideration.

For example, in August of 1977, Jorgenson and Mieko Nishimizu presented a characteristically fascinating analytical and policy paper at the Fifth World Congress of the International Economic Association.[45] Some of the general conclusions reached included:

- Japan has made gigantic strides in increasing its capital stock. In 1952 Japan's level of capital input in the production process was a bare 6.0 percent of the American, while in 1974 its quantity of capital input was over 16.7 percent of the American. The Japanese were *increasing* their capital at an annual average rate of 3.6 percent in 1952–1960 and at 11.9 percent in 1960–1974, about three times the American rate in the latter period.

- Since Japan is a smaller economy its quantity of labor input remains below that of America, but Japan with its higher rate of labor input increase is closing the gap. In 1952 it was about 34 percent; in 1974 it was 42 percent.

- Japan's total factor input in 1952 was 17.5 percent of the American; in 1974 it had grown to 29.4 percent of the American.

- By 1974 there was effectively no gap between the levels of American and Japanese technology, with the Japanese clearly forging ahead.

---

[44] See John R. Norsworthy and Michael J. Harper, "The Role of Capital Formation in the Recent Slowdown in Productivity Growth," Working Paper no. 87 (January 1979) of the U.S. Department of Labor, Bureau of Labor Statistics, Office of Productivity and Technology.

[45] A revised version has been published as "U.S. and Japanese Economic Growth, 1952–1974: An International Comparison," *Economic Journal*, vol. 88 (December 1978), pp. 707-26. See also Denison and William K. Chung, *How Japan's Economy Grew So Fast: The Sources of Postwar Expansion* (Washington, D.C.: Brookings Institution, 1976); for an earlier treatment of the topic, see Toshiaki Tachibanaki, "Quality Change in Labor Input: Japanese Manufacturing," *Review of Economics and Statistics*, vol. 58 (1976), pp. 293-99 (Jorgenson is thanked).

- In sum, Japan's remarkable increase in productivity after 1960 was because of growth in capital inputs. From 1960 to 1974 American productivity growth, such as it was, rose because of increased labor inputs—in fact the contribution of real capital input was actually lower in 1960–1974 than it had been in 1952–1960. Not so in the Far East: "the acceleration of growth in Japan during the period 1960–1973 was due to an acceleration in the growth of capital input relative to labour input."[46]

In sum, the fourth canonical view seemingly suggested that, in general, increases in output can be explained by increases in factor inputs and, in particular, the American economy has been hurt because it is deficient in its ration of incremental *capital* inputs.

Speculations about the Present (1979) American Productivity Growth Pattern

Speculation about future patterns of American productivity growth is rather restrained. In Chapter 2 of this volume Kendrick gives his current estimates of future productivity growth. Earlier his views were slightly different, but were then based on a different set of public macroeconomic controls.[47]

Three senior persons of the Bureau of Labor Statistics, writing in a May 1977 issue of the *Monthly Labor Review* possess much the same view:

With regard to the future, the BLS projections indicate that labor productivity growth to 1980 and 1985 will be somewhat lower than the average experience for the 1947–73 period: 2.4 percent and 2.7 percent projected for 1973–80 and 1980–85, compared with about 3 percent for the historical period.

A major part of the reduction in projected growth rate—about 0.3 percent—is attributable to the end of the farm-to-nonfarm shift of hours. Little if any of the 1966–73 slow-down in productivity growth can be found in changes in the rate of capital formation, although some impacts at the industry level undoubtedly arise from mandated capital

---

[46] Jorgenson and Nishimizu, "U.S. and Japanese Economic Growth, 1952–1974," p. 724.

[47] See John W. Kendrick, "The Contribution of Capital to the Postwar Growth of Industrial Countries," in *U.S. Economic Growth from 1976 to 1986: Prospects, Problems, and Patterns*, vol. 1, *Productivity*, 94th Congress, 2nd session, Joint Economic Committee, October 1976, p. 2.

expenditures for pollution control and from compliance with new health and safety standards.

There has been virtually no decline in the growth rate of total stock of capital equipment per hour of all persons. Because the equipment stock of capital has a more direct impact on productivity change, little, if any, of the slowdown in productivity growth can be attributed to a slowdown in the rate of capital formation. The effect is perhaps one-tenth of 1 percent. Until 1980, a somewhat smaller growth in equipment stock per hour of all persons is projected, and, after 1980, there will be a return to [a] more normal growth rate.

More expensive energy sources are expected to be required in the future, and thus to deemphasize an input that has grown relative to labor and capital since World War II. The same will be true in lesser degree of other raw materials, because they are often energy-intensive in their use and production. Mandated investment by industry in pollution control and expenditures to protect the health and safety of workers will cause some reduction in productivity growth. Most of these latter effects are concentrated in a few industries.

The negative effects of changing labor force composition from increases in the proportion of youths and women will taper off and, in the former case, be reversed. During the period to 1985, changing labor force composition is expected to contribute positively to productivity growth.[48]

As already noted, there is less than unanimity that productivity increases are completely tied up with increased quantitative or, even in some measurable sense, with qualitative inputs. Swings in output and, particularly, in productivity are characteristic of historical trends as well as of the impact of the business cycle and intersectoral shifts in the industrial structure. It may then be the case that, without our conscious effort but because of historical rhythms already created, productivity in the American private economy could surge during the next decade. One point worth constant recollection is that the nineteen-year, 44 percent expansion of the civilian labor force represents a phenomenon not at all likely to be continued, much less repeated. Nonetheless, it harms little to ponder the likely causes of the recent "poor" performance or the probable causes of the earlier "better" performances, or whether there is a linkage between the two. The point of departure is the essential nature of the "hard core" residual. While some aver it is basically scale economies, others (like

---

[48] Kutscher, Mark, and Norsworthy, "The Productivity Slowdown," pp. 7-8.

Denison) imply that it is applied advances in knowledge.[49] Knowledge is potential until applied, a frequently overlooked distinction when research and development (R&D) is mentioned.

R&D. Jorgenson and associates suggest that their "key to the secret" is increasing the relative amounts of capital devoted to fixed investment, including the advancement of modernity.[50] They, of course, postulate technological advance, based not so much on brilliant discoveries as on the replacement of old machines by more recent products. Renewed public emphasis on research and development is one step; historically, however, the application of technological progress has occurred (and may well continue to do so) without explicit federal or macroeconomic planning. Of course, this view does not preclude the point that federal planning might be useful.[51]

[49] U.S. Congress, Joint Economic Committee, *Special Study on Economic Change: Hearings*, part 2, 95th Congress, 2nd session, June 8, 1978.

[50] This is similar to the views of Michael D. McCarthy who prepared a report for the Council of Economic Advisers "indicat[ing] that the slowdown in productivity growth, in the 1970's in particular, can be traced to a very slow growth in the capital/labor ratio in the years 1970–75 and to a change in the [age of the] labor force mix." But the latter was perceived as only temporary in its effects. This paper was published as "The U.S. Productivity Growth Recession: History and Prospects for the Future," *Journal of Finance*, vol. 33 (June 1978), p. 977.

[51] John Kendrick summarized his version of this position in a 1976 presentation to the Joint Economic Committee of the 94th Congress: "With respect to intangible investments, probably the largest potential productivity impact would come from measures to accelerate the growth of R. & D. outlays. It will be recalled that our projection assumes a stabilization of R. & D. at about 2.2 percent of GNP. This contrasts with the relative growth of these outlays prior to the mid-1960's, when they began growing less rapidly than GNP. Private business outlays for R. & D. could be stimulated by expanding the coverage of the investment tax credit to include R. & D. Alternatively, the stimulus could be obtained at less cost to the Treasury by allowing a somewhat larger tax credit for incremental R. & D. over that of the previous year or some other base period. Elsewhere, I have also suggested that the tax credit for R. & D. outlays by manufacturers of producers' goods should be larger than standard, in view of their greater impact on productivity advance.

"On a broader plane, the Federal Government needs to develop a more comprehensive and rational policy to promote science and technology than has existed hitherto. The reestablishment in mid-1976 of the Office of Science Adviser to the President, after a lapse of several years, is an encouraging development. In particular, a consistent policy of increasing Federal funding and performance of R. & D. in areas in which private activity is insufficient is central to the governmental role. The sharp reduction of Federal funds for R. & D. beginning in 1969, which led to increased unemployment of scientists and engineers because no provision was made for phasing in new public or private programs, reflects the lack of policy planning that must be corrected in the future. The importance of R. & D. cannot be overemphasized, since invention and development to the commercial stage of new products and processes tends to raise the expected rate of return on tangible capital outlays, and thus stimulates the new investments that embody new technology." (Kendrick, "The Contribution of Capital," p. 17.)

Fiscal and Regulatory Reform. One recurrent view clearly suggests that current fiscal policy should be tilted toward undoing the likely harm of a recent history of antiprofit legislation. As mentioned earlier, the impact of potential expenditures required for safety engineering, environmental depollution, prophylaxis of and compensation for crime, insurance against product liability, and even social engineering against racial, sex, and age discrimination may fall more heavily *at this time* on owners and potential owners of industrial capital goods than on owners of residential and commercial (as distinct from industrial) property.

Capital tends to flow where its owners think it simultaneously secure and profitable. In recent years in many places much of capital investment has been in real estate. Perhaps the profitability of real estate ownership is accordingly more desirable than profitability of industrial entrepreneurship.

Moreover, in my opinion, freeing capital may not be an urgent necessity. I find little evidence of any sustained severe shortage of risk capital in the American market in spite of repeated concern that governmental borrowing was having a pronounced crowding-out effect.[52] Nor do I share the fears that foreign investors know of greener fields abroad—not in those industrialized nations that are worried about strengthening their already too strong national currencies or the growth of left-wing pro-Soviet parties, and not in most Third World nations, which are either exploding politically or in a calm enforced by counterinsurgency forces (of the left as well as of the seeming right).[53]

Labor Reeducation. Jorgenson and company also seem to suggest that the American concern with full employment and, because of our demographic structure, with increased labor inputs (as contrasted with Japan's lower rate of labor inputs) may in part explain the recent differentiated national productivity performance patterns. One frequently hears that our labor force is more heterogeneous than formerly, that in an effort to eradicate historical racial and sex inequities we have experienced a counterproductivity threshold effect, and that the sheer cost of policing these social policies (as well as those involving workplace dangers and environmental cleanup) has become excessive. Are we burdened with excessive policing, or what Adam Smith was wont to call "nonproductive labor"?

---

[52] Despite continued high interest rates, firms do not hesitate to borrow in the face of two-digit inflation in the price of capital goods.

[53] Much of the worry about the flow of capital to the American economy seems to stem from a truly ahistoric view of the autarkic character of the American economy.

Denison and, indeed, Jorgenson's group have stressed that our labor force is both younger and less experienced than it was during some of the heydays of our productivity achievement.[54] The drastic drop in fertility since 1960 and the entry of most of the eligible female population into the labor force surely suggest that, whatever its youth and inexperience have been, that phase is drawing to a close. In another quinquennium or at most a decade the profile of the American labor force will be increasing in age, and many assume that, with aging, problems will disappear.[55]

An additional point brought up in connection with labor input is the loss of the work ethic. This change is associated not with lack of age or experience but with a widespread value transformation such as the seventeenth-century alleged loss of religious fervor in England, the post-Revolutionary change in the French birth rate, twentieth-century Scandinavian skepticism about premarital sexual chastity, and the post–World War I disappearance of what Frederick Jackson Turner earlier had identified as the Frontier Spirit. These views imply that in terms of production our labor force has deteriorated, that once it seemed to police itself better than it does now, and that a whiff of Social Darwinism in the labor market (uncompensated for by overly generous Poor Laws) is desirable.

Management Renaissance. There is also a view that it is not the workers but management that has suffered critically the loss of *tone*.[56] Much of human capital (improved quality of labor) is acquired by on-the-job training. Who gives that on-the-job training? Better formally educated workers or lengthened on-the-job experience

---

[54] Younger may not mean less educated (in the formal sense), although it likely means less experienced. "There are more things in heaven and earth, Horatio,/ than are dreamt of in your [formally acquired] philosophy" (*Hamlet*, act 1, sc. 5).

[55] "One cause of slower productivity growth in recent years that is presumably of a temporary nature has been an increase in the proportion of relatively inexperienced workers in our labor force [because of the large number of new entrants into the labor force] . . . As the younger workers and adult women gain in job experience, however, the depressant effect on productivity growth of the shift in the age and sex composition of the labor force will no longer be operative. Indeed, a reversal may already be in progress." (Arthur F. Burns, *Reflections of an Economic Policy Maker: Speeches and Congressional Statements, 1969–1978* [Washington, D.C.: American Enterprise Institute for Public Policy Research, 1978], p. 37.)

[56] According to Denison and Chung: "Management is a key element in efficiency. . . . A characteristic feature of management in large Japanese firms is decision-making by consensus . . . although it may delay decisions, good or bad, it is said to facilitate wholehearted implementation by all concerned." (*How Japan's Economy Grew*, p. 83.)

are not really substitutes for good supervision. The impact of poor supervision may be suffered for quinquenniums, not merely for years. This view implies that in an earlier era management's training and supervision of workers resulted in a greater control of the production process than is now the case. Control was more comprehensive in the sense that costs of wasted time or disorganization were lower. The comparative inexperience and youth of the current labor force may be no help to productivity increases, but they are, in my view, clearly not sufficient reasons for qualitatively poorer productivity. The critical factors are the youth and inexperience (in part attributable to social policy preferences for remedial equal opportunity hiring) in *the lower echelons of management.* This change is easily forgotten when we shift to macroeconomic analysis, where management and workers are aggregated as "labor." We may reckon in forests, but it is in this sense the individual trees that must claim our attention.

The data seem to show that the age profiles of the first line of management reflect an important trend toward youth. Table 6 provides data on the class that was once called "craftsmen, foremen, and kindred workers" but that is now called "craft and kindred workers," a semantic change intended to eliminate designation by sex rather than any loss of leadership function. The data come from the usual two sources, the Census of the Population and the Current Population Survey (CPS).

In 1940, 36.4 percent of this category of workers were between the ages of forty-five and sixty-four, which we can assume to be the period of seasoned leadership; in 1960, 38 percent were of this preferred age; in 1970, the CPS estimates 39.6 percent (the census a little lower); but in 1975 the relative number had dropped to 35.3 percent. Which is quite a drop. To look at this same phenomenon from another perspective, in 1940, 33.0 percent of this leadership group was under the age of thirty-five; in 1960 it was 31.1 percent; in 1970 it was 34.1 percent (using CPS data); but in 1975 it had risen to 42.0 percent. Which is quite a rise. The 1977 data show little "correction"; the older group was still falling to 33.1 percent and the younger group was up to 44.0 percent.

So much for the American picture; unfortunately foreign data regarding the age characteristics of this critical class of workers are either not reliable or not available. It is true, however, that the younger age of the labor force (as distinct from craftsmen and foremen) is not a phenomenon comparably affecting the German or the Japanese general labor force. Reliably ferreting out these data is not an easy task, but it may be worth the cost.

TABLE 6
CRAFT AND KINDRED WORKERS: CHANGES IN NUMBER EMPLOYED, BY AGE

			Age			
	14–24[a]	25–34	35–44	45–54	55–64	65+
Census data 1940–1970 (thousands)						
1940	448.7	1,217.2	1,357.4	1,187.2	651.7	192.8
1950	791.4	2,064.1	2,074.0	1,678.5	1,118.5	360.9
1960	810.1	2,061.6	2,519.5	2,145.6	1,362.8	342.9
1970	1,398.8	2,528.6	2,553.3	2,585.2	1,698.1	342.0
Percent changes						
1940/50	76.4	69.6	52.8	41.4	71.6	87.2
1950/60	2.4	−0.1	21.5	27.8	21.8	−5.0
1960/70	72.7	22.7	1.3	20.5	24.6	0.3
CPS data 1965–1977 (thousands)						
1965	887	1,931	2,425	2,833	1,439	255
1970	1,168	2,294	2,399	2,440	1,583	275
1975	1,735	2,870	2,288	2,354	1,514	212
1977	2,025	3,208	2,494	2,384	1,551	218
Percent changes						
1965/70	31.7	18.8	−1.1	6.9	10.0	7.8
1970/75	48.5	25.1	−4.6	−3.5	−4.4	−22.9
1975/77	16.7	11.8	9.0	1.3	2.4	2.8

NOTE: The category of craft and kindred workers was previously called craftsmen, foremen, and kindred workers.

[a] In the 1970 Census data this age span is 16-24; in the CPS data the span is 16-24 for all years except 1965, when it is 14-24.

SOURCES: Census data for 1940 from *Sixteenth Census of the U.S.: 1940, Population,* vol. 3, *The Labor Force,* part I, U.S. Summary, table 65, pp. 98, 100; for 1950, 1960, 1970: *U.S. Census of the Population, Subject Reports, Occupational Characteristics,* table 4 (1950), pp. 1B-39, 1B-47; table 4 (1960), pp. 34, 44; table 3 (1970), pp. 33, 47. CPS data: Bureau of Labor Statistics, Current Population Survey, unpublished data.

111

Conclusion

Three important policy points can be made now about the American productivity situation. It is with them that I conclude this essay.

First, fluctuations in productivity growth rates are inherent, and the poorer performance of the recent quinquennium, which was preceded by the unusually high performance of the early and mid-1960s, is in the usual course of such things likely to be followed by somewhat better, although not record-breaking, figures—particularly as the consciousness of the problem grows and the veil cast by the low valuations of the dollar is lifted as the dollar appreciates.

Second, our national concern should shift from the macro indexes to an emphasis on the micro process of improving the performance of individual production units. Whether the individual solutions will depend upon improved capital inputs via new technology or better utilization of the present capital stock, the decisions will be made by managements concentrating on raising the output/input ratios. Thus, one key to the solution is clearly at the plant or firm level; macro analysis may reflect what is happening, *but one major part of the solutions is on the micro level.*

Third, insofar as there are some "solutions" on the macro level, our nation has to recognize the trade-off terms between policies involving (1) productivity growth, national economic competitiveness, and managerial efficiency and (2) workplace safety, environmental renaissance, and the administrative costs of these goals for both public officialdom and private firms. What we seem to have chosen as our preferred package is no minor matter. Let not a myopic nonconcern with history and our record of favoring quick environmental and social reforms lead us to be judged as was a similarly beleaguered pre–World War II Britain:

All in all, it is difficult to avoid the conclusion that Britain has paid a heavy long-run price for the transient glory of the Keynesian Revolution, in terms both of the corruption of standards of scientific work in economics and encouragement to the indulgence of the belief of the political process that economic policy can transcend the laws of economics with the aid of sufficient economic cleverness, in the sense of being able to satisfy all demands for security of economic tenure without inflation or balance-of-payments problems, or less obvious sacrifice of efficiency and economic growth potentialities. *A good case could even be made to the effect that Keynes was too expensive a luxury for a country inex-*

orably declining in world economic and political importance and obliged to scramble for dignified survival, to be able to afford.[57]

---

[57] Harry G. Johnson, "Keynes and British Economics," in Milo Keynes, ed., *Essays on John Maynard Keynes* (Cambridge: Cambridge University Press, 1975), p. 122; italics added.

Part Two

The Inflationary Environment

Financial Developments and the Erosion of Monetary Controls

Phillip Cagan

Summary

Beginning in the fourth quarter of 1978 demand deposits stopped growing and then actually declined. As a consequence the traditional monetary aggregates in which demand deposits are a large part showed sharply reduced growth rates. In the past such sharp declines in growth, if continued, have led to severe recessions in business activity. No one would propose such a sudden tightening of monetary policy. But the interpretation of the monetary aggregates has been thrown into considerable uncertainty by new developments in the payments system. These first became important with the rapid growth of repurchase agreements in the early 1970s and the introduction of negotiated order of withdrawal (NOW) accounts in 1972, and took another major step with the introduction of automatic transfers of savings deposits at commercial banks in November 1978. With the gradual development of an electronic transfer system, the financial transformation of the payments system will continue. The recent confusion over the monetary aggregates is an example of the erosion of monetary controls that threatens to worsen if regulatory reforms are not taken to prevent it. Changes in the conduct of monetary policy cannot adequately compensate for the absence of needed regulatory reforms.

Although data on their magnitude are still incomplete, these financial developments have clearly reached major importance. Estimates of the demand for demand deposits based on past behavior

NOTE: I am indebted to Michael Hamburger, Alvin Marty, Jeremy J. Siegel, Anna J. Schwartz, and members of the AEI policy panel whose papers appear in this volume for helpful suggestions.

suggest that new substitutes since 1973 have displaced about 10 percent of the narrow money supply (demand deposits plus currency). The Federal Reserve has undertaken a revision of the monetary data to incorporate new forms of transactions balances, but the data are incomplete. Even if comprehensive data can be acquired, monetary policy will still be greatly hampered because the growth of the means of payment has become much more difficult to predict and interpret.

In recognition of these problems, bills have been introduced in Congress with support of the Federal Reserve to subject a wide range of transactions balances to reserve requirements, to allow interest payments on demand deposits, and to pay interest on required reserves. The bills subject nonmember banks to the same reserve requirements as are imposed on member banks of the Federal Reserve System, and this has created opposition from the banking community. It is not clear that such sweeping proposals will be enacted. Even if they are enacted, it is not clear that they are sufficient to prevent the continued erosion of monetary controls.

The removal of the prohibition of interest on demand deposits is intended to make them competitive with new financial substitutes. Because of reserve requirements, however, demand deposits would remain at a disadvantage against substitutes that avoid these requirements. It remains to be seen whether interest on demand deposits and on reserves would prevent the growth of substitute assets, given the electronic developments in financial markets that are reducing the costs of shifting funds among financial instruments.

Uniform reserve requirements on all transactions balances are critical to the effectiveness of monetary controls, because they minimize the disruptive effects of shifts by holders among various transactions balances, and because they can help maintain a predictable relationship between the monetary base and aggregate expenditures, the cornerstone of an effective monetary policy.

A uniform imposition of reserve requirements on all transactions balances, however, is difficult to enforce consistently in a complex financial world. New financial developments may make the past degree of monetary control increasingly more difficult to maintain. Yet pursuit of national policies to restrain inflation and stabilize economic activity appears impossible without effective monetary controls. The creation of a regulatory environment in which the erosion of monetary controls is kept to a minimum is particularly urgent in the present period of rampant inflation.

Introduction

Recent financial developments have expanded the number and quantity of new kinds of deposit balances that provide transactions services or close substitutes for them. The electronic transfer system (ETS) to be developed over the next decade will hasten the use of these new transactions balances. The Federal Reserve's control over the quantity of these balances is much weaker than it is over the traditional money stock, M_1, consisting of demand deposits and currency. This essay discusses these developments and the consequences for monetary policy. The final section considers regulatory changes to prevent the growth of these balances from eroding monetary controls.

Development of the New Transactions Balances

History. When interest on demand deposits was prohibited by the Banking Act of 1933, an economist might have predicted that market competition would undermine the prohibition, since most such price-fixing schemes tend to be circumvented and in time to collapse. For two decades after 1933, however, market interest rates were very low, and competitive pressure to pay interest on demand deposits did not exist. Previously, interest paid on correspondent balances and many other large accounts had been around 2 to 2½ percent from 1918 to 1929, and then dropped after 1929 to below ½ percent by 1932.[1] In view of the widespread imposition of service charges during the 1930s, the ceiling of zero interest was probably at or above the market-clearing rate after 1933 until the early 1950s.

In 1951 the Treasury–Federal Reserve Accord formally ended the commitment to support the price of Treasury securities at particular levels and to maintain low interest rates, and by 1953 the policy was finally abandoned. Thereafter, with economic activity strong, interest rates on all financial assets except demand deposits began to rise and, apart from cyclical fluctuations, followed an upward trend not yet ended. As the interest loss increased for holders of demand deposits, commercial banks partially compensated in other ways. Regular business depositors were offered favorable terms on loans and various financial and payroll services. For small accounts charges for each check were reduced or eliminated if a minimum balance were main-

---

[1] James M. Boughton and Elmus R. Wicker, "The Behavior of the Currency-Deposit Ratio during the Great Depression," *Journal of Money, Credit, and Banking*, forthcoming.

tained. Nevertheless, the rising trend of interest rates on other financial assets made demand deposits increasingly unattractive, and amounts not needed to cover transactions were gradually shifted into the many attractive substitutes. The principal substitutes for households were savings deposits and for financial institutions and businesses were Treasury bills, commercial paper, and certificates of deposit. Since World War II the share of demand deposits in the total volume of short-term liquid assets has declined (Figure 1). Despite rising interest rates, however, no major inroads were made upon M_1 as the nation's principal means of payment through the 1960s, though the growing use of credit cards allowed the partial substitution of monthly check payments for currency and, to some extent, may have allowed consumers to hold smaller average deposit balances not offset by a comparable increase for credit card companies.

FIGURE 1

SHARE OF DEMAND DEPOSITS IN TOTAL LIQUID ASSETS, ANNUALLY, 1952–1978

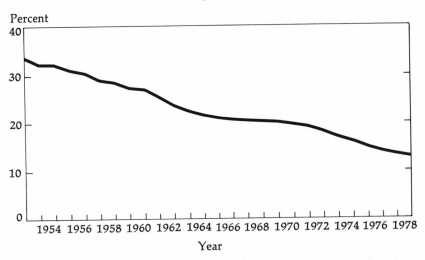

NOTE: Total liquid assets include currency, demand deposits, time and savings deposits, certificates of deposit, U.S. savings bonds, U.S. short-term securities, commercial paper, bankers' acceptances, federal funds, security repurchase agreements, and money market mutual fund shares, all held domestically outside banks and other financial institutions. Figures are for end of year.

SOURCE: Council of Economic Advisers, *Annual Report*, January 1978, table B-61.

Two developments during the second half of the 1960s accelerated the competitive pressures to provide substitutes for demand deposits. Interest rates on other assets rose to historically high levels, and the new computer technology reduced the costs of record keeping for high-turnover accounts. Proposals to remove the prohibition of interest on demand deposits have so far been successfully opposed by the large number of small banks, which lack the volume to reduce costs with the new computer technology. Finally, in 1972, increasing competitive pressure overcame the restrictions protecting demand deposits when mutual savings banks in Massachusetts forced their way into the market.

The mutuals had become eager to attract new business in the late 1960s as their deposit growth was held down by the ceilings imposed in 1966 on the interest rates they could pay. Household savings were increasingly attracted by higher interest rates elsewhere. Many mutuals must have noticed that checking services were a potential means of attracting new business wide open to competition. Earlier, mutuals in Maryland and New Jersey had established the legal authority to provide demand deposits (Indiana mutuals always had it), but few of them used it, because competition with commercial banks was not effective without offering interest. According to federal regulations, the prohibition against payment of interest on checking deposits applied to all insured commercial and mutual savings banks.[2] Although most Massachusetts mutuals are insured by a state agency, rather than the Federal Deposit Insurance Corporation (FDIC), and so are not subject to federal regulations, it seemed to be generally accepted that mutuals could not offer checking services on savings deposits. One seemingly serious obstacle was that savings deposits were (and still are) legally subject to the proviso that banks retain the right to re-

---

[2] During the 1920s commercial banks began to keep duplicate passbooks at the bank and to honor written orders for withdrawals from depositors presented by third parties. The incentive to banks to honor checks on what were classified as time deposits was that the Federal Reserve Act of 1913 imposed lower reserve requirements on time deposits; previous federal banking legislation had not distinguished between the two kinds of deposits. The practice was effectively prohibited by the Banking Act of 1933, which instructed the Federal Reserve to regulate interest and withdrawals. The Federal Reserve issued Regulation Q the same year, which stated in part that, with certain unimportant exceptions, "a member bank may permit withdrawals to be made from a savings deposit only through payment to the depositor himself (but not to any other person whether or not acting for the depositor)." The Banking Act of 1935 gave the same authority to the newly created Federal Deposit Insurance Corporation, which established similar regulations for insured nonmember banks but exempted mutual savings banks from interest ceilings until 1966, when federal legislation imposed interest-rate ceilings on all thrift institutions.

quire at least thirty-days' notice on withdrawals. Although the right has seldom been invoked, it means that savings deposits are not equivalent to demand deposits, on which checks are legally payable upon presentation. When in 1970 an innovative mutual savings bank in Massachusetts petitioned the state commissioner of banking for authority to honor negotiated orders of withdrawal (that is, checks) on savings deposits to be called NOW accounts, the petition was denied. Upon appeal to the state's supreme court, however, the denial was overturned in 1972, on the ground that state law (federal law not applying) did not restrict the form in which withdrawals could be made.[3] Thus NOW accounts were born. Given the competitive pressures, prohibition against interest on checking accounts was bound to give way sooner or later. It is striking, nonetheless, how the prohibition of checking privileges on interest-bearing savings deposits—long accepted as the law—could be suddenly voided without challenge. Although legislation was introduced in the Massachusetts legislature and Congress to reverse this decision, it did not pass. The official inaction made clear that the prohibition of interest on checking accounts had lost its political support.

Unable or unwilling to stem a rising tide of NOW accounts in Massachusetts and subsequently in New Hampshire, the federal authorities had no chance of preventing a flood. In those states and others nearby, depository institutions not authorized to offer NOW accounts and thus at a competitive disadvantage howled in protest and were placated. In 1974 all depository institutions except credit unions (commercial banks, mutual savings banks, and savings and loan associations) in Massachusetts and New Hampshire were authorized by an act of Congress to offer NOW accounts, and in 1976 this was extended to Connecticut, Maine, Rhode Island, and Vermont, and in 1978 to New York State. Credit unions were permitted in 1974 to offer shareholders the capability of writing drafts on their savings accounts (to be paid through the union's account in a commercial bank). Permission for savings and loan associations to make preauthorized payments by customers to third parties, first granted in 1970 for household-related expenditures, was expanded to cover any expenditures beginning in 1975. Commercial banks were also permitted in 1975 to make such preauthorized payments from savings accounts. Savings accounts, which once were limited to individuals and nonprofit institutions, were authorized to be held beginning in

---

[3] See Alan J. Kaplan, "The Negotiated Order of Withdrawal (NOW) Account: 'Checking Accounts' for Savings Banks?" *Boston College Industrial and Commercial Law Review*, vol. 14, no. 3 (February 1973), pp. 471-500.

1974 by state and local governmental units and beginning in 1975 by profit-operated businesses with a limit of $150,000 per business per bank. Member banks of the Federal Reserve System were authorized in 1975 to allow customers to order by telephone that funds be transferred from savings to checking accounts. (Money market mutual funds and some savings and loan associations had earlier begun a similar service of taking telephone orders to transfer funds into a customer's demand deposit in a commercial bank.)[4]

Then in 1978 the Federal Reserve and FDIC threw open the floodgates. Insured commercial banks were allowed beginning November 1, 1978, to cover overdrafts on demand accounts by automatic transfers from individuals' savings accounts. This authorization in effect permits interest on a large fraction of demand deposits without any legislation repealing the statutory prohibition, since funds can remain in a savings deposit until they pass momentarily through a demand deposit in the process of clearing checks. To make such transfers by telephone, as was previously authorized, was inconvenient for regular use and only worthwhile for covering large payments.[5] The automatic transfer services added the important ingredient of time-saving convenience. Unthinkable a few years ago, they demonstrate how rapidly an elaborate wall of regulatory restrictions, once cracked, can crumble.

Thrift institutions, concerned over the new competition, attacked the legality of these automatic transfers in court. Commercial banks also filed suit to block share drafts at credit unions and remote service units of savings and loan associations. The Appeals Court ruled that these new transactions services authorized by the regulatory agencies were in fact illegal, but postponed enforcement of the decision until the end of 1979 to enable Congress to change the law.

While Federal Reserve officials have viewed payment of interest on demand deposits as long overdue, their actions were motivated by increasing concern over the attrition of membership in the Federal Reserve System. Banks have found the costs of membership increas-

---

[4] This paragraph is based on Steven M. Roberts, "Developing Money Substitutes: Current Trends and Their Implications for Redefining the Monetary Aggregates," *Improving the Monetary Aggregates Staff Papers* (Washington, D.C.: Board of Governors of the Federal Reserve System, November 1978), pp. 147-70, and "Redefining the Monetary Aggregates," *Federal Reserve Bulletin*, January 1978, pp. 13-42.

[5] Commercial banks had earlier begun to offer to cover overdrafts on demand deposits automatically up to a prearranged limit under the rubric of making them into an instant loan from a line of credit. These overdrafts were charged interest at the high consumer-loan rates and therefore had limited attractiveness to most of the public.

ingly burdensome. The percentage of commercial banks that are members had steadily declined, from around 45 percent in the mid-1960s to 37 percent in 1977.[6] State-chartered banks have withdrawn along with some national banks that changed their charters from federal to state sponsorship to void the federal requirement that they be members. The chief cost of membership is the required reserves held as noninterest-bearing deposits with Federal Reserve Banks or as vault cash. Reserve requirements for nonmember banks imposed by each state are much lower and generally can be held in forms that pay interest (such as Treasury bills) or pay for services (balances with correspondent banks). The Federal Reserve has for some time tried to hold down the increasing burden of membership as interest rates on earning assets rose, mainly by reducing reserve requirements. The authorization for automatic transfers is a method of reducing total reserve requirements, since requirements are much lower for time and savings deposits than for demand deposits.

The Federal Reserve has in other ways accommodated member banks. Banks have long borrowed federal funds (that is, deposits at Federal Reserve Banks) from each other, and such liabilities are not treated as demand balances subject to reserve requirements or the prohibition of interest. In 1970 a Federal Reserve ruling allowed such borrowing from thrift institutions, foreign banks, government agencies, and security dealers. During the late 1960s banks had also begun to borrow from business corporations by "buying" demand deposits in their own or another bank in exchange for a security and agreeing to repurchase the security at a predetermined price which provided for interest; hence the borrowing has been termed repurchase agreement (RP). For convenience the security does not physically change hands but is pledged as collateral on the loan. Most of these loans take the form of one-day or overnight transfers of federal funds at a market-determined rate of interest. The lending corporation earns interest on an idle demand deposit, and no bank has to hold reserves against this deposit on days it has been lent. On the books of banks the corporation's demand deposit is transferred to the category of "federal funds purchased." In 1969 the Federal Reserve sanctioned this practice by stipulating that RPs will not be subject to reserve requirements or prohibition of interest (as they would be if classified as a deposit liability) so long as the collateral is a U.S. Treasury or federal agency obligation.

---

[6] Statement by G. William Miller before the Committee on Banking, Finance, and Urban Affairs, House of Representatives, July 27, 1978, *Federal Reserve Bulletin*, August 1978, pp. 636-42.

Bank borrowing of federal funds from nonbanks is a method of activating idle demand deposits for a day at a time. If a bank borrows from one of its own depositors, it borrows its own reserves; but that makes no difference, since the depositor could have lent his deposit to others and compelled the bank to cover the lost reserves by borrowing from someone else. Although the practice is declining, some corporations negotiate with banks a continuing arrangement in which unused funds left in a demand deposit at the end of each day are automatically converted into overnight RPs, available again the next morning. Reserve requirements are based on deposits on the books at the end of the day; RPs are not listed as deposits and hence require no reserves.

All these devices provide the services of checking accounts (that is, funds transferable on demand by a written order to pay) without at the same time classifying the accounts as demand deposits legally subject to reserve requirements and the prohibition against interest. In the case of automatic transfers, classification of the account as a savings deposit still subjects it to reserve requirements but at a much lower percentage than as a demand deposit.

While various rulings have facilitated these developments, they have primarily reflected the declining costs of record keeping: for banks the cost of recording a huge volume of transfers of funds, and for corporations the cost of determining daily the quantity of funds available for overnight lending. The computer technology which has reduced these costs is about to revolutionize the payments system. One can visualize most transactions being settled in the future by an immediate transfer of funds from ordinary telephones or ubiquitous remote terminals hooked into a national grid of clearing-house computers which transfer funds from one account to another. These accounts may be interest-bearing savings accounts or even money market investment funds comprising short-term highly liquid securities which are sold or purchased daily to cover net deficit or surplus clearings for the day. In such a payments system, all funds except currency can be held in interest-bearing form, and the speed of transfer will eliminate bank and mail float which amounts to billions of dollars daily. The new system will be highly efficient and low in cost per transaction. Only those transferable accounts that pay the highest rate of interest net of costs will remain in existence, because all such accounts will be equally accessible and convenient for transactions purposes.

The revolution of the payments system, though sure to bring many economic benefits, creates problems for monetary policy. The problems stem primarily from the development of new transactions balances rather than from ETS. The new developments are not simply changing the definition of money but are impeding the objectives of monetary policy. If nothing is done, the monetary control of aggregate spending will be greatly eroded. Changes in regulations under consideration to preserve the effectiveness of monetary policy are discussed in the final section.

Estimates of the Quantity Outstanding. Developments under way carry the potential of considerably expanding new transactions balances. Evidence that the expansion has already become important is suggested by changes in the relationship between the money supply and aggregate expenditures since 1972. As shown in Figure 2, the velocities of narrow money (ratios of GNP to demand deposits and to M_1) have been rising since World War II. The upward trend can be associated with the increasing opportunity cost of holding money balances as interest rates on financial assets have risen and also with steady improvements in cash management practices that have reduced average money balances per dollar of transactions. M_1 velocity can be divided into three segments that have fairly constant trends if cyclical fluctuations are ignored. Trends for the three segments are shown in Figure 2 by dotted lines. The first segment of constant trend, which began in the second quarter of 1954, excludes fluctuations associated with the aftermath of World War II and the Korean War and lasted until the second quarter of 1967. In this early segment the trend growth of velocity was 3.4 percent per year. The middle segment, in which the trend rate declined to 1.6 percent per year, continued until the second quarter of 1972. The beginning and end of the middle segment were selected by eye and could perhaps be dated a quarter or two earlier or later.

At first sight the flatter middle trend is puzzling, inasmuch as the outbreak of inflation in the second half of the 1960s might be expected to have quickened the rise in velocity. The flatter trend appears to reflect the influence on velocity growth of a slower rate of growth of real GNP after the mid-1960s, followed in the early 1970s by further increases in interest rates. The trend rate more than doubled after 1972 to 3.8 percent per year. Figure 2 shows that the changes in trend pertain largely to demand deposits and not to currency, since the velocity of demand deposits replicates the same three segments of the trend in M_1 velocity, except that the demand-deposit velocity rose to a higher trend path in 1975. (The M_2 and M_3 velocities are discussed later.)

FIGURE 2

Velocities of Various Monetary Aggregates, Quarterly, 1947–1978

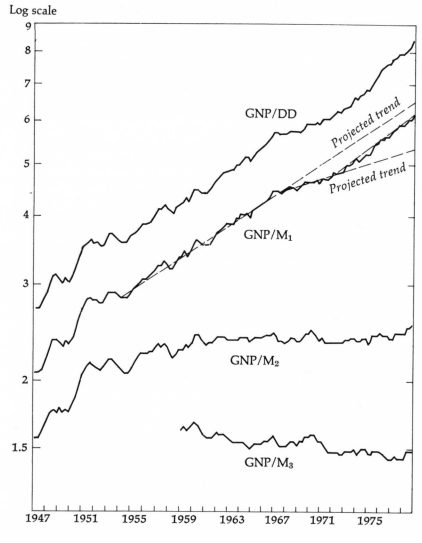

NOTE: Definition of monetary aggregates: DD is demand deposits at commercial banks; M_1 is DD plus currency held by the public; M_2 is M_1 plus time and savings deposits at commercial banks other than negotiable certificates of deposit of $100,000 or more at large weekly reporting banks; M_3 is M_2 plus savings deposits at thrift institutions (all pre-1979 definitions).

SOURCE: Department of Commerce and Board of Governors, Federal Reserve System.

The new transactions balances can be viewed either as money which should be but is not recorded in M_1 or as the availability of attractive new substitutes used in place of demand deposits. On either view the new balances can account for a lower quantity of recorded M_1 than is consistent with its historical relationship to other economic variables. Econometric estimates of the demand for money show increasing overpredictions of the amount of money demanded compared with the amount of M_1 held since 1973.[7] The overpredictions are based on dynamic simulations of standard demand equations that allow for lagged adjustments and relate velocity to real GNP (as a proxy for income and transactions) and to interest rates on savings deposits and short-term securities (as proxies for the cost of holding money). The public is apparently getting along with less M_1 than these equations say the public wants. Equations that treat the household and business sectors separately suggest that most of the overprediction pertains to the business sector,[8] which is consistent with the recent opening up of savings deposits to small businesses and the use of RPs by large businesses.

Recent estimates of the overprediction are given in Table 1. The first set is based on an equation for demand deposits in the Federal Reserve's econometric model. It has the standard form described above. Similar overpredictions are reported by other researchers using various versions of the standard equation.[9] The overprediction of the Federal Reserve equation had grown by mid-1978 to $39 billion, which was 11 percent of M_1. The basic explanation for the overprediction is that recent movements in real GNP and the interest rates used in the equation do not, on the basis of their relationship to demand-deposit velocity in earlier years, account for the more rapid growth of that velocity in recent years. The other estimate is based on an equation for M_1 velocity which uses a long-term bond yield and the dividend yield on common stocks in place of the Treasury bill

---

[7] See Jared Enzler, Lewis Johnson, and John Paulus, "Some Problems of Money Demand," *Brookings Papers on Economic Activity*, no. 1 (1976), pp. 261-80; Stephen M. Goldfeld, "The Case of the Missing Money," *Brookings Papers on Economic Activity*, no. 3 (1976), pp. 683-730; Michael J. Hamburger, "Behavior of the Money Stock: Is There a Puzzle?" *Journal of Monetary Economics*, vol. 3 (July 1977), pp. 265-88; and Gillian Garcia and Simon Pak, "Some Clues in the Case of the Missing Money," *American Economic Review*, vol. 69 (May 1979), pp. 330-34.

[8] See Goldfeld, "The Case of the Missing Money," and Garcia and Pak, "Some Clues in the Case of the Missing Money."

[9] All the studies in note 7, except Hamburger's, use a version of the standard equation.

TABLE 1

ESTIMATES OF UNDERSTATEMENT OF THE MONEY SUPPLY

(billions of dollars)

| Year | Quarter | Federal Reserve Equation | | Hamburger Equation |
		A	B	
1973	I	4.4		3.8
	II	1.8		3.2
	III	0.8		6.1
	IV	0.5		5.1
1974	I	0.9		4.5
	II	1.8		4.4
	III	7.1		3.9
	IV	12.2	8.4	3.0
1975	I	14.6	14.3	3.6
	II	13.7	15.1	1.2
	III	19.0	17.9	3.8
	IV	26.4	24.4	6.5
1976	I	32.7	28.7	7.9
	II		31.5	11.2
	III		32.8	13.5
	IV		35.0	15.0
1977	I		36.0	15.0
	II		38.0	15.5
	III		36.8	14.9
	IV		37.0	15.4
1978	I		37.3	15.3
	II		39.1	14.0

SOURCES: Federal Reserve equation: (A) Jared Enzler, Lewis Johnson, and John Paulus, "Some Problems of Money Demand," *Brookings Papers on Economic Activity*, no. 1 (1976), pp. 261-80, table 2, fit to the period 1955 II to 1972 IV; (B) Richard D. Porter and Eileen Mauskopf, "Cash Management and the Recent Shift in the Demand for Demand Deposits," Federal Reserve Board staff paper, 1978, table 1, fit to the period 1955 II to 1974 II. Hamburger equation: Michael J. Hamburger, "Behavior of the Money Stock: Is There a Puzzle?" *Journal of Monetary Economics*, vol. 3 (July 1977), pp. 265-88, table 2, fit to the period 1955 II to 1972 IV (data for updating of the simulation kindly supplied by author).

rate.[10] This equation gives a much smaller overprediction of the money supply, in part because the decline in the stock market after 1972 raised the dividend yield substantially, which according to the

---

[10] Real GNP is not included in this equation, but when it is added to another version of the equation, the residuals from the equation are not greatly affected.

equation accounts for a large reduction in the demand for money.[11] It is an unsettled question whether the rate of return on a variable-priced asset like common stocks is an opportunity cost that affects desired money holdings, particularly when, as in these years, the rise in the dividend yield reflects the public's decision to pay less for the expected stream of dividends and to sell stocks at the previous higher prices. (Because many cyclical economic variables correlate with the cycles in velocity, statistical significance in time-series regressions is suggestive but not proof of real-world effects.) Whether or not the dividend yield belongs in the equation, when it is included the over-prediction is substantial, though less than half that for the standard equation.

It is true that some estimates of the relationship between growth in the money supply and nominal GNP do not show a discrepancy for recent years. To obtain these estimates, quarterly percentage changes in GNP are regressed on percentage changes in M_1 for the concurrent and three past quarters. In simulations of this equation from first quarter 1969 to third quarter 1978, there is a cumulative overpredic-tion of GNP which amounts to 6.7 percent in 1978.[12] Consequently, predicted velocity is greater than measured velocity, which may mean that measured velocity is too low and the money supply is *over*stated by that amount. This anomaly can be explained, however, by refer-ence to Figure 2. The fitted equation is based largely on the first trend segment in M_1 velocity. If that trend is extended forward, it exceeds measured velocity in mid-1978 by 7.5 percent, slightly more than the cumulative error of the preceding equation. The equation shows slightly less overstatement because the period of fit (first quarter

---

[11] If the effect of the dividend yield is excluded by holding it constant in the simulation, the overprediction is just as large as for the other equations (see Richard D. Porter and Eileen Mauskopf, "Cash Management and the Recent Shift in the Demand for Demand Deposits," Federal Reserve Board staff paper, 1978, table 2). However, if the equation is refitted without the dividend yield and then simulated, the overprediction is closer to that of the other equations but still not as large; the difference is attributable to the inclusion of the long-term bond yield instead of a short-term rate.

[12] Hamburger, "Behavior of the Money Stock." Updated extrapolated errors from this equation were kindly supplied by the author.

In another ("St. Louis") version of this equation, two other variables are included with monetary growth to predict GNP: the full-employment change in federal expenditures and in federal tax revenues, both expressed as percentages of GNP. Using this version of the equation, Goldfeld ("The Case of the Missing Money," p. 728) found a substantial underprediction of GNP for mid-1976, con-sistent with an understatement of the money supply. However, when Hamburger (table 4 and n. 26) used a different and presumably better series for the fiscal variables developed at the New York Federal Reserve Bank, the results were then very similar to those cited in the text with the fiscal variables omitted.

1953 to fourth quarter 1968) is affected by part of the flatter middle segment of the trend. If the equation were fitted only to the middle segment, it would also show too low a level of velocity for recent years and an implied understatement of the money supply.

Econometric estimates of the understatement of the money supply therefore depend upon the particular periods used to determine the appropriate relationship among the variables. As shown in Figure 2, the trend of the first segment of M_1 velocity projected forward lies above the actual figure for 1978, and a projection of the second segment lies far below. The econometric estimates based on money-demand equations are more sophisticated than a simple trend projection, of course, but they are nonetheless derived from regression fits that conform to the flatter middle segment of the trend. Since it is uncertain what has caused the changes in trend, the extent to which the recent faster growth in velocity is to be attributed to an understatement of the money supply is also uncertain.

Yet, while the econometric overpredictions of money demand may reflect various inaccuracies, the probability that the money supply is understated seems high. Some confirmation is provided by data on the dollar magnitude of recent financial innovations. Estimates are given in Table 2 of the new kinds of accounts as well as the savings accounts recently opened up to state and local governments and businesses. The latter development provided an attractive new substitute for demand deposits not previously available to those sectors, and the increase in holdings from 1975 to 1977 was appreciable. From inquiries and surveys the Federal Reserve staff has made a rough assessment of the amount by which the Table 2 developments have displaced holdings of demand deposits rather than other assets, and concluded that the amount is substantial. The total displacement of demand deposits by these developments, including telephone and preauthorized transfers of savings deposits, is estimated to be $8.4 billion for the two years 1976 and 1977[13] (the remainder is assumed to have reduced the demand for other asset holdings). This compares with an increase of the new accounts in Table 2 from 1975 to 1977 of $18.5 billion. The Federal Reserve

---

[13] This is the sum of savings accounts newly permitted for businesses ($3.7 billion) and state and local governments ($0.8 billion), NOW accounts ($1.9 billion), demand deposits at mutual savings banks ($0.6 billion), credit union share drafts ($0.1 billion), and telephone and preauthorized transfers of savings accounts ($1.3 billion). See John Paulus and Stephen H. Axilrod, "Recent Regulatory Changes and Financial Innovations Affecting the Growth of the Monetary Aggregates," Federal Reserve Board staff memo, November 2, 1976, table 1.

TABLE 2

ESTIMATES OF NEW DEPOSITS WHICH ARE POTENTIAL SUBSTITUTES FOR
DEMAND DEPOSITS AT COMMERCIAL BANKS, 1974–1978
(millions of dollars)

Deposits	1974	1975	1976	1977	1978
NOW accounts					
at commercial banks	13	211	804	1,501	2,080
at thrift institutions	178	369	611	875	1,181
Share draft balances					
at credit unions	—	3	61	234	576
Demand deposits					
at thrift institutions	—	166	314	594	864
Savings at commercial banks					
of state and local governments	—	336	3,440	6,282	4,878
of businesses	—	—	6,013	10,123	10,757
Total	191	1,085	11,243	19,609	20,336

NOTE: Data pertain to the middle of the year.
(—): Negligible or zero amount.
SOURCE: "A Proposal for Redefining the Monetary Aggregates," *Federal Reserve Bulletin*, January 1979, pp. 13-42, table 2.

staff assessment was intentionally conservative, moreover, and the actual displacement may well have been even greater.

An additional development of major magnitude not included in Table 2 is the lending of federal funds described earlier. Net federal funds borrowed (including RPs) by commercial banks from nonbanks have grown from less than $1 billion in 1967 to $45 billion by the end of 1978.[14] If these funds came from demand deposits that would otherwise have been invested in other short-term liquid assets in response to rising interest rates, the growth of these loans does not interfere with the past relationship between money, GNP, and interest rates. Most of these loans are overnight or day-to-day maturities, however, and constitute a very close, recently developed

---

[14] Federal Deposit Insurance Corporation, *Assets and Liabilities of All Commercial Banks*, published semiannually. These call-date figures may be misleadingly low because of window dressing.

Funds raised by security dealers through repurchase agreements with nonbanks averaged $1.5 billion per day in mid-1978 (see John Wenninger and Charles M. Sivesind, "Defining Money for a Changing Financial System," Federal Reserve Bank of New York, *Quarterly Review* [Spring 1979], pp. 1-8, chart 1).

substitute for demand deposits.[15] It seems likely that, for businesses, most of the very short maturities displace demand deposits. Not all such loans are held by businesses, however—in 1977, 42 percent of them were.[16] The remainder, as noted above, are federal funds lent by thrift institutions, foreign banks, government agencies, and security dealers. It is not clear to what extent the loans of these groups are substitutes for their demand deposit holdings; to the extent the loans are substitutes, they displace recorded M_1, which is defined to include the demand deposits of most of these holders.[17]

When the new accounts shown in Table 2 and net federal funds borrowed by commercial banks are added to recorded M_1, the expanded total gives an upper bound to the effects that have occurred so far. Velocity ratios for the present M_1 and the expanded series are shown in Figure 3. Beginning in 1967, when the new accounts were inconsequential, the velocity of recorded M_1 increased at a constant rate (shown by the projected trend line) until 1972, and thereafter at a much higher rate. The velocity of the expanded M_1 followed a slower trend path until 1974, when it rose sharply to a higher level in 1975, but thereafter it appears to be returning to its original slower trend path.

Since the velocity of the expanded money supply in Figure 3 overstates the likely growth of total transactions balances, the actual velocity of total transactions balances undoubtedly lies within the widening gap between the two series shown. The new transactions balances go a long way toward accounting for the recent errors of the money-demand equations, but they are making the prediction of monetary effects on GNP more difficult.

Problems for Monetary Policy

Although federal funds borrowing appears to have had the major quantitative effect on the demand and supply of money in recent years, various other developments are bound to become important

---

[15] As of December 1977, 77 percent of these loans were overnight or day-to-day maturities, and a third of the remainder were for a week or less (Thomas D. Simpson, "Recent Developments in the Federal Funds and Repurchase Agreement Markets," paper presented to the meeting of the Southern Economic Association, Washington, D.C., November 10, 1978, table 4). See also "Repurchase Agreements and Federal Funds," *Federal Reserve Bulletin*, May 1978, pp. 353-60, tables 2 and 5.

[16] Simpson, "Recent Developments in the Federal Funds and Repurchase Agreement Markets," table 4.

[17] M_1 as presently defined includes all the demand deposits of these holders except federal government agencies treated as U.S. government.

FIGURE 3

VELOCITY OF M₁ AND EXPANDED M₁, ANNUALLY, 1967–1978

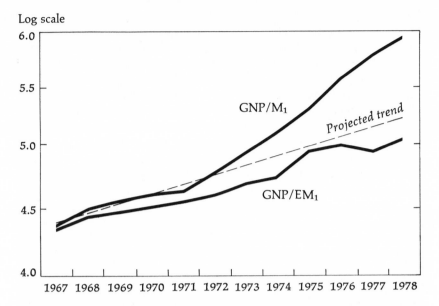

NOTE: EM_1 is M_1 plus total new demand deposit substitutes from Table 2 plus net federal funds borrowed by commercial banks from call-date reports of all commercial banks. Middle of the year data; average of second and third quarters for M_1 and GNP. Projected trend from Figure 2.

SOURCE: Department of Commerce and Board of Governors, Federal Reserve System.

in the future. Since demand deposits are at a competitive disadvantage because of reserve requirements and the prohibition of interest payments, market pressures will work to displace them as new transactions balances and related innovations are perfected and find favor with the public. The decline in the costs of transferring funds by computer technology—both the per unit resource costs of the system and the costs in time and inconvenience of the public—make radical new methods of payment economically superior. The inertia of traditional arrangements and existing institutional practices will delay these developments but cannot prevent them.

In the 1950s economists had become concerned over the possible erosion of monetary controls as a result of the growth in financial intermediation that created highly liquid, low-risk substitutes for bank deposits. The major substitutes then were shares of savings and loan associations and commercial paper issued by large corporations. In a study of those earlier developments published in 1975, Anna Schwartz and I concluded that, while such substitutes had led to a secular decline in holdings of demand deposits relative to other assets and to aggregate expenditures, the magnitude of short-run variations in holdings had not increased and had not impaired the conduct of monetary policy.[18] Those developments provided substitutes for the store-of-value function of demand deposits but did not in general provide substitutes for making transactions. The recent developments, however, do provide substitutes for the transactions function of demand deposits and can impair monetary controls.

Transitional Problems. The problem is not that the quantity of new transactions balances cannot be measured. Although complete data are at present lacking, omissions can be reported and added to the total; and the Federal Reserve has proposed new series on the money supply as a first step toward estimating total transactions balances.[19] The problem is that the substitution of new transactions balances for demand deposits will grow at an unpredictable rate. Hundreds of billions of dollars of savings deposits are now potentially substitutable for demand deposits, either because they can be converted into NOW accounts or because they can be conveniently used to cover checks written on demand deposits by automatic transfers from savings deposits. The present turnover of savings accounts indicates that most of them are inactive and that the active accounts handle current transactions far below the potential volume. Turnover will undoubtedly increase as the use of these accounts for transactions purposes expands, but the extent of the substitution for demand deposits will not be a simple matter to predict. Surveys of the volume of withdrawals and deposits in these accounts can and should be conducted, but such data are not now collected regularly and will be difficult to obtain on an up-to-date basis. Moreover, data on the current level of transactions activity in each type of account will not necessarily apply to the additions to these accounts. Consequently, the rate of displacement of demand deposits will be subject to considerable uncertainty until reliable estimates of displacement can be made, and this may require several quarters or more after the occur-

---

[18] Phillip Cagan and Anna J. Schwartz, "Has the Growth of Money Substitutes Hindered Monetary Policy?" *Journal of Money, Credit, and Banking*, vol. 7 (May 1975), pp. 137-59.
[19] "Redefining the Monetary Aggregates."

rence. The resulting uncertainty over the level of aggregate transactions and expenditures that a given measured supply of money will produce hampers the conduct of monetary policy. To be sure, policy makers have always had to face uncertainty, but the transition to new forms of transactions balances will raise the level of uncertainty about changes in velocity for many years until the transition is largely completed.

Since the growth of M_1 velocity or its expanded versions has changed and become less predictable, it might appear that policy could be effectively based on M_2 or M_3 velocity and their historical behavior. The former has maintained a constant trend since 1960 (Figure 2), except that it experiences larger percentage fluctuations around its trend than M_1 velocity does and in 1978 rose well above the band within which it had fluctuated since 1960. M_3 velocity has had a declining trend, also with sizable fluctuations. If these or some other velocities of a selected quantity of monetary assets maintain constant or predictable trend paths in the future, they could serve as indicators of monetary policy over the long run. They are far from satisfactory as guides to the short-run formulation of policy, however, and not only because of their wider fluctuations.

The savings deposits which constitute a major part of M_2 and M_3 are not closely linked to the monetary base for two reasons. First, their reserve requirements in base money are very small or nonexistent. Second, while the expansion of demand deposits depends closely upon the quantity of base money available to commercial banks, the expansion of the supply of savings deposits, though related with a lag to demand deposits through portfolio adjustments of the public, also occurs to an important extent through the saving of income flows. Thus they are created partly *as a result* of changes in aggregate income, which it is the purpose of policy to control. To the extent that the quantity of savings deposits responds to changes in aggregate income, there is no timing gain in using M_2 or M_3 as indicators of monetary policy in preference to GNP itself. Consequently, the *non*transactions savings deposit components of M_2 and M_3 are less useful to monetary policy for giving advance indication of how its actions will affect aggregate expenditures. By contrast, M_1 growth tends to lead movements in aggregate expenditures, and changes in the base have a more predictable effect on M_1 in the short run than on M_2 and M_3. It may be that the new developments will eventually transform most of M_2 and even M_3 into transactions balances, in which case they will become a feasible replacement for M_1 as indicators. But that eventuality has not yet occurred and remains uncertain, while in the meantime M_2 and M_3 will be a changing hybrid of investment funds and transactions balances with uncertain turnover rates.

During the transitional displacement of demand deposits by new transactions balances, these balances will not grow at a fixed rate in relation to the monetary base. Consequently, the base will also become a less reliable indicator of growth in total transactions balances and cannot provide any better guidance than the traditional monetary aggregates provide.

The longstanding criticism that monetary aggregates are unsatisfactory guides for conducting policy, though generally exaggerated, acquires an added relevance with the new developments in the payments system. But the conclusion sometimes drawn from this criticism—that monetary policy should reduce or abandon its concern with monetary aggregates and focus primarily or even exclusively on other economic variables—was never valid and will not provide a solution for the future.[20] The new developments that will reduce the usefulness of monetary aggregates as indicators of monetary policy will have largely the same consequences for other economic variables. The variables most often considered as alternatives to the monetary aggregates—short-term interest rates—will also become less reliable guides to the effect of monetary policy on aggregate expenditures.

The problem with interest rates as policy indicators can be described in terms of the diagram in Figure 4. The two schedules represent the combinations of the level of interest rates and aggregate expenditures for which the demand for money and the amount supplied (appropriately defined) are equal (LM) and intended saving and investment are equal (IS). The intersection of the two schedules determines the equilibrium attained by the economy in the short run for a given money supply. Monetary policy can shift the LM schedule through changes in the money supply, and in this way achieve a desired level of aggregate expenditures. An increase in the money supply shifts the LM schedule to the right, and a decrease to the left. For a given IS schedule, these shifts produce corresponding changes in the equilibrium level of interest rates and aggregate expenditures in the short run. This diagrammatic framework has some limitations, but it is useful for depicting some of the problems of monetary policy.

---

[20] Very short-run fluctuations in interest rates from day to day and week to week can still be stabilized, of course, separately from the goal of stabilizing aggregate activity. Whether the short-run stabilization of interest rates is a desirable objective of monetary policy is not at issue here.

FIGURE 4

Effect of Shifts in IS Schedule on Interest Rates and Aggregate Expenditures

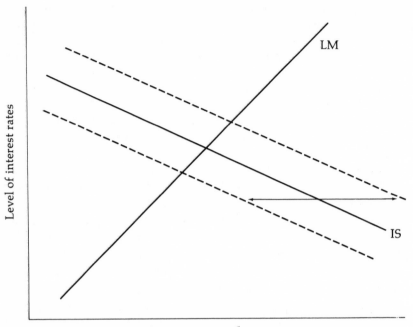

Aggregate expenditures

NOTE: Along the LM schedule the demand for money and the amount supplied are equal; along the IS schedule intended saving and investment are equal.

SOURCE: Based on William Poole, "Optimal Choice of Monetary Policy Instruments in a Simple Stochastic Macro Model," *Quarterly Journal of Economics,* vol. 84 (May 1970), pp. 197-216.

If the monetary authorities were able to estimate the varying position of the IS schedule, they could in each period select and impose the level of interest rates on the market that would achieve the desired level of aggregate expenditures for the given position of the IS schedule. Policy could then operate effectively through interest-rate targets. The inherent difficulty with interest-rate targets is that the IS schedule cannot be estimated very accurately and, even if its position were generally known, in the short run it is downward sloping and shifts about unpredictably, as illustrated by the dotted schedules in the figure.

Such shifts represent the uncertainty faced by monetary policy, which can at best be only partially overcome. Uncertainty is the basis for the argument that an active short-run stabilization policy can be counterproductive and that it is better to hold policy on a stable path toward long-run objectives.[21] Since interest rates vary over the business cycle and are subject to long-run changes as well, a stable monetary policy must be guided largely by the growth rates of monetary aggregates.

Notwithstanding the uncertainties, however, monetary policy continues for better or worse to pursue short-run stabilization objectives. In the face of unpredictable shifts in the IS schedule, policy relies on financial variables as indicators of the direction and magnitude of these shifts. A rightward shift in the IS schedule, for example, reflects an increase in intended investment relative to saving, which tightens financial markets. In terms of Figure 4, interest rates and aggregate expenditures rise toward the new intersection point with the LM schedule. Financial variables tend to reflect such movements first and so give early indications of them. To use changes in financial variables—particularly interest rates—to judge the magnitude of the ultimate effect of such shifts on aggregate expenditures, estimates of the position and slope of the LM schedule are needed. Such estimates have to be derived from past behavior.

The recent financial developments are altering the shape of the LM schedule, however. New transactions balances are shifting the schedule to the right, and the greater elasticity of substitution between them and other financial assets is flattening the slope of the schedule. The changes are also occurring at an uncertain pace and are making the LM schedule less predictable. Expressed in other terms, these changes are increasing the velocity of M_1 and making it more variable. Combined with unpredictable cyclical shifts in the IS schedule, changes in the LM schedule are making monetary policy more difficult, whether the indicators used are monetary aggregates or interest rates, or, as at present, both.

If all else fails, of course, policy can be guided by concurrent movements in aggregate expenditures and prices, as it is now, to some extent—these variables, after all, represent the ultimate goals of macroeconomic policy. But their current movements reflect economic developments and policy actions of the past, and it is generally

---

[21] Milton Friedman, "The Effects of a Full-Employment Policy on Economic Stability: A Formal Analysis," in his *Essays in Positive Economics* (Chicago: University of Chicago Press, 1953), pp. 117-32; and William Brainard, "Uncertainty and Effectiveness of Policy," *American Economic Review*, vol. 57, Papers and Proceedings, May 1967, pp. 411-25.

unsatisfactory to formulate policy on the basis of their current movements without the capability of projecting what the effects in subsequent periods will and should be.

Long-run Problems. Although changes in the payments system will erode monetary controls during the transition, it might be thought that the erosion will eventually end when a new system is fully established and further changes occur slowly. At that time the relationship between some new definition of transactions balances and aggregate expenditures might be identified as a reasonably accurate basis for the implementation of monetary policy. Although this is possible, there are reasons for doubt, and the developments now under way provide little room for complacency about the dangers to monetary policy.

If present statutes subjecting commercial bank deposits to reserve requirements and prohibiting interest payments on demand deposits are not changed, the continuing collapse of restraints on the provision of transactions services suggests that the day will come when demand deposits will be virtually eliminated. It is not clear at present how rapidly such developments will occur. They will come gradually and not all of a sudden, but there appears to be no economic or technological obstacle preventing them.[22] Nearly all demand deposits are likely to be replaced in time by a variety of deposits with financial institutions and businesses which are transferable to almost any other balance within at most a day. Some transfers will go directly to their intended destination and some indirectly through interim transactions accounts, but whether an account is one that can be legally transferred directly to third parties will be of no practical importance to the holder. Given present law, reserves will be required against the largely extinct demand deposits and time and savings deposits in all Federal Reserve member and some nonmember commercial banks, and none against all the other transactions balances. If reserve requirements are imposed on all transactions balances in banks and thrift institutions, as is under consideration, there will be a comparable tendency for these balances to be replaced by transactions balances outside these institutions, which are not subject to reserve requirements.

Even should deposits subject to reserve requirements largely disappear, the monetary base which is the vehicle for implementing monetary policy will continue to exist as presently constituted—

---

[22] Currency will undoubtedly continue to be used for some transactions and to be held by some users who prefer currency because it cannot be traced.

currency plus reserve balances with Federal Reserve Banks. It will still be held by financial institutions as required reserves against some deposits and otherwise as holdings in excess of legal requirements for purposes of making payment in federal funds and of meeting unanticipated adverse clearings that require immediate payment. If reserves do not earn interest, efficient cash management will keep them quite small. Bank reserves as a ratio of deposits would be quite low, perhaps about 1 percent compared with 10 percent or so under the present system. Most of the monetary base would be held by the public as currency.

In such a system, how would monetary policy be conducted? Presumably the way it is now, since it has no attractive alternatives. The Federal Reserve would buy and sell Treasury securities to produce changes in the monetary base. An increase in base money, for example, would be used by the initial recipients to purchase an asset from, or make a deposit with, someone else who in turn would purchase from or deposit with others. In this way the added base money would be transferred from one holder to another, increasing the quantity of balances and the volume of lending and spending until no further expansion occurred, at which point the original level of the base multiplier would be reestablished. This is the same process by which an increase in the base expands the money supply today through a multiple expansion of the banking system. As an expansion of the money supply increases expenditures, the demand for currency increases and absorbs reserves from the banking system, which the Federal Reserve typically replenishes to avoid any deviation of the money supply from its targeted growth path. The total increase in the monetary base required to produce a given expansion of the money supply would not be much higher if reserve ratios were much lower, because most of the base will still be needed to supply currency.[23] But the initial effects of open market operations would be enlarged. Since currency demand is affected after a time lag when monetary expansion raises expenditures, the initial change in the monetary base remains largely in bank reserves and leads to a multiple change in demand deposits that is the reciprocal of the reserve ratio. For a 10 percent reserve ratio, this initial multiple effect is 10 times, and with a 1 percent ratio it would be 100 times. Under a

---

[23] The base multiplier—the ratio of the money supply to the base—is given by the reciprocal of the reserve ratio plus the currency ratio minus their product: $(R/D)+(C/M)-(R/D)(C/M)$ where $M = C + D$. For a 25 percent ratio of currency to the total money supply as prevails today and a 10 percent reserve ratio, the multiplier is 3.1. With a 1 percent reserve ratio, the multiplier is still only 3.9.

system of low reserve ratios, therefore, a given open market operation can be expected to have a much larger initial effect on the money supply.

In the future system monetary policy will be handicapped in two ways. First, changes in excess reserves that are due to unpredictable redistributions of deposit holdings throughout the system tend to be proportional in magnitude to aggregate balances and will be a larger percentage of the smaller amount of total reserves. Given differences in reserve ratios, such a percentage increase of fluctuations in reserves, if not offset, will produce larger fluctuations in the aggregate balances.

Second, the lag between a change in the base through open market operations and the effect on aggregate balances will be lengthened. The change in aggregate balances results from a series of individual transactions whose size is related to the size of the initiating open market operation. At present the Federal Reserve produces an initial expansion in deposits of, say, $100 million by increasing the monetary base by $10 million. This is for a reserve ratio of 10 percent and ignores the subsequent further increases in the base to offset increased currency demand as the monetary expansion affects expenditures. Under a 1 percent reserve ratio, the same initial expansion in deposits of $100 million would require an initial increase in the base of only $1 million. The open market operation of $1 million would have an initial impact on financial markets of about one-tenth of the $10 million operation under the lower reserve ratios. The initial purchase spreads through individual financial institutions in the accounts of many individual households and businesses, in a process which lowers interest rates, increases the supply of credit, and expands the quantity of transactions balances. This process takes time. Given recent improvements in the efficiency and speed of cash management, the response of large businesses and financial institutions is becoming more rapid, but less so for other sectors. We do not know how much faster these adjustments will become, but in any event the process of redistributing $1 million of new monetary base through the financial system would take longer to build up to an increase in deposit balances of $100 million than an initial purchase of $10 million would.

Given the usual long lag of several quarters or more between changes in monetary growth and in aggregate expenditures, a longer lag between changes in the base and in total balances would be undesirable, but the addition to the total lag in monetary policy might not be overly serious. However, it complicates the first problem of larger fluctuations in the multiplier, because the time needed to identify and correct departures of monetary growth from the target rate would be lengthened. Quarterly growth targets would be harder to hit than now, though semiannual targets might still be attainable.

The stabilization of economic activity and the price level by monetary controls relies on a reasonably predictable relationship between the monetary base and aggregate expenditures. As argued above, the first part of this relationship involving the base multiplier is being undermined by new developments, but some trial and error in achieving the desired growth rate of money, necessary even now, will probably continue to be feasible. The second part of this relationship involving a change in money and the resulting effects on aggregate expenditures is also subject to a lag. Because this is a long lag, policy cannot be conducted by trial and error but must be guided by predictions of its effects. Yet the relationship underlying these predictions is also likely to be loosened. The new developments reduce the distinction, and increase the elasticities of substitution, between any designated group of transactions balances on the one side and all other assets on the other. Consequently, for given fluctuations in interest rates and economic activity, the magnitude of changes in the velocity of the designated transactions balances will increase and make predictions of monetary effects less accurate. In terms of Figure 4, this means that the appropriate LM schedule will become flatter, and shifts in the IS schedule of given magnitude will produce smaller fluctuations in interest rates and larger fluctuations in aggregate expenditures.

The new developments reflect and in turn alter the consequences of the myriad regulations in which our financial institutions are enmeshed. Over the years numerous official commissions have proposed a variety of regulatory reforms, though the conflicting interests of the financial institutions involved have prevented Congress from acting.[24] Recently the Federal Reserve has pressed for action to stem an accelerating loss of membership, and this has produced a willingness in Congress to make changes.

---

[24] Commission on Money and Credit (CMC), *Money and Credit: Their Influence on Jobs, Prices, and Growth* (Englewood Cliffs, N.J.: Prentice-Hall, 1961); *Report of the Committee on Financial Institutions to the President of the United States* (Heller Report) (Washington, D.C., 1963); Commission on Financial Structure and Regulation (Hunt Commission), *The Report of the President's Commission on Financial Structure and Regulation* (Washington, D.C., 1971); and U.S. Congress, House Subcommittee on Financial Institutions Supervision, Regulation and Insurance of the Committee on Banking, Currency, and Housing, *Financial Institutions and the Nation's Economy* (FINE), Discussion Principles, 94th Congress, 1st session, 1975, and *The Financial Reform Act of 1976: Hearings*, 94th Congress, 2d session, March 1976.

Proposed Regulatory Reforms

Proposals to Allow Interest on Demand Deposits. One set of proposals reflects the view that removal of the prohibition of interest on demand deposits would prevent the erosion of monetary controls, since this prohibition has fostered the growth of interest-paying substitutes for demand deposits. If demand deposits and currency continued to handle most payments in the economy, none of the increased difficulties for monetary control discussed above would arise. It makes a difference, however, how the prohibition is removed. The 1978 ruling allowing automatic transfers from savings to demand deposits does, in effect, allow commercial banks to pay interest to demand depositors, but under the rubric of reclassifying demand deposits as savings deposits. The result is not the same as allowing interest on demand deposits directly, because reserve requirements are much lower on savings deposits, and the growing substitution of automatic transfers for demand deposits will be difficult to predict.

The advantage to monetary policy of the payment of interest on demand deposits can be explained in terms of Figure 4. If the interest rate paid moved in unison with the general level of interest rates, the interest rate differential between demand deposits and other assets would not change. Then the LM schedule would be vertical (if currency demand is largely unaffected by interest rates), and shifts in the IS schedule would produce changes in the general level of interest rates but not in aggregate expenditures. Of course, the LM schedule would continue to shift for reasons other than changes in interest rates, and monetary policy would still face the task of offsetting these shifts, but a vertical LM schedule makes it easier to stabilize the economy.

Interest rates on demand deposits (and on other transactions deposits such as NOW and automatic transfer savings accounts) are not likely to move perfectly in unison with the general level of interest rates for two reasons. First, financial intermediation involves longer maturities on assets than on deposit liabilities, and the average rates of return on bank assets that provide the income to pay interest on deposits move sluggishly in response to market changes. Second, required reserves of member banks are held in noninterest-bearing deposits with Federal Reserve Banks, which reduces the fraction of interest earnings on assets that member banks can pass on to their depositors. As a partial offset, however, the Federal Reserve has proposed that it pay interest on a part of required reserves, at a rate equal to the average return on its earning assets.[25] Although the differential between rates paid on all transactions balances and other financial instruments is not likely to remain constant over business cycles, even a partial reduction of the variation in this differential makes the LM schedule more vertical and increases the effectiveness of monetary controls. Furthermore, unregulated interest payments on deposits and payment approximating market rates on reserves will remove most of the market pressures to develop substitutes for demand deposits which erode monetary controls.

Proposals to Extend Reserve Requirements. Without payment of interest on demand deposits, the new financial developments will continue. Even with interest on demand deposits, the financial developments are not likely to be reversed. These developments add to the unpredictable changes in total transactions balances, and uniform reserve requirements on all transactions balances have received wide support as a countermeasure. Bills proposed in Congress to impose reserve requirements on all transactions balances in depository institutions and to allow interest on demand deposits go a long way toward rectifying the erosion of monetary controls. They are limited in scope, however. These proposals would continue to impose lower reserve requirements on nontransactions time and savings deposits in commercial banks and would do nothing about transactions balances held outside depository institutions or not classified as deposits (such as RPs). Since recent financial developments are making some radical changes in the form of transactions balances, these proposals do not go far enough.

The primary purpose of reserve requirements is to tighten monetary controls over aggregate expenditures. The traditional argument for reserve requirements—and clearly their most important contribution—is to improve control over the total of transactions balances, since they are considered to have the strongest and most predictable influence on aggregate expenditures. In terms of Figure 4, the purpose is to reduce unpredictable shifts in the LM schedule. A major source of unpredictable changes in total transactions balances are redistributions among different suppliers. Reserve requirements reduce such effects on total transactions balances to the extent that requirements make excess reserves, which can vary considerably among suppliers,

---

[25] "Proposals to Facilitate the Implementation of Monetary Policy and to Promote Competitive Equality among Depository Institutions," statement of G. William Miller before the Committee on Banking, Finance, and Urban Affairs, House of Representatives, January 24, 1979.

a smaller or more constant fraction of total reserves[26] and to the extent that the requirements are uniform for marginal redistributions. In recent years banks have learned to keep excess reserves low, but excess reserves can be made even lower relative to total reserves if reserve requirements are raised.[27] In addition, since it is money held by the nonbanking public that should be controlled by monetary policy, reserves now required against net deposits held by commercial banks with each other and against deposits of thrift institutions with commercial banks are undesirable because they absorb varying amounts of the monetary base. Indeed, reserve requirements no longer play an important role in insuring the safety of deposits and are not needed for that purpose. Safety is provided by deposit insurance, an active federal funds market, and the Federal Reserve as lender of last resort. Present requirements for reserves behind non-transactions time and savings deposits are an anachronism from the past and should be eliminated.

Another potentially important contribution of reserve requirements—one that receives little attention—is to reduce shifts by the public between transactions balances and other assets by lowering the elasticities of substitution between the two groups of assets. (This would steepen the LM schedule in Figure 4 and reduce the fluctuations in velocity.) Reserve requirements can help eliminate the assets that are the closest substitutes for transactions balances and for which the elasticities of substitution are highest. Since reserves behind transactions balances reduce the amount of interest and services that issuing institutions can afford to provide (if interest on reserves is zero or inadequate), the public has an incentive to hold these balances largely to conduct transactions or, if they are not needed for that purpose, to shift into other assets which have no transactions advantages but pay a higher rate of interest. Assets of an in-between variety which offer less convenient transactions services and a somewhat higher rate of interest would, if subject to full reserve requirements, not remain in-between; they would either become fully competitive in transactions services or discontinue such services altogether to avoid reserve requirements.

This effect of reserve requirements is based on maintaining a lower rate of return on transactions balances and is inconsistent with proposals to pay interest on demand deposits and particularly on

---

[26] For this reason, proposals to abolish reserve requirements seem to me undesirable.

[27] Since excess reserves typically average about 1 percent of total deposits, a reserve requirement of at least 10 percent seems desirable.

reserves. Yet, as noted above, the payment of interest is desirable, in part for the same reason. Flexible interest payments on demand deposits and other transactions balances reduce variations in the differential rate between them and other financial assets. (This also steepens the LM schedule in Figure 4.) In addition, interest payments on deposits remove the cost differences that give the market an incentive to circumvent reserve requirements. Although transactions balances will always pay less interest because of the costs of a clearing system, the transactions services compensate holders for an interest rate that is lower by the amount of those costs.

It is likely that the advantages of interest payments on transactions balances and on required reserves outweigh the disadvantages of not enhancing the distinction between transactions balances and other financial assets that could be expected to exist with a sizable difference in rates of return. If we make this choice, however, shifts between transactions balances and very close substitutes that remain outside the coverage of reserve requirements will occur in response to variations in differential rates of return that cannot be entirely eliminated, and these shifts could be sizable and troublesome for monetary policy because of high elasticities of substitution. It is all the more important, therefore, that reserve requirements be sufficiently comprehensive to discourage the provision of *limited* transactions services on financial assets, since those services increase the substitutability of these assets for transactions balances offering full services.

Problems of Extending Reserve Requirements to All Transactions Balances. If transactions balances are defined broadly as any balance or source of funds that can be transferred on demand, the new financial developments warrant a radical expansion in the usual coverage of reserve requirements. They would, as present legislative proposals contemplate, encompass a broad range of deposit accounts—demand deposits and savings deposits transferable automatically or by written and telephone orders in commercial banks and thrift institutions. They would also, however, encompass transferable balances held in brokerage houses or anywhere else if the dollar value of the balance is virtually fixed, as is true of funds available on short notice and invested in a diversified list of short-term market instruments. The definition also applies to lines of credit available immediately and overdraft privileges (to the limit allowed). In addition, to cover arrangements like RPs in which deposits are invested for very short periods without material inconvenience to their continued use for transactions purposes, the definition would have to apply to any balance which can be transferred within a short time.

The problem is that the new developments are obscuring the historical line between transactions and other balances. If funds represented by a share of pooled investments in various kinds of market securities can be rapidly withdrawn and if, with the introduction of electronic transfer facilities, these funds can be transferred to customers' transactions accounts in short order and from there to third parties, such investment shares become readily usable for transactions purposes, and the absence of direct third-party payments is of no consequence. Such developments require that transactions balances be defined in terms of the speed and convenience of transfer—as any funds virtually fixed in dollar amount and withdrawable within a specified short time, say, a business week. Any shorter period makes them usable for present transactions purposes except where same-day or next-day funds are required.

Comprehensive reserve requirements can therefore be quite radical in their logical implications for coverage. In practice, a less radical coverage, even if not equitable, might preserve the effectiveness of monetary controls. The problem with reserve requirements on some but not all kinds of transactions balances is that they invite further market developments to circumvent the holding of reserves. In the event of such developments, the coverage of reserve requirements would later have to be extended. The advantage of comprehensive requirements at the outset is to provide a stable regulatory environment to guide future financial developments in directions that will continue to be consistent with the conduct of an effective monetary policy.

Comprehensive requirements would drive some of the financial assets on which they are imposed out of the transactions business and prevent the introduction of others; those excluded would be less efficient and less attractive to the public for handling transactions. Money market mutual funds, though primarily a vehicle for investment, have begun to offer transactions services and would lose much of their attractiveness if they were subject to reserve requirements. To be exempt from reserve requirements, any balance or fund would be prohibited from offering transactions capabilities. To qualify as a nontransactions account, the rule might be that customer orders to transfer funds be delayed for a business week, during which the funds to be transferred are held without explicit or implicit interest (which means, in effect, in a noninterest-bearing account at Federal Reserve Banks), or that the account be composed of certificates with maturities of longer than a business week. These rules would depart from traditional kinds of financial regulation, except that we already penalize the premature withdrawal of time deposits. Yet it may not be possible to avoid such rules and achieve the intended purpose. They are implied by a definition of transactions balances in terms of the time and cost of making transfers rather than in terms of the characteristics of existing assets, and are intended to discourage or cover new kinds of transactions accounts that would otherwise circumvent the reserve requirements.

Problems of preventing subterfuges would nevertheless arise. Although reserve requirements serve the public interest by facilitating the stabilization of aggregate expenditures, individual issuers and users of money have no private economic incentive to abide by such requirements. One subterfuge might arise with investment funds set up with renewable certificates maturing every eight days, just long enough to satisfy the exemption. If an individual account were divided into eight parts each of which matured on a separate day, one-eighth of the account would become transferable to cover deficit clearings on successive days. Such subterfuges would have to be made illegal, though care in writing the regulations would be necessary to do so effectively.

Two other problems are presented by passbook savings and Eurodollar accounts. Passbook savings of individuals have traditionally been withdrawable on demand, subject only to the bank's right, seldom invoked, to require advance notice of thirty days or more. The privilege of withdrawal on demand has been sanctioned by long practice, and individuals have not usually used passbook savings as important substitutes for transactions balances. Nothing new would be lost by exempting them from reserve requirements. Savings accounts of individuals might continue to be withdrawn on demand upon presentation of passbooks at banking offices but not, however, by written or telephone orders or at remote terminals.

Although reserve requirements on Eurodollar deposits in foreign branches of U.S. banks would pose legal problems of reciprocity with other countries, they are desirable to close a loophole in which balances in parent banks could otherwise be shifted to foreign branches to escape reserve requirements. The proposed free banking "port" in New York City will facilitate such evasive shifts. Exemption from reserve requirements could be consistently allowed if the minimum term of such Eurodollar deposits were longer than a business week. At present most Eurodollar deposits have maturities of a week or longer and would not be affected, though overnight Eurodollar deposits are rapidly growing in importance.

Reserve requirements designed to eliminate close substitutes for transactions balances are to some degree a hindrance to the efficiency of financial practices. But the "efficiency" which reserve requirements hinder involves principally the supply of transactions services—essentially what has always been meant by money, the total quantity of which is a legitimate governmental responsibility now subject to increasing erosion. Interference with efforts to increase the speed and convenience of shifting in and out of investments is not a real hindrance to the economy, because those efforts are largely designed to increase the liquidity of investments as a substitute for holding transactions balances and as such are wasted from the nation's point of view. Such efforts in part reflect the private incentive to avoid reserve requirements and the prohibition of interest payments on demand deposits. Commercial banks, which have traditionally been allowed to share a monopoly of money issue with the government, have the most to gain from uniform restrictions on the issue of competitive transactions services.

Beneficial developments in the efficiency of financial institutions and markets need not be hindered by restrictions on the supply of transactions balances. The innovations in electronic transfers, management of funds, and new financial instruments can continue to bring benefits to the public. If any institution wants to provide transactions services, it should be free to do so, but only under the same reserve requirements and safety standards imposed on all other issuers of money. Failure to protect the monetary franchise will allow the supply of money to fluctuate freely in response to the market demand for it. The consequence would be to weaken and ultimately to abandon the goal of economic stabilization, which is not acceptable.

Uniform reserve requirements on all transactions balances can be supported, therefore, as equitable and very important to the continued effectiveness of monetary controls. The cost is the regulatory burden of controlling the money supply, but this has always been accepted as a proper governmental function. The new financial developments are obscuring the traditional line between money and other assets, and it may not be an easy matter, or even possible, to preserve the past effectiveness of monetary controls. The desirability of stemming the erosion of these controls calls for an extension of regulations over all transactions assets. Although many financial institutions may be opposed to regulatory changes, the upheaval of new developments is making continuation of the status quo in financial regulation impossible. Uniform reserve requirements need not reduce profits of banks and thrift institutions in the long run, because the increases in reserve requirements on some transactions balances can be offset by the elimination of requirements on nontransferable savings accounts and will prevent inroads from new forms of competition. A full reform should not be long delayed, because the coming financial developments should take place in a reasonably stable regulatory environment. Changes in the environment at a later stage will entail costly and nonoptimal adjustments.

American Household Wealth in an Inflationary Period

William Fellner

Summary

This study compares trends in American household wealth during the inflationary period since 1965 with trends during the preceding years. The analysis suggests that the changes that have occurred in the recent period came mainly in response to the inflationary process, and that the trend away from the asset mix for which households previously strove thus expresses part of the burden imposed on them by inflation. This burden has arisen because the inflationary environment has placed a penalty on specific components of the asset mix.

Upward revaluations of tangible relative to financial household assets need to be stressed in the interpretation of the significant changes in the composition of household wealth. Yet the view occasionally expressed that these changes occurred because the households merely accepted the consequences of these revaluations "passively" must be rejected. Not only did shifts in the demand of households for the various categories of "old" assets play a large role in bringing about the observed asset revaluations, but the role of the current savings of households must also be remembered. Changes in asset values result partly from current savings in the usual sense—that is, not including revaluations. During the period 1965–1978 the amount

NOTE: Much of the work leading to this paper was undertaken in cooperation with Richard E. Browning of the American Enterprise Institute.

For completion of this paper, including improvements of early drafts, I am indebted to the Flow of Funds experts at the Board of Governors of the Federal Reserve System, and to national-income and capital-stock experts at the Bureau of Economic Analysis of the Department of Commerce. It would have been impossible to engage in this study without their help and advice and without their willingness to make critical comments. This, of course, leaves me alone responsible for the interpretation of the trends and for all conclusions.

153

of current savings allocated to the purchase of tangible rather than financial household wealth was large enough to represent about 40 percent of the net financial wealth owned by the households at the end of the period. Meanwhile the real value of net financial household wealth was declining not only relative to real income but even absolutely.

The shift in the asset mix was a shift away from financial assets that have one or the other of the following two characteristics:

(1) Assets such as corporate shares involve acceptance by the household of risks that rose significantly in circumstances in which business prospects became increasingly uncertain, except for the spreading conviction that prices would continue to rise at an appreciable but unspecified rate. Moreover, neither graduated taxes on dividends nor capital-gains taxes are adjusted to inflation; hence, the tax burden of the owner rises in relation to his real yields and real gains as the inflation rate rises. Stocks are included here among the financial household assets because their valuation by the households demonstrates that they are viewed as claims sharply distinguishable from the ownership of tangible assets bought, held, and sold by the households themselves. The poor performance of stock prices in the period 1965–1978 contributed importantly to the shift in the asset composition of households, but it would be wrong to assume that excluding corporate stock from the financial assets yields information about the shift in the wealth composition of households owning no stock. Stock-owning households possess considerable weight also in other asset markets, and demand shifts between these markets are frequent.

(2) Aside from corporate stock, assets belonging in the financial category consist of money and of claims on money payments mostly fixed in current dollars. Under inflationary conditions these involve the risk of reduced, even negative, real return. This risk is substantial for pre-tax returns, and it is even greater for returns after taxes that are levied on current-dollar incomes. The low return on these types of financial household assets also reflects in part the uncertainty that has risen substantially in the inflationary environment; yet at the same time it reflects statutory regulations of interest rates that only recently were made somewhat less comprehensive.

Since the mid-sixties the composition of household wealth has shifted away from financial assets of both general categories to tangible assets, such as owner-occupied homes and durable consumer goods, that mostly have both of the following characteristics:

(1) *In an inflationary environment their prices rise in current dollars, and the prices of some have in fact risen also in inflation-corrected dollars.*

(2) *Except to the extent that resale is contemplated, the expected real yield of these assets depends not on risky market prospects but on the untaxed use value accruing to the households themselves.*

Before turning to the problems of the asset mix, the study evaluates indications that the overall wealth-income ratio of the households has declined during the inflationary period. In earlier postwar periods of reasonable duration this ratio first remained unchanged and then, from 1952 to 1965, it rose. But thereafter the overall wealth-income ratio declined from its 1965 level of 4.81 to 4.19 in 1978 when disposable income is expressed at an annual rate. A very moderate increase in the saving ratio helped to keep this decline to slightly less than 13 percent. Wholly to prevent any decline of the ratio of wealth to income below the 1965 level, savings would have had to increase much more.

As for changes in the asset mix, a significant reduction of the ratio of the net financial wealth of households to their tangible wealth —a reduction from 0.81 to 0.43—stands out clearly in the data for 1965–1978. In the inflationary years immediately following World War II, this ratio had also declined to some extent before exhibiting a rise from 1952 to 1965. Another major shift in the inflationary period 1965–1978 is a reduction from 2.15 to 1.26 in the ratio of net financial household assets to disposable income. Meanwhile the ratio of tangible household wealth to the same income measure rose moderately.

The wealth and income data from which these ratios are computed are measured in current dollars. Considering, however, that the real value of financial wealth, as well as that of disposable income, is determined by the quantity of consumer goods that can be acquired with the financial wealth and the income, the 1965–1978 reduction of the ratio of financial household wealth to disposable income implies a steep reduction also in real terms. The real value of tangible household wealth can also be defined as the equivalent of its value in terms of consumer goods, and in this case the moderate 1965–1978 rise in the ratio of the tangibles to income expresses at the same time a moderate real rise. For the tangibles, however, this is merely one of two ways in which real values will be defined in the paper. If, alternatively, the ratio of real tangible assets to real disposable income is computed by deflating the tangibles by their own prices and by deflating disposable income by the prices of consumer goods in general, then the ratio of the two shows a decline for houses and lots,

155

a rise for consumer durables, and scarcely any change for tangibles in general. Whichever concept of real household wealth is applied, a significant shift occurred from the financial to the tangible component during the inflationary era following 1965. This shift was a response to changes in the relation between the real returns yielded by the various types of household wealth, with allowance for risks in an environment in which substantial price increases of unpredictable size were expected to continue.

Low-yield assets do, however, become favored at the margin of choice once their weight in the asset mix has dropped sufficiently. For example, in the inflationary period 1965–1978 households increased the share of their current savings that went into financial assets. By doing so they avoided an even greater decline of the weight of their financial wealth than that which actually took place. Yet in spite of the large increase in the weight of the tangibles due to revaluations, households continued to allocate well over one-half of their current savings to the tangible component even from 1965 to 1978.

On balance, the composition of household wealth has shown a significant trend toward assets yielding use value directly to the households and a trend away from assets that are counterparts of capital employed by enterprise productively. One must remember, however, that if the net worth of corporations is estimated on the basis of the replacement cost of physical capital, rather than at the market value placed on the equity by households and other stockholders, a substantial proportion of present business capital has no counterpart in the value of the wealth of households. Enterprises have thus been faced with deteriorating terms of financing their new investments through issuing equity.

At least by one method of valuing capital in the corporate sector, the consolidated balance sheet of the economy would, therefore, have to include an upward adjustment for this item as compared with the market value entering into the wealth of stockholders (mainly American households). On the other hand, the consolidated balance sheet would have to include a downward adjustment for the public debt because government securities are included in the assets held. It will be pointed out tangentially that for 1978 these two adjustments would nearly cancel, with the net worth of the households and the consolidated net worth of the economy at $6.4 and $6.8 trillion, respectively. This, however, disregards the physical assets of the government sector, which are not captured by the accounts.

I. The Problem and the Concepts Used

(1) The presumption is strong that many of the changes in the wealth-income relations of American households in the post-1965 period represent a reaction of households to an inflationary environment.[1] The main reason is that the changes as compared with earlier periods conform to well-known precepts concerning rational defensive moves under specific pressures. These are pressures developing in an environment in which the price level is very likely to rise at a considerable but uncertain rate, and in which appraisals of business prospects are highly uncertain.

Whether in an environment of stable prices the uncertainty surrounding business prospects would have remained unchanged, it is impossible to tell; but it is clear that the reasonable predictability of major price increases at an unspecified rate and the unpredictability of policy responses to such increases have played a large role in heightening uncertainty. Generally, in the search for an explanation of the post-1965 changes in relations involving the size and composition of household wealth and the income of households, it is not possible strictly to exclude factors other than inflation; but inflation, which was accelerating to a significant extent, is generally expected to lead to the changes that became observable, and an argument assigning a comparable role to other suspects to be mentioned in this paper would have to bear a considerable burden of proof.[2] In the given

---

[1] The data discussed in a recent study by Phillip Cagan and Robert E. Lipsey overlap with those surveyed in the present paper. See *The Financial Effect of Inflation*, National Bureau of Economic Research, General Series 103 (Cambridge, Mass.: Ballinger, 1978). The main difference between the views expressed in the National Bureau study and the interpretation developed here is that that study gives much less credence than I do to the hypothesis that the shift in asset composition expresses a deliberate, largely rational reaction of the public to inflation. The National Bureau study gives far more credence to the view (which I reject) that the public simply accepted the results of unexpected asset revaluations. There are differences in interpretation also in some other respects but quite a bit of similarity in others.

[2] Trends in the standard of living and population trends during the period 1965-1978 may, of course, also have a bearing on various changes to be discussed, though most of these influences are hard to identify. Compared with the preceding thirteen-year period, per capita real disposable income rose at a somewhat higher rate, but the contrary is true of real disposable income per family; and the later period shows a much weaker upward trend than the earlier for the same income measure expressed per family *plus* unrelated individuals. Population growth was smaller in the later than in the earlier period; the rate of new family formation was about the same, but the rate of household formation including unrelated individuals was quite a bit higher in the later period. The weight of persons 65 years old and over in the population rose at a somewhat higher rate in the later than in the earlier period. The weight of

inflationary circumstances households have moved into a position that would have been open to them in a noninflationary economy as well. Yet, judging by their earlier record, in such an economy they would have shifted into positions that the actual circumstances have made too costly or too risky for them. The defensive moves observed in the data are moves toward "second best" positions that become justified when a penalty is placed on the "first best."

While the problem of these adjustments is of general interest, it bears specifically on monetary theory and policy, since the environment has placed a penalty on financial assets, and the ratios of specific kinds of financial assets to income—of the money aggregates to income—are reciprocals of money velocities. In the literal sense, this statement applies to the economy at large, not to households viewed separately, but households own a very high proportion of the total money stock broadly defined.

(2) The paper is concerned primarily with real rather than current-dollar relations, but in major parts of the analysis current-dollar wealth-income ratios can be regarded as numerically equal to their real counterparts because the same price correction will be applied both to the numerator and the denominator.

Table 1 contains a description and a brief explanation of the concepts of saving that will perform a useful function in the analysis. When savings in the sense of concept 1 will be expressed in real terms, this will be done with reliance on the price index applied also to disposable income as defined in the national income and product accounts (NIPA)—that is, the personal consumption expenditures (PCE) deflator. Since throughout this paper income will mean the NIPA's disposable income, no distinction will have to be drawn between the current-dollar and the real saving ratio (saving-to-income ratio) when saving concept 1 is employed.[3]

---

the age classes below twenty years rose in the earlier and declined in the later period. Wealth-income trends and changes in the composition of household wealth *may* have something to do *inter alia* with demographic shifts of the kind mentioned in this note, but in the interpretation of large shifts from financial to tangible assets the most obvious problem to explore is the relation between these shifts and accelerating inflation.

[3] In principle, the income concept to be employed here should include, in addition to the NIPA's disposable income, the household-wealth accumulations in the government and railroad employee retirement funds and also the investment-fund dividends originating in capital gains. These items of very small quantitative significance should be included because the concept of savings as defined in the Flow of Funds accounts includes them and this is the saving concept to be used in the analysis. Further, the main difference between the NIPA and the Flow of Funds saving concept is that the latter includes net additions to the stock of durable consumer goods and the former does not, and

TABLE 1

Savings Concepts
(The first of which will be mostly used.)

Abbreviations: NIPA = National Income and Product Accounts; FOF = Flow of Funds Accounts; PCE = Personal Consumption Expenditures

Definitional property of concept	*Explanation*
(1) Zero level of net personal saving and of disposable income is set by requirement that value of previously acquired assets be kept intact at current prices of assets. To obtain current-dollar wealth, asset revaluations since the time of their acquisition must be added to the sum of past net savings in this sense.	Excludes asset revaluations from net saving and net income. The resulting concepts are the conventional ones used in the NIPA and in FOF. The latter, in contrast to the former, includes in savings net additions to the stock of durable consumer goods and also accumulations in the government and railroad employee retirement funds, as well as investment-fund dividends originating in capital gains. Saving ratio in relation to disposable income is computed from current-dollar magnitudes and is treated as equivalent to real ratio whenever PCE deflator is used for both savings and income.
(2) Zero level set as in 1, except that valuation of assets at prices of time of acquisition is substituted for their valuation at current prices. Current-dollar wealth is the sum of past net savings in this sense.	Includes in net saving and net income all nominal asset revaluations. Because same amount is added to savings as to income, the addition of the revaluations increases the saving ratio. The resulting ratio is merely a ratio of current-dollar magnitudes. For the real counterparts, see below.
(3) Zero level set as in 2, except that, for the valuation of assets, their prices at the time of acquisition are raised in proportion to the increase of the PCE deflator since that time. Real wealth in one of two senses referred to in this paper is sum of past net savings.	Includes in net saving and net income all real revaluations of assets. All savings as well as income are deflated by PCE deflator. This is a real counterpart of concept 2, where real wealth is illustrated not by so much housing accommodation, but by so much real consumption available for the value of houses owned.

(Table 1 continues on the next page.)

TABLE 1   (continued)

Abbreviations: NIPA = National Income and Product Accounts; FOF = Flow of Funds Accounts; PCE = Personal Consumption Expenditures

Definitional property of concept	Explanation
(4) Zero level set as in 3, except that, for valuation of tangible assets, their prices at the time of acquisition are raised in proportion to the increase of their own prices since that time. Real wealth in another sense referred to in this paper is the sum of past net savings.	This also is a real counterpart of concept 2, but here real wealth is illustrated by so much housing accommodation, and the corresponding real wealth-income ratio is the ratio of real wealth in this sense to the consumption equivalent of the real disposable income. This concept of real wealth is inapplicable to financial wealth. This concept differs from 3 only to the extent that movements of the prices of tangible wealth differ from movements of consumer goods prices.

Concept 1 is the usual concept which, as is explained in the table, has a less inclusive NIPA version and a more inclusive Flow of Funds (FOF) version. *Whenever the contrary is not said explicitly, we shall use the FOF version of concept 1, along with the NIPA disposable income concept.*

The analysis will rely in part on the other savings concept as well because in an essential respect the current-dollar wealth concept is logically consistent with concept 2 of savings, not with the conventional concept 1. The reason is that concept 2, in contrast to concept 1, includes asset revaluations into savings, and the value of wealth is the sum of past net savings *including* asset revaluations.

Yet in another respect the current-dollar wealth-income ratio is consistent with concept 1 rather than concept 2 of savings. For both the current-dollar wealth-income *ratio* and the current-dollar concept 1 saving *ratio* have a "real" counterpart that is numerically

---

logically this would call for adding here to the NIPA's disposable income the imputed yield of the stock of durable consumer goods, by a method analogous to that employed in the NIPA for rent imputation on owner-occupied houses. None of the additions described in the present note were actually made here to the NIPA concept of disposable income. The orders of magnitude are such that the adjustments would reduce an aggregate wealth-income ratio of, say, 4.00 to somewhere between 3.90 and 3.95.

equal to the current-dollar ratio itself, provided that the numerator is deflated by the same price index as the denominator—in this case by the PCE deflator. The resulting real concepts are meaningful for wealth-income relations as well as for saving-income relations because they express *the real consumption obtainable for the value of the savings and of accumulated wealth, respectively.* Consequently, the saving ratio based on the conventional savings concept 1 and the current-dollar wealth-income ratio are useful tools—as are their numerically equal real counterparts—even though employing concept 1 of savings makes it necessary to adjust the cumulated savings for asset revaluations to obtain the value of wealth.

At the same time there exist other meaningful conceptions of real wealth—illustrated by available *real housing accommodations* rather than the consumer goods available for the value of houses— and these require deflating the current-dollar value of wealth by a different price index than that used for deflating disposable income. The analysis will therefore include more concepts of savings than the conventionally employed concept 1. Likewise, it will include more concepts of the real wealth-income ratio than that which is numerically equal to the current-dollar ratio and is obtained by deflating the current-dollar wealth by the same index as the disposable income. Yet these are the concepts that will be used unless other concepts are specified.

II. Brief Review of Facts

A Guide to Table 2. The analysis focuses on the inflationary period 1965–1978 and compares it with the preceding thirteen-year period of practical price stability, 1952–1965. Some information on the postwar years prior to 1952 will help place the comparison in perspective.

Household wealth is estimated on the basis of Flow of Funds statistics for the end of the year; when this wealth is related to disposable income, the year-end disposable income is approximated by averaging the seasonally adjusted annual rate of the year's last quarter and of the next year's first quarter. For computing constant-dollar ("real") disposable income, the year-end standing of the price deflator is approximated by the same method.

The wealth data in Table 2 include the government security holdings of households. Because disposable income is the income measure here, the tax burden these holdings entail affects the income side of the wealth-income relation, but no allowance is made for the liability of households represented by the capitalized value of future tax payments caused by the public debt. In the entire economy's consolidated balance sheet, which includes the holdings of government securities as assets, the public debt *would* have to be taken into account as a liability of the public; on the other hand, the physical assets held in the government sector would have to be included in the economy's wealth. This describes one of the two main integration problems for researchers who wish to work these data into a consolidated balance sheet for the economy as a whole. The other is the problem of bridging the valuation of corporate capital by the stockholders (mainly households) with its valuation for the corporate sector. To give a general idea: for 1978 the FOF obtains a consolidated net worth of $6.8 trillion for the economy, with the tangible assets of the corporations valued at replacement cost, as against the $6.4 trillion found for households in Table 2, column 3. The result gives the impression of a very small difference but, while this reconciliation takes account of the valuation problem for corporate assets and of the liability aspect of the public debt, it does not account for the physical assets held in the government sector. Various sources suggest that, for 1977, $1 trillion may be a reasonable rough estimate of these public-sector assets, not including the military ones. We now turn to the wealth components listed in Table 2.

Tangible assets other than land are valued at replacement cost. These tangibles consist of residential buildings, including mobile homes, of consumer durables, and of some other physical assets that belong to households as owners of noncorporate business. Land as a component of the tangibles is valued at its estimated selling price. Financial household assets, including those belonging to households as owners of noncorporate business, consist of deposits and currency, of credit-market instruments, of life-insurance and pension-fund reserves, and of the corporate-stock holdings of households valued at the market price of the stocks. Net financial assets consist of these financial assets minus the debt of the households.[4] Their wealth is defined as the sum of their net financial and their tangible assets.

In a later analytical context, to be explained in connection with Table 4, noncorporate business assets will be omitted. In the present

---

[4] Use of the concept of net financial assets does not imply that behaviorally household debt is related primarily to gross financial assets. There exists, for example, an obvious link between homeownership and mortgage debt (see p. 176, below).

TABLE 2

VALUE OF HOUSEHOLD WEALTH AT YEAR-END, AND SELECTED RATIOS, SELECTED YEARS

	(1)	(2)	(3)	(4)	(5)	(6)	(7)
		Billions of current dollars				Ratio[a]	
Year	Net financial wealth	Tangible wealth	(1) + (2)	(1) to disposable income	(2) to disposable income	(3) to disposable income	(1) to (2)
1947	345.7	440.7	786.4	1.97	2.51	4.47	0.78
1952	421.3	667.7	1,089.0	1.72	2.72	4.43	0.63
1960	724.8	1,045.3	1,770.1	2.05	2.96	5.02	0.69
1965	1,064.7	1,313.0	2,377.7	2.15	2.66	4.81	0.81
1973	1,469.8	2,564.4	4,034.2	1.56	2.72	4.28	0.57
1978	1,931.0	4,504.3	6,435.3	1.26	2.93	4.19	0.43

[a] Interpreting the ratios in columns (4) through (6) as real wealth-income ratios implies measuring real wealth by the consumer-goods equivalent of the value of wealth.

If noncorporate business assets are excluded, and a crude adjustment (explained later in the text) is made to exclude noncorporate business income from disposable income, then the following wealth-income ratios of the type shown in column 6 are obtained for some of the key years: 3.72 for 1952, 4.26 for 1965, 3.47 for 1978. With the same adjustments the ratios of net financial to tangible assets (column 7) are the following: 1.21 for 1952, 1.43 for 1965, 0.76 for 1978. The essential properties of these trends thus remain unchanged.

Information on various components of these major wealth categories is found in Table 4, p. 177; on pp. 173-76; and on p. 184.

context it should be noted that omission of these assets would leave the wealth-income trends observed in Table 2 essentially unchanged (see the note to the table).

To a very minor extent these wealth data are spuriously enlarged by the inclusion of the assets of nonprofit institutions and, except where noncorporate business assets are excluded, also by the inability to eliminate from the noncorporate assets an admixture of assets owned by corporate farms. On the other hand, the figures of Table 2 do not include the present value of social security claims—a problem to which we shall return later.

Sketching the Trends. (a) First, as can be seen from Table 2, from 1965 to 1978 the wealth-income ratio declined from 4.81 to 4.19. This decline followed a rise of the ratio during the thirteen-year period prior to 1965. It is reasonable to date the decline from about 1965, though the table shows a small reduction already for 1960–1965. Closer examination suggests that the 1960–1965 reduction occurred mostly from 1964 to 1965. The wealth-income ratio of 1952 was about the same as that of 1947.

(b) Second, whereas the wealth-income ratio rose over 1952–1965 and then declined over 1965–1978, the savings ratio rose from 11.6 percent to 13.1 percent between the two periods (see Table 3). Although this comparison relies on the *Flow of Funds version of concept 1 of savings*, it should be noted that the national income accounts (NIPA) version of concept 1 also registers a rise of the saving ratio from 1952–1965 to 1965–1978—a rise from 5.9 percent to 6.5 percent. By these standards households were becoming thriftier relative to their income in a period in which their wealth-income ratio was declining.

(c) Third, from 1965 to 1978 the ratio of net financial household assets to disposable income declined sharply, and the corresponding ratio for tangible household assets rose, with the result that the ratio of net financial to tangible assets declined from 0.81 to 0.43. As can be seen from Table 2, column 7, this decline was preceded by a rise in the ratio of net financial to the tangible component in the period 1952–1965. Also, the corresponding marginal ratio declined sharply between 1952–1965 and 1965–1978: in the first period approximately 50 percent of the increase in the value of assets assumed the form of an increment of the net financial component, while in the second this proportion was less than 22 percent.

The years immediately following World War II also saw a decline in the ratio of net financial to tangible household wealth.

TABLE 3

CUMULATED DISPOSABLE INCOME AND PERSONAL SAVINGS
1953 THROUGH 1965 AND 1966 THROUGH 1978
(billions of dollars)

Period	(1) Cumulated disposable income	(2) Cumulated personal savings	(3) Ratio of (2) to (1) (percent)
1953 through 1965	4,439.4	516.5	11.6
1966 through 1978	11,415.0	1,497.6	13.1

NOTE: The first period starts here with the year 1953 and the second with 1966 because the wealth estimates relate to the end of each year. Reliance on concept 1 implies that changes in wealth include asset revaluations *beyond* savings as here defined.

SOURCE: For disposable income, the National Income and Product Tables of the U.S. Department of Commerce, Bureau of Economic Analysis; the data for the Flow of Funds concept of personal savings used here are derived from statistics made available by the Board of Governors of the Federal Reserve System, Division of Research and Statistics, Flow of Funds Section.

That period too reflected the consequences of inflation—first, the release of the suppressed inflationary pressures of the war years, and subsequently the brief inflationary outbreak in the early phase of the Korean War. However, the proportionate reduction of the ratio was even larger from 1965 to 1978 than it was from 1947 to 1952.

(d) Fourth, the shift in the composition of personal savings also seems to point in the direction opposite to that suggested by the behavior of asset values. From the period 1952–1965 to the period 1965–1978, when the composition of household wealth shifted increasingly from the net financial to the tangible component, the proportion of new savings represented by net financial assets *rose* from about 31 percent to 44 percent.

I will now present an analysis of the events that are summarized in these four propositions. The subsequent discussion will call for extending the factual background of the argument, and the data required for that extension will be in Table 4. All tables cover years of either advanced cyclical expansion or cyclical peaks. Closer examination does not suggest that cyclical sensitivity of the relations to be discussed would pose any serious problem—certainly not as compared to the problems posed by longer-run tendencies.

III. Logical Reconciliation of the Four Propositions

Of the four propositions just described the second may be suspected of conflicting with the first, and the fourth with the third. The reason is that asset values suggest trends different from those implied by current savings.

The merely apparent character of the first conflict—that between trends in the wealth-income ratio and in the saving ratio—can be best seen from the simple piece of formal analysis contained in the appendix (p. 187). But a brief general discussion will also disclose the problem as it has shaped up during the post-1965 inflationary era. This apparent conflict is a special manifestation, under inflationary conditions, of a reconciliation problem arising because the concept of wealth, unlike the usual concept of saving, includes asset revaluations, so that growth in the worth of assets after their acquisition does not show up in the cumulated savings (concept 1). This exerts a substantial influence on trends observed in an inflationary period, though its influence is not limited to these periods.

Even if the price level remained constant, an increase in the growth rate of disposable income would reduce the wealth-income ratio below the level at which it otherwise would be, unless the previously accumulated assets are revalued upward *sufficiently* or the saving ratio increases *sufficiently* (or both). The reason is that with a constant saving ratio an increase in the growth rate of income makes current income run faster ahead of the previous accumulations valued at their initial cost.

Consider a period, such as 1965–1978, of substantial inflation and also of real growth of income. If the total revaluation of assets (tangible plus financial) corresponds to less than the inflation component of the growth rate of nominal income, then the wealth-income ratio will decline unless savings grow large enough to make up this difference *in addition to* resulting in real wealth accumulation fully in proportion to the growth of real income. The saving ratio needed to prevent a decline in the wealth-income ratio in such an inflationary period would have to be *much* larger—not just 1.5 percentage points larger on the Flow of Funds basis—than that which in a preceding period of practically stable prices (1952–1965) was in fact sufficient to *raise* the wealth-income ratio. This will be so particularly if in the earlier period asset revaluations far exceeded the equivalent of the then small rate of general price increase (as had been the case).

An oversimplified numerical framework helps to illustrate the nature of the problem. This will be done with 1978 year-end conditions in mind. The net financial assets of households amounted at that date to about $1.9 trillion, with household debt at about $1.5 trillion and gross financial assets of households thus at $3.4 trillion. The money holdings of households—here defined in the broad sense to include all commercial bank and thrift-institution deposits (M-5)—made up about $1.3 trillion of this amount. To simplify the problem, I assume that all household assets except money are revalued upward in proportion to, say, a 10 percent annual inflation rate, that current-dollar disposable income also adjusts to that inflation rate, and that, aside from the inflation, savings would be just sufficient to stabilize the wealth-income ratio. Then to keep the wealth-income ratio of households from declining under inflation, an additional 10 percent of $1.3 trillion—approximately $130 billion a year—would have to be saved; this would be the amount required to compensate for the fact that money is by definition not revalued in current dollars. The required additional saving corresponds to 8.4 percent of the 1978 year-end disposable income. This represents a very large amount of additional saving in the usual sense of concept 1.

In highly simplified classroom models of fully anticipated inflation, the bulk of the required additional savings develops due to the assumption that the nominal interest rate on all money other than hand-to-hand currency rises by the 10 percentage points that express the inflation rate, and that the interest recipients save additionally the full equivalent of this increase in order to keep the real value of their assets unchanged. Because hand-to-hand currency bears no interest, its existence is recognized as an imperfection even in such a simplified analysis.

Reality usually deviates markedly from all these simplifying assumptions. In the present context it is not astonishing to observe for an inflationary period a pattern of revaluations along with an increase in the concept 1 saving ratio that is insufficient to prevent the wealth-income ratio from declining.

Along the same lines it is easy to eliminate the appearance of another logical conflict in connection with the third and fourth propositions—(c) and (d)—listed above. The ratio of financial household wealth to tangible household wealth will indeed decline in spite of increased allocation of current savings to the financial component, if revaluations raise the value of the previously accumulated tangible wealth sufficiently to outweigh the increased saving allocation to the financial component. In this case the increased allocation of savings to financial household wealth merely moderates a decline in the ratio of financial to tangible assets. Indeed, such

167

a change in saving allocation may merely perform the function of moderating a decline of the aggregate real value of net financial household wealth, as is the case when 1978 is compared with 1965.

IV. Empirical Content of the Reconciliation

The previous discussion has shown that, because the numerator and the denominator imply the identical deflator, holding the current-dollar wealth-income ratio constant means the same as holding the real ratio constant *provided* real wealth is interpreted as the equivalent of the value of wealth in terms of consumer goods. We have seen also that avoiding a decline of the current-dollar wealth-income ratio from 1965 through 1978 would have required that net savings in the usual sense of concept 1 plus current-dollar revaluations of financial plus tangible assets at least equal the increase in disposable income during the period. This section shows that this condition was not met. Given the revaluations, the net savings in the sense of concept 1 were much smaller than those that would have met the condition. This is so despite the fact that the saving ratio of 1965–1978 was somewhat larger than that of the preceding period, in which, however, the asset revaluations were significantly larger in relation to a very small inflation rate.

From 1965 through 1978, the sum of concept 1 savings and of revaluations raised the current-dollar value of household wealth from almost $2.4 trillion to somewhat more than $6.4 trillion (see Table 2, column 3). The difference of somewhat more than $4.0 trillion was brought about by concept 1 net savings amounting to $1.5 trillion (see Table 3), by current-dollar revaluations of the tangible household wealth amounting to $2.4 trillion, and by merely $200 billion's worth of current-dollar revaluations of financial assets. During the thirteen-year period ending in 1978 savings and revaluations thus jointly raised the current-dollar value of household wealth to about 2.7 times its 1965 level. At the same time the current-dollar value of disposable income rose to 3.1 times its 1965 level. Since the ratio 2.7 falls short of 3.1 by about 13 percent, the wealth-income ratio declined by close to 13 percent—that is, from 4.81 to 4.19.

To express the same facts in real terms, using the PCE deflator as the price index for both wealth and income: The $1.5 trillion concept 1 savings of the period 1965–1978 amounted to about $1 trillion in 1965 prices; raising by this amount the 1965 total household wealth of somewhat less than $2.4 trillion to $3.4 trillion would have resulted in a 44 percent real increase of the 1965 wealth if there had been no real revaluations. The analysis below shows, however, that the period's real revaluations were a *negative* magnitude amounting to about $200 billion in 1965 prices, as a result of which the $1 trillion of savings raised the real value of the 1965 wealth only to $3.2 trillion (rather than to $3.4 trillion) in 1965 prices. This was an increase of about 35 percent. Since the real disposable income of 1978 was 56 percent higher than that of 1965, the wealth-income ratio was reduced by about 13 percent of its 1965 level. The reason why the period's real revaluations of total household wealth should be estimated at minus $200 billion in 1965 prices is that in view of the 99 percent increase of the PCE deflator from 1965 to 1978, the $6.4 trillion wealth for 1978 amounts to somewhat more than $3.2 trillion in 1965 prices; deducting from this $1 trillion for the 1965–1978 savings expressed in 1965 prices leaves about $200 billion less than the $2.4 trillion shown in Table 2 as the 1965 total household wealth (financial plus tangible).

For the tangible component of household wealth viewed separately, the analogously estimated real revaluations of 1965–1978 add up to a positive amount: about $370 billion in 1965 prices. *In real terms the devaluation of net financial wealth was sufficient to explain the negative sign of the total real revaluations in spite of the substantial positive real revaluations of the tangible component.*

The prices of the goods making up the tangible component of household wealth rose in a higher proportion than the PCE deflator. This is so even if we limit ourselves to residential structures including lots and to consumer durables owned by households in a capacity *other than* ownership of noncorporate business. Among the tangibles, the items showing a relative price increase (houses and lots) have a far greater joint weight than those showing a relative price decline (consumer durables). On the other hand, considering the 99 percent increase of the PCE deflator from 1965 to 1978, the current-dollar upward revaluation of the net financial component was exceedingly small. The current-dollar value of the net financial assets rose from almost $1.1 trillion in 1965 to $1.9 trillion in 1978 (Table 2, column 1), but current-dollar revaluations accounted for only about $200 billion of this increase. The remainder of the increase resulted from the allocation of about 44 percent of the period's current savings to the net financial component, which was insufficient to prevent the aggregate real value of the net financial assets from declining. The record of the preceding period was very different: from 1952 to 1965 net financial household wealth rose from about $400 billion to almost $1.1 trillion—a $700 billion rise which, given the 24 percent cumulated general inflation of those years, corresponds to a very large real increase—and close to $500 billion of the rise resulted from upward revaluations of financial assets. In those years, contrary to the 1965–1978 record, real revaluations were of a substantial *positive* magnitude for total household wealth as well.

The values of the net financial assets behaved so differently during 1952–1965 than in 1965–1978 mainly because in the former period stock prices rose in a much higher proportion than the general price level while over the latter period stock prices fell far below the inflation trend. In the later period of rising uncertainty about business prospects household debt did not rise more relative to income than it had in the earlier period; in fact, the reverse is true. As for the other financial assets, money is by definition not revalued in current-dollar terms, and, when nominal interest rates rise, various types of fixed claims on money are devalued. But the differential behavior of stock prices is primarily responsible for the large positive real revaluation of net financial assets in 1952–1965 and for their negative real revaluation in 1965–1978. Other things equal, however, even a rise of the comprehensive stock-price indexes in proportion to the PCE deflator would not have been sufficient to prevent the wealth-income ratio from declining in the 1965–1978 period. Taking the actual behavior of stock prices for granted, the rise of the concept 1 saving ratio from its 1952–1965 level of 11.6 percent to its 1965–1978 level of 13.1 percent was far from sufficient to lead to that result (see Table 3, p. 165).

This is the interpretation of the trends suggested by use of the conventional concept 1 of saving, and it will turn out to be the preferred interpretation here. But, in terms of formal analysis, it would be equally possible to focus on the significant reduction in the concept 3 saving ratio in the transition from a period of a rising to one of a declining wealth-income ratio (see Table 1, p. 159).

Computing the concept 3 saving ratio calls for adding to savings in constant prices the revaluations in the same prices, and dividing this sum by the disposable income plus the revaluations expressed in those prices. The saving ratio in this sense was 19.4 percent for 1952–1965 and 11.0 percent for 1965–1978. Should we therefore modify the conclusion that, in the second period as compared to the first the households engaged in an additional saving effort reflecting itself in the rise of the concept 1 saving ratio from 11.6 percent to 13.1 percent, but that this additional effort was too weak to maintain the wealth-income ratio? Should we conclude instead that there occurred a significant reduction of the saving effort, reflected in the lowering of the concept 3 saving ratio from 19.4 percent to 11.0 percent?

Several reasons support the emphasis on the first of these two interpretations. The main reason is that thrift in the sense of accumulating current real asset revaluations—a large part of the thrift included in concept 3 saving for 1952–1965—is not the same thing as thrift in the sense of abstention from consuming one's real income. Most households view current aggregate real income as a component of a continuing long-run flow to which consumption and saving behavior is geared; but they have reason not to view currently observed real asset revaluations in this way. It would therefore be unconvincing to attribute increased thrift to households because they do not make an attempt currently to consume nearly as high a proportion of current real asset revaluations as is the consumed proportion of their current aggregate real income. This in itself suggests that it is less convincing to conclude that from 1952–1965 to 1965–1978 thrift declined from a level measured by the 19.4 percent saving ratio to a level measured by the 11.0 percent ratio than to conclude that a moderate rise in thrift occurred, from the 11.6 percent saving ratio for 1952–1965 to 13.1 percent ratio for 1965–1978.

So much for the empirical content of the logical reconciliation of trends in the wealth-income ratio with trends in saving ratios. The discussion now turns to the 1965–1978 decline of the ratio of financial to tangible wealth from 0.81 to 0.43 (Table 2, column 7). We have seen that this took place in spite of an increase in the allocation of current savings to the net financial component. As noted above, from 1952–1965 to 1965–1978 this allocation rose from about 31 percent of new savings to 44 percent when revaluations are excluded. This happened over a span during which the ratio of the net financial to the tangible component declined steeply, reflecting the concentration of large revaluations into the tangible component during the later period. The steep trend against financial and toward tangible household assets was somewhat moderated by the reduced allocation of current savings to the tangible component, but the public did not go far in reducing the effect of revaluations on the asset composition: it continued to allocate well over one-half of its current concept 1 savings to tangible assets. Over the period 1965–1978 it allocated more than \$800 billion current-dollar new savings to tangibles, in spite of the fact that even the aggregate real value of the net financial assets— not merely their value relative to other economic variables—declined over that period.

V. Behavioral Implications: The Propensity to Save

The saving ratio increased somewhat if the numerical estimates are based on concept 1 savings—in either the FOF or the NIPA version—and, in interpreting thrift, more significance is to be attributed to this than to the decline of the saving ratio based on concept 3. Conceptually, no sharp distinction exists between the supposition that the increase in the saving ratio served to moderate the decline of the wealth-income ratio and the supposition that it served to create reserves for a possible period of inflationary job insecurity. This type of insecurity may be interpreted as a lowering of the worker's estimate of his human capital relative to his current income.

Why was the increase in the saving effort insufficient to prevent part or all of the roughly 13 percent reduction of the wealth-income ratio during the period 1965–1978? The answer presumably is that for specific reasons—particularly the third reason discussed below—the ratio listed for 1965 in Table 2, column 6, somewhat overstates the target of the households for the subsequent period. This assumption can be supported by the following arguments.

(a) First, any implied assumption that "normally" the public tries to avoid a reduction of the overall wealth-income ratio becomes suspect for demographic reasons not only if income per household or per capita is declining—the contrary of which has been true—but also if the age structure of the population changes. In particular, a rise in the proportion of the population aged 65 years and over tends to increase the weight of those who may have planned all along to live partly on previously accumulated wealth, and this change diminishes the weight of those who are accumulating wealth for consumption in their old age. Such a change in the age structure did occur during the period 1965–1978. This line of reasoning suffers, however, from the difficulty that the weight of those aged 65 and over changed in the same direction, even if to a somewhat lesser extent, from 1952 to 1965, and over that span the wealth-income ratio rose appreciably. It is, of course, possible that the case would have to be argued in terms of changes in the demographic structure in finer detail. Yet one of the other demographic changes—the 1965–1978 decline of the weight of the age classes below 20 years, following a 1952–1965 rise—is unhelpful in an effort to explain why households should have reduced their wealth-income ratio.

(b) Second, the significant decline of the wealth-income ratio from 1965 to 1978 would disappear if the equity represented by corporate stock were estimated not as a financial item to be valued at market but by valuing the physical capital of the corporations at replacement cost. In an analysis of the valuation of *household wealth,* reasoning along these lines would, however, be unconvincing. Such reasoning would imply that shareholders estimate their stockholdings on the basis of the replacement cost of physical capital that is not under their individual control. And simply excluding stockholdings for the appraisal of trends in household wealth—thus deducting, from the wealth-income ratios in Table 2, column 6, 0.69 for 1952, 1.29 for 1965, and 0.52 for 1978—would be clearly inappropriate. It may be tempting to engage in this operation because available estimates suggest that small proportions of income recipients located high on the income or wealth scale own high proportions of all corporate stock owned by households directly. This finding comes to mind even if a considerable proportion of the total stock outstanding is owned by pension funds and by life insurance companies rather than by households directly. Yet the essential fact here is that the stock-owning households own major amounts of other wealth, and that in periods such as 1952–1965 their demand for stocks rises relative to their demand for other financial assets while the contrary is true of periods such as 1965–1978. Eliminating the value of corporate stock from the household-wealth data does not, therefore, yield numerical estimates for households with no stocks nor for any other reasonably defined group.

What remains true is that the behavior of stock prices played a large role in shaping the trend in the wealth-income ratio for 1965–1978, and that taking this behavior for granted leads to the conclusion that a very large increase of the period's current savings would have been needed to prevent the wealth-income ratio from declining. This kind of quantification of the potential effect of additional savings is not very revealing, however, because it involves disregarding the fact that, given a major change in saving habits, many economic variables affecting incomes and asset revaluations would also have assumed different values.

(c) Third, and most important, Table 2 makes no allowance for the capitalized value of social security benefits. The decline in the wealth-income ratio from 1965 to 1978 hinges on that fact. Without such allowances, the table shows for 1952, 1965, and 1978 the following sequence of wealth-income ratios: 4.43, 4.81, and 4.19; with allowances for social security wealth derived from Martin Feldstein's work, this sequence changes to 5.80, 7.06, and 7.36. The difference between the two sets of numbers is substantial and it rises over time.[5]

---

[5] See Martin Feldstein, "Social Security, Induced Retirement and Aggregate

These estimates for the social security adjustment rely on some interpolation and extrapolation, and the numbers used by Robert Barro suggest that the rise of this adjusted ratio from 7.06 in 1965 to 7.36 in 1978 may even be a slight underestimate.[6] Furthermore, these figures incorporate estimates of the capitalized value of retirement benefits alone, and these are not the only benefits obtained from the system. On the other hand, these figures involve no allowance for the cost to the households of the capitalized value of the future tax burden arising from the social security system.

To what extent households are guided in their saving behavior by the capitalized social security component of an adjusted wealth-income ratio is uncertain. They are very unlikely to consider this the full equivalent of wealth components over which they have command throughout their lifetime, but they are also very unlikely behaviorally to assign no weight whatever to them. Answers steering between these two extremes suggest that in the relevant sense there has been a decline of the wealth-income ratio, though one smaller than that shown in Table 2. This may help to explain the small saving reaction to the observed change.

These remarks concerning the relevance of the capitalized social security retirement benefits could be extended to other transfer-payment entitlements. Private pension-fund and life-insurance accumulations also raise doubts about full equivalence with other wealth components, but the 1965–1978 trend in the wealth-income ratio would not be perceptibly influenced by omitting these items from Table 2. Jointly, the ratio to disposable income of these two components declined from 0.52 to 0.47; the life-insurance component declined and the pension-fund component rose. However, as will be seen in Section VII, a similar question involving assignments of different importance to different items making up the major wealth components is raised by the relationship between items of financial wealth that possess different degrees of liquidity and that are thus imperfect substitutes.

VI. Behavioral Implications: The Shift from Financial to Tangible Household Wealth in View of Real Rates of Return

The reduction of the ratio of net financial to tangible household wealth from its 1965 value of 0.81 to its 1978 value of 0.43 could

Capital Accumulation," *Journal of Political Economy*, vol. 82, no. 5 (September-October 1974), pp. 905-26.

[6] Robert J. Barro, *The Impact of Social Security on Private Saving* (Washington, D.C.: American Enterprise Institute, 1978).

have been avoided only if households had made a bigger shift in the allocation of their current savings toward net financial and away from tangible wealth than they actually did. As was seen, from 1952–1965 to 1965–1978 they increased this allocation from 31 to 44 percent. Even the allocation of all of the 1965–1978 savings to the net financial component would not have prevented a reduction of the 1965 ratio of net financials to tangibles had such further reallocation not changed the pattern of revaluations in favor of the financial component. Yet further reallocation of current savings to the net financial component would, of course, have shifted the relative revaluation pattern in that direction, and it is therefore impossible to tell how much more of the 1965–1978 savings would have had to be allocated to the net financial component to prevent the ratio from declining. Given the total amount of saving, further reallocation could have been achieved by the acquisition of less tangible wealth coupled either with the acquisition of more gross financial wealth or with reduced new borrowing. For this pattern the environment has created no incentive.

Not only does the trend away from financial and toward tangible household assets stand out forcefully in Table 2, but the most important consideration qualifying the findings concerning the decline in the wealth-income ratio *strengthens* the findings concerning that trend. It does so because if "social security wealth" is included in household assets, then in accordance with the requirements of logic, though with some violence to the language, we should presumably lump this component together with the tangibles. After all, social security wealth consists of the capitalized value of claims that are indexed and thus represent bundles of goods. If social security wealth were included in the data, and if it were interpreted as belonging essentially in tangible household wealth, the ratio of net financial to tangible assets would decline during 1965–1978 not from 0.81 to 0.43 but from 0.44 to 0.21; and the ratio of tangible wealth to disposable income would rise not from 2.66 to 2.93 but much more steeply, from 4.91 to 6.10. Yet we shall continue to use here the data on which Table 2 is based.

The 1965–1978 reduction in the ratio of net financials to disposable income from 2.15 to 1.26 reflects a reduction in the ratio of gross financial assets to disposable income from 3.04 to 2.24 and a rise in the ratio of debt to disposable income from 0.89 to 0.98. When distributed over thirteen years, the rise in the *ratio of debt to income* was small, but two-thirds of it occurred between 1976 and 1978. Furthermore, even the period as a whole shows a large rise in the *ratio of debt to gross financial assets*—from 29.3 percent to 43.8 percent. The discrepancy between the change of these two ratios is easy to understand, since from 1965 to 1978 the current-dollar value of housing, including lots, increased in a much higher proportion than did the current-dollar value of gross financial assets, and a substantial share of housing is debt-financed. Hence debt rose in a much higher proportion in relation to gross financial wealth than in relation to income.

Table 4 provides a point of departure for an analysis of the positions in financial and in tangible wealth that the household acquired in the course of the post-1965 shift to tangibles. The analysis will focus on the inflationary period 1965–1978, but the table provides information also on two subperiods within these thirteen years and on the preceding thirteen-year period beginning in 1952.

As was said before, as long as the focus is on real wealth-income ratios in the sense of the real *consumption equivalent of the value of wealth* per unit of the real *consumption equivalent of disposable income,* both wealth and income may be deflated by the PCE deflator, and thus the current-dollar wealth-income ratios can be interpreted as real ratios. This is the only interpretation suggested here for the ratio of real *financial* household wealth to real disposable income, but it is merely one of two interpretations to be considered for the ratio of real *tangible* household wealth to real disposable income. On this interpretation of real wealth in relation to real income, the 1965–1978 decline for net financial assets was 41 percent and the thirteen-year rise for tangibles was 10 percent (see Table 4, columns 2 and 4).

The data used in Table 4 for major subcategories of tangible wealth (see columns 5 through 9) are limited to wealth of households other than that attributable to ownership of noncorporate business. A sufficient reason for this limitation is that the subcategories are not defined identically for noncorporate business as for other household wealth. In computing the wealth-income ratios for the subcategories of tangible household wealth I made a corresponding crude adjustment in the denominator of the ratios appearing in columns 5 through 9, in that I reduced the aggregate disposable income of the economy in 1952, 1965, 1973, and 1978 by 15 percent, 10 percent, 8 percent, and 6 percent respectively—the approximate shares of noncorporate business in personal income for those years.

With real wealth interpreted as the real *consumption equivalent of the value of wealth*—thus with the real wealth-income ratios regarded as equal to their current-dollar counterparts—the 1965–1978 trend for the subcategories of the tangibles can be read from columns 5 through 7 of Table 4. For residential buildings the ratio rose by

TABLE 4

Year-end Wealth-Income Ratios and Components Variously Defined

	1	2	3	4	5	6	7	8	9	Addenda		
										10	11	12
1952	1.72	80.0	2.72	102.3	0.86	0.14	0.62	92	99	245.6	392.0	0.63
1965	2.15	100	2.66	100	0.87	0.28	0.52	100	100	494.4	633.8	0.78
1973	1.56	72.6	2.72	102.3	0.90	0.28	0.54	95	123	943.6	854.4	1.10
1978	1.26	58.6	2.93	110.2	1.01	0.31	0.55	92	132	1535.0	988.0	1.55

1: Net financial household assets per unit of disposable income.
2: Same as 1 in index numbers (1965 = 100).
3: Tangible household assets per unit of disposable income.
4: Same as 3 in index numbers (1965 = 100).
5: Residential buildings per unit of disposable income, with crude adjustment for omission of noncorporate business, as explained in the text.
6: Same as 5, but for lots instead of residential buildings. An unknown proportion of the changes over these periods is due to changes in the share of households in total land ownership rather than to revaluations.
7: Same as 5 and 6, but for consumer durables instead of residential buildings or lots.
8: Residential buildings deflated by their prices and divided by disposable income which is deflated by PCE deflator. Adjusted for omission of noncorporate business, as explained in text, and expressed in index numbers (1965 = 100), rounded to integers. Consistent with concept 4, Table 1.
9: Same as 8, but for consumer durables instead of residential buildings.
10: Disposable income, in billions of current dollars.
11: Real disposable income in billions of 1972 dollars.
12: PCE deflator (1972 = 100).

Source: Derived from statistics made available by the Flow of Funds Division of the Federal Reserve Board (see Table 2); and from data made available by the U.S. Department of Commerce, Bureau of Economic Analysis, concerning the replacement-cost value of houses and of durable consumer goods in current and in constant dollars.

16 percent; for buildings and lots jointly by 15 percent; and for durable consumer goods by 6 percent.

These results, however, change significantly if real tangible household wealth is defined as its current-dollar value *deflated not by the PCE deflator but by the prices of the goods making up that wealth;* and if wealth on that definition is related to the general consumer-goods equivalent of disposable income—that is, to disposable income *deflated by the PCE deflator.* The real ratio defined in this way is a meaningful alternative for tangible household wealth, though not for the financial component. For residential buildings viewed separately this ratio declined from 1965 to 1978 by 8 percent (column 8). For consumer durables the ratio rose from 1965 to 1978 by as much as 32 percent (column 9), and this rise resulted from an even higher increase for durables other than cars and from little change in the ratio for cars. The 1965–1978 change in the ratio so defined for tangible household wealth in general, including land, can be approximated only by speculating, without reliance on data, that the thirteen-year increase in the value of the land owned by households (residential lots) represents preponderantly revaluations rather than additional area acquired from the holdings of other sectors. In this case the ratio of tangible household wealth to disposable income was approximately the same in 1978 as in 1965, with the main components weighted by their representation in the total current-dollar value.[7]

The large difference between the behavior shown in columns 5 and 6 and that shown in column 8 results from a rise of the prices entering into the construction cost of buildings, which exceeded the 1965–1978 rise of the PCE deflator—a 99 percent rise—by more than 26 percent (in relation to 1.99). This relative price increase has shown a tendency to accelerate. The difference between the behavior reflected in column 7 and that in column 9 results from a price-trend discrepancy of nearly 21 percent *in the opposite direction* for durable consumer goods (including cars as well as other durables). As was explained above, the valuation of all tangible household wealth other than land is based on replacement costs. The valuation of land (residential lots) is based on estimates of sales price. If the entire increase of the value of lots from 1965 to 1978 represented revaluations (that is, assuming no acquisition from other sectors), the cumulated relative price increase over the PCE deflator would come out at 84 percent for this component of wealth, but the underlying assumption

---

[7] As explained in the text, prior to deflating, the NIPA's disposable income was reduced by 10 percent for 1965 and by 6 percent for 1978, in order to eliminate the component consisting of the income of noncorporate business.

introduces an upward bias into the 84 percent estimate. With this upward bias the cumulated relative price increase would be about 40 percent for houses plus lots and about 22 percent for all tangible household wealth; even in reality this latter figure is likely to have been nearer to 20 than to 15 percent.

Buyers have, of course, been generally aware of the overwhelming likelihood of price rises for most goods making up tangible household wealth. But this is not the same thing as being guided by the expectation of real capital gains such as could result from merely speculative purchases of other buyers or from particularly tight supply constraints. Real capital gains in the sense used here reflect *relative* price increases—that is, the rise of asset prices greater than the general inflation rate. Forces operating on the supply side *reduced* the relative prices of consumer durables appreciably, and the shift toward these goods is therefore not suspect of having been induced by the kind of circular reasoning that could lead consumers to increase their purchases of specific goods merely because they expect other buyers to drive up their prices relative to prices in general. The shift toward houses and lots in a period in which their prices rose at a supernormal rate is more open to this suspicion, and here anticipated increases in relative prices probably have played a role in determining the demand. But even here the emphasis can fall largely on the implicit rates of return derived from use value, *as distinct from capital gains.*

It is reasonable to conclude that while the inflationary developments reduced the implicit real rate on homeownership from 1965 to 1978, they reduced it much less than they did the rate on the interest-bearing financial assets of households; and it is reasonable to conclude that the implicit rate on consumer durables was increased. Hence, aside from capital gains, the ranking for the given initial composition of assets was *(1) durable consumer goods, (2) houses, (3) financial assets,* and one would expect shifts in the asset composition to reflect this ranking. When the outcome shown in Table 4 is examined in terms of real housing accommodations and quantities of consumer durables, the ranking suggested by the shifts confirms these expectations. Consumer durables come out ahead of houses and the financials come last.[8] *On the other hand, when the outcome is examined in current-dollar terms, houses outrank the consumer durables,* and this does have to do with the steep increase of the rela-

---

[8] Compare column 8 with column 9 for the proportionate increase during the period 1965-1978.

tive price of homes that presumably became built into price expectations.[9] The financial assets trail in the ranking in either case.[10]

Why, aside from capital gains, would the shifts in implicit real rates of return favor consumer durables over the other two categories, and homeownership over the financial assets? Note first that from 1953–1965 to 1966–1978 even the pretax weighted average of the *real* rates of interests on the interest-bearing financial assets of households declined by more than two-thirds, from 1.75 percent to an exceedingly low 0.51 percent.[11] Furthermore, the recent phase included three years with significantly negative pretax real rates, so that the 1973–1978 average was negative. As for *aftertax* returns, even the 1966–1978 average must have corresponded to a negative real rate for most interest recipients who, given the period's average inflation rate and the U.S. tax system, paid taxes on an average nominal yield of about 5.80 percent. For most of those concerned, these taxes must have been much greater than 10 percent of the interest received, and must have wiped out the pretax real rate of 0.51 percent. Although legally imposed ceilings on nominal interest rates for major varieties of financial assets are unlikely to be the sole cause of the behavior of real rates of interest in the recent inflationary environment, they have contributed heavily to the emergence of such an adverse tendency. Conjectures about future trends should therefore reckon with the new availability of savings channels with unconstrained interest rates to accounts of moderate size. In contrast with the rates on financial household assets, the untaxed implicit real rate of return on homeownership must have remained positive by an appreciable margin even aside from real capital-gains prospects.

This contrast has justified the significant 1965–1978 shift away from net financial assets toward homeownership. After all, a household has by definition a home of its own; thus renting is the only alternative to homeownership. Disregarding rent-controlled properties, even the landlord must be assumed to earn profits, though he is disadvantaged relative to the homeowner. This disadvantage results from the fact that he must pay taxes on the rent, while the homeowner's imputed rent is tax-free without impairment of his right to deduct his interest costs from his taxable income. Even an increase

---

[9] Compare column 5 with column 7 for the proportionate increase during the period 1965-1978.

[10] Compare for 1965-1978 column 2 with any of the columns referred to in the preceding notes.

[11] These numbers are based on data obtained from the Board of Governors of the Federal Reserve System, Division of Research and Statistics.

steeper than 30 percent in the price of housing including lots, relative to the PCE deflator, could not be assumed to have reduced the implicit real rate of return on homeownership as much as the average real rate of interest on fixed-income securities was reduced. Some of the operating costs of houses—particularly the energy-related ones—increased more than prices of consumer goods in general, but this cannot have had a large enough effect on net rates of return to invalidate the conclusion that homeownership became more rewarding than financial assets even aside from real capital gains.

The most pronounced real shift, however, has taken place from net financial assets to consumer durables rather than to houses (Table 4, columns 2, 8, and 9). Had the asset mix remained unchanged, the decline of nearly 21 percent in the prices of consumer durables in relation to the PCE deflator over 1965–1978 would have greatly increased the implicit rate of return on consumer durables as compared with those on homeownership and net financial assets. The conclusion holds despite the somewhat greater role that energy prices play in determining the operating costs of specific types of consumer durables than it does for houses. To the extent that prospective capital gains were adequately foreseen and have motivated buyers, these prospects have weakened the case for consumer durables versus homes. Differently expressed, aside from the loss of yield to the owner as a result of later acquisition, postponing the purchase of a home was a more costly decision than postponing the purchase of consumer durables. On the other hand, for an unchanging asset mix the yield per purchase price would have become much higher for durables than for houses including lots, and the loss of current yield caused by postponement of purchases would therefore also have become much higher.

This brief survey of details supports the conclusion presented at the outset, according to which the environment has created incentives for a change in the composition of household wealth away from components that are counterparts of capital employed by enterprises and toward components that yield use value directly to the households. It bears repetition that this conclusion is valid regardless of whether noncorporate business assets are included in household assets.[12] At the same time it bears repeating that if the worth of corporate equity is estimated not at the market value that households place on it but on the basis of the replacement costs of the physical capital, then the post-1965 capital stock in the corporate sector includes a substantial

---

[12] On the numerical difference that the exclusion of these assets would make, see the note to Table 2 (p. 163).

component that has no counterpart in the wealth of the stockholders. This component reflects the substantial discrepancy between the cost that enterprises incur when acquiring new physical capital and the cost the previous stockholders can recover by floating equity.

Whereas the main events thus fall nicely in place when the reaction of the public to the post-1965 inflationary environment is stressed, it would be wrong to claim that other contributing factors played no role in the observed sharp increase in the relative weight of the tangible component of household wealth. This paper has acknowledged the possible role of other factors, particularly demographic ones, but has not explored them. In the period 1965–1978 the rate of increase in the number of households was considerably greater than it had been in 1952–1965, though only if single-individual households are added on to families.[13] Rapid formation of single-individual households is unlikely to contribute to the explanation of a change in the composition of wealth toward owner-occupied homes, but it may indeed help explain an increased demand for consumer durables at the expense of other wealth components. Exploring this avenue might well be worthwhile. But in view of the size of the shifts discussed in this study and the ease with which they can be related to motivations created by the inflationary process, other factors are unlikely to deserve a similarly prominent place in the interpretation of changing wealth-income relations and of the changing composition of household wealth.

VII. Behavioral Implications Concerning Money Holdings: Observations on Problems of Monetary Policy

Changing Trends. Among the financial household assets, money in the broad sense has the distinctive characteristic of being a particularly liquid component. Part of the money stock in the broadest sense— the M-1 component of M-5—is used as means of payment, and other parts can be transformed into means of payment at face value with little effort and cost. Some can be transformed with great ease and at negligible cost, and the practical costlessness and effortlessness of such transformations have become an increasingly prominent feature of our institutional setting.

For measured real rates of return, money holdings rank particularly low among the financial assets; indeed, that rate has all along been negative for a sizable component of the money stock in the broad sense. As a result, money provides a particularly suitable illustration

---

[13] On this and some other general demographic information, see note 2, p. 157.

of the fact, stressed above, that assets yielding a low return often become preferred at the margin of choice before their representation in the asset mix has decreased too far. Considering that excessive money creation is an essential feature of the post-1965 period, and that the money created by the authority and by the banking system must by definition be held by someone in the economy, the question of the level at which the public desires to keep its money holdings calls for relating money holdings to other variables whose magnitudes the public can influence. Given the money supply, the public can indeed raise or reduce its money expenditures on goods and services and on securities, and it can thus change its money holdings relative to these expenditures and relative to the income flow. The analysis here relates the money stock to incomes, as it did in the case of the other assets.

The story briefly summarized below suggests that money too has been yielding to the pressure toward reduced representation of financial assets among the wealth components; as compared with financial assets in general it has, however, shown some resistance to this pressure. In particular, for the period 1965–1978 as a whole, money in the broad sense continued to rise relative to income but at a significantly reduced rate. Moreover, by 1978 even the broadest money aggregates declined relative to disposable income.

One of the reasons why these trends are expressed here mainly for money in the broadest sense is that the increasing ease and declining costs of transforming various interest-bearing components of money in the broad sense into means of payment greatly complicate appraisals of the trends for the narrower money aggregates. Another reason for primary concern with the broad aggregates is that recently various types of interest-bearing claims against banks and other financial institutions—claims not included in the concept of money—have begun to assume much the same role as demand deposits available to the owner.[14] Because the weight of these claims is much smaller relative to the broadest money aggregates than relative to some of the narrower ones, their exclusion from the concept of money reduces the usefulness of the broadest aggregates much less than it

---

[14] These are partly Treasury bills held by a bank for a customer on the basis of a repurchase agreement involving the bank's obligation to repurchase the bill when the customer wants to use the money, and partly money-market funds enabling the owners of shares in the fund to write checks on their shares with assurance that the checks will be honored by the bank in which the funds are held. A substantial proportion of the assets of the money-market funds, however, is held in certificates of deposit, which are included in the broadest money aggregate (M-5).

does that of narrower ones. At present, M-5 is the notation used for the broadest aggregate, which comprises, besides currency held by the public, all deposits in commercial banks and in thrift institutions; the present M-3 is smaller only because of its exclusion of large-denomination negotiable certificates of deposit held in the weekly reporting member banks.[15]

Movements in market rates of interest would obviously have to be taken into account in any interpretation of shifts among the various narrower money categories, but what matters here is that interest-rate movements deserve to be stressed also in our present concern with the relation between the broad money aggregates and tangible house-hold wealth. The point to be repeated is that in the period 1965–1978 the rise in nominal interest rates was not nearly sufficient to prevent the imposition of a penalty on most interest-bearing financial assets compared with tangible household wealth.

The money stock of the households, which according to the FOF they hold as owners of noncorporate enterprise, accounts for a negligible fraction of the total, and in the present context it will not be eliminated from the aggregates. Nor, therefore, will disposable income be adjusted downward to make allowance for the share of noncorporate business. It is worth adding that through 1960 the M-5 aggregate was identical with the M-3 aggregate, because the large negotiable certificates of deposit making up the difference were not introduced before 1961.

From 1952 to 1965 the ratio of the M-5 holdings of households to disposable income rose from 0.65 to 0.80—that is, at an average yearly rate of 1.6 percent. The M-3 holdings of households per unit of income must have risen in a similar—probably slightly higher—proportion. During this thirteen-year period the aggregate of financial asset holdings also rose in relation to income, and little change was observed in the proportionate representation of M-5 in financial assets. Not so in the subsequent period.

When 1978 is compared with 1965—a period during which financial household wealth declined sharply relative to income—the M-5 stock of households per unit of disposable income shows a further rise, but at a significantly reduced rate. From its 1965 value of 0.80, that ratio rose to 0.87, and this corresponds to an average yearly rate of increase of 0.6 percent as against the 1.6 percent applying to the

---

[15] Changes in the construction of the money aggregates are under consideration at the present writing. Along the lines of one of the influential proposals, M-5 is the only aggregate that would remain essentially unchanged (though it would be renamed M-3). The present M-3 would no longer be computed.

earlier period. Further, data for 1978 suggest that in the economy as a whole the ratio of M-3, as well as that of M-5, to the GNP *declined*, though these ratios had been rising appreciably. As for the narrower money aggregates, their ratios to GNP have recently been declining quite a bit, notwithstanding the stability over a period of a decade and a half of one of these aggregates.[16] Appraisal of the ratios for 1979 may require allowances for a cyclical downturn.

These trends in the money aggregates suggest that household behavior with respect to money holdings has also reacted to the disincentive to acquire financial wealth in the post-1965 inflationary era. But money holdings have shown more resistance than other components of the financial asset holdings; that is, *within* the category of financial assets, the relative weight of which has become significantly reduced, money has so far increased its proportionate representation. Yet while money holdings have shown more resistance than have financial assets in general, they have not been immune to the inflationary disincentives, and the velocity problem involved in this development should be overlooked neither in general monetary analysis nor in the formulation of policies under inflationary circumstances.

Problems of Monetary Policy. In his contribution to this volume, Phillip Cagan develops an analysis of problems of monetary policy that are particularly difficult to cope with in the present inflationary period. Demand deposits, on which banks are allowed to pay no interest, have suffered a severe penalty, with the result that the public has moved partly toward interest-yielding components of the broader money aggregates and partly toward interest-yielding claims against banks and other financial institutions that are included in none of the aggregates. The analysis of household wealth developed here stresses the additional complication resulting from movements of households out of financial assets in general into tangible assets—a further velocity-raising factor of major importance of which the monetary authority must be mindful.

In these circumstances Cagan inclines toward removing the interest-rate prohibition from demand deposits but subjecting to reserve requirements these deposits as well as such other claims against financial institutions as can be transformed into demand

---

[16] The aggregate that had shown this stability in relation to GNP is the one now defined as M-2. It consists of currency and demand deposits and savings accounts, as well as time deposits in commercial banks other than large-denomination negotiable certificates of deposits. M-1, as now defined, consists merely of currency and demand deposits in commercial banks; it has been declining in relation to GNP for a long time.

deposits with almost no delay and almost costlessly.[17] Demand deposits and these other claims make up Cagan's "transactions balances." His conception of the desirable course includes at the same time the removal of reserve requirements from all bank deposits other than "transactions balances" and the creation of incentives for commercial banks to remain within the Federal Reserve system. In Cagan's appraisal the proposed changes have a good chance of raising the relative cost of maintaining "transactions balances" sufficiently to establish a reasonably predictable relation between them and the flow of expenditures for which they are needed. By determining the size of the reserves, monetary policy could then exert a more predictable influence on those balances that bear closely on the size of the expenditures flow.

I do not feel optimistic about the chances of achieving this result, because various difficulties that would be encountered along this route seem to me even greater than they do to Cagan. Finding an operational definition of all the claims that would have to be included in Cagan's "transactions balances" seems to me an effort of doubtful promise; for this reason, among others, I am doubtful about the possibility of regulating by means of reserves a narrow aggregate whose relation to expenditures could be approximated satisfactorily with formalized models.

There is no difference between Cagan and me as to the desirability of abolishing the prohibition of interest payments and other interest-rate regulations, nor about the desirability of imposing uniform reserve requirements on those asset holdings on which reserve requirements *are* imposed for the sake of regulating their quantity. But I am inclined to take it for granted that money in the broad sense is likely to become a more significant policy variable than "transactions balances" or any other narrowly defined component and, thus, I favor imposing uniform reserve requirements on *all* types of bank deposits. The changes that are apt to occur in the composition of the public's asset holdings do create disturbing velocity effects even for the broadest money aggregates, but this is a difficulty with which the monetary authority will have to continue to cope as best it can. Recently this difficulty has shown in the rise of the velocity of even the broadest money aggregates, which had a long record of declining velocity.

In practice this means that rules of thumb about the desirable rate of reserve creation and of money growth will have to remain adjust-

---

[17] Such other claims are not limited to savings accounts. See note 14.

able on the basis of experience, whose evaluation includes ad hoc personal judgment. In the present environment it is crucial that money creation should proceed at a rate leading to a gradual reduction of the rate of increase of money GNP to a noninflationary level.

Appendix: The Wealth-Income Ratio
(See Section III in text.)

We postulate an initial value for household wealth (W_0), a constant positive saving ratio (s), and a constant positive annual rate of increase (r) of disposable income (Y). For the time being we disregard price changes. Taking a preliminary look at the W/Y ratio after four periods beyond period zero, we find:

$$[1] \quad W_4/Y_4 = \frac{W_0 + sY_1 + s(1+r)Y_1 + s(1+r)^2Y_1 + s(1+r)^3Y_1}{(1+r)^3Y_1}.$$

It is clear that if, after period 4, r should rise to a higher value, and the previously accumulated stock is not revalued upward, then, with a constant s, W_5/Y_5 will be smaller than it would have been with the unchanging r. The reason is that the denominator in the fraction expressing W_5/Y_5 will be increased in a proportion in which only one of the six terms in the numerator of that fraction will be raised, the other terms in the numerator remaining unchanged. However, since the weight of the terms expressing the previously accumulated capital changes over time relative to the new accumulation, we need a more general expression to visualize the permanent effect that the change tends to bring about.

Note that an expression such as that developed in equation 1 can be rewritten along the following lines. We recognize that dividing the extreme right-hand term in the numerator by the denominator yields s; and that if thereafter we move leftward in the numerator, we obtain first s times the reciprocal of $(1 + r)$, then s times the reciprocal of $(1 + r)^2$, and so on. For four periods beyond zero, 3 is the highest power of $(1 + r)$ in this sequence. For n periods beyond zero we obtain (moving again from left to right),

$$[2] \quad W_n/Y_n = \frac{W_0}{(1+r)^{n-1}\,Y_1} + s\left(\frac{1}{(1+r)^{n-1}} + \frac{1}{(1+r)^{n-2}} + \dots + \frac{1}{1+r} + 1\right).$$

Whenever n rises by one, the right-hand side is exposed to two opposing influences. On the one hand, all terms need to be divided by

$1 + r$ and this means that, aside from the other influence, to be explained below, the wealth-income ratio would diminish in this proportion. Yet, when n rises by one, it is necessary also to add the number 1 again at the end of the bracketed sum, and since the whole bracketed sum is multiplied by s, this means raising the wealth-income ratio by s. The ratio will become *stabilized* on balance when the division of all terms for a given n by $1 + r$ diminishes the ratio by the equivalent of the enlargement of the ratio by the addition of s. This stabilization will occur at the value of n where

$$\frac{W_n}{Y_n} - \frac{W_n}{(1+r)Y_n} = s,$$

or (simplifying the left-hand side), at the value of n at which

$$\frac{r}{1+r}\frac{W_n}{Y_n} = s.$$

Hence, at the value of n at which the ratio becomes stabilized:

[3]
$$\frac{W_n}{Y_n} = s\frac{1+r}{r}.$$

The expression in equation 3 *diminishes* if a higher value of r is substituted for a lower value. The conditions under which a higher r would become associated with an unchanging W/Y, or possibly even with a higher W/Y, would have to involve upward revaluations of the previously accumulated wealth or an increase in s or both. This describes a deviation from our initial assumptions, though the analytical construct used above can be adjusted to take care of such deviations.

If r changes because of a change in s, or a change in the productivity of the inputs, or a change in the quantity of the inputs cooperating with capital, then the effect of the changes on W/Y depends on the value of parameters specified in an appropriate model, and an unchanging W/Y ratio belongs in the range of possible outcomes. However, the problem with which this study is mainly concerned calls for considering a rise in r brought about by inflation, in a framework in which W and Y are defined in current dollars and in which revaluations play an essential role.

In the simplest variety of textbook models describing an "inflationary equilibrium path"—a fully anticipated inflationary development—r would be stepped up from its noninflationary level, but W/Y *would remain unchanged except for a qualification that raises a question of only minor importance.* This "inflationary equilibrium path" involves continuing upward revaluations of all tangible wealth in the same proportion as that in which inflation is raising Y. For households owning tangible wealth in the sense in which the assets of corporations are owned by the stockholders, the hypothetical path involves upward revaluation of these ownership certificates in the same proportion. As for the claims defined in current dollars, the path involves, *in lieu of* revaluations, adding continuously to the current-dollar value of such wealth-components that part of the inflated disposable income that represents the difference between the inflated nominal interest earnings and the real interest earnings, where real interest is assumed to be unaffected by the inflation. This addition to the current-dollar financial wealth represents additional savings in the sense of the usual saving concept (see Table 1 in the main part of the study). These additional savings, however, merely keep the real value of the claims on fixed money amounts from declining.

One minor qualification relates to non–interest-bearing claims. Many types of claims defined in terms of money that in noninflationary circumstances bear no interest tend to become interest-bearing under inflationary conditions, but hand-to-hand currency does not. To a minor extent this qualifies the simple results described above.

Needless to say, the results observed for 1965–1978 deviate greatly from the results derived from such a model. The prices of corporate stock (included in our analysis in financial household wealth) fell far below the inflation rate, but even if the comprehensive stock price indexes had kept up with it, the saving rate of 1965–1978 would have been insufficient to keep the wealth-income ratio from declining below its 1965 level. This is the case even though, not including the corporate assets, tangible household wealth was revalued in a proportion greater than that reflecting the inflation rate.

Balancing the Budget

Herbert Stein

Summary

Although balancing the budget has been standard fiscal doctrine in the United States from its foundation, that has not meant annual balance in practice, and the arguments for balancing the budget did not imply annual balance. Before 1929, however, the annual deficits were small except in wartime, and policy was to reduce the war debts.

After 1929 the fluctuations of the budget position associated with fluctuations of the economy became much larger. This was partly because the revenue and expenditure programs were more elastic and partly because of a belief that such variations in the budget position would stabilize the economy. Through the 1930s and the early postwar years, however, there was interest in reconciling these larger swings from surplus to deficit with longer-run achievement of balance or surplus.

A major departure from earlier practice came with the decision not to try to repay the World War II debt. This decision was largely motivated by unwillingness to pay the taxes that would have been required, given the high taxes that were required anyway just to balance the budget. And as time passed even the idea of running surpluses in good times to balance the accepted deficits of bad times lost force. The idea of balance in the long run survived as a symbol, but it became divorced from any real objective and was considered not worth the cost of implementing it.

Since 1960, and especially since 1972, there has been a trend toward smaller surpluses, or deficits, in good times and toward larger deficits in recessions. Recently this trend in the budget has coincided with rapid inflation, slow productivity growth, and government spend-

191

ing considered by many to be excessive. This has led to the conclusion that the behavior of the budget is chiefly responsible for these evils.

While all the connections are uncertain, it is probably reasonable to say that:

- *Large and untimely increases in the deficit complicate the problem of avoiding inflation.*
- *Other things equal, productivity will grow more rapidly if the budget is in surplus on the average than if the budget is in deficit on the average.*
- *Expenditures will rise less rapidly if the decision to spend requires a decision to tax, just as they would rise less rapidly if the decision to spend entailed any other penalty for the decision maker, but the spending-taxing link does not assure optimum expenditure decisions or even necessarily lean in that direction.*

Even if faster growth of the economy and slower growth of expenditures are both accepted as desirable—and these are matters of preference—these conclusions do not require annual balancing of the budget. They require avoidance of sharp changes in the budget position, an average condition of balance or surplus, and equality of spending and taxing at the margin of decision.

Rules of budget policy can be devised which would be superior to a rule of annual balance in meeting these requirements. One such rule would require a surplus of constant amount (relative to GNP) when nominal GNP is on a stated stable path and permit variations from that surplus as would be automatically produced by deviations of the economy from that path.

Possibly no such rule—necessarily complicated and counter-intuitive—can be sold to and enforced upon decision makers. In that case a rule of annual balance may be the only alternative to our recent rulelessness in fiscal policy. However, it is premature to reach that conclusion. Moreover, even if that conclusion is reached, it would not bar surpluses at some times, or deficits in others, when approved by some extraordinary procedure. So the problem of finding standards by which to decide when surpluses or deficits are appropriate will remain.

Balancing the Budget

When the period began and whether it is now ending or has ended are uncertain, but we have been in a period of extraordinarily large budget deficits and rising federal expenditures. This has also been a period of rapid inflation and slow productivity growth and, in a common view, wasteful use of national resources by the government. There is apparently a strong opinion that these economic miseries are due in large part to the behavior of the budget. This fortifies the belief, always present in a considerable part of the population, that deficits should be reduced or eliminated and that expenditures should be reduced, or at least should grow less rapidly than they have.

The belief in the need for a change in budget policy is accompanied by another, not connected by logic, that we need to change the procedures and criteria by which budget decisions are made. This attitude reflects the conviction that recent improper budget policy is the inevitable or highly probable outcome of existing procedures and philosophies and that a durable improvement will not be achieved without a change in them. Thus, the argument is not simply that the deficit should not exceed $15 billion in fiscal 1980 and that expenditures should not exceed $525 billion. The argument is that we need new rules and procedures for deciding such things, not only for next year, but for a longer period and possibly forever.

The rules most discussed relate to balancing the budget. The typical proposal is that the budget should be balanced each year unless an exception is permitted by an extraordinary procedure, such as approval by a two thirds majority of Congress. Other kinds of rules, limiting either expenditures or taxes directly, have been proposed but have received less attention and support.

The establishment of a rule of budget policy would require the achievement of a national consensus on the matter and presumably congressional action incorporating the rule in a resolution or statute. But many supporters of a new rule want to go further and embody the rule in a constitutional amendment. They fear that the consensus which might exist now in favor of a rule might not be strong or durable enough to enforce adherence to the rule unless it had been incorporated in the Constitution.

In this essay I shall give a brief account of the history that lies beyond the present concern about fiscal behavior, discuss the criteria by which past practice and proposed changes might be judged and evaluate a budget-balancing rule as a way of improving practice in the future.

A Thumbnail History of Thinking about Budget Balancing

Some years ago, let us say for precision December 1975, a certain simple view of the fiscal history of the United States (or of the world for that matter) was part of the conventional wisdom. Before 1936 the earth had been in darkness, roamed by budget-balancing dinosaurs and wracked by deep depression. In 1936 Keynes brought enlightenment, in *The General Theory of Employment, Interest and Money.* In 1961 the New Economists, who came to Washington with President Kennedy, introduced the new doctrine to economic policy makers, and by 1965 we were safely fixed on the road to steady economic growth.

It was against this background that I wrote *The Fiscal Revolution in America.*[1] The lesson, to me, of the history of the period 1929–1964 was that the revolution in fiscal practice was really an evolution, that its intellectual basis existed before the Keynes of the General Theory, that the change in practice and ideas was due more to changing conditions and experience than to new theory, that the implementation of the change was not entirely achieved by Democratic economists who were graduate students in 1936, and that the value of the "revolution" was still uncertain.

By 1979 a quite new picture of fiscal history had emerged (no thanks to my book). In this picture there had been a Golden Age before 1936, when budgets were balanced, the economy was stable, and the brave yeoman spent his earnings frugally without the assistance of government bureaucrats. Into this Eden Keynes brought the forbidden knowledge that it was not only possible but also frequently beneficial to run a budget deficit. The New Economists brought that to Washington, and since then we have suffered runaway inflation, economic stagnation, and overwhelming government. The necessary remedy, derived from this view of history, is to return to the pre-Keynesian state of grace, and give up budget deficits.

However, this is also an overdrawn picture. There was no state of grace, in the sense either that there were no budget deficits or that the economy performed notably better than it has done in our time. There was a change in the size and frequency of deficits, but no single book or collection of books was the main cause of that. That was a pragmatic and not unreasonable response to new conditions. There have been mistakes in budget policy, as in other human endeavors. It would be wrong to blame all or most of our economic problems on mistakes of budget policy. And it is very doubtful that it is either necessary or possible to forswear budget deficits as a way of preventing such mistakes in the future.

At any time in the past, if any group of Americans (except economists since 1930) had been asked whether the federal budget

---

[1] Herbert Stein, *The Fiscal Revolution in America* (Chicago: University of Chicago Press, 1969).

should be balanced, the large majority would have answered yes. Of course, we have no polls on this subject before the 1930s, so this statement is somewhat speculative. It is, however, supported for that earlier period by the statements of government officials, economists, editorial writers, and others who presumably both reflect and lead public opinion.[2] For the period since the mid-1930s, public opinion polls clearly reveal the consistently large majority support for balancing the federal budget.[3]

Despite this overwhelming opinion, the record of even the good old days before Keynes was not one of constant balance or surplus in the budget. There were deficits in periods of economic slump, as a result of the automatic decline of revenues. These deficits were, by today's standards, small, relative to expenditures or to GNP. During the period up to 1916 the budget was in deficit in 27 percent of the peacetime years, and there were deficits in excess of 10 percent of expenditures in 15 percent of the years. Official statements indicate that recession deficits were not welcome, and there were sometimes calls for retrenchment of expenditures when revenue was declining, but this did not succeed in preventing deficits. The deficits were small not because of deliberate action to keep them small but because the major revenue source—import duties—was not very responsive to economic fluctuations.

Deficits were expected and accepted in times of war. This was true of even small wars, such as the Spanish-American War. Standard policy called for reducing the war-incurred debt in the subsequent peace. However, the standard doctrine did not tell how fast the war debt should be reduced. The debt left at the end of the Civil War was reduced by 60 percent in the fifty years before the entry of the United States into World War I. By that time the debt had been reduced from about 25 percent of GNP to less than 2 percent of GNP; obviously, most of this reduction had come from the rise of GNP. The rise of GNP was real; the price level was about the same in 1916 as in 1867.

Between the end of World War I and 1929 there was again a sharp reduction in the federal debt, absolutely and relative to the GNP. The debt was cut from about $25.5 billion in 1919 to $16.9

---

[2] See Lewis H. Kimmel, *Federal Budget and Fiscal Policy, 1789-1958* (Washington, D.C.: Brookings Institution, 1959).

[3] See Stein, *Fiscal Revolution in America,* also, Herbert Stein, "The Decline of the Budget Balancing Doctrine: How the Good Guys Finally Lost" in *Fiscal Responsibility in Constitutional Democracy,* James M. Buchanan and Richard E. Wagner, eds. (Hingham, Mass.: Kluwer Boston, 1978).

billion in 1929, or by about one-third. This was a reduction from about 30½ percent of GNP to 16½ percent. The annual rate of decline was significantly faster than after the Civil War in absolute terms and a little faster in terms of the relationship to GNP. However, the differences become much smaller if the debt reduction provided by the repayment of Allied debts to the U.S. is excluded from the 1919–1929 accounts.

This thumbnail history of pre-1929 federal deficits and debts is not intended to deny the importance of the budget-balancing doctrine. But if, as is sometimes said, balancing the budget was an unwritten part of the American Constitution before Keynes, it did not call for *annual* balance. The practice was to incur deficits in war, in depression, and for extraordinary expenditures, such as the Louisiana Purchase, and to reduce the resulting debts gradually out of subsequent surpluses.

This was not only the actual practice. It was also the practice that conformed to the commonly accepted argument for balancing the budget.[4] That argument called for balancing the budget in the long run. It did not require or imply that the budget should be balanced every year. The main ingredients in the case for balancing the budget were:

• *Preservation of the government's credit.* If the debt became too large the ability of the government to service it would come into question, higher interest rates would have to be paid, and the government might be unable to borrow in an emergency. This did not preclude borrowing from time to time; in fact, the object was to preserve the government's ability to borrow. What it did require was avoidance of large deficits over a considerable period which would raise the size of the total debt excessively.

• *Protecting the growth of the capital stock.* The secular increase of total output and incomes was seen to depend on the growth of the capital stock, which in turn depended on the supply of savings. Absorption of the savings in financing government deficits would slow down the growth of the capital stock and should be avoided. But this dictum applied to long-run trends in the stock of capital; it did not imply that private savings and private investment had to be equal, and the budget deficits zero, every year. Moreover, there was some recognition that the argument did not bar deficit financing of capital expenditures by government.

---

[4] See William Breit, "Starving the Leviathan: Balanced Budget Prescriptions before Keynes," in *Fiscal Responsibility*, Buchanan and Wagner, eds.

• *Avoiding burdens on future taxpayers.* Whether this meant something more than avoiding erosion of the capital stock left for future generations is unclear. Probably no sharp distinction was intended. In any case, since the discussion usually ran in terms of future "generations," the argument did not relate to deficits followed by surpluses every few years.

• *Preventing wasteful government expenditures.* There was fear that if they could finance expenditures by borrowing politicians would be more willing to spend than if they had to match spending decisions with decisions to increase taxes. This objective probably comes closer to requiring annual balancing than do the other objectives. Presumably it requires that expenditure decisions and tax decisions be made at the same time for the same period, and expenditure decisions were annual decisions. In the period before World War I, however, decisions were actually made about appropriations without much attention to their short-run outlay effects. Also during much of that period the federal government did not need to restrain its expenditures to avoid having to raise "unpopular" taxes. The chief revenue source was the tariff, which had strong supporters for its own sake, aside from the revenue it yielded. The revenue was often an embarrassment from the standpoint of discipline on expenditures. There were occasional warnings about the dangers of surpluses because they tempted excessive spending.

The distinctive feature of pre-1929 practice and pre-1929 doctrine was not the absence of deficits but the presence of surpluses, which from 1835 to 1929 almost, but not quite, offset the deficits.

The practice changed radically after 1929, and the doctrine moderately, but it is important for the understanding of our present position to understand what changed, when, and why.

After 1929 we had deficits far exceeding any previously run in peacetime, not only absolutely but also relative to the size of the budget and to the size of the GNP. There were several reasons for this large deficit in the years after 1929.

• We had the deepest and longest depression of American history.

• The federal revenues at the beginning of the depression were higher relative to GNP than they had ever been in peacetime American history before World War I. Therefore, a deficit equal to a certain percentage of revenues would be a higher proportion of GNP.

• This was the first depression after the income tax became the major source of federal revenues, making the revenues much more responsive to a depression and a decline of national income than they had previously been.

- In the United States, as in other advanced countries, the feeling that government had an obligation to assist people in hardship was much stronger than it had been before the war. This obligation was felt to be especially great for the veterans of World War I. Responding to this obligation raised expenditures during the depression.

The swing from surplus to deficit in the federal budget between 1929 and 1931 was equal to about 3 percent of the initial GNP. This is about as big, relative to the GNP, as the increase in the size of the deficit between 1974 and 1975, when the deficit reached $66 billion. This slide to deficit in 1931 was not a break with the previous practice. It had previously been accepted that we would run deficits during recessions and emergencies. This deficit was larger mainly because the depression was deeper and the automatic budget response to it was greater.

President Hoover resisted, not entirely successfully, expenditure increases that would have made the deficit even larger. However, for two years he accepted the large deficits that resulted automatically from the loss of revenues. In his budget message of December 1930 he said that he did not "look with great concern" upon the deficit for that fiscal year.

By 1930 there already was a school of economics—pre-Keynesian, or at least pre-General Theory—which advocated larger government expenditures, especially for public works, as a way of stimulating the economy in general. President Hoover understood this idea. However, it had no visible influence on his policy. The emergence of deficits in the early years of the depression was not the result of proto-Keynesianism.

In fact, it can be said that the big change from past practice was President Hoover's effort to reduce the deficit drastically by raising taxes, as he proposed at the end of 1931. The tradition did not seem to require it. The simplest explanation of this move was the President's belief that cutting the deficit would restore the "confidence" of the financial and business community, in the United States and abroad. This, of course, turned out to be incorrect.

President Roosevelt's deficits, at least until 1938, could also be explained as conforming to the old tradition which accepted deficits in recessions and to meet emergencies, but which did not seek deficits for their own sake, and which counted on subsequent surpluses to repay the debts incurred during the deficit period. That is, he did not believe that deficits were either unimportant or beneficial. They were an unfortunate necessity. He brought the budget close to balance as the economy recovered in 1936–1937. When the sharp recession of 1937 hit, he tried, as Hoover had done six years earlier, to restore confidence by taking a posture of fiscal conservatism and emphasizing his determination to balance the budget.

When fiscal conservatism, or the promise of it, failed to restore confidence and revive the economy President Roosevelt turned for the first time to an active fiscal policy in which expenditures were raised as a way not only of helping poor people but also of bringing about recovery. He was influenced in this direction by economic advisers who had recently absorbed the General Theory. However, whether out of conviction or out of deference to popular attitudes, he did not abandon the idea of balancing the budget. That is, the deficits of the depression were to be balanced by future surpluses.

The President and others at this time (1938–1939) sought schemes to balance the budget over the business cycle or over some longer period. The experience of the 1930s had shown that depressions could generate very large deficits and that some plan would be necessary to limit those deficits and to bring about surpluses in prosperous times if long-run balance was to be assured. A good deal of attention was paid to the idea of dividing the budget into a current part and a capital part. The current part, which would include the depreciation of capital and interest on the debt, as well as ordinary current expenditures, would be kept continuously in balance. The capital part would vary in size, cyclically, and might sometimes be in deficit and sometimes in surplus. In his January 1939 budget message President Roosevelt proposed a somewhat different division of the budget—into ordinary and extraordinary expenditures—but with a similar rationale.

This may have been window-dressing, to provide an aspect of legitimacy to the long continuation of deficits, but it also reflected interest in a rule of policy that would reconcile the fact of deficits in depressions with the traditional interest in long-run balance.

By 1939, before war finance began to dominate fiscal policy, there were four main views in this country about balancing the budget:

• Deficits are inevitable and possibly helpful in depressions, but they should be balanced by surpluses in other times.

• The deficit or surplus at any time should be high enough to bring about full employment without inflation. Whether this will add up to a surplus or deficit over any period of time will depend on the strength of private demand. Whatever comes out of this process,

199

whether a cumulative deficit or surplus, is the right answer. That is, there is no presumption in favor of long-run balance. This was the view that came to be known as "functional finance."

• Application of the principle of functional finance will in fact yield long-run deficits because the American economy has a secular tendency for private saving to exceed private investment when there is full employment.

• The budget should be balanced immediately and continuously, not because the idea of cyclical balance or long-run balance is bad economics but because, in the political process where decisions are made, long-run deficits will inevitably result if annual balances are not required.

Numerous polls of that time show that a large majority of the American people "believed" in balancing the budget, but the polls are not sufficiently precise to reveal what proportion held any of these or other possible attitudes on the subject. The literature of the period suggests that the first of these positions, depression deficits but balance over a longer period, was the official government position and was acceptable to most of the public, and that the goal of longer-run balance did exercise some restraint on year-by-year practice. Functional finance was the most common principle among economists and intellectuals. The special version of this position which forecast that the American economy would require permanent deficits was probably a minority view among economists, but many more had no objection in principle to the prescription if the forecast turned out to be correct. Insistence on immediate and continuous budget balancing seemed not to be a seriously or widely held position, although it was part of the conventional political argument against the Roosevelt administration.

The argument about budget-balancing was suspended during World War II, after which it was resumed in conditions which differed from those of 1939 in many respects.

• The federal debt was enormous, absolutely and relative to the GNP. The debt slightly exceeded the GNP, whereas it had been only about 30 percent of GNP at the end of World War I.

• The prospect was that federal peacetime expenditures would be a much larger percentage of GNP, even in prosperous years, than ever before.

• Therefore, to balance the budget, even in prosperous years, would require much higher tax rates than ever before in peacetime, mainly on individual and corporate incomes.

• As a result of economic and statistical work done in the previous decade, the country was more conscious of secular economic growth as a fact of life.

• The unemployment compensation system was more developed than ten years earlier.

• The national commitment to full employment was stronger than ever.

These conditions had important implications for budget policy. Probably the most serious was that no effort would be made to reduce the war debt, though there was some discussion of doing so. There was no proposal for establishing a sinking-fund to reduce the debt as had been done after World War I.

The reason was only partly, and probably only to a minor degree, that Americans had been persuaded by economists' arguments that the debt did not matter because we owed it to ourselves. The main reason was that the very size of the debt showed that no significant reduction could be foreseen without an additional tax burden that no one wanted to bear. To reduce the debt by 1 percent in one year would have required taxes to be about 10 percent higher than would have been necessary to balance the budget. The traditional conservatives, the business and financial community, were more concerned with their immediate tax burdens, which already seemed outrageously high, than with paying off a debt that was already water over the dam.

Moreover, consciousness of the growth potential of the American economy weakened the case for making great sacrifices to reduce the absolute size of the debt. If the debt were held constant, and the economy grew at 3 percent a year, the ratio of the debt to GNP would be cut in half in twenty-five years. In discussions of the time, there were frequent references to the success of Great Britain in growing up to its debt after the Napoleonic Wars.

The decision not to plan for reduction of the World War II debt was a fateful one. It greatly reduced the possibility that subsequent fluctuations between expenditures and receipts would wind up with a surplus or even a balance in the long run. That is, it reduced the probability that the average budget position, around which deficits and surpluses would fluctuate, would be a surplus or balance.

By the end of World War II, there was no doubt that the relation of expenditures to receipts—that is, the deficit or surplus—would fluctuate substantially with economic conditions and that these fluctuations should be accepted. The budget was large, relative to prewar experience, it was mainly financed by elastic revenue sources, individual and corporate income taxes, and it contained major expenditure programs whose outlays also would vary with economic conditions. So the size of the surplus or deficit would rise or fall with the rise or fall of the economy.

It was argued on Keynesian grounds, or on modern macroeconomic theory, that these fluctuations of the budget position would be stabilizing. But no very sophisticated theory is needed to come to this conclusion. Nothing seems more obvious than that if the after-tax incomes of individuals and businesses fall less in a recession their spending will fall less and the recession will be milder. In fact, only a sophisticated theory is needed to show that this might not be true.

However, even if the stabilizing effect of these budget fluctuations is denied or disregarded, the argument for not trying to offset them is strong. In the first place, ability to offset the fluctuations depends on ability to forecast them, which is quite imperfect. More important, offsetting them would require contracyclical variations of tax rates, which from the standpoint of the taxpayer is disturbing and inequitable. Otherwise, or also, it would require contracyclical variations of expenditure programs, concentrated on that small part of the budget that is controllable in the short run. That is likely to cause inefficiency.

Thus, fairly pragmatic considerations—basically, not wanting tax rates to be high or variable—led to the conclusion that no effort should be made to reduce the war debt or to prevent cyclical variations in the budget position. These were important but negative conclusions. They did not answer the question of the proper size of the surplus or deficit at any time.

There were two main approaches to this question. The first, which dominated economics, was strict functional finance. The deficit should be high enough for the achievement of full employment but not so high as to cause inflation. The other approach rejected this standard and sought a longer-run rule. Its reasons for rejecting functional finance were several:

• The functional-finance prescription assumed a degree of accusumed the existence at any moment of a unique optimum size of the deficit or surplus. But even if the goals of economic policy were accepted, the deficit or surplus needed to achieve them would depend on many other policy variables, such as the tax structure and most importantly monetary policy. Therefore, at least within some range, one could choose the desired surplus or deficit, if complementary choices were made in the other variables.

• The functional-finance prescription assumed a degree of accuracy in forecasting and precision in fiscal management which might not be achievable, and failure to achieve them might result in more instability than would adherence to simpler and less demanding rules of policy.

• Especially in view of the uncertainty of the forecasts involved, the functional-finance rule would provide little restraint against the bias of the political process towards high expenditures and relatively low taxes. That is, there would be a temptation to justify high expenditure and low taxes by forecasting the need for more economic stimulus, which would not be difficult to do. This would create a bias towards inflation and towards high expenditures.

• Even if the functional-finance rule resulted in economic stability, something might be sacrificed in terms of secular growth and efficiency by the failure to recognize any longer-term standards of budget policy.

These reservations led to the search for a rule of budget policy that would be less dominated by short-term objectives and forecasts than was the functional-finance rule. Although these other rules came in various formulations, they had certain common features, essentially that they aimed at budget balancing over a period longer than a year while accepting deficits in any particular year. I shall use the rule of "balancing-the-budget-at-high-employment," as set forth by the Committee for Economic Development in 1947, as an example of such rules, because it was typical and influential and because it was elaborated in more detail than were other versions.[5]

The key to the CED rule was that taxes should be set high enough so that they would yield a balanced budget and a moderate surplus when the economy was operating at high employment. When the economy was below high employment the surplus would be smaller and there might be a deficit; when the economy was above high employment the surplus would be larger. These surpluses or deficits would result from the built-in variation of revenues and expenditures as the economy fluctuated. Except in case of a severe recession or severe inflation, both presumably rare, deliberate action to change the size of the deficit or surplus was not permitted.

The variation of the budget position from surplus to deficit implied in this policy was justified in part as a contribution to economic

---

[5] See Research and Policy Committee of the Committee for Economic Development, *Taxes and the Budget, A Program for Prosperity in a Free Economy* (New York: Committee for Economic Development, 1947).

stability. However, other support for these variations—and against an effort to balance the budget annually—was offered. To try to prevent surpluses and deficits would require impossible accuracy of forecasting. It would require an undesirable variation of tax rates and expenditure programs. Also, and this was a paradoxical argument, keeping the budget constantly in balance would be an inducement to expenditure increases when boom economic conditions expanded the revenue, and these increased expenditures could not be squeezed out of the budget later when the economy declined. The principle of balancing the budget as it would be at high employment did not make either boom or recession the occasion for expenditure increases without tax increases.

For the future development of fiscal policy, and especially for the emergence of a condition of continuous and growing deficits, the important aspect of this proposal was not the automatic variation of the size of the surpluses or deficits but the fixing of the average position around which the budget would fluctuate. The CED statement contemplated that there would be a surplus in something like the standard or target state of the economy, a larger surplus when the economy was booming and a smaller surplus or a deficit when the economy was below the target level. The statement refers to the desirability of debt reduction in time of prosperity. It does not promise debt reduction on the average. However, it does seem to expect that the debt would not increase over any long period of time.

Whether the debt would increase would depend in part on the state of the economy—on the pattern of its variations around the target level. If it ordinarily ran substantially below "high employment," there would be a cumulative deficit. But the cumulative result would also depend on the specific provisions of the plan. Three provisions were crucial.

- The size of the surplus to be achieved at high employment was set at $3 billion in the initial statement. However, the statement recognized that as the economy grew this figure should be changed, and presumably increased. The $3 billion when initially prescribed was about 1½ percent of GNP. By 1979 1½ percent of GNP was about $30 billion.

- The high employment level was set at 4 percent unemployment. The CED considered that unemployment might from time to time be under that figure; it did not regard 4 percent as maximum.

- The $3 billion surplus was to be achieved at 4 percent unemployment *and a stable price level*. In a boom, unemployment might fall below 4 percent and also the price level would rise. This rise of the price level would automatically raise the surplus above $3 billion, and it would probably be more important in doing so than would the fall of unemployment below 4 percent, because there was more room for prices to rise than for unemployment to fall.

These three provisions each contained opportunities for defeating the intention to achieve long-run budget balance, and two of them were even recognized in the initial statement.

First, the requirement of a surplus at high employment might be sloughed off. While the notion that the budget should be balanced had a certain emotional force in the country, the idea of a surplus had none. The CED pointed out "the frightening possibility" that budget policy might become balance in prosperity and deficits in recession.

Second, 4 percent unemployment might turn out to be too low as a measure of the unemployment that would exist when the inflation rate was stable. If so, the moderate surplus at which the policy was aimed would be achieved only in conditions unlikely to be realized and not really desired.

Third, the policy might come to be interpreted as calling for balance at the price level actually attained, or even at some forecast higher price level. The CED warned against this, saying that it would remove the built-in stabilizing (anti-inflationary) effect of automatic increases of surpluses in times of inflation. In a world that was generally inflationary, it would remove one of the main sources of surpluses to balance off against the deficits of recessions.

The budget practice of the postwar period, to which I shall turn soon, was, of course, not dictated by the CED rule or any other plan of long-run balance. However, the practice was in some degree constrained by such plans. As matters turned out, the influence of these plans as a force working for long-term balance was undercut at all three of these points. The initial emphasis on a moderate surplus at high employment disappeared. Instead, balancing the budget at high employment came to be accepted as meeting "conservative" requirements of fiscal policy. Also, the standard of 4 percent unemployment as a measure of high employment was retained in conventional discussion of the budget long after it had ceased to be a realistic estimate. In the late 1970s the benchmark was raised. In the budget message of January 1979 high employment was estimated to be a condition in which unemployment was 5.1 percent. But by that time at least 6 percent would have been more realistic. Probably most important, the meaning of balancing the budget at high employment came to be, for the past, balancing the budget at the price level actually experienced in the past, and, for the future, balancing the budget at the price level forecast for the future, which is always higher than the existing price level.

These reinterpretations of the original "high-employment balance" rule greatly reduced the apparent deviation of budget practice from that rule. For example, according to estimates of the Federal Reserve Bank of St. Louis, the high-employment deficit in calendar 1978 was $22.7 billion. That was a year in which actual unemployment was 6.0 percent and the "high-employment" benchmark was assumed to be 5.2 percent unemployment. It was also a year in which the price level rose 7.4 percent over the preceding year. On a rough estimate, if 6 percent unemployment is taken as the high employment benchmark, and the deficit is calculated as if prices had been stable between 1977 and 1978, the high employment deficit would have been $46 billion. But at high employment, according to a reasonable interpretation of the original rule, there should have been a surplus equal to about 1½ percent of GNP, which would have been $31 billion. So the high-employment deficit was, by that standard, $77 billion greater than it should have been, rather than $22.7 billion as suggested by the original estimate. And, of course, if the high-employment deficit for 1978 had been calculated on the assumption of prices stable at the level of 1973 or 1968, rather than at the level of 1977, the deficit would have been very much higher.

The original standard was thus eroded in a way which legitimized much larger deficits in recessions and required a much smaller surplus in prosperity, or no surplus at all. I am not suggesting that if the standard had retained its original form budgetary practice would have exactly conformed to it. There were always people in positions of influence who rejected the validity of any such rule of budget policy and would have been guided by other considerations. Even they, however, felt the need to make their peace with some public sentiment for "a balanced budget." Thus, the Kennedy economists in 1962 and 1963 used the argument that the tax cut they proposed would still leave the budget in balance at full employment, although they do not seem themselves to have attached much value to balancing the budget.

So the general understanding of what "budget-balancing" meant probably had an influence on budget practice. Therefore, it is of interest to ask why the concept was so watered down as to accommodate the large and persistent deficits of the years which began in 1965. Probably the basic reason was that even the people who considered themselves the chief defenders of the idea of balancing the budget did not feel any great substantive interest in achieving balance. That is, they did not feel that there was a benefit from balancing the budget, either for the national economy or for themselves, worth paying any large cost for, especially when the cost took the form of giving up a tax reduction.

The rule of balancing the budget at high employment originated as guidance for the cyclical behavior of the budget. It was a rule designed to permit the automatic fluctuations of the budget position that would occur as the economy fluctuated and to rule out discretionary changes for countercyclical reasons. This policy could be justified on the claim that it would stabilize tax rates and expenditure programs. From this standpoint, whether the budget was set to balance, yield a surplus, or yield a deficit at high employment did not matter, and neither did the choice of the rate of unemployment to be considered high employment. In fact, one of the most important versions of the high-employment-balance rule, that proposed by Milton Friedman in 1948, called for a constant *deficit* at high employment. This was also considered by the CED. The decisive argument against it was the belief that there existed a popular sentiment in favor of budget balancing, and the desire of the CED to enlist that sentiment against functional finance and what was not yet called fine tuning. In fact, the recommendation of CED that there should be a $3 billion surplus at high employment was mainly dictated by symbolic or public-relations considerations. The CED wanted to state its rule in terms of a consolidated budget, including the trust accounts, whereas most discussion of the budget at that time referred to the administrative budget, which excluded the trust accounts. Since the trust accounts ran a surplus, to recommend a balance in the consolidated budget would have implied a deficit in the administrative budget. To avoid the charge that it favored a deficit even at high employment, the CED had to recommend a surplus in the consolidated budget.

The most common substantive argument offered in favor of surpluses in prosperous times and balancing the budget or the average of good times and bad was that a large debt required high taxes to service it, and that high taxes would have adverse effects on incentives. However, this did not turn out to be a compelling argument when achievement of the surplus or balance required paying more taxes now. This became clear in the efforts of fiscal conservatives, in business and government, to get tax reductions in 1947, in 1953, and especially in 1962 and 1963. In the last case, before the Kennedy tax cut, the issue was raised whether preserving a potential, high-employment surplus, which would increase the total savings available for investment, would do more for economic growth than a tax cut which included some reductions that would strengthen incentives for business investment. The answer given by the business community was in favor of the tax cut, even though only, say, one-fourth of the tax reduction would take forms directly helpful to investment.

By 1962, the interest burden of the debt, and the tax burden associated with it, had declined substantially relative to the GNP. In 1946, net federal interest had been 2 percent of GNP. By 1952, it had fallen to 1.3 percent of GNP and it remained around that percentage until 1972 when it began to rise slowly, reaching 1.8 percent in the first quarter of 1979.

The transition from a rule calling for a budget surplus under expected economic conditions to a rule calling for only a balanced budget, and that only under exceptionally booming economic conditions, was not entirely due to liberals and Keynesians who had never believed in the original rule anyway. It was also due to fiscal conservatives, who had an attachment to the idea of long-run balance, but who were unwilling to pay any substantial price to achieve it. The transition from the standard of balancing the budget at a stable price level to the standard of balancing the budget at whatever price level occurs, which meant abandoning the notion that inflation called for surpluses, was made without notice or objection from any part of this ideological or intellectual spectrum. At first, when inflation was slow, this change seemed to make little difference. Later, when the inflation rate was higher, the nation became accustomed to the idea that the price level never declined. Thus, to insist on a budget that would yield a surplus at a price level no one expected to see again seemed quixotic.

The Postwar Fiscal Record

There have been federal budget deficits in twenty-five of the thirty-three fiscal years from 1947 through 1979. There were deficits in twenty of the twenty-eight fiscal years from 1947 through 1974, and in that period the cumulative deficit was $127 billion. But until 1974, there was no widespread feeling of something being fundamentally and systematically wrong with our budget performance. There was grumbling, as always, about the deficit and the debt, about the rise of expenditures, and about the burden of taxes. But the situation did not seem critical.

In 1969, a common view would have been that the fiscal history of the two previous decades had been marked by two main errors.

One was the effort of President Eisenhower to get the budget back into balance quickly after the 1958 recession, which was believed to have been premature and to have precipitated the recession of 1960. This error was, of course, especially regretted by those who also regretted that it might have helped elect J. F. Kennedy president in that year. The other error was the failure of Lyndon Johnson to raise taxes or cut nondefense spending in the early years of the Vietnam War, which was believed to have initiated the post-1965 inflation.

However, neither of these errors was thought to be an argument for a fundamental change in the prevailing rules of fiscal policy, and certainly not a change towards a rule of annual balance. Eisenhower's error had been too much, or too rapid, budget balancing. Johnson's error came at a time of war finance, when under the traditional rules deficits were permitted, if not always wise.

By 1974, there was another episode to evaluate, the deficits of fiscal years 1971, 1972, and 1973, the largest peacetime deficits of our history. But they came in a recession and in a period of exceptional disturbances to the price level, and it was not clear that any lasting inferences could be drawn from that experience.

The whole period 1947–1974 looked respectable when measured by the standard of budget balance at high employment. According to estimates of the Federal Reserve Bank of St. Louis, there were high-employment surpluses in seventeen of those twenty-eight years and a cumulative high-employment surplus of $38 billion. The high-employment deficits came during the Korean War and the Vietnam War and during the recession of 1970–1973.

Of course, a high-employment surplus is an abstraction, an estimate of what would have happened if the world had been different from the way it was. Abstract surpluses do not reduce real debts. But still, the burden of the federal debt, relative to the GNP, was substantially reduced, despite the increase in the absolute size of the debt. In 1946, at the end of World War II the debt exceeded the year's GNP. By 1979, the debt was equal to about 25 percent of GNP. A considerable part of the reduction in the ratio of debt to GNP resulted from inflation which occurred after the debt was created. To that extent, the debt burden was reduced by expropriation of the creditors, which is not a tribute to fiscal policy. However, that is not all that was happening. There would have been a reduction of the debt burden if there had been no inflation after 1946. This may be estimated by inflating the absolute 1946 debt by the GNP deflator for that year (1972=100), inflating the debt increase of each subsequent year by the deflator for that year, and comparing the cumulative total with the GNP in 1972 dollars. On that basis, the debt is found to decline from 105 percent of GNP at the end of 1946 to 50 percent of GNP at the end of 1973.

And yet there is some evidence that the policy was beginning to run down well before 1974, from the standpoint of the objective of long-run budget balancing. The clearest sign of this is in the tendency to smaller surpluses at high employment. In the years 1957, 1965, and 1973 actual output was close to the output that would have been produced at high employment. But in 1957, there was a surplus equal to ½ percent of high-employment GNP, in 1965 there was essentially no surplus (.07 percent of GNP), and in 1973 there was a deficit of ½ percent of GNP. A similar decline is seen in the relation of the high-employment surplus to GNP. Moreover, 1973 was a year of higher inflation than either 1957 or 1965. It was therefore a year in which a policy of balancing the budget over the business cycle would have called for an especially large surplus.

What was commonly described as Eisenhower's error of fiscal policy generated a large high-employment surplus, and a moderate actual surplus, in calendar 1960. Deficits were small in the Kennedy-Johnson years before the Vietnam War. The contribution of the policy makers in that period was to dissipate the high-employment surplus, mainly by the big tax cut of 1974, so that when high employment was actually regained there was no longer any surplus.

With only a tiny surplus or a deficit at the top of the economic cycle, a recession would automatically produce a large deficit as the result of the built-in decline of revenues and increase of expenditures for unemployment compensation. There was also a growing tendency to augment this built-in shift to deficit with discretionary measures to reduce tax rates or increase spending. Thus, between 1956 and 1958, 78 percent of the increase in the deficit resulted from the automatic reaction, whereas between 1969 and 1971 that fraction was slightly under 50 percent, and between 1973 and 1975 the fraction was 62 percent. The active deficit-creating response was, thus, initially more moderate in 1973–1975 than it had been in 1969–1971. However, the distinctive feature of the deficits after 1973 was that the deliberately created deficits (those not resulting from the built-in stabilizers), although initially rather small given the depth of the recession, persisted and remained high, even after recovery had been achieved. Thus, in 1979 we have the phenomenon of a deficit equal to about 1½ percent of GNP in a condition of full employment and excess demand.

The deliberate creation of larger and more durable deficits in the recessions of the 1970s, and the dissipation of the surplus during the early 1960s, had several causes. Impatience to regain what was regarded as high employment was great. The inflationary consequences of rapid recovery were considered to be slight. The difficulty of undoing expenditure increases, adopted as temporary stimuli, when recovery was achieved was underestimated. Too much reliance was placed on the long-run growth of revenue to balance expenditure increases made in recessions, without appreciating how many other claims there would be on that future revenue. Finally, slight, and mainly rhetorical, value was attached to achieving a balanced budget or a surplus.[6]

By 1979 the record of fiscal action looked quite different from the way it had ten years earlier, or even five years earlier. In 1969, the postwar record looked fairly satisfactory, marred by two apparent mistakes, one resulting from overzealousness about balancing the budget and one connected with a war. One could add to the record of destabilizing budget policy the too expansive policy in 1972 and too restrictive one in 1974. Still, these could be explained as aberrations around a satisfactory long-run trend.

When the record of the period 1974–1979 is added in, however, one can see a trend towards larger and larger deficits, varying in size, of course, as the economy fluctuated but being eliminated only rarely in conditions of overheating and high inflation. One symptom of this trend is the rise in the debt burden relative to GNP. As already noted, the federal debt held by the public had fallen from 105 percent of GNP at the end of World War II to about 25 percent in 1974. But by the end of fiscal 1978 the ratio had risen again to 30 percent. In constant dollars the ratio had fallen from 105 percent to 50 percent in 1977 but had risen again to 58 percent at the end of 1978.

What Difference Does It Make?

One of the reasons for the trend to a budget policy that generates larger deficits was the fact that, although budget balancing was a slogan commanding routine assent, no one cared very much about it. After all, we had run large deficits in the 1930s, during World War II, and frequently thereafter, and it was hard to see undesirable consequences. If fact, the years up to 1965 or 1970 were years of general

---

[6] See Herbert Stein, "Fiscal Policy: Reflections on the Past Decade" in William Fellner, ed., *Contemporary Economic Problems 1976* (Washington, D.C.: American Enterprise Institute, 1976).

211

satisfaction with the state of the economy, and so there seemed no occasion to complain about the budget policy.

However, the recent period of large deficits coincides with less satisfactory performance of the economy. Thus, there is a tendency to conclude that the deficits have caused the economic ills we have been suffering. But this conclusion, although natural, is not necessarily valid, any more than it would have been valid to conclude that the earlier deficits, the 1930 to 1965 deficits, were harmless or beneficial. One must ask whether deficits do in fact cause the economic troubles attributed to them. More realistically, one must ask whether there is any frequency or size of deficits that is harmless, or beneficial, and if so, what the permissible frequency and size is.

Deficits and Inflation. Just as inflation has been the most virulent and obvious economic disease of the past ten years, it has been the evil most commonly ascribed to deficits. The question whether deficits cause inflation is very much like the question whether handguns cause murders, in two respects. First, just to ask either question is likely to arouse a strong emotional response. Second, each question has a number of possible meanings, and, to draw any policy conclusion, a careful distinction among the meanings of the questions is essential. Can handguns be used to commit murder? Are some handguns used to commit murder? Are all handguns used to commit murder? Would there be no murders, or fewer murders, if there were no guns? Are there ways to prevent murders without abolishing guns?

Parallel questions can be asked about the relation between deficits and inflation. I cannot review and evaluate all of the literature on this subject, but what stands out is that the connections are uncertain. Policy will have to be decided without absolute knowledge of the relation between deficits and inflation. That is, policy will have to reflect some judgment about the weight of the evidence. I will indicate here my view of the weight of the evidence.

If deficits cause inflation, or affect inflation, it is presumably by their influence on the growth of total demand for output—on total spending. The usual formulation is that, if the government spends more than it takes in, it is putting more money into people's pockets than it is taking from them, and this causes them to spend more than they otherwise would (not necessarily more than in the previous period), and this is inflationary.

The effect of government deficits on aggregate demand is some-times denied because they impose on taxpayers a liability to pay more taxes later to service the increased government debt. This liability imposed on some people offsets the additional wealth received by citizens to whom the government's payments flow. There is no net addition to private income or wealth and therefore no stimulus to increased total spending.

While this is a possible scenario, anyone examining his own reactions during the period of large and rising deficits will find it hard to recognize the reality of the behavior described. A government bond in the hand seems much more real and operative than the contra-liability to pay an undetermined share of some future tax at an uncertain date, if indeed the future servicing of the debt is not financed by borrowing.

A more persuasive, and more widely held view, is that deficits do not increase aggregate demand because aggregate demand is limited by the supply of money. As against the "naive" view that a deficit puts more money into the hands of people than it takes away, the point is made that financing the deficit by borrowing similarly take money away from people—from those who buy the government's securities. Much of the debate over the possibility that deficits increase aggregate demand has focused on answers to this monetarist position. There are three main counterarguments:

1. An increase in the deficit will increase government borrowing, which will raise interest rates. That in turn will reduce the quantity of money people want to hold; that is, at higher interest rates they will prefer to hold more of other assets, such as government bonds, and less money, which yields no interest. This will permit aggregate demand to rise even if there is no increase in the money supply.

2. Even if a deficit is not accompanied by an increase in the money supply it does lead to an increase in the supply of quite secure and liquid assets—namely, the government debt—and that is likely to cause an increase in private spending.

3. Although a deficit may not raise aggregate demand unless it is accompanied by an increase in the money supply, a deficit will cause an increase in the money supply.

While all of this is very controversial, it is probably true that cases 1 and 2 are not likely to explain a steep and prolonged inflation without an increase of the money supply. They may, however, explain spurts of inflation. The interesting case is the third one, in which the deficit is alleged to cause the increase of the money supply. The period of rapid inflation—the past fifteen years in the United States—was also a period of rapid monetary expansion, so to explain inflation as being mainly due to the deficits implies either that money does not matter much, which hardly anyone says any more, or that the money growth was due to the deficits.

Before leaving these cases, however, it is worth noting that case 1 relates the expansionary effect of the deficits to a rising deficit, not to the existence of even a large deficit as such. For example, suppose that in a constant no-growth economy, savings equal 15 percent of GNP, the budget deficit equals 5 percent of GNP, and, at the existing interest rates, private investment equals 10 percent of GNP. This deficit could go on indefinitely without causing interest rates to rise and, therefore, without reducing the demand for money and, the money supply being constant, raising aggregate demand.

In case 2, where demand is stimulated by the growth of public debt, any deficit would have a demand-raising effect. Whether this was too much, of course, would depend on what was the desired growth of demand. For example, suppose that potential output grows by 3 percent a year and that demand should grow by 3 percent a year to absorb the output at stable prices. If private investors want to hold public debt in a constant proportion to GNP, then the deficit should be equal to 3 percent of the debt. In 1979 that would mean an annual deficit of about $20 billion. If some small amount of inflation, say 2 percent, is taken to be inevitable or acceptable, the "needed" deficit would be larger.

A good deal of effort has been devoted to trying to determine whether deficits cause an increase in the money supply. The linkage is thought to be that deficits cause interest rates to rise, that monetary authorities wish to moderate increases of interest rates, and that they try to do this by making the money supply grow more rapidly. Studies of this relationship have been inconclusive. The factors determining the behavior of the monetary authority are numerous and variable, and some of them are hard to quantify. Therefore, the effect of one factor, the size of the federal deficit, cannot be isolated with any confidence.

Still, the proposition that deficits cause an increase in the money supply is clearly too simple.

• The linkage presumably runs through a desire to moderate an *increase* of interest rates. Neither the monetary authorities nor the public seems to be resistant to "high" stable interest rates, especially since this is usually known not to mean high real rates. In this case, it should be an increase in the deficit (or a reduction in the surplus) that would inspire the monetary expansion.

• Deficits occurring when interest rates are falling, as in the contraction phase of the business cycle, would not cause more rapid growth of the money supply.

• The supposed devotion of the monetary authorities to moderating increases of interest rates probably applies to rises of interest rates caused by private credit demands as well as to rises caused by government deficits. In that case the proposition is a criticism of monetary policy in general and suggests the need for a revision of monetary policy, rather than of budget policy.

• The simultaneous occurrence of rising deficits and accelerating monetary growth, sometimes observed, does not mean that the monetary authorities are induced or pressured into expansion by the desire to moderate interest rates. The monetary authorities may share the belief in the need for expansionist policy which led the government to raise its deficits.

• Even if the monetary authorities do not agree on the desirability of an expansionist policy at a time when deficits are rising, they may yield to pressure from the executive, the Congress, and the public for monetary expansion. The motivation for this pressure is probably not the desire to finance the deficit at stable interest rates but the desire for an expansionist policy to raise employment and output. In that case, the pressure on the monetary authority would be no less if the government were prevented by some means from running a deficit. In fact, the pressure may be greater, because without the possibility of a deficit monetary policy may be the only instrument available for bringing about the desired economic expansion.

The foregoing discussion is related to the question whether deficits cause an expansion of aggregate demand, directly or through their effect on the money supply. There is a further question whether an expansion of demand causes inflation. To that the obvious answer is that it depends on how big the expansion is and on the state of the economy when it occurs.

The implications of this discussion may be summed up as follows:

A stable deficit, even if large, is probably not inflationary, and increases in a deficit, or reductions of a surplus, are probably not inflationary if they come at a time of slack in the economy. However, large increases of a deficit, coming at the wrong time, may be inflationary, largely but perhaps not entirely because of their effect on the money supply. But this effect on the money supply does not seem to be an inevitable consequence of the deficit and might be corrected without eliminating the deficit. Moreover, if, as is frequently the case, the increasing deficit is an instrument deliberately chosen to bring about an economic expansion that the government, the public, and possibly the monetary authority all want, preventing the deficit will not prevent the economic expansion and its inflationary consequences.

The foregoing discussion has an important implication for the question of the definition of the budget and of the deficit. The inflationary consequences of deficits seem to be connected with their interest-raising consequences, the presumed route to either a reduction in the demand for money or an increase in its supply. This suggests that a deficit should be defined as a transaction that tends to raise interest rates. Not all federal borrowing does that. If the Treasury borrows $1 billion in Treasury bills to replace $1 billion of maturing bills, that does not tend to raise interest rates, and no one would consider that transaction to constitute a federal deficit. If the Treasury borrows $1 billion in bonds to replace $1 billion in bills, that presumably raises rates in the bond market and reduces rates in the bill market. Whether this is a rate increase is unclear, but probably no one would want to consider that a deficit. The interest rate effects are quantitatively so different from borrowing $1 billion to buy airplanes that both transactions cannot be lumped in the same category as "deficits."

The problem rises with respect to transactions of intermediate character, namely government borrowing to finance loans to the private sector. Suppose the government borrows $1 billion and makes $1 billion of mortgage loans to private home buyers. Does that raise interest rates and should it be considered a deficit? The government is taking money out of credit markets by its borrowing, but it is also putting money into credit markets by its lending. That presumably affects the pattern of interest rates—raising some and lowering others —but whether there is a net effect of raising interest rates in a sense that is relevant to the inflation problem is unclear.

The answer depends in part on the terms of the government's lending and the extent to which the terms generate lending that would not otherwise have occurred. If the $1 billion of mortgages made by the government would all have been made anyway, then there may be no change of interest rates at all. If the demand for mortgage money is very elastic, so that the $1 billion of government mortgages is absorbed by home buyers with little decline of interest rates, whereas a large rise of interest rates elsewhere is needed to bring forth another $1 billion of money for Treasury securities, the transactions may unmistakably raise interest rates. If the government offers its mortgages with a subsidy then some of the borrrowers will be people who would not otherwise have been part of the effective demand for credit and that may cause a net rise of interest rates. However, it will hardly ever be the case that this is true of all the borrowers.

Whether or not the loan transactions are inflationary depends also on the reaction pattern of the monetary authorities. The argument is usually made that there is pressure on the monetary authorities to increase the money supply in order to hold down interest rates. The question is which rates matter from this standpoint. Twenty-five years ago one would certainly have said that the rates on Treasury securities were the key ones. Today that is extremely doubtful. Today it is probably the mortgage interest rate that is most important because of the political power of the house-building industry and because of the national sentiment for home ownership. That is why we have large federal programs to encourage the flow of funds into home mortgages. These programs, including federal loans, may serve to protect the Federal Reserve against pressure for monetary expansion to hold mortgage rates down and thus may be anti-inflationary.

There is no escape from the fact that government finance is a basket of assorted transactions which differ from each other in many respects, including their inflationary effects. Only an arbitrary line can be drawn between those inflows and outflows that are to be considered part of the budget and those that are not. Some transactions that are included will be not very different from those that are excluded, and all of those included will not be the same. Still, if a line must be drawn to isolate a deficit that is significant for its inflationary effect, it should, in my opinion, be drawn between lending people money, on the one hand, and giving them money or buying current production from them, on the other. This conforms to the conclusion reached by the presidential commission to study the budget concept, which reported in 1967.[7] It implies that—for this purpose, at least—most if not all of what are now "off-budget" transactions should not be included in the deficit, and the small amount of loans now included in the budget and the deficit should be excluded.

Deficits and Growth. The classic case in favor of balancing the government budget or running a surplus is that doing so will promote economic growth. The argument is that financing a deficit will absorb

---

[7] "A surplus or deficit should therefore be presented in the budget, to be calculated by comparing expenditures other than loans with total budget receipts, for purposes of providing a measure of the economic impact of Federal programs." (*Report of the President's Commission on Budget Concepts*, David M. Kennedy, Chairman [Washington, D.C., 1967], p. 47.)

private savings that would otherwise flow into private investments and raise the productive capacity of the country.

This reasoning has been challenged on three grounds:

• The amount that private investors want to invest may fall short of the savings private savers want to make under conditions of high employment. In that case, insistence on balancing the budget will depress the economy, which will reduce savings but also reduce the desire to invest. The economy will come to equilibrium at a low level of real income, with private investment and private savings equal, but with private investment lower than if there had been a deficit that sustained both a higher level of total income and a higher level of savings.

There is probably agreement now that this condition is unlikely to persist for any long period of time. Given a complementary monetary policy, interest rates will bring about an adjustment of private investment and private savings to each other at high employment, on the average. The private desire to invest and the private desire to save may fluctuate relative to each other, and that divergence may not be *immediately* corrected by an adjustment of interest rates without some temporary change of real incomes. To keep the budget position—the deficit or surplus—from fluctuating temporarily in these conditions is probably neither necessary nor helpful, even if possible. But it is possible to have an economy which fluctuates around a budget surplus and a high rate of investment, rather than around a budget deficit and a low rate of investment, and the former will grow more rapidly.

• Private savings may be higher if the government runs a deficit than if the budget is balanced, because individuals see that the deficit entails higher tax burdens for them in the future and save more now to bear these tax burdens better. Introspection raises serious doubts that this behavior, however rational, is the behavior that actually occurs.

• If running a deficit permits the government to impose lower taxes, that may have a favorable incentive effect, raise the national income, and generate sufficiently more saving to finance both more private investment and the deficit. Whether this is true or not will depend on certain magnitudes—the responsiveness of work, initiative, and investment to the tax rates, the responsiveness of output to these inputs, and the responsiveness of savings to output. Whether the magnitudes are large enough to suggest that a larger deficit increases growth is doubtful. This is a more convincing argument for less spending, and for revision of the tax system, than for deficits as a way of accelerating economic growth.

At a more empirical level, the proposition that higher surpluses, or lower deficits, increase growth by increasing private investment is challenged by what happened in a year like 1975. Gross private domestic investment fell sharply between 1974 and 1975. It began to fall before the deficit began to rise, for reasons unconnected with the deficit. Actually, the rise of the deficit was largely the consequence of the decline of private investment, which depressed the economy as a whole. Interest rates declined substantially during the recession. They probably would have declined further if the deficit had been prevented or moderated. But it is hard to imagine this making much difference to investment during this time of recession and uncertainty.

However, this view of the problem is too short term. Private investment would have been larger in 1973 and early 1974—in the period of boom—if the federal government had run a surplus instead of a deficit in that period. Interest rates, which were rising, could have risen less if necessary to bring about a higher rate of private investment. This would not have prevented investment from declining in the recession of 1974–1975, but the decline of investment would have started from a higher level and probably would not have reached so low a level. Over the cycle total investment would have been larger, although the variation might have been as great.

During 1978 and early 1979 we have again been in a period in which investment demand is strong, as is total demand, and in which investment would be higher if there were a budget surplus instead of a deficit. The higher investment during this period would probably not be offset by lower investment during a subsequent recession. On the contrary, investment during the recession would probably also be higher than it would otherwise be.

The budget deficit that is relevant to this discussion is the excess of receipts over the current, or noncapital, expenditures of government. If the government increases expenditures for capital purposes, like roads, or other productivity-increasing purposes, and finances that by borrowing, the transaction does not necessarily repress total investment and total growth. Of course, these government expenditures for capital purposes may have a negative effect on growth if they displace private investment expenditures that are even more productive. But that is something which cannot be told from the size of the deficit, and there is no presumption that the government capital expenditures are less productive.

219

To have a government budget that was divided into a current and a capital sector would be helpful for making judgments about budget policy. Such accounts would be difficult to construct. Some expenditures, especially for intangibles, like education, would be difficult to classify. But that is also true, although probably less so, in the private sector.

This would not imply that the goal of policy should be to balance the current account budget. It does suggest that in deciding whether or not to balance the budget, or to run a surplus of some size, knowing whether the expenditures were for capital or current purposes would be useful. Thus, from the standpoint of promoting growth, there might be merit in saying that future increases of current expenditures must be balanced by tax receipts but that increases of capital expenditures need not be.

The fact that some part of federal expenditures is for capital purposes does not deny the probability that a trend to increasing deficits has slowed down economic growth, or will do so. This probability would only be denied if government capital expenditures had been rising as fast as the deficit. In view of the great preponderance of transfer payments in the recent increase of federal spending, this seems unlikely.

The conclusion that economic growth increases with the surplus in the current account budget or, assuming the proportions of capital expenditures in the budget to be constant, with the surplus in the total budget, does not answer the question of how big the surplus should be—or whether there should be any. Clearly the answer is not the maximum possible surplus to yield the maximum growth. Even if economic growth is a good thing, which only a few would deny, it is not desirable in unlimited quantities if it is not free. Promoting growth by running a surplus is not free. It requires someone to forgo current consumption or the benefits of current government expenditures for the sake of more output and income later. None of us, in private life, makes a choice in favor of maximum growth, and there is no reason to think such a choice would be rational if made through the government budget.

There is an intuitive appeal in the idea that investment should be equal to private saving, and that the budget should therefore be in balance. However, intuition probably does not indicate whether it is total investment or only private investment that should equal private saving, whether it is the current account budget or the total budget that should be in balance, or whether it is the federal budget only or the combined federal, state, or local budgets that should be balanced. If it is the combined budgets, there have been few and small deficits in the postwar period, and we are in balance in 1979. And, if intuition tells us that the combined current account should be in balance, that test has almost certainly been met continuously since World War II.

Intuition is not a good guide in such matters, where it leaves open so many questions. A society may rationally decide that it wants to grow more rapidly than would result if private investment were equal to private savings. In fact, it does make such a decision when it finances roads or research out of taxes. A decision to run a surplus would be a similar decision, to use taxes to raise funds which would increase investment, but in this case private rather than public investment.

A case can be made that the tax system discourages private saving by taking some of the return away from it, and keeps private saving from being carried to the point which the productivity of capital would make worth while in the absence of the taxes. This suggests that there should be a surplus to compensate for the deficiency of private saving. But this should be a surplus in the current account budget.

I have argued in the past that there was no clear national interest in changing the growth rate that emerged from private decisions and that it was not the business of the government to try to manipulate the growth rate. Some standard of long-run budget policy should be set; for example, the size of the surplus or deficit sought at high employment should be decided. This standard would affect the economic growth rate, but it should not be set in order to achieve a chosen growth rate, since that was not a proper national concern. Rather it should be set pragmatically, on the basis of what was most likely to work as a fiscal discipline. From that standpoint the conventional standard of balancing-the-budget seemed best, because it already had most popular support.

However, two things have happened in the past decade to weaken that position. The growth rate of productivity has slowed down markedly. Restoring the previous growth rate seems a more serious national objective than maintaining or increasing a growth rate that was gratifyingly high and apparently well established. Moreover, it no longer seems possible to anchor budget policy to a firmly held popular preference for balancing the budget, because that preference is not so firmly held. Therefore, it may be necessary to make a conscious national decision about the budget standard based on an evaluation of the consequences of the decision. Even if the decision should

221

be to balance the budget, taking advantage of what sentiment now exists for that standard, that rule could probably not withstand the vicissitudes of politics and economics unless it had some foundation in a real purpose to be served. That purpose would be some objective with respect to economic growth.

There is no objectively "right" answer to the social decision about the surplus or deficit and consequently about the rate of growth. A society may rationally choose to grow rapidly or slowly, just as individuals may. One can wish, of course, that the decision would be based on information. Surely this has not been the case in recent years. Those who want to balance the budget have been content to appeal to what they believe is an existing popular preference. Those who do not want to balance the budget do not attack that preference but pay lip-service to it and meanwhile proceed to generate deficits. Popular discussion is trivial, and confused between growth as meaning cyclical recovery to "full employment," usually defined too ambitiously, and growth as meaning the long-term rise of potential output. This confusion is one source of the belief held by the semiliterate that deficits are the way to growth.

Even in the relevant arena of discussion there is much ignorance. A key question is how much additional growth we get for how much additional budget surplus. Some tend to the Micawberesque answer that a surplus, however small, yields happiness, and a deficit, however small, yields misery. Economists who get beyond this and try to measure the pay-offs obtain quite different results. If instead of averaging deficits equal to 1 percent of GNP we averaged surpluses equal to 1 percent of GNP, that would increase the savings available for private investment by 2 percent of GNP. This could increase annual net private investment by about one-third. On some calculations this would raise the annual increase of output per hour of work by one-third—say from 1.5 percent to 2.0 percent. But others would estimate the productivity gain to be much smaller, because many factors other than private investment—such as research and education—also contribute to productivity growth.

The difference between a 1 percent deficit and a 1 percent surplus is, at present GNP levels, about $40 billion a year. This may seem a large amount to pay for even a high estimate of the productivity gain—raising it from 1½ percent a year to 2 percent. But workers seem willing to strike over smaller differences in the increase of their wages, and citizens may be willing to forgo tax reductions or expenditure increases for these gains.

222

Deficits and Government Spending. One of the principal concerns about increasing budget deficits, and increasing toleration of budget deficits, is that they cause or permit excessive government expenditures. There are several propositions involved in this concern:

• Government expenditures are larger than they would have been if deficits had been prohibited.

• These larger expenditures are too large, either (1) because they are larger than a majority of people would have preferred if they had been aware of the true costs, which are concealed from them by deficits, or (2) because they are too large by some other standard, which usually means larger than the person expressing the concern would have preferred.

Of course, it is possible to take a different position. One might agree that the expenditures are larger than they would have been if deficits had been impossible and still believe that the amount of expenditure is just right, or too small. This would follow from the belief that the majority of the citizens, or their representatives, chronically underestimate the value of government expenditures and are induced to approach the "right" level of expenditures only if costs are similarly underestimated.

The effect of deficits on the level of expenditure is not immediately apparent from the record. One may compare the experience of four years of fairly high employment—1957, 1965, 1973, and 1978. The federal budget was in balance in 1957 and 1965, close to balance in 1973, and further away from balance in 1978. In the period 1957–1965 the goal of balancing the budget was still fairly influential, in 1965–1973 less so, and in 1973–1978 still less so. Between 1957 and 1965 federal expenditures as a share of GNP remained constant, between 1965 and 1973 the share rose by 1.5 percent per annum, and between 1973 and 1978 the share rose at the same rate. Between 1957 and 1965 real federal expenditures (deflated by the GNP deflation) rose at an annual rate of 3.9 percent. Between 1965 and 1973 the annual rate of increase rose to 5.2 percent, but it fell again to 3.9 percent between 1973 and 1978. There does not seem to be any acceleration of the spending trend accompanying the decline of the budget-balancing rule.

Still, it seems plausible that expenditures would be smaller if the government could not run a deficit. But it is also plausible that expenditures would be smaller if the government were prohibited from taxing at all, and had to finance all its expenditures by borrowing. If the government has a wider range of revenue sources available, it is more likely to find the way of raising a given amount of revenue that is least costly and seems so to the citizens, who will therefore approve a larger amount of spending. In fact, federal spending would be much smaller today if it were not for the Sixteenth Amendment to the Constitution, which authorized a federal income tax. That amendment probably contributed more to the growth of government spending than did the erosion of the traditional taboo on deficits.

How much lower would expenditures be if deficits were forbidden? It is hardly likely that a requirement to balance the budget would have made expenditures lower than the revenues have actually been. The most likely consequence of such a requirement would have been somewhat lower expenditures and somewhat higher taxes. But if expenditures had been held to the level of actual revenues, they would have been 6½ percent lower in 1978 than they actually were. Except in years of war or severe recession, the difference would have never been more than that.

Whether this should be regarded as a large or a small amount is unclear. One way of looking at it is to observe that since World War II actual expenditures in any year seldom exceeded the actual revenues of the next year and only once, in 1952 during the Korean War, exceeded the revenues actually collected two years later. If this relationship persisted, a requirement that the budget be balanced would only mean that we reach a given expenditure level a year or two later than we otherwise would. Thus, we would not reach until 1986 the expenditure level we would otherwise have reached in 1984. This is some retardation of movement along the Road to Serfdom, but not much.

The figures look more impressive if we consider the relation of expenditures to GNP. This ratio rose from 18 percent in 1965 to 21.9 percent in 1978, an increase in the ratio at an annual rate of 1.5 percent. The ratio of revenue to GNP in this period rose at an annual rate of only 0.9 percent, and reached 20.4 percent in 1978. If the ratio of expenditures to GNP continues to rise at its recent rate it will reach 25.4 percent in 1988. However, if expenditures are held to the level of revenues, and revenues rise at the 1965–1978 rate, expenditures would reach that ratio of GNP only in the year 2002, or fourteen years later. The predictable reaction is that requiring the budget to be balanced will somewhat increase the rate of growth of revenues and bring expenditures to that ratio of GNP at a date between 1988 and 2002 which cannot be estimated—of course assuming that nothing else intervenes, a most unrealistic assumption.

The key question is not whether the ability to borrow makes expenditures larger but whether it makes them too large. This is not answered by saying that citizens or officials resist expenditures financed by a combination of taxing and borrowing less than they resist expenditures financed by taxing alone. The combination may be less burdensome in real terms. Neither is the question answered by saying that the citizens or officials do not give adequate weight to the real costs of borrowing. It is also possible that citizens or officials give excessive weight to the real costs of taxes and inadequately value the benefits of expenditures, so that if the possibility of a deficit is ruled out expenditures will be too low.

Almost anyone, however devoted to the proposition that total expenditures are too high, can think of particular expenditures that he thinks are too low and for which he would, if necessary, favor higher taxes. These are cases in which the political process has undervalued the benefits of expenditures and overvalued the costs of taxes. If so, one cannot be sure that the political process, if required to balance the budget, would not spend too little.

This is not a trivial or hair-splitting point. For example, in 1972 and 1973, there was much agreement on the desirability of holding down federal expenditures. The government was divided into two camps on this. One wanted to stay within an expenditure limit by holding down the defense budget and the other by holding down the nondefense budget. Neither side would have considered a tax *increase*, for political reasons. The result was that the expenditure total was allowed to exceed what either camp wanted, but neither side had to yield as much as it feared of its preferred programs. The deficit and total spending were both larger than either camp would have preferred. But each camp considered the outcome better than would have resulted if no deficit had been possible or if a lower spending limit had been enforced.

I do not think it possible to deduce that expenditures are too high from the fact that deficits are permitted and are incurred. Nevertheless, it is possible to conclude from other evidence that expenditures are too high, as I do. One may be concerned with the large absolute and relative size of government as a threat to individual freedom. One may look at a large number of specific programs and conclude that they are wasteful or harmful. And having concluded that, one may seek ways of restraining expenditures and putting obstacles in the path of decisions to spend.

One possible obstacle to expenditures would be a requirement that expenditures be balanced by tax revenues. There are other possible obstacles. One could impose by statute or constitutional amendment a ceiling on expenditures, require a two-thirds vote of Congress for spending legislation, give the President an item veto, restore the President's authority to impound funds, or impose penalties of various kinds on officials who vote for higher spending. Indexing the income tax would be an obstacle to spending because it would reduce the revenue increase that comes automatically in inflation. The case for the balanced budget requirement as an obstacle is not that it has any special rationality. Requiring expenditures to be balanced by taxes does not require any careful measurement of the real costs and benefits of expenditures. It is only another obstacle that makes the costs seem more than they would otherwise seem, which may be higher or lower than they really are. The advantage of the balanced budget obstacle, as compared with other obstacles, is simply that the balanced budget obstacle may be easier to impose and enforce, since there is already sentiment for it in the country.

Imposing the requirement that the budget be balanced is a legitimate way to hold down government spending. It should not be regarded as a "neutral" procedure for getting the right amount of spending, without any prior judgment about the direction in which spending is to be adjusted.

Two further points should be made in this connection. One is that the expenditure-limiting objective of balancing the budget does not require annual balance. We are primarily concerned with the long-run trend of expenditures, and the "disciplinary" function of the balanced-budget requirement could be served by a longer-run rule, such as that the tax rates should be adequate to balance the budget at some average condition of the economy.

The other point is that the expenditure-limitation function requires balancing the budget at the margin. It requires that the decision to raise or lower expenditures be matched by a decision to raise or lower taxes. That does not rule out deficits, as long as the deficits are not a function of the expenditure level—that is, as long as higher expenditure does not permit a higher deficit.

Conclusions

We have considered three objectives to which the requirement of a balanced budget might be addressed—avoidance of inflation, promotion of growth, and restraint of government spending. These three objectives are of somewhat different characters. The avoidance of inflation, or at least the avoidance of unpredictable inflation, is in the nature of a categorical imperative. A policy which does not accept this objective is probably inconsistent with orderly economic life. However, the other two objectives, more growth and less spending, can be rationally supported or opposed.

None of these objectives requires *annual* balancing of the budget.

Avoidance of inflation is consistent with a large stable deficit and with occasional variations from surplus to deficit of some magnitudes. Moreover, the inflationary consequences of even untimely and excessive rises of the deficit can be limited by monetary policy. Nevertheless, large swings of the budget position that are not closely or automatically connected with changes in economic conditions would put an excessive strain on the stabilizing capacity of monetary policy.

Promotion of more rapid economic growth, if that is considered a worthwhile goal to pursue by overall budget policy, requires balance of the budget, or a surplus on the average over long periods. It does not require annual balancing, but only that the budget position revolves around a state of balance or surplus.

Restraint of government spending does not require actual annual balance, because what is at issue is the long-term growth of spending. Execution of a policy to achieve this objective may be furthered by a requirement of annual balance on an "as-if" basis, such as requiring that the taxes be adequate to balance the budget at some standard condition of the economy. This would prevent annual decisions from departing too far from the longer-range objective. But it would not preclude actual deficits if the economy was below the standard condition.

It should be noted that these three objectives involve different aspects of the budget's behavior. The inflation objective involves *stability* of the *total* budget position; the growth objective involved the *level* of the *total* position, that is, size of surplus or deficit; and the spending objective involves the *equality* of the *marginal* position, that is, equality of changes in revenues and expenditures.

The three objectives probably also refer to three different definitions of the budget. At least, I have suggested that the inflation objective relates to a budget which excludes loan transactions, and the growth objective relates to a budget which excludes capital transactions. The expenditure-restraint objective relates to whatever is to be restrained, which probably means the present total plus what are called the "off-budget" transactions.

Despite everything said in this essay about the reservations that must be attached to the balanced budget doctrine, there is no doubt in my mind that our recent policy has been seriously deficient. Particularly in 1966–1968 it unnecessarily complicated the task of monetary policy in preventing inflation. In 1972 and in 1977–1979 it contributed to inflation also, although on these occasions the main force was a national desire for too rapid recovery, which the Federal Reserve shared at least in part, and which would have manifested itself in more monetary expansion even if the budget had been in balance.

From the standpoint of one who believes that at this juncture of history, although not forever, promoting more rapid growth is desirable, the large and rising deficits of the past fifteen years have been harmful, and the trend promises more harm in the future. And from the standpoint of one who finds a large part of total federal spending wasteful, the ability to incur deficits has been too permissive.

Still, the requirement that the budget be balanced annually, or be balanced unless a deficit is approved by two-thirds of the Congress, seems to me far from an ideal solution. It is a system which holds out no promise of ever having a surplus, except by occasional accident but which would yield frequent deficits and, given the starting point of no surplus, *should* yield frequent deficits.

We have generally had large deficits when, despite the popular slogan of "balance the budget" there was strong support for them. A Lyndon Johnson who could get appropriations to fight the war in Vietnam could have obtained a two-thirds majority to run a deficit. A Richard Nixon who was under political attack for not pursuing a sufficiently expansive policy in 1972 would have been able to get a two-thirds majority for running a deficit. The same can be said about 1975 and 1977. In 1975 failure to get approval for running a deficit would have required absurd efforts to raise taxes and cut spending.

In the medium term the requirement would not yield a balanced budget on the average, although it might somewhat moderate the trend to larger average deficits. Its effect on the growth of expenditures is problematical. The requirement would not prevent the commitment to large expenditure increases in recessions, when an "exception" would probably be in force, and these commitments would make achievement of balance in the next prosperity "impractical" and so call for an exception, unless inflation generated enough revenue to cover the expenditures.

Doubts about the wisdom of the budget-balancing requirement are increased when the requirement is considered as a constitutional amendment. This involves keeping the requirement in force for a very long time. The case for balancing the budget, on the average, may be compelling at this time, when the rate of productivity increase has fallen, the recent increase of federal spending has been exceptionally rapid, and we are suffering a violent inflation. The case may be quite different in the year 2000 or 2070. There is probably no existing part of the Constitution whose validity is so conditional—so dependent on possibly changing economic circumstances and national priorities.

Is it possible to devise a rule of policy which reflects our long-run goals better than either the present ad-hoc decision making or the annual-balance doctrine? If such a rule could be devised, could it be made reasonably binding on policy?

The answer to the first question is surely affirmative. Probably few would disagree with that, and especially few of those who support the requirement for balancing the budget. Most supporters of a balanced-budget requirement would, I think, agree that it is not the best of rules. They advocate it as the only rule that they believe can be enforced politically as an alternative to the present anarchy.

Although there are undoubtedly other places to start in devising a superior rule of budget policy, one place to start is with the CED recommendation of 1947. Two major defects of the 1947 policy were revealed by subsequent experience.

First, it was a mistake to define the conditions under which the moderate surplus was to be achieved as 4 percent unemployment. The more general meaning of the rule was that the desired budget position (the size of the surplus) should be constant when the economy is on its desired path. If this were achieved, the budget would not be a destabilizing force tending to push the economy off the desired path. When the economy diverged from the desired path, this rule would not call for changes of tax rates or expenditure programs to get the budget back to the standard surplus position. If monetary policy succeeded in keeping the economy on, or varying around, the desired path, the desired budget position would be achieved on the average.

The problem was that 4 percent unemployment did not describe the desired path. It was not only that this number did not continue to be achievable. It was that the desired unemployment objective is a condition which cannot be expressed in advance by any number. Moreover, and more important, the 4 percent unemployment standard did not adequately deal with the fact of inflation. The CED had suggested that the budget surplus should be calculated as if prices were stable. But this was soon forgotten. In any case 4 percent unemployment and price stability were not compatible. And it was unrealistic to suggest that policy called for balancing the budget in 1967 or 1977 at the price level of 1947.

A better standard would be to maintain a constant surplus, as a percentage of GNP, as the economy moves along a target path of nominal GNP. This implies that the desired path of the economy is well described by the path of nominal GNP. The reason for this is that the rate of unemployment can accommodate itself, and reach its optimum level, at any stable, predictable path of nominal GNP. If a path of nominal GNP is achieved which is consistent with a stable price level, the optimum unemployment rate will also be achieved, whereas setting the target as a defined unemployment rate does not determine anything about the inflation rate.

Choosing the desired path of nominal GNP requires estimating the growth rate of potential output and the rate of inflation which will be accepted as "essentially" stable and nonaccelerating. The annual growth rate of potential output in the next five or ten years is now unusually uncertain, but even so it is unlikely to be outside the range 2 to 4 percent. Probably 2 to 3 percent would be an acceptable inflation rate. If so, a growth rate of 5 to 6 percent for nominal GNP could not yield unsatisfactory results. If inflation were more rapid, output would fall below potential, which would tend to slow the inflation. A rise of unemployment would tend to slow down the inflation rate, increasing the rise of real demand and restoring high employment. Of course, starting from our present condition, in which nominal GNP has been rising by more than 10 percent a year, a gradual transition to a lower rate would be needed.

Prescribing a target growth rate for nominal GNP may seem a roundabout approach to budget policy. But even if there were no problem of budget policy, agreement on, and commitment to, such a path would be highly desirable. It would serve as a guide for monetary policy, which is now lacking, and if adopted for that purpose would provide some confidence that we will not go on oscillating violently along a rising trend of inflation. Such a target of policy would also be a substitute for the unrealistic and dangerous commitments of the Humphrey-Hawkins Act.

More generally, the suggestion is that there should be a known target path for the economy, on which at least the President and the chairman of the Federal Reserve agree and which the Federal Reserve will seek to achieve, and that the budget policy should be to set tax rates so that they would yield a moderate surplus if the economy were on that path.

The second major defect of the 1947 statement was its failure to make sufficiently clear the case for a budget surplus. The CED recommended a surplus, but without any strong argument that it served a positive purpose. It was regarded, accurately, as mainly window dressing, and soon discarded, even by its authors. This time an affirmative national decision should be sought, on grounds of promoting economic growth, in favor of achieving a moderate surplus under ordinary conditions.

Whether any plan as complex as this can be put into effect is fairly open to question. The plan would not have to be sold to all the American people or even to a majority of them. It would have to be understood and accepted by the relatively small number of "authorities" to whom the public looks for guidance in such matters.

There are some encouraging facts. The trend of deteriorating fiscal discipline is not very old, not so old as to qualify as an ineradicable feature of democracy. Some change of attitudes is obvious. That is what now propels the budget-balancing movement, and the force of this movement might be harnessed to a more elaborate plan designed to achieve the real goals of budget balancing. Also, especially in Congress there is considerable evidence of interest in procedures for taking a longer-run view of budget policy.

A rule calling for an annually balanced budget may be the only possible alternative to our recent undisciplined course. But it would be premature to accept that conclusion before a more serious effort is made to devise and institute a better idea. In any case, a balanced-budget rule would presumably not prevent a surplus at any time or a deficit at some times. Therefore, even with such a rule better national understanding of the conditions under which surpluses or deficits are appropriate will be essential.

Wage Standards and Interdependence of Wages in the Labor Market

Marvin H. Kosters

Summary

Current anti-inflation policies include an effort to use wage and price standards to limit increases in costs. Since labor costs account for the predominant share of total costs, the influence of standards is strongly contingent on how labor costs are affected by the wage standard.

Unless controls are applied with a stringency and rigidity that would lead to shortages and serious disruption of efficiency, the course of inflation depends more importantly on the economic context in which wage-price standards are employed—particularly aggregate demand conditions—than on marginal differences that may result from variations in the design and implementation of such standards. Similarly, the effects of wage standards on labor costs and inflation should be considered in the context of forces influencing wage behavior in the labor market.

The impact of a wage standard on union wage settlements is frequently considered important because of their possible pattern-setting influence on other wages and because wage trends for the future are set under multiyear contracts. Differences in wage-setting arrangements between union and nonunion situations are accompanied by differences in the way the wage standard is applied. One effect of these differences in the treatment of pay increases under the wage standard is that the standard is less stringently applied to wage settlements negotiated by unions than to wage increases for most other workers.

The potential significance of these differences in the application of the wage standard for labor cost increases throughout the economy can be assessed by examination of forces influencing wage increases in the labor market. Under one view of labor market adjustment processes, wage increases negotiated by major unions are seen as establishing a pattern to which other wages in the economy tend to conform. That is, patterns established by major union settlements are widely imitated by comparable wage increases in other, less organized sectors of the economy. An alternative view is that one of the bargaining goals of major unions is to obtain a target wage premium relative to other wages in the economy. That is, wage-setting under collective bargaining is characterized in part by an effort to establish and maintain equilibrium wage differentials in comparison with wages in the less organized and nonunion sectors of the economy.

The contribution to smaller average wage increases throughout the economy that could be made by restraining major union wage settlements depends on which interpretation of wage behavior better characterizes the channels through which interdependence between wages in different sectors of the economy exert an influence in the labor market. The evidence on the effects of relative wage relationships supports the view that wage increases in the more highly organized sectors of the economy are influenced by their relation to wages in other sectors. However, the view that wage settlements in highly organized industries exert an important pattern-setting influence on wages in other sectors is not supported by the evidence.

According to this evidence, wage increases for the majority of workers who are outside the more highly organized sectors of the economy would not be significantly affected by the extent to which the wage standard actually contributes to reducing the size of wage increases negotiated by major unions. The effects on average wage increases of more stringent application of the wage standard to pay increases under major union settlements, if this could be achieved, would apparently be limited largely to the direct effects on wages under the labor contracts involved.

Introduction

Inflation rose to the top of the economic policy agenda during 1978 by virtue of its acceleration during the year as well as its persistence since the late 1960s. By the end of the year, the consumer price index had more than doubled since 1967, and rates of price increase were rising toward a third cyclical peak since that time. Moreover, a new, higher inflation plateau was viewed as a possibility because of the many multiyear collective bargaining agreements scheduled for negotiation in 1979 and 1980.

The policies that were developed to deal with this surge in inflation included monetary and fiscal policies to reduce aggregate demand growth and wage and price standards. Aggregate demand restraint is generally regarded as an indispensable element in an anti-inflation strategy, but the wage-price standards are viewed by the administration as an important complement to demand restraint. There are various viewpoints from which the possible complementary contribution of wage-price standards could be assessed, such as their general stringency, methods for inducing compliance, and their potential for adverse effects on productivity or supply. Wage-price standards are only one element in the complex of market forces and institutional arrangements that influence wage and price behavior, however, and the process through which they might exert an influence in this context is a more fundamental issue.

Wage-price standards are intended to contribute to reduced inflation by reducing the push of costs instead of, or as a complement to, reducing the pull of demand. Because labor costs bulk so large, standards would impinge on only a small fraction of costs if they were not applied to wage increases. With the exception of "low" wages, wage standards are in principle usually extended to wage increases throughout the economy. Differences in wage-setting arrangements between union and nonunion situations, however, lead to differences in the way wage standards are applied to collective bargaining situations. These differences are usually taken into account by giving precedence to contractual claims and formal arrangements, as well as by introducing sufficient flexibility to deal with the practical realities of avoiding disruptive work stoppages.

The pattern of response to current market conditions of wages negotiated under collective bargaining agreements differs from that of nonunion wages, in part because union wage adjustments are usually established at less frequent intervals. These differences in wage behavior are often a source of the rationale for standards. Restraint of wage increases under multiyear labor contracts is frequently sought because these wage increases are believed to establish patterns that might induce comparable wage increases for other workers while the contracts are in force. This element in the rationale for wage standards is usually belied to some extent, however, by their design and administration.

Although the effects of wage standards on overall wage behavior may seem to be compromised by differences in treatment for different wage-setting arrangements, the consequences for average wage increases depend on the influence exerted by union wages on wage behavior elsewhere in the economy. Are wage increases outside the major union sectors strongly influenced by how their wages compare with wages negotiated by major unions? Or are wage increases negotiated by major unions instead strongly influenced by how their wages compare with other wages in the economy? According to the evidence presented here, the latter influence is important while the former is negligible. That is, imitation by less unionized workers of pattern-setting wages negotiated in the more unionized sectors of the economy apparently exerts much less influence in the labor market than pressures for establishment and maintenance of wage differentials in the more unionized sectors relative to wages in the less unionized sectors. Consequently, average wage increases in the economy would not appear to be critically affected by differential application of the standards to wage increases negotiated under collective bargaining agreements, and the impact of more stringent application of the wage standard to union situations would be limited mainly to its effects on wages in the unionized sectors of the economy.

Recent Wage Developments

The information presented in Table 1 shows developments in a number of wage series during the past ten years, which include essentially two complete business cycles. The wage series were chosen to show differences in wage behavior over these cycles between more highly organized and less unionized sectors.

Measures of wage changes for the broader averages show rises in the rate of wage increase toward cyclical peaks in 1974 and again in 1978. They also show lower average rates of wage increase from 1975 to 1977 than in 1974, and less erratic annual average rates of wage increase during this period than from 1970 to 1973. Examination of the data on wage changes by extent of unionism reveals a tendency for smaller wage increases for nonunion workers and workers in less unionized industries during periods of relatively higher unemployment and smaller price increases. This tendency is particularly evident in the period from 1975 through 1977. For workers in the more highly organized sectors, however, the slowdown in wage increases after 1974 was quite small, and wage increases were larger in 1971 and 1972 than before the 1970 recession.

Wages of workers covered by collective bargaining agreements could be expected to respond less quickly to changes in economic conditions because the agreements often extend over more than a year. The timing of expiration of agreements, of course, influences

TABLE 1

UNEMPLOYMENT, CHANGES IN PRICES, AND SELECTED WAGE SERIES,
1969–1978
(annual percentage change, except for unemployment rate)

Item	1969	1970	1971	1972	1973	1974	1975	1976	1977	1978
Unemployment rate	3.5	4.9	5.9	5.6	4.9	5.6	8.5	7.7	7.0	6.0
Consumer price index[a]	6.1	5.5	3.4	3.4	8.8	12.2	7.0	4.8	6.8	9.0
Average hourly earnings index[b]	6.7	5.6	6.9	7.7	6.6	8.3	6.2	7.6	7.7	8.2[c]
Combined industry categories[b,d]	6.6	5.9	7.0	7.5	6.4	9.1	8.0	7.5	7.8	8.2[c]
Extent of unionism[b,d]										
Construction	9.8	8.7	8.0	6.8	5.1	7.8	5.0	6.6	4.2	6.4[c]
High union	5.5	5.1	8.8	9.4	6.9	10.2	10.1	8.0	9.8	9.0[c]
Medium union	6.1	5.4	6.5	7.1	6.4	9.3	8.4	8.2	8.1	8.3[c]
Low union	6.5	5.6	5.3	6.2	6.7	9.2	7.1	6.7	7.7	8.2[c]
Effective wage adjustments										
Major collective bargaining agreements	6.5	8.8	9.2	6.6	7.0	9.4	8.7	8.1	8.0	8.2
Manufacturing										
Union establishments[e]	5.3	6.4	7.1	5.4	6.4	8.7	8.1	7.8	7.7	N.A.
Nonunion establishments[e]	4.6	4.7	4.0	4.4	6.0	7.7	5.9	6.1	6.0	N.A.
Labor cost index										
Union[b]	N.A.	N.A.	N.A.	N.A.	N.A.	N.A.	N.A.	8.1	7.6	8.0
Nonunion[b]	N.A.	N.A.	N.A.	N.A.	N.A.	N.A.	N.A.	6.8	6.6	7.6

N.A.: Not available.

[a] December to December percentage changes.

[b] Fourth quarter to fourth quarter percentage changes.

[c] Computed from second quarter of 1977 to second quarter of 1978 because industry categories were regrouped for subsequent data.

[d] Index based on industries for which average hourly earnings data were available since 1947. For detailed description of the categories for the extent of unionism, see Table 2.

[e] Percentage increase during the year.

SOURCE: Bureau of Labor Statistics.

the pattern of wage increases for unionized workers and, consequently, for the broader index as well. The behavior of construction
wages is somewhat eccentric in relation to business cycles during this
period, apparently because construction wages have reflected developments within the construction sector more closely than overall
economic and labor market conditions.[1] The data for wages of union
workers and workers in the more highly organized industries show,
in general, only a weak tendency toward slower rates of increase
during the periods between cyclical. peaks. These differences in
behavior between more unionized and less unionized sectors have
resulted in unusually high relative wages for the more unionized
sectors by 1978.

Wage Standards

Standards for wage and price behavior have usually had the prox-
imate aim of restraining wage increases.[2] Standards for prices have
typically been structured to maintain some relationship between cost
increases and price increases so that if labor cost increases are reduced
by the wage standard, this reduction would be reflected by correspondingly smaller price increases. Thus, while the overall objective
of wage-price standards is stabilization of prices, lower price inflation
can be achieved only if there is a parallel reduction in labor cost
increases—a reduction to which the wage standard is intended to
contribute.

How the wage standard is intended to influence the size of wage
increases presumably depends on the diagnosis of the problem of
adjustment in the size of wage increases in response to changes in
overall market conditions. If average wage increases would otherwise adjust only sluggishly to current conditions in the labor market,
for example, introduction of a wage standard could be viewed as an
effort to bring about more rapid adjustment to restrictive aggregate
demand policies. If expectations about inflation trends, and policies
that support them, contribute to sluggish adjustment when government
policies turn toward restraint, establishment of wage-price standards

---

[1] For a discussion of developments in construction activity and in the construction
labor market during this period, see Marvin H. Kosters, "Wage and Price Behavior: Prospects and Policies," in William Fellner, ed., *Contemporary Economic
Problems 1977* (Washington, D.C.: American Enterprise Institute, 1977),
pp. 196-98.

[2] This is a common feature of incomes policy proposals, including tax-based
incomes policies. See, for example, Arthur M. Okun and George L. Perry, eds.,
Curing Chronic Inflation (Washington, D.C.: Brookings Institution, 1978).

could be viewed as providing explicit information about wage and price trends that would be consistent with the market conditions which government intended to bring about through policy restraint. For diagnoses of the problem along these lines, the main emphasis would be placed on the contribution that standards could make to better information on future market conditions, and their influence would depend strongly on the credibility of such information. The role of wage-price policies in this context would be to foster maintenance of equilibrium in labor and product markets by encouraging more rapid adjustment to anti-inflationary aggregate demand policies.

The role of wage-price standards could alternatively be considered in terms of how they might deal with disequilibrium. Under a surge in demand that might be regarded as temporary and subject to reversal (for example, unexpectedly buoyant demand near a cyclical peak or a wartime emergency), wage and price standards could be invoked in an effort to limit the rise in the price level. The temporary, short-term market disequilibrium induced by the standards could be accepted as the price paid in an attempt to mitigate the costs of adjustment that would be entailed by higher inflation and subsequent policies to contain it.

The use of wage-price standards on a continuing basis as a tool to restrain inflation, however, would appear to reflect a diagnosis in which more persistent disequilibrium is envisaged, or in which inducing disequilibrium to offset other persistent forces in the market environment is an objective. Establishing wage-price standards with a view to achieving higher employment and output levels than could otherwise be maintained could be regarded as an attempt to induce and maintain tighter labor markets and lower unemployment than would be consistent with equilibrium. Efforts to attain higher resource utilization by pursuing policies that, at least implicitly and in retrospect, produced temporary disequilibrium of this kind have turned out to be self-defeating.

The use of wage-price standards on a continuing basis could also be viewed as an effort to offset persistent departures from fully efficient wage and price patterns—departures that may be attributable to institutional or other factors that prevent or inhibit timely adjustment to efficient patterns. In some instances, for example, market power exerted in highly organized sectors of the economy could imply a large equilibrium wage differential. Such a result could emerge and persist in regulated industries where domestic competition is limited by entry restrictions or in sectors where protection from import competition can be obtained to avert serious domestic job losses in response to large wage differentials. The ability to negotiate large wage premiums may also create strains within the labor market because of differences in wages for otherwise similar work in other sectors. If, for whatever reasons, policies cannot be devised and implemented to address problems of this type directly by introducing more competition, wage and price standards could be employed in an effort to offset the undesirable effects of insufficient competition. In the absence of fundamental changes to introduce additional competition, of course, the pressures against which wage standards would be contending could be formidable.

The rationale for the use of wage-price standards is usually shaped by the circumstances under which they are introduced, and the manner in which a wage standard is intended to influence wage increases is usually not articulated with much precision. Nevertheless, it is possible to distinguish between different strategies or mechanisms through which wage standards might influence overall wage trends, and to examine the implications of different conceptual approaches in light of evidence on wage behavior. The main issue that will be discussed is the relationship between union wage settlements and overall wage trends.

Wage standards might be considered to influence overall wage trends by directly reducing the size of major union wage settlements. If settlements under major collective bargaining agreements are viewed as setting patterns that exert an important influence on other wages in the economy, restraint of major union settlements could be expected to be translated into smaller wage increases in other sectors of the economy. The main alternative way in which wage standards might influence overall wage trends is through a broad and general effect on wage increases in the economy, with the standards initially reducing the size of wage increases chiefly in small union situations and for nonunion workers. If union bargaining goals include achieving and maintaining some wage differential (or wage premium) between union wages and other wages in the economy, a strategy oriented toward reducing wage increases in less organized sectors of the economy could over time be expected to lead to correspondingly smaller union wage settlements. These alternative strategies should be distinguished from a strategy aimed at achieving proportionate reductions in the size of wage increases for all sectors. Other possible strategies include, for example, an effort to truncate the high end of the distribution of wage settlements to avoid provocatively large settlements that might lead to imitation or leap-frogging, but more subtle strategies of this type are beyond the scope of this discussion.

The first strategy to be considered is that of establishing a wage standard intended to influence overall wage behavior primarily through its direct influence on wage settlements under major collective bargaining agreements. This strategy might be inferred from public statements emphasizing the critical importance of these major settlements by those responsible for administering the program and from the emphasis on highly visible collective bargaining situations by the news media.[3] This interpretation of the strategy for wage standards is also suggested by recent wage behavior and changes in relative wage positions. The slowdown in average wage increases since the recession of 1974–1975 was heavily concentrated in sectors not covered by major multiyear labor contracts, bringing wages established by many of these contracts to relatively high levels. Moreover, the timing of the announcement of the standards in late 1978 suggests that they were established to influence the new round of major collective bargaining settlements.

The design of the present standards, however, suggests that they should not be interpreted as oriented primarily toward directly influencing major collective bargaining settlements. First, the standard provides exceptions for situations involving skill shortages, tandem relationships, and low-wage workers. Major unions are in a better position to document and present their claims for such exceptions in a bureaucratic administrative environment than are workers in most other groups. Second, workers under major union agreements typically have larger packages of fringe benefits than do other workers, and in certain cases costs of health and pension plans are given more favorable treatment under the standard than are wage costs. Third, the pay standard's treatment of payments under cost-of-living escalator provisions favors workers under major multiyear labor contracts where formal provisions are most prevalent. Compliance with the pay standard is measured on the basis of a 6 percent rate of increase in consumer prices, even though recent rates of price increase have been considerably larger, and larger price increases realized in the future would bring larger wage increases without

---

[3] For example, the director of the Council on Wage and Price Stability, Barry Bosworth, has said: "We just cannot afford to go through another big round of major labor contracts calling for annual wage increases near 10 percent. What we are trying to do is reduce these settlements down to the range of what other workers have been getting, or about 7 percent annually." (Testimony of Barry P. Bosworth before the House Committee on Banking, Finance, and Urban Affairs, Subcommittee on Economic Stabilization, June 21, 1978.)

affecting compliance with the standard. Finally, pay increases under the terms of existing contracts are considered in compliance with the standard. These features of the pay standard suggest that it was not designed to reduce overall wage increases primarily through its influence on the size of major union settlements.

The main alternative interpretation of the channel through which a wage standard might operate to reduce wage increases is that its effects on average wage increases would come primarily through the direct influence of the standard on wage increases in the less organized and nonunion sectors. Wage increases for the great majority of workers in the economy are established under decisions outside the major union sectors. Thus, if smaller wage increases for this large share of the work force are induced by the wage standard, the effect on average wage increases in the economy could be significant, and a corresponding effect on prices might be realized if price increases are strongly conditional on labor cost increases in the short term.

It might be more realistic to expect employers with relatively small numbers of workers or nonunion workers to comply with the wage standard, to the extent that it provides some temporary assurance that other firms would not offer wage increases in excess of the standard to attract valuable employees. Cooperation in compliance with the standard would be likely to break down over time, of course, if the potential market rewards from offering larger wage increases to retain or attract productive employees became important. Collusion, in this case to keep down wage increases for a broad category of workers, is always difficult to enforce and tends to break down over time. To the extent that a slowdown of wage increases in the less organized sectors of the economy was induced by the wage standard, a corresponding slowdown in wage increases under major union settlements could be expected to emerge if pressures toward equilibrium wage differentials in the labor market play a significant role in wage-setting in highly organized sectors. Such a sequence of wage and price developments would, of course, be contingent on sufficiently restrained aggregate demand policies to avoid pulling up prices at rates more rapid than would be consistent with short-term labor cost increases.

There is little basis for judging which of these two alternative strategies is more appropriate as an interpretation of the intended effects of the wage standard. Analysis of wage behavior can, however, provide some insight into factors that have influenced wage increases in the past. If the wage standard, by design or default, has little influence on the size of major multiyear collective bargaining settlements, for example, is the pattern-setting influence of these settlements on other wages likely to be important? Or, alternatively, are union wages significantly influenced by wages in less organized sectors? These questions are addressed by examining evidence on the responsiveness of wage increases to labor market conditions and relative wage patterns.

Factors Influencing Wage Changes

Analyses of the determinants of wage increases have identified factors such as slack in the economy (usually as measured in terms of unemployment rates) and rates of price increase (which, along with wage increases, are also affected by slack) as significantly influencing rates of wage increase. In this analysis short-term changes in rates of wage increase are examined in terms of the effects of changes in unemployment, changes in rates of price increase, and relationships among wages in major sectors of the economy. The main ideas used in setting the framework for the analysis are that short-term changes in the rate of wage increase can be expected to be influenced by (1) the short-term strength of demand within the business cycle, (2) the level of the operating rate of the economy, and (3) relationships among wages in the economy, to the extent that pattern-setting or establishing equilibrium wage differentials are important.

The following expression incorporates these factors into a form changes in inflation.

$$\Delta \dot{W} = a + b(\Delta U) + c(\Delta \dot{P}) + dR + u$$

where $\Delta \dot{W}$ is a change in the rate of increase in wages, ΔU is a change in the unemployment rate, $\Delta \dot{P}$ is a change in the rate of increase in prices, and R is a measure of the wage level relative to that for a reference group.[4] The variables are defined for two-quarter spans, with changes in rates of increase for wages and prices measured

---

[4] The wage measure is computed from industry average hourly earnings data for industries classified by extent of unionism, with wage indexes formed by using the fixed weights from the Bureau of Labor Statistics average hourly earnings index of 1967. The unemployment rate is for males twenty-five to fifty-four years of age, and the consumer price index is used for computing the price variable. The relative wage measure is:

$$R = 1 + (ln\ W/W_r)_{t-2} - \overline{(ln\ W/W_r)},$$

where the last term is the average proportionate difference in wages relative to a reference group, r, for the period.

relative to their rates of increase during the immediately preceding two-quarter span. The relative wage measure is lagged two quarters.

The variables measuring changes in unemployment and in the rate of price change are intended to take into account general labor market conditions. The change in unemployment is viewed as an indicator of short-term changes in labor market demand during business cycles. The change in the rate of change in prices is viewed as an indicator of the effects of the operating rate of the economy or of economic slack, but its role deserves additional discussion.

In conventional economic models the amount of slack in the economy—as measured, for example, by an unemployment rate—is regarded as the major underlying influence on the tendency for inflation to accelerate or decelerate. This tendency for changes in the rate of price increase in response to slack normally is expected to become evident only after a lag. The change in the rate of price increase can therefore be viewed as an indicator of economic slack insofar as the effects of slack have been translated into price acceleration or deceleration. It must be recognized, however, that the rate of change in the rate of price increase not only is an indirect measure of slack, but also is contaminated by other influences. For example, actual changes in the rate of increase in prices should be viewed as reflecting cyclical changes in demand (ΔU in this equation) in addition to the effects of current and past levels of slack in the operating rate of the economy. Moreover, because the effects of a variety of short-term factors (such as the influence of weather on food prices) are also reflected in measures of short-term changes in rates of price increase, only a component of the variation in measured short-term price changes can be regarded as reflecting the effects of slack. For these reasons the effects of slack on changes in the rate of wage increase are greatly attenuated in estimates of the effects of short-term changes in inflation.

There are several elements in the rationale for using changes in the rate of inflation instead of a more direct measure of slack, such as an unemployment rate, in the analysis. From a statistical point of view, correlation among the independent variables is reduced. The length and form of time lags most appropriate for estimating the effects of slack on changes in rates of wage and price increase are uncertain and possibly not stable over time, although this problem is also applicable to the relation between changes in the rate of wage increase and in the rate of price increase. From an economic point of view, both the level of slack at which changes in the rate of wage and price increase are induced and the responsiveness of inflation to a given amount of slack are uncertain and may vary over time, in part because expectations of inflation and the credibility of efforts to restrain it are likely to be influenced by experience. Some of these problems are mitigated to some extent by focusing directly on changes in the rate of price increase as an indicator of the extent to which variation in slack has been translated into acceleration or deceleration of inflation.[5]

The main purpose of the unemployment and price variables is to take into account general conditions of demand in the economy and in the labor market in order to permit examination of the effects of wage differentials (or relative wages) on wage behavior in industry categories distinguished primarily by differences in extent of unionism. The industries included in different categories for the extent of unionism are described in Table 2. Relative wages, R, are used in the analysis as measures of the proportionate wage differential between wages for the extent-of-unionism category analyzed in the regression and wages for another category that serves as a reference group. The variable is defined so that, for example, a one percentage point change in the rate of wage increase, if continued for a year, would compensate for a one percentage point divergence of the variable from its average, with a trend in the ratio during the estimation period reflected in the constant term of the equation.

Wages in different sectors of the economy have not increased at precisely the same rates at all times, and as a result relative wages

---

[5] This interpretation of the role of the price variable is quite different from the usual interpretations of its role in regressions that examine the influence on wage increases of the *rate* of price increase. *Changes* in the rate of price increase obviously reflect many short-term factors. But they may also depend on whether the actual operating rate of the economy exceeds or falls short of the level of resource utilization consistent with no change in the rate of price increase. Changes in the rate of wage increase can in general be expected to show a more limited response to price increases that arise from sectoral demand conditions or temporary reductions in supply, particularly those that may be subject to reversal such as food price increases, than to price increases that reflect the pressure of aggregate demand on the overall production capacity of the economy. Consequently, I interpret the price coefficient as primarily reflecting the effects of this latter component of changes in the rate of price increase on changes in the rate of wage increase.

The framework for estimation used here is similar in many respects to that employed by Phillip Cagan in his adaptive expectations formulation of a model to examine the response of prices and wages to slack demand. Cagan, however, uses a variable for the level of unemployment in addition to a variable measuring the change in unemployment. See Phillip Cagan, "The Reduction in Inflation by Slack Demand," and the discussion by William Fellner, "The Core of the Controversy about Reducing Inflation: An Introductory Analysis," in William Fellner, ed., *Contemporary Economic Problems 1978* (Washington, D.C.: American Enterprise Institute, 1978).

TABLE 2

Construction (relative weight, 0.11)

Contract construction (15–17)

High union (relative weight, 0.25)

Metal mining (10)	Primary metal industries (33)
Bituminous coal (12)	Electrical equipment and supplies (36)
Ordnance and accessories (19)	Transportation equipment (37)
Paper and allied products (26)	Railroad transportation (4011)

Medium union (relative weight, 0.32)

Food and kindred products (20)	Petroleum refining (291)
Tobacco manufactures (21)	Rubber and plastics products (30)
Apparel and other	Leather and leather products (31)
textile products (23)	Stone, clay, and glass products (32)
Lumber and wood products (24)	Fabricated metal products (34)
Chemicals and allied products (28)	Machinery, except electrical (35)

Low union (relative weight, 0.33)

Textile mill products (22)	Miscellaneous manufacturing
Furniture and fixture (25)	industries (39)
Printing and publishing (27)	Wholesale trade (50)
Instruments and related	Retail general merchandise (53)
products (38)	Apparel and accessory stores (56)

NOTE: Numbers in parentheses after industries are Standard Industrial Classification (SIC) codes. Industries were placed into categories according to the following criteria: *High union:* All industries that are at least 75 percent unionized according to Bureau of Labor Statistics estimates, or are 50 to 75 percent unionized and at least 60 percent covered by major collective bargaining agreements (as indicated by the ratio of workers covered by major agreements to production worker employment). *Medium union:* Industries that are 25 to 75 percent unionized and 10 to 60 percent covered by major collective bargaining agreements. *Low union:* All industries that are 25 percent or less unionized or are 25 to 50 percent unionized and less than 10 percent covered by major collective bargaining agreements.

The industries used in the analyses were those for which average hourly earnings data were available throughout the period since 1947. Several major industries were excluded because information on average hourly earnings was available only since 1958 or 1964. The relative weights used for wage series for extent-of-unionism categories were taken from those used in the average hourly earnings index for 1967. The industries included in the analysis accounted for 53 percent of the total weights for the average hourly earnings index of 1967.

SOURCE: Information on unionization and coverage by major agreements is contained in Bureau of Labor Statistics, *Directory of National Unions and Employee Associations of 1973*, p. 81; and Douglas LeRoy, "Scheduled Wage Increases and Escalator Provisions in 1977," *Monthly Labor Review*, January 1977, p. 24.

among sectors vary over time. Sources of this variation include differences among sectors in the responsiveness of wage increases to general market conditions, as well as factors not explicitly taken into account in this analysis, such as the frequency of wage adjustments and the timing of wage negotiations. To see the implications for coefficient estimates of different channels through which relative wages influence wage behavior, consider the effects of a rise in wages in the high-union sector compared with their "normal" relationship with wages in the low-union sector. If wages in the high-union sector exert a strong pattern-setting influence on wages in other sectors, this rise in relative wages would be expected to produce a more rapid rate of wage increase in the low-union sector (which would tend to restore a "normal" relative wage relationship). In this case the relative wage coefficient in the regression for wage increases in the low-union sector would be statistically significant and relatively large (positive and in the range between zero and unity). A relatively small and nonsignificant coefficient, on the other hand, would be consistent with an absence of pattern-setting influence by the high-union sector. Conversely, for a regression examining wage increases in the high-union sector, a relatively large (negative) and statistically significant coefficient would be expected if the rise in relative wages led to a reduction in the size of wage increases in the high-union sector. A small and statistically insignificant coefficient, on the other hand, would imply an absence of influence on wage increases in the high-union sector of departures from "normal" relationships between high-union and low-union wages. The size and statistical significance of relative wage coefficient estimates in the different regressions, accordingly, provide evidence on the channels through which relative wage relationships exert an influence on wage behavior.

Econometric Estimates

The regression estimates, in general, show the expected pattern of signs. That is, cyclical expansion tends to accelerate wage increases, reduced slack (as reflected in a more rapid rate of price increase) also produces wage acceleration, and divergences in relative wages from average relationships produce a tendency for the rate of wage increase to change in the direction that would work toward elimination of such divergences. While the main focus of the analysis is on relative wage effects, estimates of unemployment and price effects will be discussed first. (The regression estimates are reported in detail in the appendix to this chapter, along with the precise definitions of the variables. Estimates from the regressions are reported in the text in Tables 3 and 4.)

The estimated coefficients for the change in unemployment are sufficiently large to be economically important and are, in general, statistically significant for regressions for the entire period from 1950 to 1978 (Table 3). Levels of statistical significance are generally lower for the last half of the period (vanishing for construction), although the sizes of the estimated coefficients are not sharply lower. In broad terms, the magnitudes of the estimates suggest a reduction in the rate of wage increase of three- to five-tenths of a percentage point for a one percentage point increase in the unemployment rate (for males aged twenty-five through fifty-four). While differences

TABLE 3

SELECTED ESTIMATES OF UNEMPLOYMENT AND PRICE COEFFICIENTS FROM WAGE REGRESSIONS

Industry Group Serving as the Dependent Variable, $\Delta \dot{W}$	Period for Estimation					
	1950.1 to 1978.2		1950.1 to 1964.4		1965.1 to 1978.2	
	ΔU	$\Delta \dot{P}$	ΔU	$\Delta \dot{P}$	ΔU	$\Delta \dot{P}$
1. Average hourly earnings index	-0.454	0.167	-0.334	0.163	-0.531	0.130
	(4.54)	(2.74)	(2.56)	(2.32)	(2.96)	(1.14)
2. Combined industry groups	-0.422	0.190	-0.467	0.217	-0.244	0.111
	(4.43)	(3.26)	(4.37)	(3.58)	(1.29)	(0.92)
3. Construction	-0.251	0.293	-0.337	0.342	0.012	0.138
	(1.54)	(2.98)	(2.22)	(3.64)	(0.03)	(0.55)
4. High union	-0.546	0.168	-0.619	0.178	-0.365	0.090
	(3.20)	(1.53)	(2.83)	(1.35)	(1.22)	(0.44)
5. Medium union	-0.481	0.096	-0.353	0.243	-0.509	0.0003
	(4.70)	(1.57)	(3.30)	(3.36)	(2.32)	(0.002)
6. Low union	-0.328	0.257	-0.358	0.285	-0.293	0.182
	(3.86)	(4.58)	(4.06)	(5.28)	(1.56)	(1.44)

NOTE: These coefficients for the last four regressions were estimated in equations that include a measure of relative wages in addition to these variables. The low-union sector serves as the reference group except for regression 6, in which the change in the rate of increase in low-union wages is the dependent variable, and the high-union category serves as the reference group. The numbers in parentheses are absolute values of t statistics. (See appendix to this chapter for additional detail.)

TABLE 4

ESTIMATED EFFECTS OF RELATIVE WAGES ON CHANGES IN RATES OF WAGE
INCREASE, FOR ESTIMATION PERIOD 1950.1 TO 1978.2

Industry Group for Which Changes in Rate of Wage Increase are Estimated	Reference Group with Which Wages Are Compared for Estimating Effects of Relative Wages on Changes in Rate of Wage Increase		
Sector	Construction	High union	Medium union	Low union

Sector	Construction	High union	Medium union	Low union
Coefficient estimates				
Construction	—	−0.030	−0.020	−0.024
		(1.18)	(0.95)	(1.13)
High union	0.050	—	−0.100	−0.079
	(1.93)*		(1.76)*	(1.94)*
Medium union	0.016	0.006	—	−0.206
	(0.96)	(0.14)		(2.63)*
Low union	0.010	0.010	0.006	—
	(0.91)	(0.52)	(0.12)	
Annualized estimates of effects				
Construction	—	−0.06	−0.04	−0.05
High union	0.10*	—	−0.21*	−0.16*
Medium union	0.03	0.01	—	−0.45*
Low union	0.02	0.02	0.01	—

NOTE: The estimates reported in the table show the response of wage increases in the sector designated on the left to the proportionate difference from the "normal" relationship between wages in the sector designated at the top of the table and wages in the sector used as the dependent variable (designated on the left). Thus the rows indicate the effects of different relative wage relationships on wage increases for the sector designated on the left, and the columns indicate the effects of relative wages on wage increases in each of the sectors designated on the left, with wages in the sector designated for each column as the reference point for the relative wage comparison.

The larger and more significant coefficients appear in the top half of the table and to the right of the diagonal. The asterisks (*) indicate sufficient statistical significance for reasonable confidence that the coefficients differ significantly from zero; *t* statistics in parentheses.

among industry categories are not pronounced, the estimated response to unemployment changes is usually larger for more unionized than for the low-union industries (again, with construction a special case). According to these estimates, cyclical changes in labor market demand have a systematic and significant influence on rates of wage change.

The signs of the coefficients for changes in the rate of price change reported here are uniformly positive. However, their magnitude is in general quite small, and there is considerable variation in size among industry groups. Estimates frequently fall short of statistical significance, particularly for the period from 1965 to 1978. The size of the estimates ranges from about three-tenths to essentially zero. Taken at face value, the estimates at the top end of the range indicate that a one percentage point change in the rate of inflation is translated into three-tenths of a percentage point change in the rate of wage increase in the same direction.

The size and statistical significance of the estimated price coefficients drop sharply for the last part of the period compared with the earlier years. Smaller effects are estimated for both halves of the period for the high-union than for the low-union industries, but size and statistical significance are reduced in both cases for the later years. Thus, insofar as the price coefficients can be interpreted as reflecting the effects of economic slack, these estimates do not support the view that there has been a reduction in responsiveness to slack stemming primarily from a change in wage behavior in highly organized industries.

Both the magnitude of these price coefficients and the decline in their size in the latter part of the period should be interpreted cautiously as estimates of the effects of slack on changes in the rate of wage increase. Only a fraction of the variability in rates of price increase can be regarded as attributable to the influence of slack, as noted earlier, because short-term variability reflects transitory influences from other sources, such as food and energy price increases, as well as short-term demand changes within the business cycle. More variability from transitory sources of this kind during the latter part of the period could be expected to reduce confidence in short-term changes in inflation as indications that such a trend might persist; in addition, it could be expected to reduce the speed of adjustment to short-term changes in inflation. Since wages have moved up roughly in parallel with prices over reasonably long periods, the main conclusion that can be drawn from the magnitude of the price coefficients and the reduction in their size during the latter part of the period is that the rate of increase in wages can be reduced only through maintaining policies of restraint long enough to generate confidence that lower inflation is a realistic expectation, because short-term changes in the rate of inflation are increasingly discounted in the wage-setting process.

Estimates of the effects of relative wages (wages in the sector analyzed relative to wages for various reference groups) on changes in the rate of increase in wages are presented in Table 4, along with annualized estimates of these effects. The estimates reported in the table are based on regressions for the entire period from 1950 to 1978. While there are differences in the size and statistical significance of the estimates for the two subperiods (1950–1964 and 1965–1978), the pattern of primary interest for this discussion is shown by all the estimates.

In general, the estimates show more sensitivity of wages in highly unionized sectors to wages in less unionized sectors than of wages in less unionized sectors to wages in more highly unionized sectors. That is, coefficients of the relative wage variable tend to be larger and are more likely to be significant when wages for less unionized workers serve as the reference group for analysis of wages of more unionized workers than when this relationship is reversed. In terms of the table, larger, more significant coefficients appear only in the top half and to the right of the diagonal, with smaller and less significant coefficients in the bottom half and to the left of the diagonal. This pattern also prevails for estimates for both subperiods (see appendix below).

The order of magnitude of the estimates of relative wage effects can be illustrated by considering the annualized estimates reported in the bottom panel of Table 4. These estimates show, for example, that if wages in the medium-union sector relative to wages in the low-union sector were one percentage point below their "normal" ratio, nearly half (0.45 percentage points) of the discrepancy would be restored during one year by more rapid wage increases in the medium-union sector. The estimate of the corresponding fraction for the high-union sector (with low-union wages again used as a reference point) is 0.16 percentage points. In contrast to these results, when the effect of relative wages on the rate of increase in low-union wages is estimated using high- and medium-union wages as reference points, low-union wages show virtually no response. (The annualized estimates are 0.02 and 0.01, respectively, and they do not differ statistically from zero.)

To summarize the implications of these examples, the rate of increase of wages in the high- and medium-union sectors is apparently influenced by how their wages compare with wages in the low-union sector. For wages of workers in the low-union sector, on the other hand, relative wages (with high- or medium-union wages used as a reference point) have virtually no influence on their rate of wage increase after the influence of general labor market conditions is taken into account.[6]

Wage settlements by major unions have frequently been viewed as having implications for inflation that extend far beyond their effects on wages of workers covered by the settlements. It is thought that major union settlements set a pattern to which wages elsewhere in the economy tend to adjust. The evidence presented here does not support this view. The evidence instead lends support to the view that wage increases in the less organized and nonunion sectors are influenced primarily by market conditions, but that wage differentials do have an influence on wage-setting in the more unionized sectors. While in these respects the evidence contradicts much of the conventional wisdom on this subject, it is consistent with evidence from some other studies.[7]

Conclusions

The rise in inflation during 1978 led to anti-inflation policies that included the establishment of standards for wage and price behavior. The standards were introduced at a time when wages in the union sectors were relatively high and a new round of collective bargaining was getting underway for major unions negotiating multiyear contracts. Those responsible for administering the standards placed considerable emphasis on the pattern-setting importance of major union wage negotiations.

---

[6] The pattern of signs in Table 4, negative above the diagonal and vice versa, is consistent with a tendency for "normal" proportionate relationships to be restored. The difference in signs results from the fact that for the estimates above the diagonal, relative wages are based on reference groups with lower wage levels so that a positive discrepancy for the relative wage variable implies a slowdown in the rate of wage increase, with these relationships reversed for estimates below the diagonal.

[7] In an analysis of union and nonunion wage increases in manufacturing, Robert Flanagan found union wage increases significantly influenced by proportionate differences in union and nonunion wages, but no corresponding significant influence for nonunion wages. See Robert J. Flanagan, "Wage Interdependence in Unionized Labor Markets," *Brookings Papers on Economic Activity*, no. 3 (Washington, D.C.: Brookings Institution, 1976), pp. 635-73. In his analysis of wage increases negotiated in a sample of union contracts, Daniel Mitchell found significant relative wage effects. See Daniel J. B. Mitchell, "Union Wage Determination: Policy Implications and Outlook," *Brookings Papers on Economic Activity*, no. 3 (Washington, D.C.: Brookings Institution, 1978), pp. 537-82. See also George E. Johnson, "The Determination of Wages in Union and Nonunion Sectors," *British Journal of Industrial Relations*, vol. 15, no. 2 (July 1977), pp. 211-25.

The wage standard is likely to have little direct effect on the size of major union settlements, in part because the standard is designed and administered so that it impinges less strongly on pay increases for major unions than for most other workers. The commonly held view that wages in the more highly organized sectors of the economy exert an important pattern-setting influence on wages in other sectors is not supported, however, by evidence on the effects of labor market conditions and of relative wages on rates of wage increase. Instead, rates of wage increase in the less organized sectors of the economy are apparently influenced mainly by labor market conditions, while wages in the less organized sectors exert some influence on wage increases in the more highly organized sectors. Consequently, a failure of the wage standard to influence the size of wage settlements negotiated by major unions is likely to have little effect on average wage trends or inflation prospects. Moreover, modification of their design so that they would bear more heavily on major union situations would not change this judgment, even if securing compliance with standards modified in this manner were in practice feasible.

Appendix

In the three tables in this appendix, regression estimates are reported for the period 1950.1 to 1978.2, and for two subperiods, 1950.1 to 1964.4 and 1965.1 to 1978.2. For the first subperiod the annual rate of increase in the consumer price index averaged 1.6 percent and for the second subperiod, 5.5 percent.

The basic data used to compute the variables for the regressions were quarterly, seasonally adjusted data on average hourly earnings by industry, the unemployment rate for males twenty-five through fifty-four years of age, and the consumer price index. The average hourly earnings data were not adjusted for overtime, but wage indexes for the extent-of-unionism categories were constructed using fixed weights (from the 1967 Bureau of Labor Statistics average hourly earnings index) for the industries included in each category.

The quarterly observations for each of the variables were defined as follows:

$$\Delta \dot{W} = \dot{W}_t - \dot{W}_{t-2} = \frac{W_{t-2} - W_t}{W_{t-2}} - \frac{W_{t-4} - W_{t-2}}{W_{t-4}}$$

$$\Delta U = U_t - U_{t-2}$$

$$\Delta \dot{P} = \dot{P}_t - \dot{P}_{t-2} = \frac{P_{t-2} - P_t}{P_{t-2}} - \frac{P_{t-4} - P_{t-2}}{P_{t-4}}$$

$$R = 1 + (lnW/W_r)_{t-2} - \overline{(lnW/W_r)}$$

TABLE 5

ESTIMATES OF EFFECTS ON THE RATE OF WAGE CHANGE OF CHANGES IN UNEMPLOYMENT AND IN THE RATE OF PRICE INCREASE AND OF RELATIVE WAGES

(estimation period 1950.1 to 1978.2; 114 observations)

Dependent Variable $\Delta\dot{W}$	Independent Variables			ρ^a	Durbin-Watson Statistic	Reference Group for R
	ΔU	$\Delta\dot{P}$	R			
1. Average hourly earnings index	−0.454 (4.54)	0.167 (2.74)	—	0.411 (4.69)	1.56	—
2. Combined industry groups	−0.422 (4.43)	0.190 (3.26)	—	0.396 (4.52)	1.66	—
3. Construction	−0.251 (1.54)	0.293 (2.98)	−0.024 (1.13)	0.359 (3.85)	1.61	Low union
4. High union	−0.546 (3.20)	0.168 (1.53)	−0.079 (1.94)	0.315 (3.34)	1.72	Low union
5. Medium union	−0.481 (4.70)	0.096 (1.57)	−0.206 (2.63)	0.526 (6.23)	1.57	Low union
6. Low union	−0.328 (3.86)	0.257 (4.58)	0.010 (0.52)	0.284 (3.00)	1.70	High union
7. Construction	−0.255 (1.56)	0.294 (2.98)	−0.020 (0.95)	0.358 (3.85)	1.61	Medium union

8. High union	−0.555 (3.21)	0.169 (1.53)	−0.100 (1.76)	0.332 (3.50)	1.72	Medium union
9. Medium union	−0.480 (4.56)	0.095 (1.51)	0.006 (0.14)	0.516 (6.13)	1.55	High union
10. Low union	−0.327 (3.85)	0.257 (4.57)	0.006 (0.12)	0.285 (2.99)	1.70	Medium union
11. Construction	−0.250 (1.53)	0.293 (2.99)	−0.030 (1.18)	0.361 (3.89)	1.61	High union
12. High union	−0.586 (3.43)	0.169 (1.54)	0.050 (1.93)	0.302 (3.20)	1.72	Construction
13. Medium union	−0.487 (4.64)	0.096 (1.53)	0.016 (0.96)	0.514 (6.09)	1.55	Construction
14. Low union	−0.336 (3.94)	0.256 (4.59)	0.010 (0.91)	0.282 (2.98)	1.70	Construction

[a] Autocorrelation coefficient.

TABLE 6

ESTIMATES OF EFFECTS ON THE RATE OF WAGE CHANGE OF CHANGES IN
UNEMPLOYMENT AND IN THE RATE OF PRICE INCREASE
AND OF RELATIVE WAGES

(estimation period 1950.1 to 1964.4; 60 observations)

Dependent Variable $\Delta\dot{W}$	Independent Variables			ρ	Durbin-Watson Statistic	Reference Group for R
	ΔU	$\Delta\dot{P}$	R			
1. Average hourly earnings index	−0.334 (2.56)	0.163 (2.32)	—	0.565 (4.81)	1.14	—
2. Combined industry groups	−0.467 (4.37)	0.217 (3.58)	—	0.502 (4.28)	1.48	—
3. Construction	−0.337 (2.22)	0.342 (3.64)	−0.066 (1.55)	0.360 (2.81)	1.60	Low union
4. High union	−0.619 (2.83)	0.178 (1.35)	−0.092 (1.23)	0.368 (2.80)	1.64	Low union
5. Medium union[a]	−0.353 (3.30)	0.243 (3.36)	−0.142 (1.97)	—	.862	Low union
6. Low union	−0.358 (4.06)	0.285 (5.28)	0.009 (0.30)	0.436 (3.36)	1.57	High union
7. Construction	−0.351 (2.32)	0.340 (3.63)	−0.100 (1.69)	0.366 (2.84)	1.60	Medium union

8. High union	−0.671 (2.98)	0.157 (1.20)	−0.274 (1.86)	0.465 (3.48)	1.61	Medium union
9. Medium union	−0.448 (3.55)	0.128 (1.81)	0.015 (0.17)	0.613 (5.25)	1.33	High union
10. Low union	−0.363 (4.09)	0.285 (5.28)	0.033 (0.43)	0.442 (3.41)	1.56	Medium union
11. Construction	−0.380 (2.56)	0.341 (3.70)	−0.201 (2.09)	0.350 (2.70)	1.61	High union
12. High union	−0.681 (3.17)	0.198 (1.54)	0.422 (2.68)	0.476 (3.61)	1.62	Construction
13. Medium union	−0.449 (3.61)	0.128 (1.86)	0.073 (1.04)	0.650 (5.62)	1.31	Construction
14. Low union	−0.363 (4.16)	0.287 (5.35)	0.022 (0.84)	0.446 (3.44)	1.57	Construction

a The results reported for this regression do not include adjustment for first-order autocorrelation. When the autocorrelation adjustment was used, it led to an estimate for ρ of 0.977, a Durbin-Watson statistic of 1.58, and an unstable (large and negative) coefficient for R, although the unemployment and price coefficients were not greatly affected.

TABLE 7

ESTIMATES OF EFFECTS ON THE RATE OF WAGE CHANGE OF CHANGES IN UNEMPLOYMENT AND IN THE RATE OF PRICE INCREASE AND OF RELATIVE WAGES

(estimation period 1965.1 to 1978.2; 54 observations)

Dependent Variable $\Delta\dot{W}$	Independent Variables			ρ	Durbin-Watson Statistic	Reference Group for R
	ΔU	$\Delta\dot{P}$	R			
1. Average hourly earnings index	−0.531 (2.96)	0.130 (1.14)	—	0.230 (1.57)	1.79	—
2. Combined industry groups	−0.244 (1.29)	0.111 (0.92)	—	0.211 (1.42)	1.79	—
3. Construction	0.012 (0.03)	0.138 (0.55)	−0.112 (1.82)	0.343 (1.84)	1.63	Low union
4. High union	−0.365 (1.22)	0.090 (0.44)	−0.078 (1.58)	0.189 (1.30)	1.81	Low union
5. Medium union	−0.509 (2.32)	0.0003 (0.002)	−0.132 (1.33)	0.367 (2.51)	1.68	Low union
6. Low union	−0.293 (1.56)	0.182 (1.44)	0.010 (0.32)	0.200 (1.37)	1.76	High union
7. Construction	0.071 (0.16)	0.134 (0.53)	−0.103 (1.80)	0.331 (1.76)	1.65	Medium union

8. High union	−0.336 (1.13)	0.084 (0.41)	−0.117 (1.57)	0.196 (1.33)	1.81	Medium union
9. Medium union	−0.419 (1.95)	−0.004 (0.03)	−0.018 (0.34)	0.339 (2.26)	1.70	High union
10. Low union	−0.281 (1.45)	0.180 (1.43)	0.035 (0.41)	0.201 (1.37)	1.76	Medium union
11. Construction	0.088 (0.20)	0.132 (0.53)	−0.090 (1.78)	0.339 (1.83)	1.65	High union
12. High union	−0.428 (1.38)	0.082 (0.40)	0.067 (1.59)	0.200 (1.36)	1.81	Construction
13. Medium union	−0.455 (2.05)	−0.008 (0.06)	0.020 (0.58)	0.358 (2.40)	1.69	Construction
14. Low union	−0.314 (1.66)	0.179 (1.42)	0.006 (0.21)	0.205 (1.40)	1.76	Construction

where W and W_r are wage measures for higher-wage and lower-wage categories, respectively. One wage measure is for the extent-of-unionism category used as the dependent variable in the regression, while the other is for the extent-of-unionism category that serves as the reference group for examining relative wage effects.

The industries used in the regression analysis were those for which data on average hourly earnings were available throughout the period since 1947, and the criteria for assigning industries to extent-of-unionism categories are described in Table 2. The first regression in each table includes all the industries included in the average hourly earnings index, while the second regression, combined industry groups, includes only the industries in the various extent-of-unionism categories using the relative weights reported in Table 2. The regressions were estimated by using an iterative procedure to adjust for first-order autocorrelation in the residuals. Numbers in parentheses are absolute values of t statistics.

The Present Economic Malaise

Gottfried Haberler

Summary

In sharp contrast to the twenty years after World War I, the first quarter century after World War II was a period of unprecedented prosperity for the whole Western world. World trade grew by leaps and bounds, and the less developed countries participated fully in the world prosperity. The world recession of 1973–1975 has changed the euphoria and optimism of the 1960s to pessimism and gloom. Some speak of a new crisis of capitalism, and many fear a replay of the Great Depression.

The present malaise is astonishing: although the 1973–1975 recession was the longest and severest of the postwar recessions, it was definitely not a depression comparable to the Great Depression of the 1930s and earlier ones. Furthermore, the recovery since 1975, often described as sluggish and incomplete, has carried the U.S. economy to substantially full employment.

In 1945 it was not generally foreseen that the world was on the verge of a long period of great prosperity. Most Keynesian economists had accepted the hypothesis of secular stagnation and expected that deflation would be a serious problem in the postwar period, although Keynes had never fully committed himself to the secular stagnation theory and had become apprehensive of inflation as early as 1937. Actually there has been no deflation in the postwar period in the sense of either a declining price level or a negative monetary growth, although there have been mild recessions during which the rate of inflation declined but never became negative.

The rate of inflation has gone up from each cycle to the next. There have been many warning voices, but the influential Keynesian economists have belittled the dangers of inflation. As late as 1972 James Tobin called inflation a painless and efficient method of reconciling inconsistent claims on the national product.

The main cause of the economic malaise is the persistence of a seemingly intractable inflation and the coexistence of rising prices and high unemployment—stagflation. Three other reasons for the malaise are discussed: low productivity growth, inadequate productive private investment, and troubles in the international monetary area. These three developments can be traced to the same roots as the main cause of the malaise.

The highly inflationary character of the last recession was an unsettling phenomenon because it posed a nasty dilemma: easy monetary-fiscal policy to reduce unemployment accelerates inflation, while a tight money-fiscal policy to curb inflation increases unemployment. This policy dilemma has caused a feeling of helplessness and malaise. This paper tries to demonstrate that there is no crisis of capitalism, no malfunctioning of the market economy, but a crisis of government policies. The stagflation dilemma is the predictable consequence of faulty government policies.

Every inflation, including stagflation, is a monetary phenomenon in the sense that there has never been a significant inflation that has not been caused or accommodated by excessive monetary growth, and no inflation or stagflation can be stopped without monetary restraint. The longer it lasts the more intractable inflation becomes, because money illusion is eroded and inflationary expectations are sensitized. The widely held view that inflation can be stabilized at a level of, say, 5 percent or more is an illusion. Not every creeping inflation must become a trotting or galloping one, but after a while inflation loses its stimulating power and Keynesian policies become increasingly ineffective. A steady, fully anticipated inflation is a mirage, but the policy of reducing the rate of inflation in a very leisurely fashion over many years is not much better.

Monetarists stop at this point and say the only way to curb inflation is to reduce monetary growth and to accept transitional unemployment or a recession as the price for regaining stability. They are right that the price has to be paid and that the Keynesian prescription to overcome stagflation by more rapid monetary expansion plus an incomes policy in the sense of wage and price controls is not workable. But monetary-fiscal restraint is not sufficient for a politically acceptable and economically efficient policy of subduing inflation. The stagflation dilemma would never have become serious if government policies had not moved most Western economies so far *from the competitive ideal. In a truly competitive economy stag-flation at the present scale would be impossible, for under compe-tition wages and prices would decline under conditions of excess supply, not rise as they do now. If it were not for government interventions, the private sector, apart from public utilities, would be more competitive today than it was fifty years ago because rapid advances in transportation technology and the enormous growth of world trade have undermined monopoly positions. But government policies have made labor unions so powerful that even real wages have become very rigid downward, and a strong real wage push has developed. Many other pressure groups such as organized agri-culture are being accommodated by government policies. The general unwillingness to adjust to changing conditions and growing readiness to yield to special interest demands find clearest expression in a variety of import restrictions and direct subsidies to, or government takeover of, noncompetitive firms.*

Tight money could, nevertheless, check inflation, but it would create so much unemployment that it would be almost impossible to carry the anti-inflationary policy to a successful conclusion. Experts differ on how serious the situation is. But Keynesians and mone-tarists should be able to agree that macroeconomic policies will work more efficiently if the economy could be moved closer to the competi-tive ideal.

The sharp decline of productivity growth and the low level of productive private investment have contributed to the economic malaise. These are complex phenomena; but there can be no doubt that the enormous growth of the public sector, the sharp increase in government employment, and the exploding propensity to control and regulate the economy are to a large extent responsible. The low level of private sector investment is largely due to the growth of the public sector, to high marginal tax rates, double taxation of dividends, and the taxation of overestimated profits resulting from faulty ac-counting practices that fail to take account of inflation.

In a truly competitive economy, however, low productivity growth would not lead to inflation or unemployment because, given an appropriate monetary policy, the growth of wages and other money incomes would adjust to the low productivity growth. Only government policies that foster and tolerate union power and yield to other pressure groups make inflation or unemployment, or both, the inevitable consequence of lagging productivity growth and low investment.

Real or imagined troubles in the working of the international monetary system of managed floating contribute to the present malaise. The large U.S. trade deficit, despite the decline of the dollar, and the stubborn Japanese surplus are widely regarded as a malfunctioning of the system of floating exchange rates. Actually, the decline of the dollar and the U.S. trade deficit are due to the fact that since 1977 the United States has pursued more inflationary policies than Germany, Japan, and Switzerland, the three principal strong-currency countries. U.S. inflation declined from 12 percent in 1974 to under 6 percent in 1976, but then started to accelerate when the new administration shifted priority from fighting inflation to more rapid expansion. The three strong-currency countries, on the other hand, continued the fight against inflation. In Switzerland inflation was reduced to practically zero, in Germany to between 2 and 3 percent, and in Japan to 3.5 percent. The divergent monetary policies produced what is misleadingly called a "growth differential," that is, more rapid recovery from the recession in the United States than in the three strong-currency countries which accepted temporary slack as the price they had to pay for subduing inflation.

The dollar held its own until September 1977, when the growing inflation differential between the United States and the three strong-currency countries became unmistakable. The market realized that the currency of an inflationary country is bound to depreciate. The dollar is vulnerable to a loss of confidence because it is still the foremost reserve currency, and huge dollar balances held abroad are subject to diversification when the dollar is expected to decline.

In October 1978 the foreign exchange markets became jittery, and the administration was forced to shift gears from more rapid expansion to fighting inflation. On November 1, 1978, the "dollar rescue" operation was announced, promising a tighter monetary-fiscal policy and setting up a $30 billion fund of foreign currencies for interventions in foreign exchange markets. The dollar strengthened after November 1, 1978, and the foreign exchange market calmed down. The long-term success of the new policy will depend primarily on whether the Federal Reserve follows through with the policy of monetary restraint that it signaled by raising the discount rate on November 1, 1978. If the U.S. inflation rate shows no sign of abating soon, we must expect a resumption of the dollar's decline, probably not in a smooth, orderly fashion but in intermittent lurches accompanied by panics and disorderly market conditions.

There is no reason to become panicky about the trade deficit, which has sharply declined since the first quarter of 1978. By moder-

ating the inflation and the speed of the expansion, the trade deficit has lengthened the current business cycle upswing that has carried the economy to virtually full employment. This appraisal has been criticized on the ground that in 1977 the deflationary drag of the trade deficit would have materialized if it had not been deliberately offset by a government budget deficit. This criticism is analyzed below and shown to be invalid.

All this does not mean that the United States can or should go on indefinitely running a large trade deficit. It does mean, first, that the disappearance of the trade deficit will be an inflationary factor (which may be welcome in a recession, although it would reduce the anti-inflationary effect of the recession), and, second, that we should not ask for import restrictions. The 10 percent import surcharge recommended by some experts would be roughly equivalent to a 3 percent devaluation of the dollar. It makes no sense to deplore the inflationary effect of the dollar's depreciation, and then to turn around and call for a measure that would be equivalent to its further depreciation.

The conclusion is that the decline of the dollar, the trade deficit, and the turbulence in foreign exchange markets are not due to a malfunctioning of the system of floating exchange rates. Those developments are the consequence of mismanagement of national policies in major countries, too much inflation, and widely diverging inflation rates. The main responsibility for leading the world out of the present malaise rests squarely on the United States. The American inflation must be reduced at least to the German and Japanese level.

Introduction

The first quarter century after World War II, 1945 to 1970 or 1972, was a period of almost unprecedented growth and prosperity for the whole Western world. Simon Kuznets summed up his magisterial lecture, "Two Centuries of Economic Growth: Reflections on U.S. Experience," as follows:

> Even in this recent twenty-five year period of greater strain and danger, the growth in peace-time product per capita in the United States was still at a high rate; and in the rest of the world, developed and less developed (but excepting the few countries and periods marked by internal conflicts

and political breakdown), material returns have grown, per capita, at a rate higher than ever observed in the past.[1]

World trade grew by leaps and bounds as never before, and contrary to what is often said or implied the less developed countries have fully participated in world prosperity.[2]

The excellent performance of the United States and the world economy after World War II is in sharp contrast to what happened in the interwar period. True, recovery from war destruction after World War I was unexpectedly rapid, but the prosperity lasted barely ten years, 1919–1929, and was interrupted by the severe depression of 1920–1921, the so-called first postwar depression. Then came the Great Depression of the 1930s, the second postwar depression, from which the U.S. economy did not completely recover before the outbreak of World War II. There have been no depressions, only recessions, since 1945, if by depression we mean a decline in economic activity of the same order of magnitude as the first and second depressions after World War I or earlier depressions.

But what about the last, sixth, recession from November 1973 to March 1975?

The general mood certainly has changed. The euphoria and optimism of the 1950s and especially the 1960s have given way to apprehension, pessimism, and gloom. Some speak of a new crisis of capitalism,[3] others of the beginning of a Kondratieff downswing or of a replay of the Great Depression, and many economists complain that the economy does not work any more as it used to.

On the face of it, the present widespread pessimism, or malaise, is surprising. The 1973–1975 decline, although the longest and on most counts the severest of the postwar recessions, was definitely not a depression. It was entirely different from the Great Depression of the 1930s and earlier depressions.[4] True, the contrast between the

---

[1] Richard T. Ely Lecture, *American Economic Review*, vol. 67 (1977), p. 14. See also Simon Kuznets, "Aspects of Post-World War II Growth in Less Developed Countries," in A. M. Tang, E. M. Westfield, J. E. Worley, eds., *Evolution, Welfare, and Time in Economics*, Essays in Honor of Nicholas Georgescu-Rogen (Lexington, Mass.: D. C. Heath, 1976), chap. 3.

[2] On this last point see my paper, "The Liberal International Economic Order in Historical Perspective," in Ryan C. Amacher and others, eds., *Challenges to a Liberal International Economic Order* (Washington, D.C.: American Enterprise Institute, 1979).

[3] Robert L. Heilbronner begins a long, much-noticed article on "Boom and Crash" by saying: "Another worldwide crisis of capitalism is upon us" (*New Yorker*, August 1978). See also his booklet, *Beyond Boom and Crash* (New York: Norton, 1978).

[4] For a detailed comparison, see Geoffrey H. Moore, "Lessons of the 1973–1976 Recession and Recovery," especially Table 1, Selected Measures of Duration,

last and earlier postwar recessions has been greater in Europe and Japan than in the United States. But there, too, the 1973–1975 decline was very mild compared with earlier depressions; it was definitely merely a recession.[5]

The recovery after 1975 is generally regarded as sluggish and slower than those after the earlier postwar recessions. But the business cycle upswing has now lasted for more than four years, which makes it the longest peacetime upswing in the postwar period and the second longest since 1854.[6] Moreover, on closer inspection the expansion since 1975 has not been much different from earlier ones.[7] Employment is at record level and unemployment is low. Again the contrast between the last and earlier postwar cyclical recoveries has been greater in Europe and Japan than in the United States. Especially in the strong-currency countries—Germany, Switzerland, Japan, and the countries whose currencies are pegged to the mark—the recovery from the recession has been slower because these countries have made a more determined and sustained effort to subdue inflation than has the United States. The resulting inflation differential has been the main cause of the weakness of the dollar (see the section below entitled "Troubles in the International Monetary System"). But in Europe and Japan, too, the present state of affairs cannot be described as a depression or stagnation comparable to, or even faintly resembling, the situation in the 1930s or earlier depressions.

Given this general picture, what accounts for the widespread gloom and pessimism? Before answering that question, I will try to put the current malaise into a broad perspective.

The Current Malaise in Broad Perspective

After the end of World War II it was not generally foreseen that the world was on the verge of a long period of great prosperity. On the

---

Depth, and Diffusion of Business Cycle Contractions, 1920–1975, in William Fellner, ed., *Contemporary Economic Problems 1977* (Washington, D.C.: American Enterprise Institute, 1977).

[5] The terminology of recession-depression is of recent origin. In the earlier business cycle literature an analogous distinction was made between "Kitchin" and "Juglar" cycles (J. A. Schumpeter), "major" and "minor" cycles (Alvin Hansen), and "deep" and "mild-depression cycles" (Milton Friedman). In the pre-1914 period there were some borderline cases, but on the whole the distinction between recession and depression, although one of degree, happens to be quite unequivocal.

[6] See U.S. Department of Commerce, *Business Conditions Digest*, Washington, D.C., June 1978, p. 103.

[7] See Geoffrey H. Moore, "A Recovery Scoreboard," *Morgan Guaranty Survey* (published by Morgan Guaranty Trust Co., New York), May 1978.

contrary, probably the majority of economists expected a repetition, though perhaps in a milder form, of the same dismal pattern of cyclical developments that followed World War I. Most Keynesians had embraced the theory of secular stagnation. There was a far-reaching convergence of Keynesian and Marxian thought on the disease afflicting the capitalist economy—chronic underconsumption or oversaving.[8] But in regard to remedies, Keynes and his liberal (or should I say conservative?) followers such as Sir Roy Harrod differed from the Marxists. They thought that through cyclical or permanent government deficit spending the disease of chronic oversaving could be kept at bay. But the radical wing of the Keynesian school—the Marxo-Keynesians, as Schumpeter called them—thought and still think that the capitalist, free market system is beyond repair.[9]

Many non-Keynesians, too, were afraid that the pattern of a first and second postwar depression would emerge again. Thus, many economists' eyes were constantly scanning the economic horizon for signs of a coming slump, and in each slowdown or recession many thought they discerned the omen of an impending severe depression. There were of course exceptions, but most economists foresaw dangers of deflation, not of inflation. This attitude helped to impart an inflationary bias to macroeconomic policies throughout the postwar period.

---

[8] Keynes himself was never fully committed to the stagnation thesis, and he was always ready to change his views in the light of changing conditions. Thus in 1937 he became alarmed about inflation, although the rate of inflation was low and unemployment still very high compared with what Britain experienced in recent years. See T. W. Hutchison, *Keynes versus the 'Keynesians'* . . . *An Essay on the Thinking of J. M. Keynes and the Accuracy of Its Interpretation by His Followers* (London: Institute of Economic Affairs, 1977). In his famous posthumously published article, "The Balance of Payments of the United States," *Economic Journal*, June 1946, pp. 172–87, Keynes expressed optimism that "the classical medicine would work" and castigated the views of his erstwhile radical followers (who in the meantime had become his critics) as "modernist stuff gone wrong and turned sour and silly."

[9] The radicalization of the Keynesian school has been described by the late Harry G. Johnson in several papers, a collection of which has been published posthumously in Elisabeth S. Johnson and Harry G. Johnson, *The Shadow of Keynes: Understanding Keynes, Cambridge and Keynesian Economics* (Oxford and Chicago: Basil Blackwell and University of Chicago Press, 1978); see Part V, "Keynesian Economics."

The radicalization of the Keynesian school is by and large a British phenomenon. Keynes's American followers belong to the liberal or conservative wing. Joan Robinson, the most prominent British Marxo-Keynesian, calls them "bastard-Keynesians." This does not mean that there are no radical economists in the United States, but the American radicals have broken allegiance to Keynes and have organized themselves in the Union of Radical Political Economists (URPE).

As deflation and depressions again and again failed to materialize, Keynesian economists and policy makers became confident that the business cycle had finally been subdued by skillful fine-tuning of the economy.[10] The 1960s were the heyday of Keynesianism.

Actually, the postwar period was one of rising prices—of inflation, accelerating first slowly and later rapidly. The price rise slowed down in recession but was never reversed. Successive recoveries from recession started from successively higher rates of inflation.[11]

Many voices have warned about the dangers of inflation, but the influential Keynesian economists discounted these dangers. The comparative efficiency and harmlessness of inflation were proclaimed by the dean of American Keynesians, James Tobin. In his brilliant presidential address to the American Economic Association in December 1972, he said: "Inflation lets this struggle [for mutually inconsistent claims on the national product] proceed, and blindly, impartially and non-politically scales down all its outcomes. There are worse methods of resolving group rivalries and social conflict." [12]

Tobin spoke on the eve of an inflationary commodity boom of major proportion which preceded the oil price rise. In the light of this experience he seems to have changed his mind on the harmlessness of inflation.[13] It is easier for economists to revise their theories than to persuade governments to accept the revision, and it is still harder for governments to change the course of policy.

---

[10] This was not the first time the business cycle had been declared dead. For example, there was much talk of a "new era" when the price level remained stable from 1921 to 1929, and many economists thought that the business cycle had at last been eliminated.

[11] See Moore, "Lessons of the 1973–1976 Recession and Recovery," Table 6, A Chronology of Peaks and Troughs in the Rate of Inflation, p. 142, and Table 7, Relationship between the Business Cycle and Inflation, p. 145.

[12] *American Economic Review*, vol. 62 (March 1972), p. 13. The worse methods Tobin had in mind were extensive controls. This judgment surely is correct, but unfortunately continued accelerating inflation—and inflation always has a tendency to accelerate or else it loses its stimulating power—tremendously increases the political pressures for controls.

[13] In 1978, looking back to the 1960s, Tobin said: "Speaking for myself, an outsider then and now, I acknowledge that I had been overoptimistic about the trade-off [between inflation and unemployment] and too skeptical of accelerationist warnings." James Tobin, "Comment of an Academic Scribbler," in a symposium on "Keynesian Policies, the Drift into Permanent Deficits and the Growth of Government," Karl Brunner, ed., *Journal of Monetary Economics*, vol. 4 (1978), p. 622.

The Main Cause of the Present Malaise

Several reasons can be given for the widespread pessimism or malaise. I shall first indicate and analyze what I regard as the main cause and then mention two other reasons often cited, which on closer analysis can be traced to the same roots as those of the main cause.

The main reason of the malaise is, I suggest, the persistence of a seemingly intractable vicious kind of inflation, namely, the coexistence of sharply rising prices and wages on the one hand, and large unemployment and excess capacity on the other hand, both in the aggregate and in particular industries—a situation commonly called stagflation.[14] At least on the present scale, stagflation is a new phenomenon. Thus, the last recession, although definitely not a depression, had a most disturbing feature: it was highly inflationary with the price level rising sharply throughout. The recession started in November 1973, but the rate of inflation accelerated and reached its peak of 12 percent eight months later, in July 1974. Thereafter the inflation rate declined rapidly to a little under 5 percent in 1976 but never came near to zero.[15] This was an extreme case of stagflation, but the phenomenon existed throughout the postwar period.

Stagflation is in sharp contrast to earlier experience. In "classical" depressions and recessions, before World War II, the price level used to fall (or in mild recession at least remain stable); it did not rise or even accelerate, as was the case recently.

Stagflation poses a nasty dilemma for macroeconomic policy: If tight monetary-fiscal policy is used to combat inflation, unemployment is pushed up; if easy monetary-fiscal policy is applied to reduce unemployment, inflation is intensified. This dilemma did not exist in classical recessions and depressions, at least not in an acute form or over long periods.

What accounts for the increased seriousness and intractability of the inflation problem? I shall develop my answer in three steps.

First, every inflation *and* stagflation is a monetary phenomenon in the sense that there has never been one of significance that has not

---

[14] Since I have discussed the problem of stagflation in greater detail elsewhere, I confine myself here to what I regard as the essentials. See Gottfried Haberler, "Stagflation: An Analysis of Its Causes and Cures," American Enterprise Institute Reprint no. 64, reprinted from Bela Balassa and Richard Nelson, eds., *Economic Progress, Private Values, and Public Policy: Essays in Honor of William Fellner* (New York; North-Holland, 1977), and "The Problem of Stagflation," in William Fellner, ed., *Contemporary Economic Problems 1976* (Washington, D.C.: American Enterprise Institute, 1976).

[15] For details see Moore, "Lessons of the 1973–1975 Recession and Recovery."

been originally caused by or, if started in some other way, accommodated by a significant rise in the money stock, and no inflation or stagflation can be stopped without reducing monetary growth.

Second, the longer an inflation lasts the more intractable it becomes, because money illusion disappears and inflationary expectations are sensitized. In other words, after a certain point inflation tends to accelerate. This does not mean that every creeping inflation must inexorably become a trotting and then a galloping inflation but that inflation tends to lose its stimulating effect unless it is stepped up. More precisely, only an unanticipated inflation has a stimulating effect, and the longer an inflation lasts, the more fully it will be anticipated.

It follows that the theory of the harmlessness of a steady anticipated inflation is untenable.[16] This theory has been put forward on many occasions and still seems to be widely accepted, sometimes in the milder form that a very slow reduction of the rate of inflation extending over many years is a viable and desirable option.

During the great debate on inflation in the 1950s, the late Sumner H. Slichter took the position that we have to resign ourselves to continued creeping inflation of about 3 percent a year. He blamed it all on wage push by trade unions. An intolerable amount of unemployment would be required to bring the rate of inflation down near zero, but he was confident that the Federal Reserve would prevent inflation from accelerating. He recommended the issue of government bonds with a purchasing power guarantee and the use of escalator clauses in labor and other contracts to minimize the social consequences of steady inflation.

Slichter was criticized on the ground that unions and other pressure groups would not be satisfied with, say, a 6 percent rise in money wages when they saw that half the rise was lost through inflation. They would soon ask for, say, 9 percent, and the monetary authorities would once again be faced with the dilemma of either permitting inflation to accelerate or "creating" unemployment. Given wage push and the demands of other pressure groups, it was thought that the dilemma was inescapable.[17]

In the early 1970s Slichter's theory of the permanent but harmless inflation was revived in much more sophisticated form by Robert J.

---

[16] In an important paper Martin Feldstein shows that the welfare cost of permanent inflation is much greater than is commonly assumed ("The Welfare Cost of Permanent Inflation and Optional Short-Run Economic Policy," *Journal of Political Economy*, forthcoming).

[17] See my pamphlet, *Inflation, Its Causes and Cures*, enlarged edition (Washington, D.C.: American Enterprise Institute, 1966), p. 95.

Gordon, James Tobin, and others.[18] In the new version the distinction between anticipated and unanticipated inflation was made explicit. "Anticipated inflation is harmless inflation," according to Tobin. He criticized the anti-inflationists—the "accelerationists" as they were called—on the ground that their "argument rests on an appealing but unverified assumption that you can't fool all the people all the time." He did not exclude the possibility that "money illusion is a transient phenomenon," but added that "the period of adjustment is measured in decades." [19] In other words, you can fool all the people for decades! That this is a gross underestimation of the intelligence of the common man has been conclusively demonstrated by subsequent developments.[20] It took only a few years to erode money illusion sufficiently to make Keynesian policies less and less effective except in the very short run. There can be hardly any doubt about that, although, as so often happens, a good argument is in danger of being spoiled by extreme exaggerations. Some proponents of the theory of "rational expectations" go much too far when they deny any effectiveness of a monetary policy of expansion on the ground that it will immediately be fully anticipated by market participants.[21]

There is a theory that stabilizing a nonnegligible inflation for an indefinite period is a viable policy option. This view, which Arthur Okun called "the mirage of a steady inflation," seems to underlie much of the current anti-inflation policy—at least in the milder form

---

[18] See Robert J. Gordon, "Steady Anticipated Inflation: Mirage or Oasis?" *Brookings Papers on Economic Activity*, no. 2 (Washington, D.C.: Brookings Institution, 1971), as well as earlier papers quoted there and Gordon's statement before the U.S. Congress, Joint Economic Committee, *Hearings*, July 21, 1971. James Tobin gave his approval to Gordon's "able testimony" (see Joint Economic Committee, *Hearings*, September 9, 1971, p. 337) and expressed similar sentiments in James Tobin and Leonard Ross, "Living with Inflation," *New York Review of Books*, May 6, 1971. Gordon's theory was criticized by William Fellner, "Phillips-Type Approach or Acceleration?" and Arthur M. Okun, "The Mirage of Steady Inflation," in *Brookings Papers* cited above. The problem is reviewed in somewhat greater detail in Gottfried Haberler, "Incomes Policy and Inflation: Some Further Reflections," *American Economic Review*, vol. 65 (May 1972), pp. 234-41 (American Enterprise Institute Reprint no. 5, 1972).

[19] Tobin and Ross, "Living with Inflation," p. 24.

[20] See William Fellner's contribution to the present volume for a demonstration that American households have reacted to the inflation.

[21] For a criticism of the theory of rational expectations, see Kenneth J. Arrow, "The Future and the Present in Economic Life," *Economic Inquiry*, vol. 16 (April 1978), pp. 157-69. But not all monetarists take such an extreme position. Friedman himself is much more cautious; see *The Monetarist Controversy: A Seminar Discussion Paper by Franco Modigliani, Discussion by Milton Friedman*, Federal Reserve Bank of San Francisco, Economic Review Supplement, Spring 1977, p. 13. The time has come for an Axel Lejonhufvud or a Terrance Hutchison to write on Friedmanian Economics and the Economics of Friedman.

that inflation can be subdued in a very leisurely fashion over a period of many years. For example, G. William Miller, chairman of the Federal Reserve Board, was recently reported to have said that it would take seven to eight years to bring inflation down close to zero and Rüdiger Dornbusch, in a statement before a congressional committee, declared that "we should be concerned about inflation, not to reduce the level of the rate of inflation but to prevent by all means an acceleration in inflation." [22]

This view is not shared by all policy makers. For example, Barry Bosworth, director of the Council on Wage and Price Stability, is under no illusion that merely stabilizing the recent rate of inflation is a viable option. Although he did not explicitly say so, this is the clear implication of what he said about "the split that has developed between the very large wage increases of the major unions in the industrial core of the economy and those in the rest of the economy." [23] He mentioned several other important cases of the grossly uneven impact of inflation on different social classes and sectors of the economy and the price structure. The consequence is that those who have suffered from inflation are trying to catch up. Thus inflationary pressure is kept up. The upshot is that only a fairly accurately and uniformly anticipated inflation could be harmless. But this is, in the words of Alfred Marshall (used in another context), "not inconceivable but absolutely impossible."

After a certain point every inflation tends to accelerate, a fact that goes a long way toward explaining the phenomenon of stagflation. Indeed, monetarists are inclined to stop at this point: there remains nothing further to explain, they say, and the only cure for stagflation is the same as for any kind of inflation—reduction of monetary growth. I believe, however, that a good deal more remains to be explained about the persistence and magnitude of the problem in recent years.

The third step in my argument is that the problem of stagflation would not exist, at least not in the severe form that we experienced recently, if we had not moved so far away from a truly competitive, free market economy. Deviation from free markets is, of course, not of recent origin, but since the Great Depression the movement away from a competitive market economy has been very fast and far-reaching.

---

[22] See U.S. Congress, House of Representatives, *Hearings before the Committee on Banking, Finance and Urban Affairs*, 95th Congress, 2nd session, March 7-9 and April 10, 1978, p. 42.

[23] *A Conversation with the Honorable Barry Bosworth: Coping with Inflation* (Washington, D.C.: American Enterprise Institute, 1978), p. 9.

This does not mean that the private sector of the economy as such has become less competitive than it was, say, fifty years ago and that monopolies or oligopolies have become more numerous and powerful merely because of the natural tendency of increasing advantages of large-scale production. The opposite is true. If it were not for government interference, the private sector as such would be more competitive than it has been. The tendency for large-scale production to create monopolistic situations has been largely offset by the rapid advances in the technology of transportation and communication. Because of the enormous growth of international trade, especially in manufactured goods, and because of the emergence of new industries in developed and less developed countries, there is little room for private monopolies or oligopolies except in the public utility area.

That we have moved so far away from a truly competitive free market economy is entirely due to the enormous growth of the public sector and to government policies that are creating, fostering, and protecting private monopoly positions. These policies have sharply reduced the area of competition and free markets and have made wages and many prices unresponsive to changes in demand and supply.

This development has gone farthest in the labor market. The greater power of labor unions (labor monopolies) is largely due to government policies. Not only have money wages become almost completely rigid downward, but real wage resistance and real wage push have developed. This is partly the consequence of inflation itself, which has led to widespread wage indexation, and partly the result of government policies. Through minimum wages, generous unemployment and welfare benefits, the Davis-Bacon Act that requires the government to pay highest union wages, and in many other ways, the government has made real wages rigid downward and has strongly supported union wage push by making it easier for unions to use the strike weapon.

Labor unions and the support they get from the government are probably the greatest obstacle to regaining price stability. But they are by no means the only culprits. Other groups also exert heavy political pressure on the government to boost the prices of their products and their real income. Organized agriculture is the best known and most important example.

At the back of this development is the increasing unwillingness to adjust to changing conditions, the increasing propensity to use political pressure, including street demonstrations and violence, to force the government to intervene in order to keep alive uncompetitive firms and industries, and the growing readiness of governments to yield to such pressures. As Harry Johnson said, "there now appears to be a commitment not only for every man to be employed, but for him to be employed in the occupation of his choice, in the location of his choice and, it would sometimes seem, at the income of his choice." [24]

That development finds its clearest expression in protectionist pressures and the government's readiness to yield to them. Instead of adjusting to changing conditions by letting uncompetitive firms go out of business and uncompetitive industries contract, the government protects such firms and industries not only by import restrictions in the form of tariffs, quotas, "trigger-price system" (the latest U.S. import restriction on steel), so-called "voluntary" agreements forced on foreign exporters to reduce their sales ("orderly market agreements"), and other devices, but also increasingly by subsidies to, or takeover by the government of, lame-duck firms and industries that should be allowed to contract or be liquidated.

All this reduces the area of competitive markets, increases the rigidity of wages and prices, and thus blunts the effectiveness of macroeconomic policies to subdue inflation. The degree to which competition has been eliminated and the economy has lost flexibility varies greatly from country to country, and so does the judgment of economists. Monetarists take a relaxed view. They do not believe that the potency of monetary policy has been seriously impaired. To regain price stability some transitional unemployment, perhaps a mild recession, will have to be accepted in order to douse inflationary expectation and to induce labor unions to accept a reduced wage growth roughly in proportion to the average growth in labor productivity.

The question on which there is disagreement is not whether monetary restraint can subdue inflation. Few would doubt that it can. The disagreement is about the magnitude of the transitional

---

[24] Foreword by Harry G. Johnson in G. Denton, S. O'Clieircacian, and S. Ash, *Trade Effects of Public Subsidies to Private Enterprise* (London: Trade Policy Research Center, 1975), p. xiii. The unwillingness to adjust is the main theme of two remarkable studies by Richard Blackhurst, Nicolas Marian, and Jan Tumlir, *Trade Liberalization, Protectionism and Interdependence*, General Agreement on Tariffs and Trade (GATT) Studies in International Trade, no. 5 (Geneva, 1977); and the same authors, *Adjustment, Trade and Growth in Developed and Developing Countries*, GATT Studies in International Trade, no. 6 (Geneva, 1979). See also the trenchant analysis by Melvyn B. Krauss, *The New Protectionism: The Welfare State and International Trade* (New York: New York University Press, 1978).

and possibly permanent ("natural") unemployment that we have to accept if we rely on monetary-fiscal policy alone to bring down inflation. Unlike the monetarists, pessimists like myself believe that if nothing is done to bring the economy closer to the competitive ideal, we shall have to accept a comparatively high level of unemployment. This will make it politically extremely difficult to pursue a consistent anti-inflationary monetary policy. But I agree with the monetarists that the Keynesians are wrong to assume that they can escape the dilemma by refusing to take the monetary medicine. More rapid monetary expansion plus some wage and price controls (incomes policy) would only lead to accelerating inflation and more serious trouble later. There is no *permanent* trade-off between unemployment and inflation.

Be that as it may, most economists, both Keynesians and monetarists, should be able to agree that general macroeconomic policies to subdue inflation, and monetary restraint in particular, would operate more effectively and smoothly and would create less transitional (or permanent) unemployment, if the economy could be brought closer to the competitive ideal and if by the removal of the worst impediments to competition a greater measure of wage and price flexibility would be assured. Each group could use its favorite jargon: the Keynesian could say that structural reforms would improve the trade-off between unemployment and inflation, while the monetarist could insist that there is no permanent trade-off but concede that structural reform would reduce the level of transitional (or natural) unemployment.

There should also be agreement that in an ideal, fully competitive economy there could be no stagflation. There can of course be inflation, but the persistent coexistence of rising prices and unemployment would be impossible because in competitive markets prices and wages would decline when supply exceeds demand. It is true few markets are fully competitive in the strict theoretical sense, and the labor market has been imperfect even before union power and government policies made wages as rigid as they are now. But there can be hardly a doubt that the rigidity of the body economic has sharply increased. Melvyn Krauss speaks of the *rigor mortis oeconomicus* that is beginning to set in as a consequence of the extreme policies of the welfare state and the new protectionism.[25]

By unemployment I mean genuine, involuntary unemployment. The distinction between involuntary and voluntary unemployment is

---

[25] Krauss, *The New Protectionism: The Welfare State and International Trade*, p. 106.

not difficult conceptually,[26] but in practice the line separating the two is often difficult to draw, especially in the case of "frictional" unemployment, that is, of workers who lost their jobs and are in search of another suitable opening. Since I have dealt with these problems elsewhere, I confine myself here to saying that in my opinion the distinction between voluntary and involuntary unemployment is essential even though, like most concepts in the social sciences, the practical application of the distinction presents difficulties.

To summarize, the main cause of the present malaise is the seemingly intractable and anomalous combination of inflation and unemployment. But this is not due to a basic defect of the free market, free enterprise economy. On the contrary, it is due to the fact that the growth of the public sector and government policies have moved the economy too far from the competitive ideal. In other words, our present troubles do not signify a crisis of capitalism; they indicate a crisis of government policy. The cure is not more government planning but fewer government interventions; not more controls and more regulations, but decontrol and deregulation. The recent deregulation of air traffic has demonstrated spectacularly what can be achieved by deregulation: rapid growth of air travel, higher profits for the airlines, and a boom in the aircraft industry.

Two other reasons are often given for the present malaise. The first is the recent decline in productivity growth and the closely related, disappointingly low level of productive private investment since the last recession. The second reason is certain difficulties in the international monetary area: the persistent U.S. trade deficit in the face of a rapidly declining dollar and a stubborn Japanese surplus despite a sharply rising yen. Some observers regard them as deviations that defy conventional principles of balance of payments adjustment. But on closer analysis those phenomena, too, turn out to be the consequence of the same root cause: the decline of the competitive, free market economy because of the growth of the public sector and misguided government policies.

---

[26] One conceptual complication may be mentioned. When unions push wages above the competitive level, the resulting unemployment can be described as "voluntary," and possibly rational from the viewpoint of the union—that is, the unions may regard the unemployment that they create as the price they have to pay for a larger income of the group. But unemployment is involuntary and a hardship from the standpoint of the workers who lost their jobs. For an ingenious attempt to separate voluntary and involuntary unemployment in a particular case, see Geoffrey H. Moore, "A New Leading Indicator of Unemployment," *Morgan Guaranty Survey*, November 1978.

The Decline in Productivity Growth and the Low Level of Investment

The trend of national productivity has faltered during the past decade.[27] While output per man-hour grew at an average annual rate of over 3 percent from 1947 to 1967, it has since then increased at only half that rate. Investment in plant and equipment in the private sector has played a much smaller role in the current business cycle upswing than in earlier upswings since World War II.

It stands to reason that the decline of the productivity growth had an unfavorable effect on inflation and unemployment. With a higher productivity growth wages could rise faster without causing unemployment or inflation. To put it the other way around, a given wage push causes more inflation or more unemployment with a slower productivity growth than with a faster one.

Evidently both declining productivity growth and lagging investments are pervasive and exceedingly complex phenomena whose causes, too, are pervasive and complex. Fortunately, no exhaustive study is required for the present purposes; it will suffice to identify a few factors that are surely very important.

The causal factors to which the decline in rate of productivity growth is usually attributed are: (1) the increased share in the labor force of women and teenagers whose productivity is much less than that of prime-age males; (2) the lagging volume of investment; and (3) the enormous growth of the public sector, the sharp increase in government employment, and the exploding propensity of the government to control and regulate the economy. Arthur Burns aptly refers to this last factor as a veritable "regulatory frenzy, with members of Congress and officials of the executive agencies vying with one another in devising new economic controls." He described the growth of regulations as follows:

> At the federal level alone, at least ninety agencies are now involved in this activity. The *Federal Register*, which records new regulations, ran to 3,400 pages in 1937, but swelled to about 10,000 pages in 1953 and to 65,000 pages in 1977. In this year's federal budget the amount allocated to regulation is . . . more than twice the expenditure in 1974. To this figure must be added not only the corresponding expenditures by state and local governments, but also the huge costs of compliance imposed on private industry.

---

[27] For present purposes only the broad facts need be recalled; for details see the contributions of Denison, Fellner, Kendrick, and Perlman to the present volume.

The Center for the Study of American Business at Washington University [St. Louis] estimates that these compliance costs amounted to over $60 billion in 1976 and that they may come to over $90 billion this year.[28]

Burns points out that to the financial cost of government regulations must be added the fact that many business executives find so much of their time and energy absorbed by coping with regulatory problems that they cannot sufficiently attend to their proper entrepreneurial functions such as developing new products and better technologies.

For the lag of productive private investment, too, government policies are clearly responsible to a very large extent. There is, on the one hand, the regulatory explosion and, on the other hand, the mounting tax burden resulting from rapidly increasing government expenditures, including mushrooming transfer payments. It is now widely recognized that, partly as a consequence of prolonged inflation, the decline of investment is largely attributable to high marginal tax rates, the double taxation of dividends, and the taxation of overestimated or nonexistent profits resulting from faulty accounting rules that fail to take account of inflation.[29]

It follows that the disappointing productivity growth and investment lag are to a very large extent the consequences of excessive government interventions and faulty tax policies. But even if it were possible to identify other causes—or if the slow productivity growth is accepted as the price we have to pay for a better environment, or a more acceptable income distribution, or for any other worthy objective—in a competitive, free enterprise economy a lower productivity growth would not lead to inflation or unemployment. In a fully competitive economy, given an appropriate noninflationary monetary policy, the growth of money wages and other money incomes would adjust to the slower productivity growth. Only government policies that foster or tolerate union power and wage

---

[28] See Arthur F. Burns, *The Condition of the American Economy* (Washington, D.C.: American Enterprise Institute, 1978), pp. 7-8. The role of government policies in causing the virtual collapse of productivity growth is brought out forcefully in William Fellner's contribution to this present volume, "The Declining American Productivity Growth: An Introductory Note," see pp. 3-12.

[29] Two important papers by Martin Feldstein show how inflation and the existing tax system interact to discourage saving and investment and so reduce the level of productivity growth. See Martin Feldstein, *The Stagflation Problem*, Testimony of the Joint Economic Committee of the U.S. Congress, April 30, 1979, processed; and Martin Feldstein and Lawrence Summers, "Inflation and the Taxation of Capital Income in the Corporate Sector," National Bureau of Economic Research Working Paper no. 312 (New York, 1979), processed.

push and yield to other pressure groups make inflation or unemployment, or both, the inevitable consequence of lagging productivity growth and low investment.

In summary, our earlier conclusion still stands: The present economic malaise is not due to a defect of the free market, free enterprise economy; on the contrary, the trouble is that government policies have moved the economy too far away from the competitive ideal. The malaise does not reflect a crisis of capitalism, but a crisis of government policy.

Troubles in the International Monetary System

Real or imaginary troubles in the working of the existing international system of widespread managed floating have greatly contributed to the current economic malaise.[30] In particular the U.S. trade and current account deficits that persist despite a sharp depreciation of the dollar and the Japanese surplus that persists despite a sharp appreciation of the yen are widely regarded as anomalies. They are thought to indicate a malfunctioning of the adjustment mechanism and to require massive official interventions in the exchange market or even unorthodox adjustment measures such as import surcharges (an across-the-board import tariff of 10 percent on manufactured goods has been suggested) or quantitative import restrictions.

I shall argue that turbulences in the foreign exchange markets in recent years have their roots not in a basic defect of the system of floating exchange rates but in the failings of national policies in some of the leading countries—the same policies that have presented stubborn inflation and stagflation—and to mismanagement of the float.

To begin with, the breakdown of the Bretton Woods system and the advent of managed floating of the currencies of all major industrial countries were the consequences of the wave of high inflation that started in the United States in the middle 1960s and engulfed the whole Western world. Countries simply could not agree on a common high rate of inflation that would be required to keep exchange rates stable in a highly inflationary environment.

The opposite theory, which asserts that floating brought on inflation, puts the cart before the horse. Policy makers who saw in

---

[30] This section is based on my contributions to *Contemporary Economic Problems 1977*, "The International Monetary System after Jamaica and Manila," and to *Contemporary Economic Problems 1978*, "Reflections on the U.S. Deficit and the Floating Dollar," where some of the problems are discussed in greater detail.

floating a license for engaging in inflationary policies soon discovered that this was an illusion. On the contrary, under floating the pains of inflation were increased because unlike under a fixed-rate system, it is impossible to alleviate the pains of inflation temporarily by "exporting" some of the inflation to other countries in the form of a trade deficit that is financed by running down reserves. Thus, floating provides a strong inducement to curb inflation. Needless to add, there is no guarantee that inflation will actually be curbed. A strong inducement to disinflate can always be overwhelmed by even stronger pressures to inflate.

The basic facts of the problem of the dollar are well known. In 1975 the United States had a trade surplus of about $9 billion, in 1976 a deficit of over $9 billion, a swing of $18 billion in one year. In 1977 the trade deficit shot up to $31 billion, and for 1978 it was $34 billion. The balance on current account showed a surplus of $18 billion in 1975, a surplus of $4 billion in 1976, a deficit of $15 billion in 1977, and $16 billion in 1978.

For a considerable time the dollar held its own despite the mounting trade and current account deficits. Until the summer of 1977 the overall depreciation of the dollar from the Smithsonian level (December 1971) as measured by the effective (trade-weighted) exchange rate was quite small, although the deutsche mark, the yen, and Swiss franc had already appreciated substantially. It was generally realized that a large part of the trade deficit was due to a more rapid recovery from the 1974–1975 recession in the United States than in Europe and Japan—a development that was expected to reverse itself sooner or later.

Then in 1977 it became increasingly clear that another more fundamental factor was involved: An inflation differential had developed and was growing between the United States on the one hand, and the three strong-currency countries, Germany, Japan, and Switzerland, on the other. The U.S. inflation rate had declined from its peak of about 12.6 percent in July 1974 to a little below 6 percent at the end of 1976. But under the new administration the priorities of macroeconomic policy were shifted from fighting inflation to more rapid expansion. As a consequence, the rate of inflation got stuck at 6 percent or so and then began to increase again, first slowly then more rapidly to reach the two-digit level in 1979. The three strong-currency countries, on the other hand, persevered in their fight against inflation. Thus the rate of inflation declined to practically zero in Switzerland, 2.5 percent in Germany, and 3.5 percent in Japan.[31]

---

[31] These figures relate to the consumer price index. For Japan the consumer

In retrospect it is clear that what is misleadingly called the "growth differential" between the three strong-currency countries and the United States was due to differences in attitude and policies with respect to inflation: The three persevered in their anti-inflation policy and accepted temporary slower growth as the price for lower inflation, while the United States shifted gears too soon. The result was almost two-digit inflation and forced a reversal of policy to fight inflation in October 1978, which will cause a slowdown of the economy and probably a recession in 1979.

The unfavorable influence of the inflation differential on the current balance is likely to be slow in developing, but its effect on the capital balance and on the exchange rate can be quite strong and rapid, as soon as the market realizes that the currency of an inflationary country will have a long-run tendency to depreciate. The dollar is especially vulnerable to a loss of confidence because it is still the world's foremost official and private international reserve and transactions currency. As a consequence there exist huge foreign-held dollar balances. The holders of these balances have a strong inducement to diversify the currency composition of their holdings when they expect the dollar to depreciate. The persistent and growing inflation differential and the policies responsible for the inflation differential are the principal factors that determine the expectations about future exchange rate movements.

What matters is not the U.S. inflation rate compared with that of a broad average of countries or even with the countries of the Organization for Economic Cooperation and Development (OECD) as a group—this comparison is quite favorable for the United States. What matters is the comparison with the three potential reserve currency countries. Their currencies are fully convertible—not of the mouse-trap variety, which are easy to get into but hard to get out of, but the opposite, which are hard to get into but easy to get out of. In fact, the volume of dollar balances subject to diversification is open-ended because not only foreign-held but U.S. dollar balances are subject to diversification.

Thus, the dollar dropped sharply, mainly vis-à-vis the three strong currencies: From October 1977 to October 31, 1978, the German mark appreciated vis-à-vis the dollar by 27.7 percent, the Swiss franc appreciated by 53.6 percent, and the Japanese yen by

---

price index greatly understates the inflation differential because the index of wholesale prices, especially of manufactured goods, consistently lags behind the consumer price index. In fact, the manufactured goods price index has recently declined in Japan.

42.3 percent. The trade-weighted depreciation of the dollar (multi-lateral weights) was 19.2 percent.[32] In October 1978 the foreign exchange markets became quite jittery, and on November 1, 1978, President Carter announced a sharp reversal of economic policy, the so-called rescue operation for the dollar, consisting of a tightening of monetary policy and mobilization of a $30 billion fund of foreign currencies by the United States for interventions in the foreign exchange markets. (This intervention fund consisted of an increase in swap lines of $7.6 billion with the central banks of Germany, Japan, and Switzerland; drawing on the U.S. reserve position in the International Monetary Fund and selling special drawing rights (SDRs); and issuance of foreign currency denominated securities in foreign capital markets.)

With the strong assistance of central bank interventions by the United States as well as by the three strong-currency countries, the response of the foreign exchange market was dramatic. From October 31, 1978, to December 8, 1978, the mark declined against the dollar by 8.2 percent, the Swiss franc declined by 12.9 percent, and the yen by 9.7 percent. Overall, the dollar appreciated by 7.9 percent.

It is, however, generally recognized that the future of the dollar will depend on how effectively the "fundamental factors" are tackled. In view of the huge volume of the dollar balances subject to diversification, even a $30 billion intervention fund will not halt the slide of the dollar for long, unless the U.S. inflation rate soon shows clear signs of coming down to approach in the not too distant future the inflation rate in the strong-currency countries.

I shall not speculate here on the chances of the inflation rate's declining except for two remarks: First, obviously any decline in the inflation rate will largely depend on whether the Federal Reserve will follow through with the policy of monetary restraint that was signaled by the rise of the discount rate in November 1978. Second, the widely expected recession or at least marked slowdown in the rate of growth of the U.S. economy in 1979 will probably strengthen the dollar temporarily, even if the rate of inflation does not decline quickly, because the volume of U.S. imports usually reacts strongly and quickly to a slowdown in economic activity. This quick reaction is due to inventory adjustments and is, therefore, a short-run phenomenon. A lasting improvement must await the disappearance of the inflation differential.

---

[32] See Morgan Guaranty Trust Co., *World Financial Markets* (New York, December 1978), p. 2.

If the U.S. inflation shows no signs of abating soon, we must expect a continuation of the pattern of the last year and a half—a tendency of the dollar to slide, probably not in a smooth, orderly fashion but in intermittent lurches accompanied by panics and disorderly market conditions.[33] My general conclusion then is that the decline of the dollar and the turbulence in the exchange markets is due to mistakes of domestic policies, specifically to the U.S. failure to subdue inflation. This in turn is due to lax monetary management and to the policies described earlier that have given rise to the phenomenon of stagflation.

To round out the international monetary picture, some alternative explanations and remedies for the decline of the dollar need discussion. American officials like to attribute to the oil price rise a major share of the responsibility for the weak dollar. That oil has nothing to do with the weakness of the dollar is conclusively demonstrated by the fact that the three strong-currency countries depend completely on imported oil and that Canada, an energy-rich country, has an even weaker currency than the United States. Lacking domestic production of oil, the three strong-currency countries were not tempted to follow the U.S. example of encouraging energy consumption and discouraging domestic production by keeping the domestic price of oil artificially down. That the oil price rise has nothing to do with weakness of the dollar is further demonstrated by the fact that U.S. imports of non-oil commodities have risen much faster than imports of petroleum and petroleum products. From the third quarter of 1976 to the third quarter of 1978 oil imports have risen by 15 percent while non-oil imports jumped by about 50 percent. Imports of manufactured goods grew especially rapidly.

The above argument will perhaps be criticized on the ground that it neglects the indirect effect of the oil price rise on the dollar through accelerating U.S. inflation. But that criticism proves my point: U.S. monetary policy has accommodated the inflationary pressure stemming from the rise of the oil price while the three strong-currency countries resisted it.

When the Carter administration was confronted with a large trade deficit and a weak dollar, its first reaction was to bring pressure on the strong-currency countries to adopt expansionary policies in order to reduce their surpluses, eliminate the pressure on the dollar, and stimulate the world economy. The so-called locomotive approach was based on the assertion that because of the existing slack in the

---

[33] See my contribution to *Contemporary Economic Problems 1978*, p. 225.

strong-currency countries an expansionary monetary and fiscal policy would not risk accelerating inflation. This theory is, however, wrong on two counts. First, we do not live in a Keynesian world; in the era of stagflation it is not true that the existence of some unemployment permits monetary expansion without raising the price level. Second, even if it were possible to bring about a real expansion by monetary expansion without raising the price level, the dollar problem would be alleviated but not solved because the inflation differential would remain unchanged.[34]

It is true, however, that if the strong-currency countries inflated their economies sufficiently, they would solve the dollar problem. This could be accomplished in various ways. For example, the German and Japanese central banks could support the dollar in the foreign exchange market or could lend enough marks and yen to the U.S. authorities to enable them to intervene strongly in the foreign exchange market, thus pumping up the money supply in Germany and Japan. Another method would be for Germany to underwrite the French, Italian, Irish, and Danish inflation in the European Monetary System (EMS) that has recently gone into effect. The German government (as distinguished from the Bundesbank and large segments of the German public) seems ready to do just that.[35] Britain may still be willing to lend a helping hand by joining the EMS and letting Germany finance its deficit. However, solving the dollar problem by inflating the strong currencies rather than by

---

[34] For details about the locomotive approach and the escalated version, the so-called convoy approach, see ibid.

[35] Roland Vaubel says in his brilliant paper, "Die Rückkehr zum neuen Europäischen Währungssystem," *Wirtschaftsdienst* (Hamburg, January 1979), pp. 26-27: "The subsidies [to weak members of the EMS] will have to be shouldered primarily by the Federal Republic of Germany. In the past Federal Chancellor H. Schmidt always rejected with indignation the intended role as 'European paymaster.' What has induced him now to push himself into that role? What are the purposes for which he is willing to spend so much of his (or rather of the taxpayers') money?" Vaubel then speculates about possible motives. One explanation, which he calls a "not very well-meaning conspiratorial theory," is that the government would not mind an inflationary boomlet as a help for the approaching election.

The standpoint of the Bundesbank has been made clear by its president, Otmar Emminger. In a speech in Frankfurt he said: "The EMS must be managed in such a way that the domestic stability of the individual members is not impaired. . . . We should not deceive ourselves that we could build a 'zone of greater monetary stability' on a harmonised average level of general inflation. This kind of harmonisation would soon break apart. Harmonisation of monetary goals can only mean a downward convergence to the lowest level of inflation" (*Deutsche Bundesbank Auszüge aus Presseartikeln*, no. 14, February 19, 1979, p. 5). This clearly means that the Italian, French, and other EMS members' inflation rates should be reduced to approximately the German level.

disinflating the weak currencies would heat up world inflation, hardly a sound basis for sustained world prosperity.

Further discussion of the locomotive policy is, however, no longer necessary because the policy has been authoritatively redefined by one of its original architects. Richard N. Cooper, under secretary of state for economic affairs, declared at the Claremont Monetary Conference in October 1978 that the locomotive approach does not mean that the strong-currency countries have to pursue an expansionary monetary-fiscal policy if they are afraid of inflation; it merely means that they have a choice between domestic expansion or letting the exchange rate go up. This is a reasonable position but a far cry from the original version of the locomotive approach.

There remains the question of the large U.S. trade deficit. Does this deficit, despite the sharp depreciation of the dollar, not indicate a malfunctioning of the adjustment mechanism under floating? Judgment concerning the equilibrium exchange rate and the "proper" balance of payments are notoriously fallible, and purchasing power comparisons are uncertain guides because of lags ("J-curve" effects) and the multiplicity of different price indexes that may be used.

Let me point out, however, that as measured by the effective (trade-weighted) exchange rate the dollar did not change much since the end of 1975 until about September 1977. (In the second half of 1975 it had even somewhat appreciated.)[36] Furthermore, in the second and third quarters of 1978 there was a strong, broadly based improvement both in the trade and current account balances. Especially notable is the dramatic shift in the balance of manufactured goods trade from a deficit of $13 billion (annual rate) in the first quarter of 1978 to a surplus of $1.5 billion in the three months ending October 1978.[37] The improvement in the balance of manufactured goods trade is especially important for two reasons. This balance is usually not subject to erratic shifts, and its deterioration in 1977 and early 1978 was the main reason for the widespread pessimism that has induced protectionist proposals. The recent changes suggest that the U.S. trade balance has moved into the upward branch of the J-curve, although the improvement may be interrupted or delayed by the higher cost of oil imports or by changes in the more volatile exports of agricultural products. The deficit on current

---

36 See *OECD Economic Outlook*, no. 24 (December 1978), pp. 60 and 130. Morgan Guaranty figures and an index of exchange value of the dollar (using multilateral trade weights) computed by the Federal Reserve Board tell the same story.

37 See Morgan Guaranty Trust Co., *World Financial Markets*, p. 3.

account, too, declined sharply in 1978. In the second, third, and fourth quarters it was $3.3, $3.7, and $1.3 billion respectively compared with $7.6 billion in the first quarter. In view of these developments it is, to say the least, premature to speak of an anomalous reaction of the balance of payments to the depreciation of the dollar or of a malfunctioning of the adjustment mechanism under floating.

Be that as it may, there is no reason to become panicky about the trade deficit. In my contribution to the 1978 edition of *Contemporary Economic Problems*,[38] I criticized the Keynesian theory put forward by some experts that the trade deficit was a serious drag on the economy and that its disappearance or decline would automatically translate, dollar for dollar, into higher employment and output. I pointed out that we live not in a Keynesian world but in a world of stagflation and (since 1978) virtually full employment. In such a world an increase in overall effective demand emanating from the foreign trade sector of the economy adds to inflationary pressures just as much as an increase in effective demand caused by a larger budget deficit or an easy money policy. I argued that the trade deficit had a (mild) anti-inflationary effect; it has somewhat moderated the speed of the cyclical upswing and, thus, has helped to make the current cyclical expansion the second longest in the postwar period. In 1978 this expansion carried the U.S. economy close to full employment.

I have been asked how my appraisal of the impact of the trade deficit on the economy can be reconciled with the statement of the Council of Economic Advisers that in 1977, given the fact that "net private saving was near zero . . . a Federal deficit of nearly $50 billion was required to counterbalance the aggregate surpluses of State and local governments and the excess of receipts over expenditures stemming from our international trade and payments." [39] The answer is simple: The council's statement that the budget deficit counteracted the deflationary effects of the trade deficit is quite compatible with my statement that the trade deficit counteracted the inflationary impulses stemming from the government deficit.

I assume that the council's statement should not be interpreted, as some experts have done, to mean that the budget deficit was *deliberately* made large in order to counterbalance the trade deficit plus the state and local budget surpluses. Such an interpretation would imply an overly naive faith in fine-tuning the economy. When

---

[38] See the section entitled "Current Account Deficits under Floating—Burden or Benefit?" pp. 215-17.

[39] Council of Economic Advisers, *Annual Report*, January 1978, p. 89.

the administration drew up its budget proposals for 1977 it surely did not know what the trade deficit plus the combined state and local surpluses would be and that the net private sector savings would be near zero. It would be even more far-fetched to assume that, in the political rough and tumble in the Congress from which the budget finally emerged, the right forecasts were made about the three factors mentioned—trade deficit, state and local surpluses, and private sector savings—and were firmly kept in mind to make sure that the federal budget deficit would precisely offset the trade deficit and state and local surpluses.[40] Therefore, my statement (that the trade deficit, far from being a serious drag on the U.S. economy, has helped to bring about virtually full employment by moderating and thereby lengthening the upswing) cannot be dismissed—as some experts have done—on the ground that the depressing effect of the trade deficit would have materialized if the government, in its infinite wisdom, had not arranged for a precisely offsetting budget deficit.

All this does not mean, however, that the United States will or should continue forever to run a large trade deficit. It does mean that a decline of the trade deficit—whether it results from a more rapid expansion abroad, the depreciation of the dollar, or a recession at home—is an expansionary factor. It will not automatically translate, dollar for dollar, into higher employment and output as the Keynesians assume, but will largely cause prices to rise higher than they otherwise would.[41] It means, above all, that we should not panic, as

---

[40] The excellent paper by Jai-Hoon Yang, "Budget Deficits and Trade Deficits: Is There a Link?" (Federal Reserve Bank of St. Louis, *Review*, October 1978, p. 10), points out that "the statement that the Federal deficit serves to offset the sum of State and local government savings and the trade deficit is a correct *accounting* statement only if net private saving is zero" and that "an accouting identity . . . provides no useful clue, by itself, for identifying the set of factors which contributed to the recent emergence of deficits in both the trade account and Federal budget." The paper attributes, somewhat ungenerously, to the council "the view that the trade deficit is somehow determined independently of the factors impinging on other accounts in the identity and that the other accounts, notably the Federal budget, must adjust to preserve the accounting relationship." A more generous interpretation is to assume that the council was aware that its table on page 89 states an accounting identity. This interpretation is suggested by the fact that in the table the budget deficit is presented as identically equal to the trade deficit plus state and local surpluses, plus the near-zero net saving of the private sector, with no statistical discrepancy being mentioned. It is true, however, that the council's language sounds like an ex post justification of the large budget deficit.

[41] It could be argued that an improvement of the trade balance because of a recession at home (rather than expansion abroad or depreciation of the dollar) will have no inflationary effect. This is true in a special sense in the short run. Consider two alternative impacts a recession may have on the trade picture: By chance or by policy design it may cause a decrease in demand either for

some experts have done, and ask for import restrictions—such as a 10 percent import surcharge or even quantitative restrictions—to eliminate the deficit. In its macroeconomic impact on aggregate expenditure, price level, and the trade balance, a 10 percent import surcharge (across-the-board import tariff) would be roughly equivalent to a 3 or 4 percent depreciation of the dollar.[42] It therefore makes no sense to recommend an import surcharge on the ground that the downward float of the dollar has failed to correct the imbalance.[43]

In summary, the decline of the dollar and of other major currencies—for example, the Italian lira and the British pound—and the turbulence in the foreign exchange markets do not indicate a malfunctioning of the system of floating exchange rates. These developments are due to the mismanagement of the national policies in the countries concerned—to too much inflation all around and to widely diverging inflation rates. And inflation has become a stubborn stagflation not because of a basic defect of the free market, capitalistic system but, on the contrary, because government policies have moved the economy too far away from the competitive, free market ideal and have made wages and many prices rigid and unresponsive to changes in the demand and supply. Since the U.S. economy looms

---

imported oil or for domestic coal. In the first case the trade balance improves, and employment and output in the coal industry is maintained. In the second case the trade balance is not improved, and output and employment shrink in the coal industry. Thus, the improvement of the trade balance can be said to have "caused" an increase in output and employment compared with the level that otherwise would have resulted. But by the same token it reduces the antiinflationary effect that the recession would have had in the longer run.

Under the assumed (strictly Keynesian) conditions, the improvement in the trade balance translates dollar for dollar into higher levels of output and employment and no increase in prices. In the longer run, however, under almost full employment and under existing stagflationary conditions, the outcome is different.

[42] This follows from the well-known proposition that a 10 percent devaluation is equivalent to a 10 percent across-the-board import tariff plus a 10 percent export subsidy. But it should be kept in mind that in practice the tariff plus subsidy is never strictly across-the-board. Services are not covered, and there are always exceptions such as for basic food and other necessities. Therefore, the tariff-subsidy scheme has distorting (microeconomic) effects. The equivalence applies only to the broadest macroeconomic implications.

[43] On January 25, 1979, the chairman of the Federal Reserve Board, G. William Miller, said in a statement before the Committee on the Budget, House of Representatives, that interventions in the exchange market (after November 1, 1978) had "succeeded in strengthening the dollar" but that the decline of the dollar since September 1977 had added about one percentage point to the inflation rate in 1978. On January 30, 1979, five days later, testifying before the Joint Economic Committee, Mr. Miller said that he would prefer to limit imports through an import surcharge if the dollar weakened further (*Washington Post*, January 31, 1979). He seems to be unaware of the inconsistency of the two statements.

so large in the world economy and since the dollar is the foremost international reserve and transactions currency, the main responsibility for leading the world out of the present malaise rests squarely with the United States.

If the United States succeeded in reducing its inflation rate to, say, the present German level, a large area of comparative price stability would emerge consisting of the United States, the present strong-currency countries (Germany, Japan, Switzerland), the countries whose currencies are pegged to the mark (the Netherlands, Belgium, and Austria), and the many countries whose currencies are pegged to the dollar. The creation of such a large bloc of substantial price stability would go a long way toward putting the world economy on a firm basis. Since there would no longer be a presumption for a long-run decline of the dollar and, therefore, no strong inducement to diversify dollar balances into other currencies, remaining or re-emerging imbalances could be handled by mild fluctuation in exchange rates without running the risk of loosening another wave of massive diversification of dollar balances. Thus, the dollar would continue, or resume, its role as the world's foremost reserve and transactions currency, a function that is highly beneficial for the world as well as for the United States.

Part Three

Special Problems

World Agricultural and Trade Policies: Impact on U.S. Agriculture

D. Gale Johnson

Summary

World trade in agricultural products has increased significantly since 1950, though at a slower rate than total world trade. The composition of agricultural trade has changed, with the relative importance of agricultural raw materials declining and both food and feed products increasing. Grains account for about 40 percent of the agricultural exports of the United States, and we account for more than 60 percent of the world's grain exports. Most of the substantial increase in world grain exports in this decade has been provided by the United States.

Agricultural trade is inhibited by a large number of trade restraints. Protection rates of 100 percent or more are common for products produced in the temperate zone. Because of high rates of protection, the European Community (EC) has significantly increased its degree of self-sufficiency for all grains and has become a net exporter of wheat. The high rates of protection for grains, combined with nominal or nonexistent rates of protection for nongrain feed materials in the European Community, have restricted the use of grains for feed. However, since soybeans are a nongrain feed, the United States has realized much larger soybean exports than it would have if protection rates had been more comparable on grain and nongrain products.

The United States has a very high rate of protection for sugar and dairy products, and in both the United States and the European Community high dairy product prices have resulted in surpluses that are often highly subsidized to permit exportation.

293

Trade liberalization for agricultural products would result in a major expansion of our exports. The effect on our imports of agricultural products would be much more modest.

A largely neglected consequence of the existing forms of agricultural protection is the increase in international price instability. In most countries agricultural price and trade policies are designed to stabilize domestic prices and consumption through varying the amount of net trade. Thus changes in world supply and demand for a product are prevented from affecting internal prices, and consumers and producers have no reason to react to changes in international market prices. Such policies, which affect more than half the world's consumption of grain products, impose all the effects of world production and demand variability on the international markets and on the countries that permit their domestic prices to vary with international prices. The result is much greater price variability in international markets than there would be if there were free trade or if protection were achieved by tariffs that were a percentage of the import price.

The net export surplus in our agricultural trade is currently $15 billion. Large agricultural export surpluses are a recent phenomenon. Between the two world wars the United States was a net importer of agricultural products; except for World War II and the years immediately following, the United States continued to be a net agricultural importer until 1956.

There appears to be an anomaly in our trade relations with the rest of the world. The United States is a major net exporter of agricultural products and of high technology products such as airplanes, computers, and complex machinery but a net importer of raw materials and a wide variety of standardized manufactured producer and consumer goods. Our major comparative advantages appear to be in two quite disparate areas—high technology products and a primary industry, namely agriculture.

Appearances are misleading, however, because agriculture has become a high technology sector. It has a high ratio of capital to labor, rapid changes in methods of production, a high rate of adoption of new inputs, and a large flow of resources into research. These characteristics of agriculture became significant after World War II and began to influence the development of agriculture during the 1950s.

Other factors were also important in creating the conditions for agriculture's comparative advantage. One was the removal of most governmental interferences (high price supports and export subsidies) in the domestic and international markets for the major farm export products, especially grains, soybeans, and cotton. A second factor was the striking resource adjustments in agriculture that resulted in lower costs of production at the same time the incomes of farm people increased relative to the rest of the population. A major part of the resource adjustment occurred through the large increase in the importance of off-farm employment and income of farm people.

Modern agriculture is highly complex. Change is rapid, and adjustment to new conditions is continuous. This calls for farm managers who have the capacity to react quickly and effectively. The past two decades have seen a sharp increase in the level of education of farm operators, many of whom have completed college.

If appropriate policies are followed, American agriculture can maintain its comparative advantage. The interrelated requirements of a high technology industry are more difficult to transfer to other countries than are standardized methods of production. In addition, many of the crop varieties and production methods used in agriculture are most effective in particular locations and thus their transfer from one part of the world to another is difficult.

Introduction

During the past decade there have been some remarkable changes in the international trade performance of American agriculture. The competitive position of our agriculture has improved markedly while many other sectors of our economy have had increasing difficulty in maintaining exports or in competing with imports.

Agriculture now has a large export surplus; no other sector of the economy even approaches the size of that surplus. While employing less than 4 percent of the nation's labor force, agricultural exports are approximately 20 percent of all merchandise exports. But our agriculture has not always displayed such a high degree of competitiveness in international markets. The substantial comparative advantage of agriculture has emerged only during the present decade. Between the two world wars the United States imported more agricultural products than it exported, and a similar situation prevailed during the 1950s.

Why has there been such a dramatic shift in the competitive position of U.S. agriculture? A major objective of this paper is to explain that shift. But before presenting the major factors that may have been responsible for the recent export performance of agriculture, recent developments in world and U.S. agricultural trade will be presented. Particular emphasis is given to the great importance of exports to the economic well-being of our farmers. This is followed by a discussion of the numerous and severe restrictions affecting agricultural trade, in terms of the quantities of products that enter international trade and the price instability in international markets. Following a discussion of the development of agriculture's trade surplus, I analyze the factors that may explain the recent comparative advantage of American agriculture. Three factors are considered most significant. Since the 1950s, U.S. agricultural price policies have been designed, at least to some degree, to facilitate exports. The substantial resource adjustments that have occurred in agriculture since the end of World War II have been important in lowering production costs for several major crop products. Finally, and perhaps most important, agriculture has been transformed into a high technology sector of the economy. The availability of new knowledge, rapid changes in its capital structure, a high ratio of capital to labor, and a significant increase in the educational qualifications of farm operators and managers have transformed our agriculture and greatly increased its capacity to produce and to adjust to changing conditions.

Recent Developments in World and U.S. Agricultural Trade

Both the quantity and value of world trade in agricultural products have increased significantly since 1950. Because of the low income elasticity of demand for agricultural products, however, the share of agricultural trade in total world trade declined by half between 1951–1955 and 1971–1975—from 32 to 16 percent.[1]

Trade in agricultural products occurs primarily between the developed market economies. During 1971–1975 these countries accounted for 71 percent of agricultural imports and 62 percent of exports. The centrally planned economies accounted for about a tenth of imports and 9 percent of exports, with the developing countries responsible for the remainders. The developed market economies have significantly increased their share of exports since 1956–1960, when they accounted for half of total agricultural export. Their share of imports has remained approximately constant over the same period. The increased share of exports of the developed market economies came at the expense of the less developed countries.[2]

Significant shifts in the commodity composition of world agricultural trade have occurred since 1950. The largest relative gain has

---

[1] U.S. Department of Agriculture, Economic Research Service, *World Economic Conditions in Relation to Agricultural Trade*, no. 12 (August 1977), p. 25.

[2] *World Economic Conditions*, no. 13 (no date), p. 33.

been in the trade of feed, which reflects the significant expansion of livestock production. There has been a very marked decrease in the relative importance of agricultural raw materials, which include cotton, tobacco, rubber, and industrial vegetable oils. Their percentage of total trade declined from 29 percent in 1950 to 23 percent in 1960 and to 11 percent in 1976. Exports of food products increased from 40 to 55 percent of total agricultural exports between 1950 and 1976 compared with the growth of feed in total exports from 5 to 14 percent.[3]

The changes in the commodity composition of U.S. agricultural exports have been at least as marked as for the world as a whole. The United States in 1950 was even more dependent on the export of agricultural raw materials than the world, and since then the decline in relative importance has been as great as for the world total. Food products showed no change in proportion, but the importance of feed increased to offset fully the relative decline in raw materials.[4]

Between 1961–1965 and 1977 the quantity of world agricultural exports increased by 57 percent, unit value by 157 percent and total value by 286 percent. For Canada and the United States the increase in quantity was 81 percent, unit value 122 percent, and total value 293 percent. In contrast, the quantity of agricultural exports from developing countries increased by 30 percent and from the centrally planned economies by 38 percent.[5]

Grains account for approximately 40 percent of the value of U.S. agricultural exports, and in recent years the United States has accounted for more than 62 percent of world grain exports. The changes in the sources of world grain imports and the destination of grain exports are given in Table 1 for the years immediately before the period of world food difficulties in the early and mid-1970s and for 1976/77 through 1978/79 (years thus indicated are July–June). World exports of grain increased by 74 percent; the United States supplied 78 percent of the total increase in the quantity exported.

The increased net grain imports were primarily in the centrally planned economies (47 percent), North Africa and the Middle East

---

[3] Ibid., p. 36.

[4] Ibid., p. 37.

[5] Food and Agriculture Organization of the United Nations, *Trade Yearbook 1975*, vol. 29, p. 3 and *1977*, vol. 31, p. 35. The measures of changes in the quantity of exports (or imports) and unit values are indexes with weights based on 1961-1965 data. Thus the quantity index is weighted by 1961-1965 international prices in U.S. dollars. The total value measure is derived independently by pricing the actual exports or imports. The total value index measures the change in the current values of exports or imports expressed in U.S. dollars. Exports are priced f.o.b. (free on board) and imports are priced c.i.f. (cost, insurance, and freight).

TABLE 1

NET EXPORTS AND IMPORTS IN WORLD GRAIN TRADE, 1969/70–1971/72 AND 1976/77–1978/79

(million metric tons)

Country	1969/70– 1971/72	1976/77– 1978/79	Percent Change	Percent of Total Change
Net exporters				
United States	38.8	83.1	114	78
Canada	14.6	17.9	23	6
Argentina	8.2	13.9	70	10
South Africa	1.4	2.7	93	2
Oceania	10.7	12.2	14	3
Southeast Asia	3.3	4.1	24	1
Total	77.0	133.9	74	100
Net importers				
European Community	16.1	12.7	−21	−7
Other Western Europe	6.9	8.9	29	4
Japan	14.4	22.5	56	16
Eastern Europe	7.4	11.3	53	8
U.S.S.R.	−4.0	12.0	—[c]	31
China	3.1	7.3	135	8
Latin America[a]	4.9	11.8	140	13
North Africa/Middle East	9.2	17.9	95	17
Central Africa	1.8	3.6	100	3
East Africa	0.3	0.3	0	0
South Asia	5.1	3.7	−28	−3
East Asia[b]	8.4	13.1	56	9
Rest of world	2.3	2.7	19	1
Total	75.9	127.8	68	100

[a] Excluding Argentina.

[b] Excluding Japan.

[c] Status changed from net export to net import.

SOURCE: U.S. Department of Agriculture, Economics, Statistics, and Cooperatives Services, *World Agricultural Situation*, no. 18 (December 1978), p. 38.

(17 percent), Japan (16 percent), and Latin America other than Argentina (13 percent). Two areas—the European Community and South Asia—reduced their grain imports over the period. A very large share of the increased world imports of grain resulted from the shortcomings of agriculture and agricultural policies in the centrally

planned economies and the rapid growth of demand in OPEC or OPEC-supported countries.

The United States is the world's largest exporter of agricultural products and by a wide margin. The value of its agricultural exports in recent years has exceeded that of the next three largest exporters— France, Netherlands, and Australia.[6]

The United States is not only the world's largest exporter of agricultural products but is also the fourth largest importer. Japan, the United Kingdom, and West Germany, with much smaller populations, import somewhat more agricultural products than we do.[7] During the 1978/79 year our agricultural exports exceeded $30 billion and our agricultural imports were approximately half that. The balance of payments surplus generated by agriculture was approximately $15 billion.[8]

Something less than half of our agricultural imports consist of products that we do not produce—coffee, tea, cocoa, rubber, spices, and bananas, primarily. The remainder include products that we do produce but in insufficient quantities to meet demand at reasonable prices. The most important imports of competitive products are beef and veal, pork, dairy products, fruits, vegetables, sugar, wine and beer, and various vegetable oils. In the case of vegetable oils we are large net exporters; the imported vegetable oils have characteristics somewhat different from those of the oils we export. We are also net exporters of fruit and fruit products and export approximately the same value of vegetables and products as we import. Imports of fruits and vegetables are either products such as pineapples, which we do not produce, or seasonal supplies of products such as strawberries and tomatoes.

Crop products account for approximately 90 percent of the value of all agricultural exports. Our exports of livestock products are relatively small, and nearly half of such exports consist of hides, fats, oils, and greases.

As noted earlier, there has been a significant shift in the composition of our agricultural exports since World War II. In 1950 cotton and tobacco accounted for 44 percent of agricultural exports; in 1977/78, for 10 percent. In 1950 grains accounted for 29 percent and oilseeds 6 percent of agricultural exports; in 1977/78 grains

---

[6] Ibid., pp. 9-11.

[7] Ibid.

[8] U.S. Department of Agriculture, Economics, Statistics, and Cooperatives Services and Foreign Agricultural Service, *Outlook for U.S. Agricultural Exports*, February 16, 1979. Estimates are partly projections.

accounted for 40 percent and oilseeds nearly 28 percent.[9] A quite remarkable development of the last few years has been the rapid growth of production and exports of sunflower seeds. As indicated in Table 2, 68 percent of the 1977 sunflower seed output was exported. Production increased more than twelvefold between 1974 and 1978. In fiscal 1978 the value of exports was approximately $225 million and in fiscal 1979 increased by at least $100 million.[10] Sunflowers were such an insignificant crop in 1973 that the U.S. Department of Agriculture did not publish annual data on acreage and production. The production of sunflowers is largely a response to export markets and illustrates the capacity for adjustment that exists in American agriculture.

Exports are critical to the economic well-being of American agriculture. The crop output from 30 percent of all harvested land (about 330 million acres) has been exported in recent years. There is no possibility that the crop output from 100 million acres or even half that area could be absorbed within the domestic economy at prices that would permit profitable production. The importance of exports of individual farm products, as measured by the share of production exported, is shown in Table 2. Exports accounted for more than 50 percent of the 1977 production for rice, sunflowers, wheat, and soybeans. Corn production accounts for nearly a quarter of total harvested area, and 30 percent of corn output was exported.

As noted earlier, U.S. agricultural exports now exceed agricultural imports by $15 billion. While our share of world nonagricultural export trade has declined from a little more than 20 percent during 1951–1955 to 11 percent during 1971–1975, our share of world agricultural exports has remained approximately constant at 20 percent since the end of the Korean War except for a low period during 1969–1971 and a high period during the early 1960s.[11] Since 1953 agricultural exports as a share of our total commodity exports have followed almost exactly the same pattern as the share of our agricultural exports in total world agricultural exports, fluctuating around

---

[9] U.S. Department of Agriculture, Economic Research Service, *U.S. Foreign Agricultural Trade Statistical Report, Fiscal Year 1974*; and U.S. Department of Agriculture, Economics, Statistics, and Cooperatives Services, *FATUS* (Foreign Agricultural Trade of the United States), various issues. The terms "grain" and "oilseeds" include both the raw products and products derived from the raw products. Thus oilseed exports include the product itself, such as soybeans, but also oils and oilmeals derived through processing.

[10] Ibid.; and U.S. Department of Agriculture, Economics, Statistics, and Cooperatives Services, *Fats and Oils Situation*, no. 294 (February 1979), pp. 12-13, and earlier issues.

[11] *World Economic Conditions*, no. 12 (August 1977), p. 25.

TABLE 2

EXPORTS OF SELECTED U.S. AGRICULTURAL COMMODITIES COMPARED WITH PRODUCTION, 1974–1978
(thousand metric tons, except cattle hides)

Commodity	Production					Exports (Year ending September 30)					Exports as Percent of Production				
	1973	1974	1975	1976	1977	1974	1975	1976	1977	1978 [a]	1974	1975	1976	1977	1978
Rice milled	3,033	3,667	4,100	3,782	3,120	1,694	2,214	1,950	2,229	2,107	56	60	48	59	68
Sunflower seed	—	274	545	468	1,330	N.A.	151	312	403	906	N.A.	55	57	86	68
Wheat [b]	46,560	48,496	57,764	58,305	55,133	27,806	30,404	31,127	25,334	33,575	60	63	54	43	61
Soybeans [b]	42,117	33,102	42,113	35,042	47,947	21,484	16,439	20,977	20,384	26,691	51	50	50	53	56
Cattle hides (number)	34,700	37,700	41,800	43,582	42,770	18,203	21,758	23,894	25,085	23,665	52	58	57	57	55
Almonds (shelled basis)	70	104	84	129	142 [c]	32	49	50	61	62	45	47	59	47	43
Cotton, raw	2,825	2,513	1,808	2,304	3,133	1,206	859	699	988	1,317	43	34	39	43	42
Tallow, inedible	2,197	2,569	2,177	2,619 [a]	2,822	1,080	896	930	1,226	1,557	49	35	43	47	41
Prunes, dried	186	129	135	134	142	54	45	58	48	53	29	35	43	36	37
Tobacco, unmanufactured	706	807	885	866	776	314	274	273	290	273	44	34	31	33	35
Corn, grain	144,036	119,416	148,062	159,173	161,821	31,006	28,822	43,126	42,454	49,108	22	24	29	27	30
Grain sorghum	23,450	15,817	19,127	18,283	20,083	5,925	5,362	5,789	6,225	5,357	25	34	30	34	27
Beans, dried	738	922	791	807	739	144	226	132	185	199	19	25	17	23	27
Hops, including extract	25	26	25	26	25	12	11	12	13	6	47	43	47	48	25
Lemons and limes	805	652	1,054	647	936	195	198	204	241	220	24	30	19	37	24
Peanuts	1,576	1,664	1,750	1,701	1,690 [c]	243	258	137	265	319	15	15	8	16	19
Edible offals	1,063	1,157	1,130	1,225	1,220	130	140	152	183	183	12	12	13	15	15

N.A.: Not available.

[a] Preliminary.

[b] Export data include unmilled equivalents of products.

[c] July-June data.

SOURCE: *FATUS* (December 1978), p. 34.

20 percent of the total. During fiscal year 1979 agricultural exports were slightly in excess of a fifth of total exports, down from 25 percent in 1974 but up from 16 percent in 1970. The change in our trade pattern is not one that could have been foreseen. Three decades ago it would have been difficult to predict that the world's largest and most technologically advanced industrial nation would maintain its share of agricultural exports while losing almost half its share of nonagricultural exports.

Interventions in Agricultural Trade

Most agricultural products that are produced in the temperate zones are subject to substantial degrees of protection and trade interventions. Nominal rates of protection of 100 percent or more are common. Such rates are achieved by numerous devices—import quotas, variable levies, tariff duties and fees, embargoes, state trading export subsidies, and sanitary and health regulations.[12]

Some forms of protection do not require direct restraints on trade but operate through domestic subsidies that apply to all or a major share of domestic production.[13] The U.S. programs for wheat and feed grains operate in this way. For the 1977 wheat crop payments averaged about $18 per ton ($0.49 per bushel); the average price received by farmers was $85.50 per ton ($2.33 per bushel). Thus the payments were equal to 21 percent of the price received. For the 1978 program the target price of wheat was increased from $2.90 to $3.40 per bushel. Since the market price was substantially higher in 1978/79 than in the previous year, the payments average $11 per ton ($0.34 per bushel). Payments under the feed grain programs were much more modest, averaging about $4 per ton for both the 1977 and 1978 programs.[14]

In comparison with certain other countries the protection afforded grain producers in the United States is small, indeed. Perhaps the

---

[12] For an excellent and comprehensive review and analysis of nontariff barriers to trade in agricultural products see Jimmye S. Hillman, *Nontariff Agricultural Trade Barriers* (Lincoln: University of Nebraska Press, 1978).

[13] For a description of the farm commodity programs, see my article, "The Food and Agriculture Act of 1977: Implications for Farmers, Consumers, and Taxpayers," in *Contemporary Economic Problems 1978*, William Fellner, ed. (Washington, D.C.: American Enterprise Institute, 1978), pp. 167-209.

[14] U.S. Department of Agriculture, Economics, Statistics, and Cooperatives Services, *Wheat Situation*, no. 247 (February 1979), p. 2, and *Feed Situation*, no. 272 (February 1979), p. 16. The payments include deficiency payments based on the difference between target prices and farm prices and disaster payments for crop failure. No deficiency payments were paid for corn in 1978.

extreme case of protection is provided by rice in Japan. For the 1976 crop the wholesale price for paddy rice in Thailand was $123 per ton and the farm price in the United States $154.50 per ton; the Japanese producer price was approximately $700 per ton.[15] Although this represents an extreme, nominal protection of grain production in the European Community is also high, as indicated in Table 3. The European Community is a major producer and user of grain, consuming nearly 9 percent of the world's grain.

As provided in the Common Agricultural Policy (CAP), threshold prices are established for grains as well as for several other farm products. The threshold price is the minimum price at which imports can enter the European Community. If the import price is below the threshold price, a levy is imposed that equals the difference between the threshold price and the import price. The levy is based on the lowest adjusted price for grain c.i.f. Rotterdam. Prices are monitored daily, and each import price is adjusted to reflect differences from a standard quality of grain to which the threshold price applies. The levy is adjusted daily if any grain import price changes by more than 0.60 units of account (about $0.75) per ton.

As indicated in Table 3 the levies and thus the domestic prices of grain vary substantially from country to country. The domestic prices are only approximately equal to the import price plus the levy, however, and cannot be calculated from the table. In 1977 average wheat prices varied from a high of $250 in West Germany to a low of $165 in the United Kingdom. Corn prices varied from $142 in the United Kingdom to $213 in West Germany. For both corn and wheat the West German price was 50 percent higher than in the United Kingdom. There is very little that is common in the Common Agricultural Policy, but that is not the main point I wish to make. Table 3 shows very high rates of nominal protection for wheat and corn for all of the Common Market, except for corn in the United Kingdom. If there were a common policy for grains the levy in 1977 would have been about $111 per ton for wheat and $93 for corn.

As indicated by the large difference in national grain prices within the EC, there is very little left of the Common Agricultural Policy. At least the prices are not common as they were briefly in the late 1960s. The differences in national prices reflect two factors. The first is that the recent entrants to the EC—Denmark, Ireland, and the United Kingdom—were given a period of five years to adjust their

---

[15] Food and Agriculture Organization, *Monthly Bulletin of Agricultural Economics and Statistics,* various issues. The price for rice in Japan was adjusted for the difference between brown and paddy rice.

TABLE 3
Wheat and Corn Import Prices and Levies, European Community, 1977

| | Wheat (at import price of US$113 per ton) | | Corn (at import price of US$106 per ton) | |
	Levy	Levy/Import price (percent)	Levy	Levy/Import price (percent)
West Germany	137	121	107	101
Netherlands	124	110	95	90
France	94	88	71	67
Belgium	123	109	95	90
Italy	89	79	62	58
Denmark	112	99	82	77
United Kingdom	59	52	38	36
Ireland	102	90	73	69

NOTE: Import prices are based on Rotterdam c.i.f. price; actual import price varies slightly from country to country.
SOURCE: *FATUS* (April 1978), pp. 32-40.

agricultural prices to the EC level. During 1977 such adjustments were still in process; the adjustment period ends in 1979. The second and more important factor has been the development of "green" exchange rates. Threshold prices are established in units of account; the unit of account was equal to the U.S. dollar in 1972 and is now worth about $1.31. The original concept of the CAP was that the relative value of the currencies of the member countries would remain unchanged or, if there were a change, that prices in national currencies would be changed to maintain a constant value in terms of units of account. This is not what has occurred. Countries such as France or the United Kingdom whose currencies have been devalued relative to the unit of account have insisted on translating the unit of account into the national currency at a past rate of exchange to prevent an increase in agricultural and food prices. Countries whose currencies have appreciated, such as West Germany and Netherlands, have not permitted the rise in the value of their currency to be reflected in lower agricultural prices.

The high rates of protection for grains in the EC has resulted in a high and increasing rate of self-sufficiency in grains. For all grains the percentage of self-sufficiency (production as a percentage of use) increased from 83 percent in 1966/67–1970/71 to a projected 97 percent for 1978/79. For wheat the self-sufficiency ratio increased from 90 to 114 percent—the EC is now a net exporter of wheat.[16] In the early 1960s the EC-9 had net imports of 21.5 million tons of grain; in 1978/79 imports were 5 million tons.[17]

One factor responsible for the decline in grain imports has been the price distortions introduced by the CAP. The United States has gained export volume from one distortion and lost from another. The price distortions result from differences in the relative prices of grains, oilmeals, and other nongrain feeding materials within the EC compared with the relative prices in international markets. The distortions in relative prices occur because oilmeals and oilseeds and a variety of other nongrain feeding materials enter the EC either free or at a low duty, while the grains are subject to variable levies that generally range from 50 percent up. As a consequence, the fraction of total livestock concentrate feed from sources other than grain has increased significantly during the past decade.

The extent of the price differentials between grains and oilmeals in the United States and West Germany is shown in Table 4. The differences would be about the same for the Netherlands and smaller for the United Kingdom and France. Since October 1977 the price of soybean meal has been *lower* than the price of corn in Germany; in the United States the price ratio is approximately two to one. A consequence of these pricing policies is that in the European Community the quantity of oilmeal fed was 23 percent of the quantity of grain fed in 1976 and 1977 while it was only 12 percent in the United States.

A number of other nongrain feeds enter the EC either free or at a low duty. The importation of manioc (tapioca or cassava) by the EC-6 countries increased from 95,000 tons in 1962 to 1.4 million tons in 1970. In 1977 the EC-9 imported 4 million tons of manioc, and most of the imports went to the original six EC countries, principally Netherlands and Germany.[18]

---

[16] U.S. Department of Agriculture, Economics, Statistics, and Cooperatives Services, *Agricultural Outlook*, no. 38 (November 1978), p. 18.

[17] *World Agricultural Situation*, no. 18 (December 1978), p. 38. Data are for current members of the European Community. These include Belgium, Luxembourg, West Germany, France, Italy, Netherlands, United Kingdom, Ireland, and Denmark.

[18] *Agricultural Outlook*, no. 38 (November 1978), p. 19; and *FATUS* (July 1972), p. 6. Manioc imports in 1978 were estimated to be 5 million tons (*World Agricultural Situation*, no. 18, p. 14). The duty on manioc is approximately 6 percent. The original EC countries were the first six listed in the previous footnote.

TABLE 4

CORN AND SOYBEAN MEAL PRICES, UNITED STATES AND WEST GERMANY
(US$ per ton)

Year (October–September)	Soybean Meal		Corn		Relative Price— Soybean Meal to Corn	
	United States[a]	West Germany[b]	United States[c]	West Germany[d]	United States	West Germany
1976/77	200	238	90	194	2.22	1.22
1977/78	164	204	89	223	1.84	0.91

[a] Wholesale price at Decatur, Illinois.
[b] Import price.
[c] Wholesale price at Chicago, Illinois.
[d] Import price including variable levy.
SOURCE: U.S. Department of Agriculture, *World Agricultural Situation*, no. 18 (December 1978), p. 15; and U.S. Department of Agriculture, *Agricultural Outlook*, no. 40 (January-February 1979), p. 28.

On the one hand, the United States gained from the fact that imports of soybeans and soybean meal by the EC were larger than they would have been if EC relative prices were similar to those in the international markets. On the other hand, the United States lost because feed grains were displaced by the EC import of manioc in such large quantities. Since manioc has a much lower protein content than the average feedgrain, it needs to be supplemented with substantial amounts of high protein feeds to produce a satisfactory livestock ration. Thus the large-scale import of manioc also served to increase the imports of oilmeals.

The costs per ton of producing soybeans and other oilseeds are substantially greater than the costs of producing feed grains. The relative prices of soybeans and corn in the United States are indicative of relative costs since the United States is the world's largest producer of both products. The price policies of the EC, as well as of Japan and Western European countries generally, result in a significant waste of the world's agricultural resources. The annual value of the excess consumption of oilmeals in the EC alone is approximately $1 billion.

The grain and oilmeal pricing policies have an additional effect on low-income countries. The production of oilmeals, except for fishmeals, is associated with the production of vegetable oils. The excess consumption of oilmeals thus has a depressing impact upon the price of vegetable oils, which many low-income countries produce. The low-income countries gain much less from the oilmeal demand than the United States since the ratio of oilmeals to oil is much lower for their oil bearing plants than for the plants grown in the United States.

The discussion of grain and oilmeal pricing policies is illustrative of other distortions that exist in agricultural trade. Other important examples are sugar, beef, and dairy products. The United States is currently engaged in highly restrictive trade practices for both sugar and dairy products. While we no longer have import quotas on sugar, as we did for nearly three decades until the beginning of 1975, a variety of tariffs, fees, and subsidies have been used to keep domestic prices from 50 to 100 percent above import prices. We control the imports of dairy products through highly restrictive quotas on all but a tiny fraction of the available types of dairy products. As a consequence, dairy product prices in the United States are substantially higher than in the international markets. Imports are controlled to be approximately 2 percent of consumption. Some kinds of cheese are not subject to import quotas if the price exceeds a specified level. Thus those who like—and can afford—high-priced cheeses have relatively free access to the world markets. But those whose tastes run to more mundane—and cheaper—cheeses, such as cheddar, are restricted to American supplies and must pay much more than similar cheeses sell for in international markets.

The United States remains a slightly net importer of dairy products, and in the past two fiscal years net treasury costs of the price support program have ranged from about $450 million to a little more than $700 million.[19] The estimated treasury cost of the EC price support operations for 1977 and 1978 were approximately $4 billion for each of the years, up from about $1.5 billion in 1975. As the *Economist* stated:

> The EEC's prices for dairy products are set at up to five times the world market prices, and the community guarantees that it will buy up all the milk that its dairy farmers produce but cannot sell. Result: a surplus of some 16 percent of output this year [1978] which must be subsidized for sale to consumers, stocked in the notorious butter and skimmed-milk-powder mountains or dumped on world markets with massive export subsidies. And the commission reckons that the sur-

---

[19] U.S. Department of Agriculture, Economics, Statistics, and Cooperatives Services, *Dairy Situation*, no. 373 (December 1978), p. 22. The data are for fiscal years 1977 and 1978.

plus will get worse, as consumption stagnates and production grows at nearly 2 percent a year.[20]

This does not imply that the EC dairy policy is more restrictive or disruptive than that of the United States. The higher costs of the EC dairy program are due to a larger total output and the costs imposed on dairy farmers by the high EC prices of feed grains. While prices received by farmers for milk in recent years have been higher in most EC countries than in the United States, EC farmers face substantially higher costs for grain than do our farmers.

All the major industrial countries protect their sugar producers, and all major industrial countries are high-cost producers of sugar. In 1977/78 the EC produced almost 2 million tons (a little more than 20 percent) more sugar than it consumed.[21] The internal price was approximately double the world price.

One of the consequences of the high U.S. sugar price has been the development of a new process of producing a corn sweetener, namely high fructose corn syrup. While corn sweeteners have long been produced in the United States, largely as a byproduct of other corn products such as starch, the recent high prices of sugar relative to the price of corn has resulted in a major expansion of an important substitute for refined sugar. From less than one pound per capita production in 1971, high fructose corn syrup increased to the dry weight equivalent of eleven pounds per capita in 1978. At this level of consumption it is equal to 11 percent of refined sugar consumption.[22] The expansion in its production has come at the expense of imported sugar and not domestically produced cane and beet sugar.

The creation of the high fructose corn syrup industry has created a new pressure group for higher domestic sugar prices. The long-run level of production of this substitute for refined sugar depends upon the relative prices of sugar and corn. Given the recent quite stable level of corn prices, an increase in the price of sugar means an increase in the profitability of producing the substitute syrup. Since domestic producers of sugar rightly assume that the expanded production of the syrup will influence only the level of imports for many years to come, the new-found competition is seen as a friend rather than a potential enemy. This creation of price interference and economic inefficiency is but another example of some of the unintended effects of inappropriate economic policies. Producers of corn

---

[20] *Economist* (30 September–6 October 1978), p. 60.

[21] Ibid. (1 April–7 April 1978), p. 60.

[22] U.S. Department of Agriculture, *Sugar Sweetener Report*, vol. 3, no. 12 (December 1978), pp. 19 and 34.

are almost certainly mistaken in welcoming this new outlet for their product, since the reduction of sugar imports has both short-run and long-run negative effects upon the level of agricultural exports.

Although some attempts have been made to utilize econometric models of world supply and demand for agricultural products to determine the effects of trade liberalization upon the quantities and prices of agricultural exports, one should not rely very heavily on the results. For many countries free trade or a moderate nominal level of protection, such as 10 or 20 percent, would involve such large changes in prices that past experience of adjustment of output and consumption to modest price changes may give little guidance for estimating the effects of very large changes.

One study of the effects of varying degrees of trade liberalization on agricultural production, consumption, and trade was done in preparation for the U.S. negotiations in GATT.[23] Completed in 1973, the study is based on a mixture of judgment of knowledgeable individuals and the use of available empirical and analytical information on supply and demand responses. While not too much emphasis should be given to the projections for 1980, they give a rough indication of the general order of the impacts of differing degrees of trade liberalization. Three cases were compared to base projections for 1980, which assumed a continuation of the policies of the early 1970s. One case involved complete liberalization of trade in agricultural products for the United States, Western Europe, Japan, Canada, and Australia with continuation of the policies then current for the rest of the world. The one exception to the assumption of complete trade liberalization was for sugar. Even in this very courageous study, sugar resisted inclusion in anything so unreasonable as an exercise for estimating the effects of free trade!

The study projected that U.S. agricultural exports in 1980 would be approximately doubled by free trade compared with exports under a continuation of the trade and farm policies then current. Imports of agricultural products were projected to increase by about a fifth and the positive balance of trade (in 1970 prices) to increase by $8 billion. The study projected a large increase in dairy imports and a shift from net imports to net exports of livestock products as a result of liberalization. The projection indicated a shift from substantial net imports of beef to net exports primarily because of a

[23] *Agricultural Trade and the Proposed Round of Multilateral Negotiations*, report prepared at the request of Peter Flanagan, assistant to the President for International Economic Affairs, Committee on Agriculture and Forestry, U.S. Senate, 93d Congress, 1st session (Washington, D.C., 1973).

more than tenfold increase projected for the Japanese per capita consumption of beef—equivalent to about 60 percent of U.S. per capita consumption.

The projections of the effects of trade liberalization on U.S. agriculture seem reasonable in indicating a large expansion in exports and a modest expansion of imports. Had the preparers of the report bitten the bullet, so to speak, and assumed free trade in sugar, the projected increase in the value of imports would have increased 30 percent instead of 20 percent. It should be repeated that the exercise referred only to the high-income private market economies; the policies in the rest of the world were assumed to be unchanged.

Trade Interventions and International Price Instability

Thus far, as is common in most discussions of interventions in international trade, I have considered primarily the effects on the quantity and value of trade and the efficiency with which resources are used. Until quite recently the effects of certain types of interventions on price variability or instability in the rest of the world have been neglected.[24] If there are variations in either supply or demand for an agricultural product, domestic price stability can be achieved in two different ways—storage and, more usually, variations in net international trade.

The two methods of achieving internal price stability have very different effects on prices in international markets and in other countries. When storage is used, as it was during the 1960s by the United States and Canada, to stabilize prices, it has the effect of making the supply highly elastic within a very limited price range. In effect, as a major part of their price support policies the two governments offered to buy whatever was supplied at a given price and to sell whatever was demanded at a slightly higher price. Thus not only were domestic prices held within a rather narrow range, but so were international prices of wheat and feed grains for a period of twelve years.

If imports or exports are varied to stabilize internal prices, the effect is to increase price variability in the rest of the world. If internal prices are fully stabilized by controlling trade, this means that the price elasticity of demand for imports or the price elasticity of supply of exports, whichever is relevant, is zero. Put another way, the quan-

---

[24] See my article, "World Agriculture, Commodity Policy, and Price Variability," *American Journal of Agricultural Economics*, vol. 59, no. 5 (December 1975), pp. 823-28.

tity of imports is insensitive to the international price or the quantity of exports is independent of external prices. Trade quantities are determined by what is required to stabilize internal prices. None of the variations in world supply and demand, whether the variations occur in the country or outside it, is absorbed by the country or region that stabilizes internal prices.

Why are the elasticities of import demand or export supply zero when domestic prices are stabilized? Two simple examples will suffice to illustrate. The European Community uses variable levies to control international trade in order to achieve internal price stability. A threshold price is established, and the levy varies to equal the difference between the specified price and the landed import cost. If the threshold price were $120 per ton and the landed import cost of the same product were $80, the variable levy would be set at $40. If the landed import cost were $140, an import subsidy of $20 per ton would be paid. Regardless of the external price, domestic buyers would be faced with the price of $120, and supply would be equal to demand at that price. Suppose that within the European Community production declined by 2 million tons; if EC demand were stable, imports would increase by 2 million tons regardless of the external price. Or if the commodity were one that the EC exports, exports would decline by 2 million tons.

The second example is more specific, namely the actual experience of the Soviet Union in 1972–1973. The 1972 Soviet grain crop was 168 million tons, some 13 million tons below the 1971 crop. Net grain imports were increased by 19 million tons, or more than the decline in grain production. Why was this so? First, the policy of the Soviet Union is to stabilize the prices that it pays to producers and the prices charged to consumers. In recent years, it has made a significant effort to equalize the supply and demand for grain at the designated prices. Second, the demand for grain, especially for feed, has been growing by approximately 5 percent annually in recent years. Thus, equating supply with demand for grain at unchanged prices in 1972–1973 required a larger supply than in the previous year. Consequently, grain imports were increased enough to meet both the shortfall in production and the increase in demand. The Soviet Union did not adjust its use of grain at all in response to the world grain production shortfall in 1972–1973 from the previous year, even though it was responsible for approximately 40 percent of the decline in world grain production.

Policies of domestic price stabilization, such as adopted in the European Community, the Soviet Union, Japan, and several other

311

countries, destabilize international prices at all times—not just when production declines below trend levels. When world grain supplies are ample, price stabilization policies do not permit domestic use to increase and thus absorb part of the added available supply. Thus international market prices are lower than they would be if prices in such countries were permitted to decline and the quantity demanded were increased.[25]

It should not be concluded from the previous discussion that protection, as such, is the cause of international price instability. It is the form of protection, not the average level of protection, that is the source of international price instability. Assume that the EC variable levy system has provided an average rate of nominal protection of 50 percent over a number of years. If an ad valorem (percentage of import value) tariff had been used instead of the variable levy, the contribution of the EC to international price instability would have been the same as under free trade in the same product. With the ad valorem tariff, when international prices changed, producers and consumers in the EC would have had the same relative incentives to change production and consumption decisions as if there were free trade. But with the variable levy it is the degree of protection that varies when international prices vary; the internal prices to which consumers and producers respond do not change. Under the Common Agricultural Policy the degree of nominal protection for some grains has varied from more than 100 percent to negative rates of protection in recent years. The negative rates of protection occurred when import prices exceeded the threshold prices and an import subsidy was required. In 1973 and 1974 it was also necessary for the European Community to apply export levies on wheat to prevent exports that would have resulted in an increase in internal prices.

Increasing the variability of prices in international markets and in the countries whose prices vary with international prices increases the demand for storage. The amount of storage is a function of expected price variability—the greater the variability the greater the demand for storage. If there were free trade in grains or if domestic prices varied with international prices, the economic level of storage

---

[25] For three efforts to provide quantitative estimates of the price effects of stabilizing domestic agricultural prices, see Shun-yi Shei and Robert L. Thompson, "The Impact of Trade Restrictions on Price Stability in the World Market," *American Journal of Agricultural Economics*, vol. 59, no. 4 (November 1977), pp. 628-38; Paul R. Johnson, Thomas Grennes, and Marie Thursby, "Devaluation, Foreign Trade Controls, and Domestic Wheat Prices," ibid., pp. 619-27, and "Insulating Trade Policies, Inventories, and Wheat Price Stability," *American Journal of Agricultural Economics*, vol. 60, no. 1 (February 1978), pp. 132-34.

would be much lower than with current agricultural and trade policies. The increased price variability results in a waste of resources by artificially creating a demand for stocks.

Development of Agriculture's Trade Surplus

The large net export surplus in U.S. agricultural trade is a recent phenomenon. Starting with fiscal year 1974 the net trade surplus has exceeded $10 billion annually. In fiscal 1973, the net positive trade balance was $7.2 billion, more than treble that of the previous year. Since 1973 the net export surplus has continued to increase and reached $15 billion in fiscal 1979.[26]

During the last half of the nineteenth century the United States followed the pattern associated with developing countries. As late as 1880 agricultural exports accounted for 80 percent of total exports, and there was a significant excess of agricultural exports over agricultural imports. In the years immediately prior to World War I agricultural exports still accounted for approximately half of total exports. Even as late as the mid-1920s, when the United States had emerged as a major industrial nation, agricultural exports were 40 percent of total exports.

However, 1922 was the beginning of two decades (save but one year) during which the value of U.S. agricultural imports exceeded the value of agricultural exports. It was not until the early years of World War II that the United States once again became a net exporter of agricultural products. This development was almost certainly caused by the disruptions of production and transport during the war rather than any fundamental improvement in the comparative advantage of U.S. agriculture.

The net export of agricultural products lasted only a few years. In 1950 imports once again exceeded exports and continued to do so through 1956, even though during most of this period the United States supplied substantial quantities of agricultural products to other nations at low cost or free through its aid programs. It was not until the early 1960s that agricultural exports would have exceeded agricultural imports if there had been no P.L. 480, the food aid program. It is not possible to pinpoint the exact year when the transition would have occurred since some of the food aid shipments displaced commercial exports.

What was responsible for the large increase in the net agricultural surplus during the 1970s? One of the major objectives of this essay

---

[26] *Outlook for U.S. Agricultural Exports* (February 16, 1979), p. 2.

is to explain why American agriculture has emerged with such a large export surplus. For the moment, however, we shall consider only the role of prices and quantities and any changes that may have occurred in our trade barriers that might have influenced the quantity of imports. The next section will consider factors that may explain the significant change in the comparative advantage of agriculture during the 1970s.

In 1971 the value of agricultural exports was $8.0 billion; imports $6.1 billion. By 1977 the value of agricultural exports had trebled, and the value of imports had somewhat more than doubled. The growth in the value of exports was due to a 54 percent increase in quantity and a 94 percent increase in prices. Import volume increased by 19 percent while import unit values increased by 104 percent.[27] Thus, the growth of export volume was almost three times as great as the growth of import volume while export prices increased somewhat less than import prices.

The significant increase in the U.S. net agricultural trade balance has been the result of maintaining a constant or slightly increasing share of world exports and a declining share of world imports. One possible explanation for our declining share of world imports of agricultural products might be that our barriers to imports increased during the 1970s. This explanation has little or no validity. The farm products that were heavily protected during the 1960s, such as dairy products and sugar, are the same products heavily protected during the 1970s. Most of our agricultural imports enter either duty free (rubber, coffee, cocoa, tea, palm oil) or at rates of 5 percent or less. In 1976 the average import duty on dutiable farm products (one half of imports) was 7 percent; a decade earlier the duty averaged 10.8 percent.[28]

The only apparent significant increase in the protection of agricultural products in the 1970s compared with the 1960s has been for beef. But this increase has been more apparent than real. We do have import restrictions on beef and veal in the guise of voluntary export restraints by the major exporters. The restraints have had some effect on beef and veal imports during the 1970s, but the effects have been small. During part of the 1970s the restraints were removed, and in 1974 imports were below those that would have been permitted under the program. The maximum restraint in any year was

---

[27] *FATUS* (March 1978), pp. 45-46, and (September 1978), pp. 112-14. The quantity indexes are for fiscal years; the unit values for calendar years. Publication of these series has been discontinued, at least temporarily.

[28] *FATUS* (August 1977), pp. 80-84.

probably 10 to 20 percent, with the lower figure the more probable. In 1978, in the face of rising domestic beef prices, the restraints on beef imports were increased by 200 million pounds, or more than 15 percent.[29] In announcing the 1979 restraint level, the U.S. Department of Agriculture estimated that in the absence of restraints the imports of beef and veal subject to the restraints might have been 6 percent greater.[30] There are significant imports outside the restraint system, primarily cooked and processed beef from countries subject to hoof and mouth disease. Imports of cooked and canned beef are not controlled at all, and duties are very low, generally less than 5 percent.

As noted above, the quantity of agricultural exports increased by more than 50 percent from 1971 through 1977, which accounted for a significant part of the increase in the value of exports. This growth was due to production increases for major export products and a decline in domestic utilization of some of the same products. While total agricultural output increased by 12 percent between the first two years of this decade and 1977 and 1978, livestock output remained unchanged. Thus crops accounted for all the increase in output, and essentially all the increased crop output was available for export. Significant production increases were realized for four major exports—feed grains, food grains, oilseeds, and cotton, with the largest increase for oilseeds.

During 1977 and 1978 the United States used lower absolute amounts of all grains than during the first two years of the decade.[31] While the domestic use of soybeans has increased gradually during the decade, the export of soybeans increased from 52 percent of production for the first two years to 58 percent in 1977 and 56 percent in 1978.[32] Thus restraint in the domestic demand for the major export products also contributed to the expansion of agricultural exports, though the major factor was output growth.

Comparative Advantage of U.S. Agriculture

The United States stands in a singularly unique trade relationship with the rest of the world. It is a major net exporter of agricultural products and a large net importer of other raw materials. It is a

---

[29] U.S. Department of Agriculture, Economics, Statistics, and Cooperatives Services, *Livestock and Meat Situation*, no. 221 (June 1978), p. 4.

[30] U.S. Department of Agriculture, *News*, December 29, 1978.

[31] *World Agricultural Situation*, no. 18 (December 1978), p. 38.

[32] *FATUS* (November 1973), p. 34.

major net exporter of high technology products such as airplanes, computers, sophisticated military hardware, and complex machinery but a large net importer of a wide variety of standardized manufactured producer and consumer goods. Our major comparative advantages seem to be in two quite disparate areas—high technology products and a primary industry, namely agriculture.

There may well be less of an anomaly in our trade pattern than the previous sentence implies. It can be argued, and I will so argue, that American agriculture is today a high technology sector of our economy. While there is no clear definition of high technology, most would agree that certain characteristics are associated with such an industry or sector: a relatively high ratio of capital to labor; rapid changes in the methods or techniques of production; a high rate of adoption of new and improved inputs; and a relatively large annual flow of resources into research. Where these characteristics prevail, the transfer of technology to other countries is difficult compared with, say, the production of such products as radios, television sets, textiles, or steel. Admittedly the description of a high technology sector is imprecise and impressionistic, but yet the characteristics indicated may be helpful in putting the comparative advantage of U.S. agriculture in proper perspective.

Three inappropriate explanations of the comparative advantage of U.S. agriculture are frequently offered. It is quite common for foreigners, especially those from Western Europe and Japan, to attribute the high productivity of American agriculture to the enormous amount of excellent land and the generally favorable characteristics of our climate. It is true that we are blessed with much land of excellent quality; there exists nowhere else in the world an equivalent area of high-quality land such as exists in the American corn belt. Another explanation for the high productivity is the large size of American farms compared with those in Western Europe or in most other parts of the world outside the centrally planned economies. This statement is empirically valid. A third explanation is that American agriculture employs relatively few workers, and the ratio of land area per worker is very much greater than almost anywhere else in the world. Comparable ratios exist only in Canada and Australia.

Although the facts on which these explanations are based can be verified, they were equally valid, at least in a relative sense, when the United States was a net importer of agricultural products. The explanations probably rest on the mistaken impression that the United States has been a net exporter of agricultural products throughout the past century or more. But, as has been noted, agriculture's substantial comparative advantage has emerged only recently.

The reemergence of U.S. agriculture as a net exporter in the early 1960s was due, in my opinion, to three important factors: (1) modification of our agricultural price, incomes, and exchange rate policies; (2) significant resource adjustments in agriculture after World War II; and (3) the emergence of U.S. agriculture as a high technology sector. Each was important, and there have been significant interrelationships among the three.

Policy Modifications. During the 1950s, price supports for the major grains and cotton were established at levels significantly above market clearing prices. Large stocks were accumulated by the government even though efforts were made to reduce production. Exports declined during the early 1950s, and efforts to reduce the accumulation of stocks included the expansion of food aid and the payment of export subsidies on commercial sales. Starting in the late 1950s price support levels were lowered, and by 1966 price supports for most commodities were at or below international prices. When the price supports were above market clearing levels, export subsidies were used to maintain an acceptable level of exports or the quantity of exports was adversely affected. When price supports significantly influenced the domestic price, exports were largely determined by the kind and extent of governmental intervention. When price supports were lowered, the market was permitted to function in allocating the available supply between domestic and export uses, and there can be little doubt that exports increased significantly as a consequence.

Schuh has argued that the overvaluation of the U.S. dollar prior to the 1971 devaluation had imposed substantial costs upon agriculture, restraining the growth of exports and adding to the resource adjustments required to obtain a satisfactory level of labor returns in agriculture.[33] The overvaluation of the dollar resulted in a lower level of prices of farm products in the domestic market and in greater difficulty in competing for resources with all sectors of the economy except the other export-oriented industries. There can be little doubt that the devaluation of the dollar in 1971 and the floating of the dollar in 1973 encouraged agricultural exports and improved the relative profitability of agricultural production in the United States. Consequently, the change in exchange rate policy clearly contributed to the size of the net agricultural trade surplus in recent years, even

---

[33] G. Edward Schuh, "The Exchange Rate and U.S. Agriculture," *American Journal of Agricultural Economics*, vol. 56, no. 1 (February 1974), pp. 1-13.

though other factors may have been primarily responsible for the transition from a net import to a net export position.

Resource Adjustments. The significant resource adjustments that occurred in agriculture after World War II were described in my article in *Contemporary Economic Problems 1977*. These changes included a rapid reduction in the labor input per unit of farm output and an increase in the amount of capital per worker. Very importantly, agriculture became more fully integrated into the economy, and the off-farm income of farm people increased significantly so that by the mid-1960s approximately half the net income of farm operator families was derived from off-farm sources. Although real farm prices declined by more than 20 percent from the early 1950s to 1970, the per capita disposable income of the farm population increased from about 60 percent of the nonfarm population's in the early 1950s to about 75 percent by 1970.

A High Technology Sector. What is today described as modern agriculture is a recent development. The first of the new high-yielding varieties—hybrid corn—became available only during the mid-1930s. It was not planted on half the corn area until 1942. The second important new high-yielding variety—grain sorghums—did not become available until the mid-1950s. Grain yields in the United States in 1930 were very little greater than they had been six decades earlier. The benefits of agricultural research until the 1930s were relatively small and were confined primarily to labor-saving inventions. Output-increasing innovations did not occur until there were significant breakthroughs in plant breeding. Once the yield potentials of several major economic crops were increased significantly, numerous other innovations and adjustments occurred that resulted in substantial increases in yield and output.

Between 1910–1914 and 1937–1941 crop production per acre increased by 8 percent; from 1937–1941 to 1950–1954 by 15 percent; from 1937–1941 to 1960–1964 by 51 percent and to 1975–1978 by 100 percent.[34] Almost all the increase in output per acre of cropland occurred after 1955 and much of it since 1964.

Farm output per hour of farm work increased even more dramatically over the same period—by 660 percent between 1937–1941 and 1976. Again most of the improvement occurred after 1955, though

---

[34] U.S. Department of Agriculture, Economic Research Service, *Changes in Farm Production and Efficiency 1977*, Statistical Bulletin no. 581 (November 1977), p. 19; and *Agricultural Outlook*, no. 40 (January-February 1979), p. 18.

less so than for the increase in crop production per acre. Output per farm worker nearly doubled between 1937–1941 and 1950–1954 and then doubled again by 1960–1964 and again by 1976.[35]

Modern agriculture is highly dependent upon the services of many other sectors of the economy. It depends upon major continuing research efforts in both the public and private sectors. It depends upon competitive and innovative input sectors that continuously introduce new and improved products and supplies them on a timely and assured basis. It depends upon an efficient marketing and transport sector that minimizes costs of delivering inputs to farms and of delivering the output of farms to processors and consumers. American agriculture is favored on all of these scores. This is not to say that similar circumstances do not exist in any other part of the world, but only a limited number of countries provide as effective a setting for agriculture as is available for U.S. agriculture. Certainly the agricultures of the centrally planned economies are not supported with the same degree of effectiveness. Nor are the agricultures of the developing countries similarly favored.

American agriculture is supported by a large and varied set of research institutions. In 1974 approximately a quarter of the world's agricultural research expenditures was made in the United States. The share of this research undertaken in the industrial sector is much larger in the United States than in any other economy. The firms that do the relevant research are primarily in the agricultural input industries. Such firms obviously draw upon both the basic and applied research of the federal and state agricultural research institutions. A substantial amount of research being undertaken in the input-producing firms means a relatively rapid productive utilization of recent research results. It can also be argued that there is more competition among agricultural research institutions in the United States than in the rest of the world, even within the publicly supported sector. Each state has one or more agricultural experiment stations, and the federal government has a number of different research enterprises. While some of the support for state research comes from the federal government, funds supplied by state governments dominate.

The amount of capital per farm worker has dramatically increased since 1950. In constant 1978 dollars the value of production assets per farm worker has increased from $40,000 in 1950 to $150,000 in 1978. If one excludes all land and buildings, the increase has been

---

[35] *Changes in Farm Production and Efficiency 1977*, p. 45.

from approximately $9,000 in 1950 to $28,000 in 1978. A large part of the increase in capital per worker occurred after 1960. Production assets per worker in 1978 dollars as of 1960 was $55,000 and other than land and buildings, $14,000.[36] In 1976 the 500 largest industrial corporations had $39,000 of assets per employee; production assets per farm worker were almost $125,000 by the end of 1976.[37]

A further indication of the capital intensity of U.S. agriculture is the relative importance of annual capital consumption to net product. In 1977 capital consumption, including capital consumption allowance, was 40 percent of agriculture's net national product.[38] For all nonfinancial corporations capital consumption, including the capital consumption allowance, was approximately 12 percent of net domestic product. The high relative capital consumption of agriculture occurs even though its major production asset, namely land, is not considered in the estimates of capital consumption. Perhaps the most important implication of high ratio of capital consumption allowances to net product in agriculture is that it indicates a rapid turnover in the stock of capital equipment and the degree to which the capital stock represents the newest and most modern equipment available.

Important as material capital may be in a high technology sector, human capital is at least as important. One form of human capital is utilized in the development of new knowledge, primarily in the public and private research institutions. But the material capital and the new knowledge must be combined with other resources by the farm operator or entrepreneur.

Modern agriculture is highly complex. Change is rapid; adjustment to new conditions is continuous. There is a continuing flow of new knowledge and new inputs. Agriculture is subject to wider price variations than most other sectors of the economy and, in addition, is subject to numerous natural conditions over which it has no control. Efficient allocation of resources is both complicated and difficult, requiring a high level of skill. By comparison with other sectors of the economy, farm firms are relatively small. This means

[36] Calculated from Board of Governors of the Federal Reserve System, Division of Research and Statistics, *Agricultural Finance Databook: Annual Series* (September 1976), table 512.1; and U.S. Department of Agriculture, Economics, Statistics, and Cooperatives Services, *Balance Sheet of the Farming Sector, 1978*, Supplement no. 1, Agricultural Information Bulletin no. 416 (October 1978).

[37] U.S. Department of Commerce, Bureau of the Census, *Statistical Abstract of the United States 1977*, p. 563; and *Balance Sheet of the Farming Sector, 1978*, p. 27.

[38] *Survey of Current Business* (December 1978), pp. 1-3.

that the increasing productivity of agriculture depends upon the capacities of hundreds of thousands of entrepreneurs.

The effects of education on productivity may be divided into two parts—the worker effect and the allocative effect. According to Finis Welch, the worker effect refers to improvement in production as education is increased, with other factors of production held constant. Education may also improve allocative efficiency or ability to acquire and utilize information about costs and the productive characteristics of other inputs, including the characteristics of unfamiliar inputs such as new seed varieties or new machines or new methods of cultivation. Welch concluded that agriculture "is probably atypical inasmuch as a larger share of the productive value of education may refer to allocative ability than in most industries."[39]

Welch's analysis of data for U.S. agriculture shows that the return to the operators with the most education, namely college graduates, is substantially higher than for all other educational levels. A significant part of the increased return to the college graduate is attributed to expenditures on research, which contribute to the changing and dynamic characteristics of agriculture. In effect, as Schultz has argued, "the value of schooling in farming depends on the opportunities that farmers have to modernize their production." As Schultz has noted, modern agriculture is in a continuous state of disequilibrium because it undergoes rapid changes as new knowledge and new inputs become available. Before complete adjustment can be made to any set of conditions, new potentialities have been made available. He concludes: "There is enough evidence to give validity to the hypothesis that the ability to deal successfully with economic disequilibria is enhanced by education and that this ability is one of the major benefits of education accruing to people privately in a modernizing economy." [40]

In a recent article, Welch summarizes a number of studies of the returns to education in agriculture related to allocative efficiency. His conclusion was:

Based on what by now is a large body of accrued evidence, it seems clear that in U.S. agriculture—a particularly dynamic technical setting—education enhances allocative efficiency. Furthermore, increased scale increases incentives for "correct" decisions and results not only in the "purchase" of

---

[39] Finis Welch, "Education in Production," *Journal of Political Economy*, vol. 78, no. 1 (January/February 1970), p. 47.

[40] Theodore W. Schultz, "The Value of the Ability to Deal with Disequilibria," *Journal of Economic Literature*, vol. 13, no. 3 (September 1975), pp. 841 and 843.

more education for operators of larger farms but in related investments that enhance response.[41]

Since the end of World War II there has been a significant absolute and relative increase in the educational levels of farm operators in the United States. Simultaneously there has been a substantial increase in the scale or size of farms. Since 1960 gross sales per farm, measured in constant dollars, have more than doubled. Another measure of farm scale—farm output per farm—increased 86 percent between 1960 and 1977.[42]

There has been a significant increase in the years of school completed by farmers and farm managers during the past two decades. For male farmers and farm managers twenty-five years old or more, the median years of schooling completed in 1960 was 8.7 years; in 1970, 10.6. For all males in the labor force the increase was from 11.0 to 12.3 years. By 1970 the years of school had exceeded twelve years for three age groups—twenty-five to twenty-nine, thirty to thirty-four, and thirty-five to forty-four. In 1960 the median years of schooling for the thirty-five to forty-four age group was 9.9. Available data indicate a continued increase in years of school completed through 1975, especially for the forty-five to sixty-four age group—from 9.0 years in 1970 to 10.9 years in 1975.[43]

The increase in educational attainment for farm operators represents two factors. The first is that the gap between years of school completed by urban and rural residents has been largely eliminated over the past three decades. The second is the influence of mobility. If one follows the age cohorts from 1960 to 1970, the data indicate that farm operators in the forty-five to fifty-four age group in 1970 completed 0.9 more years of school than did the same cohort a decade earlier. Quite obviously, the farm operators who remained in agriculture had more years of schooling than those who left for other economic activities.

---

[41] Finis Welch, "The Role of Human Investments in Agriculture," in *Distortions of Agricultural Incentives*, Theodore W. Schultz, ed. (Bloomington: Indiana University Press, 1978), p. 274.

[42] Based on *Changes in Farm Production and Efficiency 1977*, pp. 6-7; *Agricultural Outlook* (December 1978), p. 21; and U.S. Department of Agriculture, *Agricultural Statistics 1977*, p. 422.

[43] U.S. Department of Commerce, Bureau of the Census, *Census of Population 1960*, vol. 5B, *Educational Attainment*, table 8; and ibid., *1970*, table 11. For each age group under forty-five, the percentage of farm operators and managers who had completed at least four years of college doubled between 1960 and 1970. For the cohorts aged thirty-five to forty-four and forty-five to fifty-four in 1960, the decline in the number of farm operators was 33 percent and 42 percent, respectively. The decline in the number with four or more years of college was 17 percent and 20 percent.

Transferring Agricultural Technology. A characteristic of modern agriculture is that many significant improvements are location specific. In other words, crop varieties and some production practices are specifically adapted to the soil and climatic conditions of limited geographical areas. In order to take advantage of the matching of local conditions with the most appropriate varieties, production methods, and equipment, agriculture must be supplied with the continuing output of sophisticated research and with the required inputs. American agriculture is greatly favored on both counts.

An important implication of the location specificity of much of modern agriculture is that it is difficult effectively to transfer varieties and production methods from one part of the world to another. Although modern research has produced crop varieties that are less sensitive to certain climatic conditions, such as length of day, than were crop varieties developed as recently as two decades ago, the advantages of technological leadership remain very great.

Maintaining Agriculture's Comparative Advantage. If appropriate governmental policies are followed, U.S. agriculture should retain its comparative advantage into the indefinite future. Continued support of agricultural research is essential, as are price and incomes policies that permit the market to allocate available supplies between domestic and foreign consumers and permit farmers a high degree of freedom in utilizing their resources in an efficient manner. Agriculture's comparative advantage would be more striking if its major products faced trade barriers in its export markets similar to those enjoyed by most industrial products. We should, of course, reduce those of our own barriers that interfere with efficient use of the world's agricultural resources. We have much to gain from a substantial reduction in trade barriers, including our own.

Concluding Comments

World agriculture has been subjected to numerous shocks and changes in the past decade. The 1970s began with large stocks of grains held in the major grain-exporting nations; international grain prices in real terms were only a little above the lowest levels of the Great Depression, and the major exporters took measures to reduce the production of grains, especially of wheat. A very small reduction in world grain production in 1972 was followed by a sharp increase in world grain trade, the rapid depletion of the grain stocks held by the exporters, and the doubling of grain prices within a year.

The higher grain prices were relatively short-lived; prices started to decline in mid-1976 and by the last quarter of 1977 had returned to the low levels of the early 1970s. Since the end of 1977 grain prices, especially wheat prices, have strengthened but in early 1979 are still the lowest real prices since the depression of the 1930s except for the very low prices of the late 1960s and early 1970s.

The relatively low prices persist alongside a level of international trade in grains that is more than half greater than during the early part of the 1970s. But world trade in grain, which has recently been as much as 180 million tons out of production of 1,350 million tons, could be significantly greater if the agricultural and trade policies of several nations were modified to permit more liberal trade.

The Natural Gas
Policy Act of 1978:
An Economic Evaluation

Walter J. Mead

Summary

The pricing provisions of the Natural Gas Policy Act of 1978 are clearly a mixture of new costs and new benefits for the nation. The NGPA is a poor piece of legislation in terms of resource allocation, but it replaces the Natural Gas Act of 1938, which was also poor for resource allocation.

The new act, frequently described as a decontrol law, in fact brings under price control supplies that flowed freely in intrastate commerce under the previous act. It then proceeds in three steps to decontrol gas classified as high-cost or new, but retains control permanently for most classes of old gas, including old intrastate gas that formerly was free of control.

Under the old NGA, wellhead prices of interstate gas were set by the Federal Power Commission below market clearing levels. At these artificially low prices, consumer demand for gas was stimulated and supplies were retarded, in relation to what they would have been under free market conditions. Thus, the control system created a shortage that is part of what is now called the "energy crisis." Under past controls, U.S. natural gas reserves reached a peak in 1967 and have since followed a 4 percent annual rate of decline. Annual domestic gas production peaked in 1973 and is now on a 4.9 percent rate of decline. Because intrastate gas prices were not controlled, gas has generally been available in producer states, although at higher prices. This availability has led to a misallocation of plant investments as gas-using industries shifted some of their production facilities into gas-producing states.

Under the new NGPA, pricing procedures are extremely complex, and regulations have created approximately thirty-three tiers of natural gas prices at wellhead. Effective in January 1979, mandated prices range from a minimum rate of $0.204 to $2.243 per thousand cubic feet (Mcf) for stripper well production, with price distinctions based on nine separate factors. In addition, pipeline firms must discriminate between certain industrial and other customers. The thirty gas-producing states are now required to classify natural gas production on the basis of five factors.

Price escalation is provided so that the real cost of most gas will remain constant. However, bonus escalation is allowed for high-cost gas, new gas from new leases, and stripper well production. These three classes receive an additional 3.5 to 4 percent annual price increase.

Price decontrol is legislated in three phases effective on November 1, 1979, for certain classes of high-cost gas, on January 1, 1985, for some classes of new gas plus some old intrastate gas, and on July 1, 1987, for another class of new gas. For all other categories (primarily old gas) price control is to be permanent. This includes some old intrastate gas which was free of control under the previous act. All price controls may be reimposed for an eighteen-month period at any time between July 1, 1985, and June 30, 1987.

Under the new act, wellhead prices are not likely to increase as fast as was permitted during the 1974–1978 period. Under the NGPA, most classes of gas will remain at a constant real price until decontrolled. This will include nearly 100 percent of production during the first year of the new act. In contrast, during the last four years of the old act, the real price of natural gas at wellhead was allowed to increase at a compound annual rate of 23 percent.

The NGPA will continue to hold natural gas prices below free market levels for residential consumers for as long as gas is produced from old wells. This has great political appeal and may be a sufficient explanation for the congressional action. It is counterproductive, however, for resource conservation. It continues to encourage wasteful consumption of a valuable nonrenewable resource. It legislates "unfair competition" for substitute energy technologies including solar, wind, bioconversion, and the like. It also leads to increased demand for oil, primarily for industrial uses, and thereby leads to increased dependence on foreign supplies and to greater balance of payments pressures.

The new act is a substantial improvement on the supply side. It decontrols high-cost gas on an early schedule, and new gas is fully decontrolled by July 1, 1987. While this is an improvement over the NGA, it is less efficient than free market conditions.

Administrative costs will clearly increase under the new act because of the expansion of controls to include intrastate gas and the complexity of administering thirty-three different price tiers. The cost of adjudicating the inevitable legal disputes will also be high. The costs to the government and to the complying industry of administering energy control programs are likely to be approximately $4 billion per year, paid in the long run by taxpayers and consumers.

There are no clear offsetting benefits for resource allocation efficiency. The primary arguments offered in support of price controls are concerned not with efficiency but rather with income redistribution, that is, with avoiding windfall profits and adverse impacts on the poor. Both arguments are shown to be only partially valid, although politically powerful.

On the basis of efficient allocation of resources, the NGPA appears to be an improvement over the Natural Gas Act. However, it will lead to more waste of valuable natural and human resources than under free market conditions.

Introduction

After an intense debate lasting eighteen months, and a host of compromises that attempted to balance the advantages of competing interest groups, Congress finally passed the Natural Gas Policy Act (NGPA) which became law on November 9, 1978. The act itself covers sixty pages of fine print; additional volumes of detailed regulations must be issued by the Federal Energy Regulatory Commission (FERC). As of this date, the FERC has issued 364 pages of regulations, with more to come.

In approving the act, Congress "washed its hands" of the natural gas pricing problem. The frustrations generated in the struggle over the act mean that Congress will not soon reexamine or amend any element in the NGPA. To reopen any single issue in this complex legislation would so disturb the existing political equilibrium that one adjustment would call for another. Therefore, industry, consumers, and the bureaucracy must accommodate and live with this legislation for the foreseeable future.

Natural gas is second to oil as a major source of energy in the U.S. economy. As indicated in Table 1, gas accounts for 31.6 percent of all U.S. primary energy production and 25.5 percent of consumption. Natural gas reserves in the United States (excluding Prudhoe Bay, Alaska) reached a peak in 1967 and have since been declining at a 4.6 percent annual rate. Production peaked out in 1973 and is on a

TABLE 1

U.S. Primary Energy Production and Consumption, 1978

	Natural Gas (dry)	Crude Oil	Coal	Hydro-electric Power	Nuclear Electric Power	Geothermal Power and Others	Total
Domestic production							
Btu (10^{15})	19.254	20.610[a]	15.136	2.949	3.012	0.071	61.031
Percent	31.6	33.8	24.8	4.8	4.9	0.1	100.0
Customary measure	18.857 trillion cubic feet	3,554[a] million barrels	661 million tons	283 billion kwh	280 billion kwh	3.3 billion kwh	61.031 Btu (10^{15})
Net energy imports							
Btu (10^{15})	0.904	13.555[b]	(1.042)[c]	0.180		0.120[d]	16.555
Customary measure	0.885 trillion cubic feet	2,165 million barrels	(45.5)[c] million tons	17.1 billion kwh		5.6 billion kwh	16.555 Btu (10^{15})
Domestic consumption							
Btu (10^{15})	19.779	37.526[e]	14.044	3.131	3.002	0.191	77.672
Percent	25.5	48.3	18.1	4.0	3.9	0.2	100.0

[a] Includes natural gas liquids.
[b] Excludes imports for the Strategic Petroleum Reserve.
[c] Parentheses indicate "negative" imports, that is, exports.
[d] Coke made from coal.
[e] Petroleum, including crude and refined products.
Source: U.S. Department of Energy, *Monthly Energy Review*, February 1979.

3.7 percent rate of decline. These dramatic reductions in natural gas reserves and production are partly the result of long-standing federal policies that first artificially stimulated production through tax subsidies (percentage depletion allowance and expensing of intangible drilling costs) and then artificially retarded production and stimulated demand by imposing price controls.

The objective of this chapter is to provide an economic evaluation of the pricing provisions of NGPA. First, I will set forth the standards for evaluation. In the second section the predecessor Natural Gas Act (NGA) and its results will be examined for purposes of comparison. In the third section the pricing provisions of the act will be identified as simply as possible. Finally, the most important economic consequences of new pricing legislation will be evaluated relative to the standards set forth in the first section, and conclusions will be drawn.

Standards for Evaluating the NGPA

Because natural gas is an exhaustible natural resource, the evaluation of NGPA will be in terms of optimum resource allocation in general, and resource conservation in particular.

Everyone is in favor of "conservation," but it is a term rarely defined by those who publicly endorse it. In some circles, conservation is thought to be attained only when resources are locked up. In the political arena of Washington, D.C., a more modest view of conservation appears to prevail, equating conservation with less use. But this definition is without a theoretical framework and regresses ultimately into a plea for no use at all.

The commonplace view of conservation has been stimulated intellectually by some leading geologists. For oil, coal, and natural gas, Hubbert has constructed bell-shaped normal curves of production over time and argued that the rate of production "must begin at zero, rise until it passes over one or more maxima, and finally decline gradually to zero."[1] In the case of crude oil his model indicates that 80 percent of U.S. reserves will be produced over a period of sixty-five years ending late in the present century and that production will fall to near zero by the year 2060.[2] Hubbert's model makes no allowance for either sharp price increases, which would obviously occur as a

---

[1] M. King Hubbert, "Energy Resources," in Committee on Resources and Man, National Academy of Sciences/National Research Council, *Resources and Man*, Preston Cloud, ed. (San Francisco: W. H. Freeman & Co., 1969), p. 167.

[2] Ibid., p. 183.

result of his anticipated resource depletion, or major technological improvements for efficient energy recovery, which should be stimulated by sharply higher prices.

More recently a series of doomsday projections have appeared, based partly on impending resource exhaustion. For example, the Club of Rome group, on the basis of present growth trends in resource depletion and other factors, projected that "the limits to growth on this planet will be reached sometime within the next one hundred years."[3] The Club of Rome work has been criticized by economists who point out that the model contains no effective price system. Thus it does not take into account that consumers would economize on increasingly scarce (higher-priced) resources, consumers and producers would search out cheaper substitutes, and producers would be led by sharply higher prices to introduce major technological innovations.

An economic interpretation of resource conservation will be used here to evaluate the NGPA. Conservation in an economic sense may be applied both over time and at any point in time. Over time, optimum resource conservation occurs when society maximizes the present value of its resources. Thus, decisions on whether to produce and utilize resources in the present or in the future are resolved in favor of the use that maximizes their present value. The implication of this maximizing principle is that the value of oil, natural gas, and coal in the ground (its price minus its marginal extraction cost) will increase over time at a compound annual rate equal to the social opportunity cost of capital. This orderly pattern will be disturbed only by unexpected changes in supply or demand and as resource owners adjust to new information.

A profit-maximizing resource owner will save resources (that is, conserve) for future production when he expects the *in situ* value of his resource to increase faster than expected returns on his alternative investment opportunities. On the other hand, if the expected reward for leaving resources in the ground for future use is less than his expected reward from current production and reinvestment of the proceeds in his best alternative investment, then he would favor current over future production.

As a nonrenewable resource becomes increasingly scarce and shows signs of a continuing decline in availability (higher future prices), this anticipated future scarcity will lead to reduced present outputs and higher present prices. This adjustment process will con-

---

[3] Donella H. Meadows and others, *The Limits to Growth* (New York: Universe Books, 1972), p. 23.

tinue until resource owners no longer have a profit incentive to reduce present production in favor of the future. At that point, *in situ* values of such resources will be rising at a compound annual rate corresponding to the opportunity cost of capital. Thus, a market system is a planning mechanism that tends to allocate resources efficiently over time—that is, to promote resource conservation.

Given an equilibrium over time, resource conservation at a point in time will be advanced as private operators attempt to maximize profits. Profit maximization requires that a production manager expand or contract resource inputs until the marginal physical product per dollar of resource cost is equal for all resources used. Expressed in another way, this requires a minimization of input per unit of product output (alternatively, a maximization of output per unit of resource input).

Under conditions stated below, maximum efficiency and profit maximization are identical, and both concepts are synonymous with resource conservation. Optimum resource allocation both over time and at a point in time would occur under private ownership and private profit-maximizing assumptions if (1) there are no significant externalities affecting either anticipated costs or revenues, (2) markets are effectively competitive, and (3) governments do not significantly distort the price mechanism through price fixing, nonneutral taxes, subsidies, or other interference, except to correct for externalities identified in (1).

Where significant externalities exist, market failure is said to take place. Then there is no perfect correspondence between a social and a private optimum. This condition has led many observers to recommend government interference in the form of subsidies, taxation, regulation, or outright government ownership. For example, in the case of crude oil and gas, the resource in the ground is migratory. Where a reserve is subject to multiple ownership, regulation of production or mandatory unitization appears to be necessary.[4] Unitization requires that the "common property" (the entire reservoir) be managed as a unit with an agreed upon distribution of the net revenue among the reservoir owners.

However, efforts to correct for externalities through various forms of government interference may succeed only in introducing further distortions. Even if economists could agree on the appropriate internalizing values to recommend for congressional action, the recommendations must pass through the political process. Congres-

---

[4] Stephen L. McDonald, *Petroleum Conservation in the United States: An Economic Analysis* (Baltimore: Johns Hopkins University Press, 1971).

sional hearings must be held to give all interest groups a chance to be heard. Congressmen must be responsive to dominant pressures brought to bear on them from constituent interest groups. What emerges from the political process may bear no relation to the optimum internalizing mechanism proposed.

What finally becomes legislation must then be administered. The process by which a regulatory agency is captured by the group to be regulated has been well documented by political scientists. Bernstein wrote, "The history of [regulatory] commissions indicates that they may have survived to the extent that they have served the interests of the regulated groups."[5] Thus, what goes into Congress is not what comes out, and what is administered is a further modification. The record of administering oil import quotas provides an excellent example of the progressive deterioration and ultimate collapse of a program that from the beginning never advanced the general welfare.[6]

Economists and political scientists have been slow to point out that use of the political process to correct for market externalities introduces a new set of political externalities. Congressmen do not bear all the costs or receive all the benefits of legislation passed with their votes. Thus, an optimum solution to the externalities problem is unlikely to be achieved in the political process. Attempts to internalize externalities will frequently result in resource misallocation greater than if no corrective action had been attempted. If so, then the conservation goal will not be attained through the political process.

Where monopoly power exists, prices may be distorted and resource misallocation may occur. With respect to the energy industry, most recent studies indicate that the U.S. petroleum industry is effectively competitive.[7] If monopoly power in fact existed in the U.S. petroleum industry, then "over-conservation would be the expected result."[8]

---

[5] Marver Bernstein, *Regulating Business by Independent Commissions* (Princeton: Princeton University Press, 1955), p. 73. See also, Anthony Downs, *Inside Bureaucracy* (Boston: Little, Brown, 1967).

[6] For a thorough description of the oil import quota program and its operation, see Douglas R. Bohi and Milton Russell, *Limiting Oil Imports: An Economic History and Analysis* (Baltimore: Johns Hopkins University Press, 1978).

[7] For a review of the literature, see W. J. Mead, *Energy and the Environment: Conflict in Public Policy* (Washington, D.C.: American Enterprise Institute, 1978), pp. 9-15.

[8] Milton C. Weinstein and Richard J. Zeckhauser, "The Optimal Consumption of Depletable Natural Resources," *Quarterly Journal of Economics*, vol. 89 (August 1975), p. 389. For a similar conclusion see Joseph E. Stiglitz, "Monopoly and the Rate of Extraction of Exhaustible Resources," *American Economic Review*, vol. 66 (September 1976), p. 655.

Probably the major distortion-creating resource misallocation is government interference itself. Apart from regulations and nonneutral taxation, government frequently interferes directly with the price system—sometimes to raise prices above their competitive levels, as in the case of market-demand prorationing and import quotas in the oil industry; and sometimes to hold prices below their competitive level, as in the case of the present control of oil and gas prices. Regardless of which policy is pursued, the results are likely to be resource misallocation. An artificially high price on one product leads producers or consumers to shift their buying away from the high-priced item and toward its close substitutes. Artificially low prices cause the opposite effect. In either case, the goal of conservation is not well served.

The primary issue in an economic evaluation of the new natural gas legislation is this third cause of misallocation—government interference.

Law and Regulations Prior to NGPA

The Natural Gas Policy Act, which became the basis for Federal Power Commission (FPC) control over the wellhead price of interstate natural gas, was enacted by Congress in 1938. This act was initially applied only to regulation of interstate gas pipelines. However, a U.S. Supreme Court decision in 1954 determined that the act also mandated federal control over the wellhead price of natural gas sold in interstate commerce.

The dominant political pressure leading to FPC price setting appears to have been from eastern consumer interests. Natural gas prices have consistently been held below their market equilibrium level. By January 1974 the average wellhead price of gas flowing into interstate commerce was only $0.24 per thousand cubic feet (Mcf). In terms of British thermal (Btu) content, this is equivalent to a crude oil wellhead price of $1.34 per barrel. But at the time the average refiner acquisition cost of imported crude oil was $9.59 per barrel. From 1974 to 1978 substantial price increases were permitted under FPC regulation. By the first quarter of 1978, the controlled price of "new gas" flowing into interstate markets was fixed at $1.47 per Mcf. This translates into $8.24 per barrel of crude oil. But the cost of imported crude oil had risen to $14.50 per barrel.

Under these regulation constraints, producers found it unprofitable to develop high-cost new gas supplies. Proved reserves of natural gas reached a peak in December 1967 (292.9 trillion cubic feet [Tcf]) and have declined at a 4.0 percent annual rate through 1977 (181.1 Tcf, excluding 27.8 Tcf at Prudhoe Bay, Alaska). Domestic natural gas production reached a peak in 1973 (22.6 Tcf) and has since been declining at an annual rate of 4.9 percent.

The extent of the shortage of natural gas induced by price controls is unknown. In some parts of the nation, new residential gas hookups have not been available for more than ten years. Residential consumers who have natural gas hookups have generally been able to buy all the gas they want at low prices. Presumably, these favored users have treated gas as a cheap commodity and have consumed it to the point where their marginal benefit equals their (low) marginal cost. This result is inconsistent with a conservation goal.

At the same time, intrastate gas has not been subject to controls. No new gas discoveries onshore have been dedicated to interstate commerce when more profitable uncontrolled intrastate prices have been available. This artificial distinction between intrastate and interstate gas has misallocated the flow of new gas, causing it to be used excessively in producer states. This circumstance led to a second misallocation—of capital—as industrial users of gas have diverted capital investments (new plants and plant expansion) toward producer states.

Although intrastate gas sales have been free of price controls one should not conclude that prices in the intrastate markets reflect prices that would be determined in the absence of controls. Given low controlled prices for interstate gas and freedom of all onshore producers to sell their gas in either interstate or intrastate markets, new onshore supplies have been offered in intrastate markets. Consequently, intrastate prices are artificially depressed by amounts that differ from state to state depending on local conditions of supply and demand. Table 2 shows the record of recent new intrastate contract sales for leading gas-producing states. Under free market conditions, prices for natural gas under current supply-demand conditions would reflect the prices of substitute fuels and the so-called law of one price. Prices would be uniform except for transportation and other real cost differences. But Table 2 shows a $0.52 spread from lowest to highest price.

Pricing Provisions of the NGPA

The NGPA consists of six parts: wellhead pricing; incremental pricing; additional authorities and requirements; natural gas curtailment policies; administration, enforcement, and review; and coordination

TABLE 2
New Contract Intrastate Natural Gas Sales in Leading Gas-Producing States, September 1978

State	Dollars per Thousand Cubic Feet
California	1.45
Oklahoma	1.46
Kansas	1.50
Louisiana	1.94
Texas	1.97

Source: Department of Energy, *Monthly Energy Review* (February 1979), p. 95.

with the Natural Gas Act and effect on state laws. This analysis will be limited to pricing provisions of the act.

In general, the NGPA brings all intrastate gas (about 40 to 45 percent of total domestic gas sales) under federal controls, then provides for decontrol of some old intrastate gas and new gas on January 1, 1985. Specific classes of new "high-cost" gas are to be decontrolled on November 9, 1979. Decontrol of new intrastate shallow gas (5,000 feet depth or less) is to be delayed until July 1, 1987. For all other classes of gas, price controls are made permanent.

Details of Price Controls. A detailed examination of price control provisions in the new act reveals their enormous complexity and technical distinctions. Table 3 shows thirty-three tiers of price controls that mandate prices effective in January 1979, ranging from a minimum rate of $0.204 to $2.243 per Mcf for stripper well production.[9] Distinctions are made on the basis of nine separate factors: old versus new gas; interstate versus intrastate; time at which drilling was commenced; lease sale date in the case of outer continental shelf (OCS) production; large versus small firms; Indian and state-owned production versus all other; vertical depth of production; distance from existing productive wells; and geographical area.

There is a significant departure from past gas regulatory procedures, which were of the cost-based public utility type. Congress

---

[9] There is wide disagreement on the number of price classes established in the NGPA. Estimates run from twenty-six to about thirty-five. The range of estimates reflects confusion in the law and uncertainty about FERC present and future regulations.

TABLE 3

Maximum Lawful Prices for Natural Gas, January 1979, Provided by the Natural Gas Policy Act of 1978 and FERC Regulations

Item No.	Authority Section	Category of Natural Gas	Maximum Lawful Wellhead Price (dollars per million Btu)
		OLD GAS	
		Interstate only	
1	104	Gas produced in 1973–1974 and now produced by a small firm	1.387
2	104	Gas produced in 1973–1974 and now produced by a large firm	1.064
3	104	Replacement contract gas or recompletion gas, now produced by a small firm	0.775
4	104	Replacement contract gas or recompletion gas, now produced by a large firm	0.596
5	104	Flowing gas, now produced by a small firm	0.395
6	104	Flowing gas, now produced by a large firm	0.334
7	104	Permian Basin gas, now produced by a small firm	0.465
8	104	Permian Basin gas, now produced by a large firm	0.407
9	104	Rocky Mountain gas, now produced by a small firm	0.465
10	104	Rocky Mountain gas, now produced by a large firm	0.395
11	104	Appalachian Basin gas, north subarea contracts dated after October 7, 1969	0.370
12	104	Appalachian Basin gas, other	0.346
13	104	Minimum rate gas	0.204
14	109	Gas committed to interstate commerce on November 8, 1978, for which a "just and reasonable" rate under the Natural Gas Act was not in effect	1.639
15	106	Rollover gas, now produced by a small firm	0.715
16	106	Rollover gas, now produced by a large firm	0.607

No distinction between interstate and intrastate

17	109	Not otherwise covered	1.639

Intrastate

18	106	Rollover contract	—[a]
19	106	Rollover gas where seller is an Indian tribe or a state government	2.096
20	105	Sales under existing or successor contract where November 9, 1978, price was at or below $2.06 per million Btu	—[b]
21	105	Sales under existing or successor contract where November 9, 1978, price was greater than $2.06 per million Btu	—[c]

NEW GAS

Interstate

22	102	Natural gas discovered on or after July 27, 1976, and produced from a new outer continental shelf (OCS) reservoir on an old OCS lease	2.096
23	102	New OCS leases (issued after April 20, 1977)	2.096

No distinction between interstate and intrastate

24	109	Prudhoe Bay, Alaska, gas	1.639
25	102	New onshore reservoirs (discovered on or after April 20, 1977)	2.096
26	102	Gas discovered onshore if more than 2.5 miles from or 1,000 feet below an existing well in production between 1970 and April 20, 1977	2.096
27	103	Onshore production wells where surface drilling started on or after February 19, 1977	1.980
28	107	High-cost gas[d]	2.096[e]
29	109	Gas produced from any new well not otherwise covered	1.639

Intrastate

30	103	Onshore production after 1984 from wells at or less than 5,000 feet and not committed to interstate commerce as of April 20, 1977	—[f]

(*Table 3 continues on the next page.*)

TABLE 3 (Continued)

Item No.	Authority Section	Category of Natural Gas	Maximum Lawful Wellhead Price (dollars per million Btu)
		NO DISTINCTION BETWEEN OLD AND NEW GAS	
		Interstate	
31	110	Gas dedicated to interstate commerce on November 8, 1978, and production started after 1974	1.639
32	110	For gas committed to interstate commerce on November 8, 1978, and for which there was not a "just and reasonable" rate in effect on that date, the maximum lawful price may be exceeded to recover certain gathering allowances, allowances for delivery of offshore gas, and production-related costs.	Unknown
		No distinction between interstate and intrastate	
32	108	Stripper well production	2.243
33	109	Gas not committed to interstate commerce on November 8, 1978, and not subject to an existing contract on that date	1.639

a For January 1979, the higher of the maximum lawful price paid under the expired contract, adjusted for inflation, or $1.128.
b If November 9, 1978, price was at or below $2.06 per million Btu, then the lower of the existing contract price on November 9, 1978, or the maximum lawful price for new gas ($2.096 effective January 1979).
c If November 9, 1978, price was greater than $2.06, then the higher of the maximum lawful price for new gas ($2.096 effective January 1979), or the contract price on November 9, 1978, adjusted for inflation using the GNP deflator.
d High-cost gas includes the following classifications: gas produced from below 15,000 feet, if surface drilling began after February 18, 1977; gas produced from geopressured brine; gas produced from coal seams; gas produced from Devonian shale; and other gas determined by the FERC to present extraordinary risks or costs.
e The FERC has authority to grant higher prices if an additional incentive is needed because of high cost.
f Midway between the maximum lawful price computed for new gas under item 22 above and the price computed for new onshore production wells under item 27 above.
SOURCES: The Natural Gas Policy Act of 1978, Title I, Subtitle A; and Federal Energy Regulatory Commission, "Interim Regulations," *Federal Register*, December 1, 1978, pt. 8.

moved instead to legislate maximum prices plus prescribed price escalation by month.

Congress has also legislated a new distinction for prices paid by consumers, whereas the old NGA concerned only prices received by producers. The incremental pricing provision of Title II indicates the intent of legislation that low-cost gas supplies will flow first to households while high-cost supplies will be used as industrial boiler fuel. Gas costing more than $1.65 per million Btu as of December 1978 (the base price is escalated at the rate of inflation for subsequent months) will be allocated to industrial boiler uses until the price to those users rises to their cost of fuel oil.[10] Costs above the price of fuel oil will be allocated to other customers, including residential and small commercial users, and will be rolled into prices they pay.

Price Escalation. Price escalation corresponding to the general rate of inflation is provided for all thirty-three price tiers. The effect of this escalation is to hold the present wellhead price of gas constant in real terms, thereby maintaining the present artificially low real price. In addition, three classes of production—high-cost gas (produced from a depth of more than 15,000 feet only), new onshore and OCS gas from new leases, and stripper well gas (production at less than 60 Mcf per day)—receive an additional 3.5 percent annual bonus escalation through April 1981 and 4.0 percent annually thereafter until decontrolled.

For gas subject to bonus escalation, the real price will be permitted to increase by approximately 30 percent through 1984. From the legislated base of $1.75 per million Btu in April 1977, new gas prices (deflated) will rise to approximately $2.27 per million Btu (wellhead) by the decontrol date, January 1, 1985. By any reasonable projection, this bonus escalated price will be substantially less than free market prices in 1985 and therefore lead to new political problems associated with decontrol. Any "balloon effect" on prices will raise anew the twin issues of windfall profits and impact on the poor.

Price Decontrol Authority. Decontrol of natural gas prices is provided in three stages.

First, not later than twelve months after November 9, 1978, high-cost natural gas not dedicated to interstate commerce on April 20, 1977, is decontrolled. Included in this category are gas produced from a depth of 15,000 feet or greater if drilled after February 18, 1977, and gas produced from geopressured brine, from coal seams, and from Devonian shale.

---

[10] At 1,021 Btu per cubic foot, $1.65 per million Btu = $1.62 per Mcf.

Second, effective on January 1, 1985, three categories of gas are to be decontrolled: (1) new natural gas, including OCS gas from leases issued on or after April 20, 1977, and onshore gas produced from any new wells drilled after February 18, 1977, at least 2.5 miles from the nearest existing well, or at least 1,000 feet below the deepest existing well within 2.5 miles; (2) new onshore production wells where surface drilling began after February 18, 1977, production was not committed or dedicated to interstate commerce on April 20, 1977, and gas is produced from a depth of more than 5,000 feet; and (3) intrastate contracts having a price in excess of $1.00 per million Btu on December 31, 1984, and not committed or dedicated to interstate commerce on November 8, 1977. Categories (1) and (2) above have no significant production as of November 9, 1978, but by the decontrol date in 1985 may account for 20 to 30 percent of domestic gas production. Category (3) quantities are unknown but should account for at least half the intrastate production.

Third, on July 1, 1987, decontrol is provided for new onshore production wells producing gas from a depth of 5,000 feet or less, if not committed or dedicated to interstate commerce on April 20, 1977.

For all other categories of gas there is no provision for price decontrol. The principal category of gas subject to permanent price control is old gas sold in interstate commerce, including gas produced from the OCS. Presumably most old intrastate gas would be decontrolled under the one-dollar provision identified in point (3) above. Further, all old gas will eventually be economically depleted and wells will be abandoned. Gas produced from Prudhoe Bay, Alaska, is specifically exempt from decontrol. However, price controls on any future Prudhoe Bay gas are likely to be inoperative (given expected high costs of transport) because the wellhead price of such gas is unlikely to exceed the $1.45 maximum lawful price plus inflation escalation provided by the legislation.

Standby Price Control Authority. The president or Congress, by concurrent resolution, may reimpose price controls at any time between July 1, 1985, and June 30, 1987. This authority may be exercised only once and for a period of eighteen months. The maximum lawful price under reimposition is the new gas price for various classifications.

Economic Evaluation of the NGPA

Control and Decontrol. Is the NGPA correctly described as a decontrol law? For the first year of the NGPA, federal price controls are extended from control over 55 to 60 percent of U.S. natural gas production to control over 100 percent of production. After one year, new high-cost gas is decontrolled. At a maximum, this supply is unlikely to amount to more than 1 percent of November 1979 supplies. Then on January 1, 1985, two classes of new gas plus old intrastate contracts in excess of $1.00 (formerly free of control) are to be decontrolled. Finally, new onshore shallow wells are decontrolled in 1987. All old interstate gas plus some old intrastate gas formerly free of control are subject to permanent controls. Thus, the NGPA is a decontrol measure for some interstate gas at present under controls, but extends controls over intrastate gas at present uncontrolled. By expanding some controls and continuing others permanently, the act creates resource misallocation effects characteristic of price controls described elsewhere in this chapter.

Rate of Increase of Gas Prices. Are gas prices likely to increase faster under the NGPA than under the old NGA? Under NGA regulations, interstate natural gas prices, on average, were permitted to increase at a 31 percent compound annual rate from June 1974 through June 1978. In constant dollars, average prices increased 23 percent per year. The record of current average wellhead gas prices from 1947 through June 1978 is shown in Figure 1. There is no way of knowing what successive Federal Power Commissions would have allowed under the NGA. From April 1977 onward, however, the new law holds most classes of natural gas at constant real prices and permits only new gas, gas produced from more than 15,000 feet, and stripper well production to increase to a 3.5 to 4.0 percent annual rate in real terms while decontrolling high-cost gas on November 9, 1979. This information suggests that under the NGPA average price increases for natural gas will be substantially lower than was permitted by the Federal Power Commission under the old NGA from 1974 to date.

While no definitive statement can be made about the relative average price of gas under the old NGA and the new NGPA, high-cost gas supplies will be quickly stimulated at higher prices than would appear to have been likely under the NGA, and new gas will show similar supply and price behavior after decontrol in 1985. These two developments are consistent with optimum resource allocation.

Probable Consumer Reactions. What are the probable consumer reactions to the NGPA? Artificially low prices for natural gas will continue to stimulate consumer demand for this nonrenewable resource. For reasons given in the next section, under the new law this demand will not be satisfied and consumers will continue to suffer from a

FIGURE 1

Average Annual Wellhead Price of U.S. Natural Gas

Current dollars per thousand cubic feet

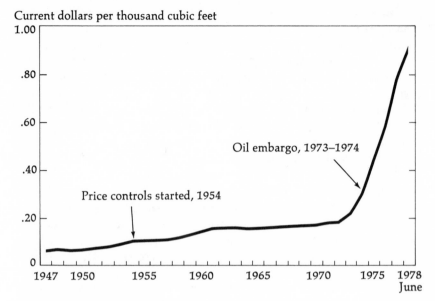

Source: U.S. Bureau of Mines.

gas shortage at least through 1984. With respect to conservation this means that some consumers with effective political power will obtain gas at bargain prices and will presumably consume it wastefully. Given a shortage, those consumers with inadequate political power will be forced to seek out substitutes. The most common substitute is oil (no. 2 distillate, residual fuel oil, and other refined petroleum products). Because there is an open-ended supply of crude oil in the form of imports, natural gas price controls and the consequent shortage will lead to increased dependence upon foreign oil suppliers and added balance of payment problems.

A natural gas shortage also creates problems to which the political system is likely to respond by stimulating developments of energy supplies from nonconventional sources. Table 4 lists estimated April 1977 costs for six potentially large sources of new natural gas. Under free market conditions, gas would be produced from only the first three of these sources. But with the gas shortage expected under price control, higher-cost sources are likely to be drawn upon. The NGPA provides for incremental pricing to indus-

TABLE 4

ALTERNATIVE SOURCES OF ADDITIONAL HIGHER-COST NATURAL GAS

| | Cost | |
| | April 1977 dollars per Mcf | January 1979 dollars per Mcf |
Source		
Canada	1.91[a]	2.40[b]
Devonian shale, Appalachia	2.00–2.50[c]	N.A.
Mexico	2.60[d]	3.00[d]
Algeria (liquefied natural gas)	3.88[e]	N.A.
Synthetic gas from coal	3.50–4.50[f]	N.A.
Prudhoe Bay, Alaska		
At 5 percent per year construction cost overrun	4.79[g]	N.A.
At 10 percent per year construction cost overrun	5.37[g]	N.A.

N.A.: Not available.

[a] Department of Energy, *Monthly Energy Review* (November 1978), p. 77.

[b] Projected from July 1978 price.

[c] Office of Technology Assessment, *Enhanced Recovery of Oil and Devonian Gas.*

[d] Computed from a price of $0.35 per gallon for no. 2 fuel oil prices, New York harbor, as reported in the *Oil and Gas Journal.*

[e] W. J. Mead, *Transporting Natural Gas from the Arctic: The Alternative Systems* (Washington, D.C.: American Enterprise Institute, 1977), p. 3.

[f] White House Task Force, "Report of the Working Group on Supply, Demand and Energy Policy Impacts of Alaska Gas," July 1, 1977, p. 121.

[g] Further assumes $1.45 per Mcf wellhead payment to producers, plus $0.18 per Mcf tax payment to Alaska. See W. J. Mead, "An Economic Analysis of the Northwest Alcan Pipeline Project," in American Society of Civil Engineers, *An Overview of the Alaska Highway Gas Pipeline: The World's Largest Project* (forthcoming 1979). A 10 percent per year cost overrun corresponds with the Alyeska Pipeline experience.

trial users. Pass-through of high-cost gas is mandated, and very high-cost gas will be hidden in the rolled-in (average pricing) procedure. Gas users will thereby be misinformed about the true cost of the gas they use.

Probable Producer Reactions. How are producers likely to react to the NGPA? Optimal supplies of new gas from domestic resources will also be retarded by continued price control. This will be the case so long as regulated prices for new gas, stripper well production, and augmented supplies from more efficient recovery practices are below market clearing levels. The NGPA attempts to avoid this

343

problem in part by decontrolling new high-cost gas effective November 9, 1979, by granting inflation plus bonus price increases for new gas, and by permitting stripper well prices to apply to augmented production occurring as a result of improved recovery techniques. But these higher prices will remain below equilibrium levels until decontrol is actually achieved. Consequently, resources will be misallocated and the goals of conservation will not be attained.

Congress has attempted to allow the highest prices for new supplies believed to have the highest supply elasticity and to impose low prices on previously discovered gas which is believed to have an inelastic supply function. An economic argument in support of multi-tiered price controls can be made where sectoral differences in supply elasticity for the same commodity can be correctly estimated. Under such conditions, the resource misallocation effects may be small and consumers may benefit by minimizing their outlays for gas supplies. This rationale for "regulatory monopsonization," together with its necessary conditions, have been elaborated for crude oil price controls.[11]

Of greater significance may be producer reactions which Congress has not foreseen. Further, the legislation is general and must be implemented with detailed regulations to be written not by Congress but by the FERC bureaucracy. Adverse supply reactions to detailed regulations emerge with the passage of time. If they were known in advance, one would optimistically believe that they would be avoided by both Congress and the implementing bureaucracy.

Since all adverse supply reactions resulting from legislation and regulations cannot be foreseen, I will illustrate the problem by drawing on past experience. Under gasoline price regulations, only about 40 percent of the cost of new refinery facilities for producing unleaded gasoline could be passed through to the gasoline user. With no return permitted on approximately 60 percent of the new investment, the clear signal to management was: do not invest in such facilities. This regulation posed no immediate problem, but the facilities not built will not be on stream after the normal construction lag period. We entered that period in the summer of 1978 (before the Iran crisis), and shortages of unleaded gasoline began to appear. If refiners, under government pressure, adjust existing refinery output to yield more unleaded gasoline, then the total output of gasoline per unit of crude input is reduced because relatively more crude is required to make

[11] E. W. Erickson, W. L. Peters, R. M. Spann, and P. J. Tese, "The Political Economy of Crude Oil Price Controls," *Natural Resources Journal*, vol. 18 (October 1978), pp. 791-94.

unleaded gasoline. But when the yield of gasoline falls, a correspondingly smaller percentage of the crude oil cost is available for pass-through, creating an additional disincentive to produce unleaded gasoline. This is where we find ourselves in early 1979.

Long after this problem surfaced, the regulatory agency undertook to draft new regulations designed to remove disincentives restricting unleaded production. In March 1979 the Economic Regulatory Agency (ERA) issued new regulations designed to correct this problem. The ERA determined that as much as 110 percent of the increased crude costs attributable to gasoline could be allocated to gasoline prices. In addition, refiners are permitted to allocate to gasoline a percentage of nonproduct costs greater than the volumetric ratio. This rule was made effective retroactively to January 1, 1979, and is intended to encourage increased investment in refining capacity and to prevent shortages of gasoline, especially unleaded. However, it is not known what effects will be induced by this new tilt.

Biologist Garrett Hardin has reminded us that "you can't do just one thing." One regulation leads to unforeseen problems which call for offsetting regulations, which in turn create new unforeseen problems. The illustration above, drawn from experience with oil price regulation, is a proxy for the kind of problem that we should expect from the new NGPA but are unable to foresee at this point.

Resources are also misallocated by virtue of a distinction made by FERC between large and small producers, and between native Indian and state producers and all others. As shown in Table 2, small producers are allowed higher prices relative to large producers for various classes of interstate gas. The premium varies from a low of 14 percent to a high of 30 percent. The NGPA provides for no such discrimination. The FERC, in its regulations, instead cited section 157.40 of the old NGA which allowed small producers a maximum of 30 percent price premium. In the case of intrastate rollover gas where the seller is an Indian tribe or a state government, a maximum premium over all other intrastate rollover contracts is 86 percent ($2.096 as against $1.128 per million Btu for January 1979). Price discrimination favorable to Indian tribes and state governments is authorized by the NGPA (section 106b).

Under free market conditions, discrimination occurs on the basis of relative efficiency or other real cost or quality differences. If large firms are less efficient than small firms, then in the long run competition will force such high-cost producers to withdraw from the market. But with price discrimination on political grounds, incentives lead to expansion by favored small producers, Indians, and possibly states, without regard to efficiency.

Producers are also affected by the distinction between old and new gas. The rationale of the congressional distinction is that gas discovered in the past will be produced so long as its incremental revenue is greater than its incremental cost of production. Hence, higher prices are not needed for old gas, except for the stripper phase of production, and therefore are functionless. On this line of reasoning, Congress has reserved higher prices for stripper production and new gas, which would not be produced unless both development and incremental production costs were covered.

It must be assumed, however, that oil company managers are rational and will be aware that some of their anticipated profits will be taken from them as government in the future reclassifies new gas as old gas and mandates prices sufficient to cover only incremental production costs. To the extent that managerial decisions are based on the fear of reclassification of gas categories, a suboptimal level of investment in exploration and development will occur.

Under free market conditions, producers would allocate their scarce capital between deep and shallow wells on the basis of anticipated rates of return on these alternative investments. The NGPA will distort this optimum investment flow by its price distinction on account of depth.

Producers also react to uncertainty, which is a true social cost. Insofar as it reduces uncertainty, the NGPA appears to be preferable to the NGA. The new act provides for selective decontrol, whereas formerly one could only speculate about decontrol, and for most of the thirty-three tiers of natural gas identified in Table 3 it mandates a relatively precise escalation of future prices. Under the old act, prices were determined by the Federal Power Commission, and price increase varied widely from time to time and with changes in the political complexion of the commission. Although, on balance, uncertainty is reduced in the NGPA, an eighteen-month reimposition of controls is authorized. Further, there is a possibility that as January 1, 1985, approaches, Congress will reexamine the politics of decontrol and the effects on consumers who are receiving low-price gas, and it may reimpose controls on a long-term basis.

Probable Reactions of Bidders for Leases. How are bidders for federal gas leases likely to react to the NGPA? Until Congress in 1978 amended the Outer Continental Shelf Lands Act, OCS oil and gas leases were commonly sold on the basis of bonus bidding plus payment of a fixed royalty. Some onshore leases were sold on the same basis. Under the amended OCS act, use of auction bidding on the bonus is to be limited, and other specified bidding systems must be used for not less than 20 percent and not more than 60 percent of the total area offered for leasing each year.

Price controls that hold natural gas prices below free market levels make leases less valuable. As a consequence, auction bidding with price controls will produce lower payments to government than under free market conditions. A recent study of 839 federal oil and gas leases issued in the Gulf of Mexico over the years 1954–1962 concluded that competitive bidding for these leases produced high returns to the government. Lessees bid too much. Proof of this point is found in the conclusion that the *before tax* rate of return to the lessees was 9.5 percent.[12] This is substantially below normal competitive returns. If prospective bidders in future lease sales believe that natural gas and oil prices are to be controlled at artificially low levels, then the amounts bid will be lowered. Further, to the extent that there is additional uncertainty resulting from the capricious application of price controls, then bidders are likely to employ higher discount rates in computing their bonus bids. Thus, the effect of price controls is to reduce the flow of income to the government. If this lower income flow to the government is a trade-off against the level of taxes, then taxpayers bear some of the costs of price control.

From these findings one can infer that all gas produced from leases issued in the future should be completely and immediately freed of price controls. The effect would be that the economic rent arising out of higher prices would be transferred to government as the lessor. Even on old leases, government collects a royalty that is always expressed as a percentage of gross income. In the case of outer continental shelf gas leases, the royalty is at least 16.67 percent of wellhead value. Onshore leases generally require royalty payments amounting to 12.5 percent of wellhead value. Hence, even on old leases some of the costs of continued controls are borne by the government and consequently by taxpayers.

Administrative Costs. Are administrative costs likely to change under the NGPA? Some features of the new act may be less costly to administer than the old because the act departs from a cost-based public utility type of regulation and provides for phased decontrol.

---

[12] R. O. Jones, W. J. Mead, and P. E. Sorensen, "Free Entry into Crude Oil and Gas Production and Competition in the U.S. Oil Industry," *Natural Resources Journal*, October 1978.

In general, however, it will be much more expensive by virtue of the facts that it brings intrastate gas under control, establishes multiple tiers of pricing categories, creates new classification functions to be performed by all producing states, and adds new incremental pricing provisions.

Responsibility for determining how gas is to be classified has been given primarily to state agencies. The FERC is authorized to define terms; then state agencies will classify gas subject to FERC and possibly court review. This process creates enormous new administrative problems. Currently thirty states produce natural gas, and agencies within each state must classify the gas in five categories: new natural gas; OCS gas differentiated by lease date, reservoir discovery date, and reservoir penetration date; new onshore production wells; high-cost natural gas; and stripper well production. The need for some degree of uniformity among the thirty state interpretations of these five categories will impose an expensive administrative burden, and the inevitable court challenges will lead to new and very costly litigation charges for both industry and government. These are real social costs for the nation.

Expensive problems of administration are anticipated because of the Title II incremental pricing provision. The NGPA requires that not later than November 9, 1979, the FERC issue rules implementing the statutory requirement that high-cost gas be allocated to industrial boiler fuel users. Until such regulations are issued, their administrative problems cannot be appraised in detail.

This incremental pricing provision appears to reflect either innocent or intended deception by Congress. By shifting the immediate burden of high-cost gas from consumers to business, Congress appears to be protecting the public. In the long run, however, product prices must equal all costs of production plus competitive profits. Therefore, consumers will ultimately bear the burden of high-cost gas. The added burden of administering and complying with the incremental pricing provision will be shared by consumers and taxpayers. There are no apparent offsetting benefits.

Further, administration of the incremental pricing provision involves a circularity problem. Compliance requires that each pipeline firm have pricing information on end-use profiles for all its customers. Information must be available on gas supplies from other pipelines delivering gas to the same end-users, as well as on the costs of alternative fuels. Information must be available on how fixed costs and input costs are allocated to industrial boiler users and how much of each pipeline's incremental cost pool has been allocated to particular customers. Then price adjustments must be made between industrial and residential consumers when the industrial price rises above a price that varies from month to month. The inherent complexity and perhaps administrative impossibility of applying the incremental cost provision will multiply administrative costs and litigation expenses for both the government and for complying firms.

The social cost of administration consists of costs incurred by the government, costs of compliance incurred by private industry, plus the cost of inefficiency generated by the administrative process itself. Until cost experience is developed, we can only speculate about the true social cost. Research by Weidenbaum and DeFina indicates that the annual cost of regulation in the old Federal Energy Administration in 1976 amounted to $186 million.[13] Although the authors were unable to estimate compliance costs associated with FEA regulations, on the basis of estimated costs of compliance and government administration for several other major categories of regulation they concluded that the private compliance cost was approximately twenty times the government's administrative cost.[14] Application of this rule to the estimated FEA administrative costs indicates that private industry compliance in 1976 cost approximately $3.7 billion, and the total cost of regulation (not including the cost of resource misallocation generated by FEA controls) amounted to approximately $3.9 billion.

These numbers are so large that few can comprehend their meaning. One way to place these costs in a meaningful context is to relate them to familiar forgone opportunities. For example, the cost of building a new elementary school is approximately $2 million. Thus, the estimated cost of FEA regulation in 1976 was sufficient to build approximately 2,000 new elementary schools in the United States. This cost is repeated each year. Regulation under FEA is a trade-off against new schools (or highways or parks) which might have been built. Presumably, because of the vastly expanded role of government under new energy legislation enacted in 1978, the cost of regulation under the new Department of Energy will be significantly larger than the costs referred to above.

By diverting valuable human and other resources from production to regulatory functions and to compliance with regulations, Congress is contributing to the declining productivity growth rates observed by

---

[13] Murray L. Weidenbaum and Robert DeFina, *The Cost of Federal Regulation of Economic Activity* (Washington, D.C.: American Enterprise Institute, May 1978), p. 5.

[14] Ibid., p. 2.

other authors in this book. The social cost of regulation is the loss of goods and services that could otherwise be produced by those same resources.

No estimates are available as to the offsetting benefits of energy regulation. There may be none. The main thrust of regulation is income redistribution. Any redistribution benefits are uncertain and have not been evaluated. With respect to resource allocation, the regulatory system encourages consumers to demand more and at the same time retards the development of new higher-cost gas supplies. There are adverse balance of payments effects as well as adverse conservation effects where politically favored consumers obtain a nonrenewable resource at low prices and consume it wastefully.

Windfall Gains and Impact on the Poor. How valid are the "windfall gains" and "impact on the poor" arguments? Two powerful political arguments in support of the price control system relate to the windfall profits that supposedly would accrue to big oil companies as a result of decontrol and to the allegedly beneficial impact of controls on the poor. While in today's political environment these arguments are potent politically, they are only partially true.

First, the windfall argument itself was created by price controls. If price controls on natural gas had not been instituted in 1954, the price increases that the market would have brought about would already have been absorbed, painfully but naturally. The major impact on the market occurred as a result of international events in the early 1970s associated with the roughly fourfold increase in the price of crude oil. Similar increases have occurred in market prices for coal and uranium in the energy area, and timber in the nonenergy natural resource area. Similarly, residential housing prices in California have increased approximately fourfold in the same period. While these developments have brought benefits to some and losses to others, in these cases prices were not and are not subject to control, and there have been relatively few charges of windfall profits.

Second, oil companies are almost never owners of natural gas resources. Normally, they are lessees and pay the resource owners a royalty which is usually a function of wellhead value and is calculated on gross rather than net income. Consequently, a large part of any windfall gain will flow to the resource owner. But the resource owner in most cases is the federal government. The federal government owns the entire outer continental shelf out to the limit of operability, according to the Geneva Convention, as well as the entire public domain onshore. In declining positions of importance as resource owners are state governments, native American groups, railroads, and private individuals, primarily ranchers and farmers. Decontrol would increase royalty payments to the landowner. Recent research indicates that for new leases the entire economic rent accruing from decontrol would flow to landowners and not to oil company lessees.[15]

Third, the concept of windfall profits depends heavily on the time period used. Most of any unexpected gain in the true value of natural gas occurred in the early 1970s, as shown in Figure 1. The initial cause of rapid price increases was a shift in control of oil production from private operating companies, as concessionaires, to host governments. But the more enduring cause was the increasingly apparent scarcity of nonrenewable oil (and gas) reserves. The operation of competitive markets and applied capital theory would have brought about a substantial increase in the value of oil and gas reserves.

The free market wellhead price of natural gas increased from $0.06 per Mcf in 1947 to an estimated $2.60 per Mcf in 1978. When these values are adjusted for inflation (using the wholesale price index) the compound annual rate of growth in wellhead prices was 9.3 percent in real terms. Information is lacking on the trend in recovery costs, which are commonly joint costs with oil production. Therefore, no precise conclusion can be drawn regarding the competitive normality of profits from holding reserves for future production. Similarly there is no support for the allegation of windfall profits when a long time period is considered. Price increases were reflections of an efficient market mechanism allocating scarce resources over time.[16]

Fourth, the residual gain in windfall profit achieved by an oil company is subject to corporate, federal, and state income taxation. Following the Tax Reduction Act of 1975, integrated oil companies lost the tax advantage of a percentage depletion allowance except for certain cases covered by price controls. Congress permitted this tax advantage to be retained by nonintegrated producers.

Income from gas production by integrated companies is now subject to normal corporate income tax treatment.[17] Therefore, ap-

---

[15] Jones, Mead, and Sorensen, "Free Entry into Crude Oil and Gas Production."

[16] For a new interpretation of the optimal price of crude oil, see Ali D. Johany, "OPEC Is Not a Cartel: A Property Rights Explanation of the Rise in Crude Oil Prices," unpublished dissertation, University of California, Santa Barbara, June 1978.

[17] The expensing of intangible drilling costs is still allowed, but this tax feature is related to exploration rather than to production.

proximately half of any windfall gains accruing to large oil companies would immediately flow to federal and state governments as additional income taxes.

Fifth, over time the problem of windfall gains will disappear if price controls are removed. Old oil production is subject to decline at rates amounting to 10–15 percent per year. For new oil and gas leases, the economic rents accruing from higher prices would be captured by the landowner as shown above.

The argument that price controls have a favorable impact on the poor is also politically potent and only partially true. First, many poor people have no natural gas hookup. Consequently, artificially low prices are of no value to them and decontrol would have little or no impact on them.

Second, in the southwest, a major consumer use of natural gas is to heat swimming pools. Relatively few poor people have swimming pools.

Third, in the summer months, gas-powered air conditioners are a significant element in the demand for gas in some parts of the country. Again, poor people do not generally have air-conditioned homes.

Fourth, in winter months the major residential use of natural gas is for space heating. The larger the house, the greater the use of gas for this purpose. Poor people do not generally have large homes. They may, however, have poorly insulated homes.

Fifth, if the public wishes to increase subsidies to the poor, a direct subsidy in the form of a negative income tax, or even an expansion of the present multiple federal and state welfare programs, would be more efficient.[18] From the point of view of optimum resource allocation and conservation, it is wasteful to use artificially low energy prices for indirect income redistribution.

Allocation of Natural Gas. Does the NGPA efficiently allocate natural gas among states? Under the old NGA, new gas supplies to interstate pipelines were not available except from new OCS gas production, which was mandated to interstate use. While the price of intrastate gas in producer states was rising more rapidly, new hookups were available. In contrast, new hookups for industrial users have generally not been available from interstate sources. With the distinction

---

[18] For a discussion of the present welfare programs relative to the proposed negative income tax, see Barry R. Chiswick, "The Income Transfer System: Impact, Viability, and Proposals for Reform," William Fellner, ed., *Contemporary Economic Problems* (Washington, D.C.: American Enterprise Institute, 1977), pp. 398-406.

between interstate and intrastate eliminated in the NGPA, presumably new supplies will become available outside of producing states. Price differences will then reflect transportation cost differences. However, the picture is further clouded by the new incremental pricing rules (yet to be issued), which may distort what is potentially a more optimal allocation of gas among states, leading to more optimal flows for new industrial plants. Apparently natural gas will be more efficiently allocated among states under the new NGPA than under the old NGA, but without any advantage over free market pricing.

Mexican Natural Gas. How is the NGPA related to possible importation of Mexican natural gas? The large discoveries of oil in Mexico included large supplies of associated gas. In 1977 six U.S. gas transmission companies signed letters of intent with Pemex, the Mexican national oil company, providing for the importation of as much as 2 billion cubic feet of natural gas per day. The price tentatively agreed to was $2.60 per Mcf. This price was unacceptable to the Carter administration because its proposed NGPA legislation would set a variety of ceiling prices well below $2.00 per Mcf for domestic gas producers, and in 1977 Canadian gas import prices varied from $1.85 to $2.16 per Mcf. Consequently, applications to import Mexican gas were denied and the letters of intent expired on December 31, 1977.

The $2.60 import price was based on a Btu conversion from the price of no. 2 fuel oil landed in New York. This import price appeared to reflect prevailing market values during 1977. By refusing Mexican gas at $2.60 per Mcf, the U.S. consumer is faced with even higher cost alternatives shown in Table 4. In fact, the government has approved liquefied natural gas imports at prices above $3.50 per Mcf and appears to be proceeding with administrative approval for construction of the even more costly natural gas transportation system from Prudhoe Bay. To the extent that the NGPA delayed or reduced Mexican gas imports, the real cost of energy to the consumer was increased.

Beneficiaries and Losers. Who benefits and who loses under the NGPA? The first beneficiaries will be those customers outside producer states who, under the NGA, have been unable to obtain new gas hookups at any price. Second, because the new incremental pricing provisions provide favored pricing treatment to certain classes of consumers, including residential households, schools, and hospitals, beneficiaries will include nonindustrial gas consumers, consumers of hospital services, and taxpayers who share the burden of school and hospital finance.

The principal losers under the NGPA include the following groups:

First, consumers of industrial products will pay higher product prices because the producing firms will pay rolled-in prices reflecting high marginal cost for incremental gas supplies. After a short adjustment period, the forces of competition will pass these higher costs on to consumers.

Second, taxpayers in general will be losers because royalty and bonus payments to state and federal governments will continue to reflect low regulated prices. Further, tax receipts from producing oil companies (lessees) and private royalty owners (lessors) will be lower than they would be without controls. Whether these losses are greater or less than under the NGA is unknown.

Third, nongovernment royalty owners will similarly receive relatively low royalties and lease bonuses. Indian tribes and states are favored relative to other royalty owners, but even they will receive royalty and bonus payments below what the free market would provide.

Fourth, gas producers will continue to forgo the residual gains on existing leases, which would accrue to them as producers under free market conditions.

Fifth, if administrative costs incurred by both government and complying industry are greater than under the NGA, then everyone loses by this diversion of productive human resources.

Sixth, of greater importance, everybody loses to the extent that scarce resources are misallocated over time or at a point in time. Resource misallocation causes resource input used in production to be higher per unit of output than would occur under free market conditions. Consequently, resource conservation is sacrificed and standards of living are lower than would occur in the absence of controls.

Seventh, while the intent and effect of natural gas price controls is to hold gas prices below competitive market clearing levels, the effect on price inflation in general is the opposite. Following from the fifth and sixth points above, if valuable human resources are diverted from producing consumer goods and services to the administration of controls, then the same amount of money will be "chasing after" fewer goods. The result must be a higher level of inflation in general. Presumably everybody loses as a result of more inflation.

Conclusions

While the Natural Gas Policy Act is a mixture of new costs and benefits for the nation, on balance it appears to be a slight improvement over the old Natural Gas Act. Its major benefit is a decontrol schedule for new gas and for some classes of old gas. The provisions for early decontrol of high-cost gas are especially important.

Unfortunately, the new act also extends controls to intrastate gas and permanently controls some classes of old gas, both interstate and intrastate. The extremely complex control system, initially identifying about thirty-three tiers of prices, imposes heavy administrative costs that must ultimately be borne by consumers and taxpayers. This social cost appears to be a deadweight loss. Valuable human and other resources are diverted to regulatory functions that are of doubtful value to the nation. Indeed, this diversion of resources from the useful production of goods and services for consumers contributes to the declining national productivity trends observed by other authors in this book.

By legislating permanent price controls, Congress makes permanent the existing natural gas shortage. By holding natural gas prices below market clearing levels, consumers are encouraged to demand more gas than they would want if prices were allowed to reflect the real value of this nonrenewable resource. Thus, legislated low prices are inconsistent with the objectives of resource conservation.

The Economic Progress of Immigrants: Some Apparently Universal Patterns

Barry R. Chiswick

Summary

The study of the economic progress of immigrants in the country of destination is relevant for understanding not only the adjustment of the immigrants themselves, but also their initial and ultimate impact on the receiving country's economic growth and distribution of income. In addition to humanitarian considerations, such as refugee relief and family reunification, a rational and humane immigration policy needs to take into account the progress and impact of the immigrants.

Hypotheses are developed as to the economic progress of immigrants in comparison with the native born, and of the sons of immigrants in comparison with the sons of native-born parents. These hypotheses are then tested through comparative analyses of eleven different immigrant groups—seven racial and ethnic groups in the contemporary United States, immigrants in the United States at the turn of the century, and immigrants in contemporary Canada, Great Britain, and Israel. The intragroup procedure permits an analysis of economic progress among immigrant generations without confounding the findings with differences in the racial-ethnic mix of first-, second-, and higher-generation Americans. In addition, the procedure tests the proposition that the substantial differences in immigration histories do not call for separate hypotheses to explain the relative progress of the foreign born in each group. The findings indicate that a single,

NOTE: This article is drawn from a larger project on the earnings, employment, and impact of immigrants, financed by the Employment and Training Administration, U.S. Department of Labor (Grant no. 21-17-78-40). The views expressed here are solely those of the author.

relatively simple model can explain their progress regardless of ethnic group.

Two key determinants of economic progress are identified. The first is the transferability to the country of destination of skills acquired in the country of origin, whether in school or on the job. The second is the self-selection of immigrants on the basis of innate ability and motivation for economic advancement. Immigrants from countries with a language, culture, technology, and economic and legal structure similar to that in their destination would find their skills more readily transferable than those from countries with greater differences. Although economic migrants tend to be favorably self-selected on the basis of high innate ability and economic motivation, this self-selection is less intense for refugees with similar demographic characteristics, whose migration is primarily influenced by the political and social environment. In addition, persons migrating primarily for economic reasons are more likely to have transferable skills than are refugees.

When immigrants first arrive they have lower earnings than the native born with similar demographic characteristics because of the less than perfect transferability of skills. The disadvantage is greatest for refugees from countries with a different language and economy (for example, Cuban and Chinese refugees in the United States) and least for economic migrants from countries with a language and economy similar to the destination (for example, immigrants to the United States from English-speaking countries). With the passage of time, however, immigrants acquire knowledge of the language and customs of the country of destination and adjust their skills and credentials to the new environment. They also acquire skills that are relevant only in the particular workplace in which they are employed. Labor market experience in the country of destination has the largest impact on earnings for those whose skills acquired in the country of origin were least transferable.

The initial earnings disadvantage of immigrants may be over-come by the favorable characteristics implied by self-selection. This effect is apparently sufficiently strong for economic migrants that their earnings actually exceed those of native-born persons with the same demographic characteristics after they have been in the country eleven to sixteen years. Some of the greater innate ability and motivation of the economic migrants is transmitted to their native-born children—their sons earn more (by 5 to 10 percent) than the sons of native-born parents. Among refugees, the smaller transferability of skills and the less favorable self-selection apparently result in lower earnings. Although with the passage of time their earnings approach those of the native born, the catch-up either never occurs or requires several decades. In addition, the native-born sons of refugees do not exhibit the earnings advantage found for the native-born sons of economic migrants.

Although consistent patterns are found among first- and second-generation Americans within racial-ethnic groups, there are striking differences in earnings among groups. Some immigrant groups appear to be more successful than others. The reasons for these variations are beyond the scope of this study.

Although it was not possible to examine the relative success of immigrants admitted to the United States primarily because of kinship ties rather than their productivity characteristics, it is likely that their earnings pattern would be somewhat less favorable. One implication of the analysis is that if "productivity," or the likelihood of economic success, were used as the criterion for rationing admissions, more of the immigrants would come from countries whose similarities to the United States make their skills readily transferable, and the immigrants would be very favorably selected. Immigrants admitted under a productivity criterion would tend to experience greater economic success relative to the native born with similar characteristics than was found in the data under study. Even those admitted under a strict kinship tie criterion would be expected to adjust more or less completely after the passage of some time because they too are motivated primarily by economic considerations in the decision to immigrate. Although the disruption implied by refugee status may never be fully overcome, the earnings of refugees would nevertheless approach those of native-born persons as adjustments are made.

Introduction

U.S. immigration policy has historically been based primarily on the premise that immigrants have a favorable impact on the country's economic development.[1] This was the basis of the Open Door policy practiced from colonial times until the late nineteenth century. The earliest restrictions were intended to bar the entry of persons who would lower the nation's productivity—the sick, disabled, indigent, and criminal. Even the ethnocentric national origins quota system was

---

[1] For a summary of U.S. immigration policy since colonial times, see Barry R. Chiswick, "Immigrants and Immigration Policy," in William Fellner, ed., *Contemporary Economic Problems 1978* (Washington, D.C.: American Enterprise Institute, 1978), pp. 285-325.

influenced by concerns with productivity, although apparently based on a prejudiced reading of the data.[2]

The 1965 amendments to the Immigration and Nationality Act sharply changed U.S. immigration policy. The end of the national origins quota system that had been applicable to the Eastern Hemishere (and Western Hemisphere dependencies) since the 1920s resulted in a relative decline in immigration from Europe and a substantial increase in immigration from South and East Asia and from the current and former dependencies in the Caribbean. For other reasons immigration from Mexico, Cuba, and other parts of Latin America has also increased. From 1955 to 1965, half the nearly 3 million immigrants were born in Europe, but in the next decade the proportion declined to 28 percent of nearly 4 million immigrants (see Table 1). Whereas at the turn of the century the term "new immigration" referred to those from southern and eastern Europe, it now refers to immigration from Third World countries. In the decade 1955–1965, 7.5 percent of the immigrants were from Asia, but in the next decade 25 percent were from Asia. The share of immigration from Mexico and the Caribbean increased from 25 percent to 35 percent. Hispanic, black, and Asian immigrants are likely to continue to play an increasing role in U.S. immigration.

These amendments, together with subsequent legislation, also changed the mechanism for rationing immigration visas among the applicants from a country. The system is now more heavily weighted toward accepting those who are related to a U.S. citizen or resident alien, with less emphasis given to the immigrant's skills.

The 1965 amendments were passed at an unusual time in American history. In an era of expanding civil liberties, the racial and ethnic discrimination implicit in the national origins quota system was becoming increasingly inconsistent with both the domestic anti-discrimination legislation and the desired friendly relations with the emerging Third World countries. It was also an era of optimism in public policy. The amendments may have had a favorable impact on productivity in the United States by providing opportunities for immigration to skilled and highly motivated workers from countries which previously had very small quotas. The greater emphasis that it placed on kinship ties than on productivity may have had the opposite effect.

---

[2] For a sense of the debate at the time, see the article by Paul H. Douglas (then a professor and later senator from Illinois), "Is the New Immigration More Unskilled than the Old?" *Journal of the American Statistical Association*, vol. 16 (June 1919), pp. 393-403. Douglas's answer was no.

TABLE 1

IMMIGRATION TO THE UNITED STATES BY COUNTRY OF ORIGIN, FISCAL YEARS 1956–1975

	1956–1965		1966–1975	
Place of Origin	Number (thousands)	Percent	Number (thousands)	Percent
Europe	1,409	49.0	1,067	28.0
Germany	310	10.8	102	2.7
Greece	58	2.0	129	3.4
Italy	197	6.8	217	5.7
Poland	87	3.0	50	1.3
Portugal	29	1.0	121	3.2
United Kingdom	249	8.8	157	4.1
Other	479	16.6	291	7.6
Asia	215	7.5	944	24.8
China[a]	49	1.7	205	5.4
India	5	0.2	101	2.7
Japan	49	1.7	43	1.1
Korea	16	0.6	138	3.6
Philippines	28	1.0	239	6.3
Other	68	2.3	218	5.7
Africa	23	0.8	59	1.6
Egypt	7	0.2	25	0.7
Other	16	0.6	34	0.9
North America[b]	1,051	36.5	1,492	39.2
Canada	322	11.2	160	4.2
Mexico	420	14.5	538	14.1
Cuba	132	4.6	290	7.6
Dominican Republic	40	1.4	126	3.3
Haiti	13	0.5	55	1.4
Jamaica	15	0.5	124	3.3
Other	109	3.8	199	5.3
South America	168	5.8	216	5.7
Colombia	47	1.6	64	1.7
Ecuador	23	0.8	43	1.1
Other	98	3.4	109	2.9
Oceania	12	0.4	28	0.7
Total	2,878	100.0	3,808	100.0

NOTE: Detail may not add to total because of rounding.

[a] China includes Taiwan and Hong Kong.

[b] For North America other than Canada, there were 729,000 immigrants (25.3 percent) for 1956–1965 and 1,332,000 immigrants (35.0 percent) for 1966–1975.

SOURCE: Immigration and Naturalization Service, U.S. Department of Justice, 1978.

More than a decade has passed since the 1965 amendments, and there is a different perspective on the limitations of America's resources. In addition, the issue of illegal aliens has heightened public interest in immigration policy. Interagency and congressional task forces and commissions have been formed, or are soon to be formed, to study immigration policy. Even if legislation is not changed because these studies conclude that current law is optimal, the periodic reevaluation of policy is fruitful.

An analysis of the impact of immigrants on the average level and distribution of income among the native population shows that immigrants with higher levels of skill are more likely to raise the average level of income and decrease the inequality of income among the native population.[3] A preliminary analysis of the earnings of foreign-born white men in the United States also showed that the skills of immigrants are not static. Foreign-born men were compared with native-born men with the same demographic characteristics. Although the immigrants had lower earnings when they first arrived, as time passed they acquired skills relevant to the U.S. labor market, and the earnings gap between the foreign and native born narrowed. After about thirteen years in the country the earnings of the foreign born actually exceeded those of the native born.

Can the findings regarding the economic progress of white men be generalized to other immigrant groups? If these findings, which suggest an overall favorable impact of immigrants, are relevant only for white male immigrants they are of little value for policy makers, regardless of their value to historians of contemporary America. On the other hand, if it appears that these findings are not unique to a single demographic group at a single point in time, but rather reflect broad patterns that are likely to be reproduced in new immigrant groups, then they are of considerable value.

In addition, it is useful to know whether the criteria for admitting immigrants into the United States are relevant for understanding their economic progress and impact. Immigration visas may be rationed on the basis of the person's likely productivity in the country, whether the person has relatives in the country, or for humanitarian reasons, such as refugee relief. It is important to understand more fully the progress of immigrants admitted under different criteria in order to aid their adjustment more effectively, to recognize more accurately the costs and benefits of alternative policies, and to help form an overall immigration policy. While a humane immigration policy must

---

[3] See Chiswick, "Immigrants and Immigration Policy."

surely include a recognition of the importance of kinship ties and refugee relief, the implications of these policies as distinct from one giving a greater weight to productivity need to be recognized.

We cannot currently analyze the economic progress in the United States of future immigrants. To gain some insights into the future, however, it is possible to analyze the progress in the contemporary United States of Hispanic, black, and Asian immigrants, and to examine the progress of immigrants in other times and in other places. In this analysis it will be possible to differentiate economic migrants from refugees. If similar patterns of progress are found in a variety of settings, there is greater confidence that these patterns will persist in the future.

The purpose of this chapter is to extend the analysis of the economic progress of immigrants. The analysis is in terms of the earnings of male immigrants of various racial-ethnic groups in various settings, in comparison with native-born men with similar demographic characteristics. The earnings of the native-born sons of immigrants are also compared with the earnings of the sons of native-born parents. The first section discusses the international transferability of skills and self-selection on the part of immigrants. This leads to the development of hypotheses regarding the pattern of earnings between the native and the foreign born, and how this varies by country of origin, time in the place of destination, and type of immigration. The section closes with a discussion of the statistical framework.

The next section tests these hypotheses through a detailed examination of the economic progress of seven immigrant groups in the contemporary United States—foreign-born whites (singling out Cubans and Mexicans for special attention), blacks, Chinese, Japanese, and Filipinos. The analysis generally uses a one-in-a-hundred sample from the *1970 Census of Population* to compare the earnings in 1969 of these foreign-born men with their native-born counterparts.

This is followed by an analysis of the economic progress of immigrants in other times and other places: the United States at the turn of the century, and contemporary Canada, Great Britain, and Israel.

The final section sets out some implications for immigration policy that emerge from this study.

Hypotheses and Statistical Framework

For the comparative analysis of the earnings of foreign-born and native-born men with the same demographic characteristics, it is hypothesized that the earnings differential would depend, in part, on the transferability to the United States of the skills acquired by the foreign-born in school and on the job in the country of origin. It would also depend on the extent to which there is self-selection in favor of those with greater innate ability or work motivation. The transferability of skills and the self-selection of immigrants are key factors in the analysis. Their implications for the earnings of the foreign born are first developed; then the statistical framework used to test these hypotheses is presented. Although the discussion in this section is in terms of immigrants to the United States, the points are applicable to immigrants to any country.

Transferability of Skills. In general, those with more schooling appear to have more allocative efficiency, that is, they are more efficient in making decisions regarding the optimal allocation of resources.[4] They also appear to have more worker efficiency, that is, they are better able to perform tasks, perhaps because they learn skills in a shorter time and perform them with less error. The extent to which schooling enhances productivity would, in part, be related to the quality of the schooling itself: up to some point more hours of schooling per year, a lower student-teacher ratio, and more knowledgeable teachers increase the productivity of schooling. However, the productivity also depends on where and how the worker applies the knowledge acquired in school.

For the present purposes, the international transferability of the skills acquired in school is of considerable interest. For a given cohort of immigrants this transferability may be thought of as having two components: the extent to which skills acquired in school are transferable from one country to another within occupational or training categories and the occupational composition of that cohort. Presumably, all schooling has some elements that are country specific and some that are transferable internationally, but their relative importance would vary among the levels and types of education. A Russian criminal lawyer, for example, may have received a high-quality education in Moscow, but the training will have little market value in the United States. On the other hand, a mathematician from Russia with the same number of years of schooling may find his skills well rewarded in the United States. An immigrant cohort of persons with readily transferable skills will achieve greater and more rapid success in the United States than an otherwise identical cohort

---

[4] See, for example, Theodore W. Schultz, "The Value of the Ability to Deal with Disequilibria," *Journal of Economic Literature*, September 1975, pp. 827-46.

consisting of workers with skills that are of value primarily in their country of origin.

Immigrants can acquire schooling in either the country of origin or in the country of destination. Schooling acquired in the United States is more likely to be relevant for U.S. labor markets. But since the quality and transferability of previous schooling in part determines the productivity of U.S. schooling, those with previous schooling that is less transferable to the United States may gain less from schooling here.

This discussion suggests that it is useful to classify immigrants by the extent to which immigrant cohorts are weighted toward transferable skills or occupations. For the classification according to transferability of skills two country-of-origin groups are used, English-speaking countries and all other countries. The presumption is that for any given occupation the skills (including language) acquired in London, England, and Kingston, Jamaica, are more likely to be readily transferred to the U.S. labor market than the skills acquired during the same number of years of schooling in Berlin, Germany, or Port-au-Prince, Haiti.

For the classification according to the distribution of skills, it is useful to think in terms of "economic" and "noneconomic" migrants. All immigrants may be said to base their decision on the optimization of their economic well-being, if this is defined broadly to include personal safety and freedom. But here the distinction between economic and noneconomic motivations is the extent to which real money income (narrowly defined economic well-being) rather than political or social factors influences the migration decision.[5]

Since the earning power of one's skills plays a primary role in economic migration and a secondary role in refugee migration, a cohort of the latter is likely to include a larger proportion of workers with skills that have little international transferability. Refugee migration generally arises from a sudden or unexpected change in political conditions, which appear to change more suddenly and more sharply than economic conditions. As a result, refugees are less likely than economic migrants to have acquired readily transferable skills and are more likely to have made investments specific to their country

---

[5] For analyses of the motivations and skills of the Cuban and Vietnamese refugees, see Richard Brody and others, *Cubans in Exile: Disaffection and the Revolution* (Stanford, Calif.: Stanford University Press, 1968); and William T. Liu, *Transition to Nowhere: Vietnamese Refugees in America* (Nashville, Tenn.: Carter House Publishers, 1978). For a review of refugee migrations in the post–World War II period, see Gaynor I. Jacobson, "The Refugee Movement: An Overview," *International Migration Review*, vol. 2, no. 4 (Winter 1977), pp. 514-23.

of origin. Economic migrants are younger on average than refugees, since migration tends to be more profitable the sooner it is done. Delay involves forgoing the higher earnings in the place of destination and shortening the remaining working life. In addition, delay results in increasing investments specific to the country of origin, thereby reducing the gain from migration.

It is not always easy to identify individuals as either economic migrants or refugees, because the classification depends in part on the person's motive for migrating. It is possible, however, judgmentally to classify immigrants from some countries at some points in time as predominantly refugees and others as predominantly economic migrants. In the 1970 U.S. census data the primary refugee group among whites is the Cubans (since 1959), while among Asian-Americans the largest proportion of refugees are Chinese. There were no major refugee movements to the United States from English-speaking countries in the past several decades. Because one cell in our two-by-two classification is empty, there are three categories of immigrants; economic migrants from English-speaking countries, economic migrants from other countries, and refugees.[6]

The effect of the transferability of schooling on earnings implies the hypothesis outlined in the first row of Table 2. That is, the effect of schooling on earnings is expected to be greatest for those whose schooling is most transferable to the U.S. labor market (the native born) and would decline with the degree of transferability—next highest for English-speaking economic migrants, then other economic migrants, and least for refugees.

The discussion of the effect of the transferability of the skills acquired in school applies with equal force to the skills acquired through formal or informal on-the-job training in the country of origin. In this analysis there is no direct measure of the magnitude of job-related training, but the indirect measure, years of labor market experience in the country of origin, is used in its place. The native born will of course have their labor market experience in the United States; among the foreign born, those from countries with technologies and economic systems that most closely resemble the United States will tend to have skills that are readily transferable. Refugee populations will include a larger proportion of workers with skills acquired on the job in the country of origin that have little applica-

---

[6] For the purpose of this analysis, among whites the English-speaking countries are Britain, Ireland, Canada, Australia, and New Zealand. Among blacks the English-speaking countries are in the Caribbean area.

TABLE 2

HYPOTHESES REGARDING THE ECONOMIC PROGRESS OF IMMIGRANTS
TO THE UNITED STATES

Partial Effect on Earnings, or Parameter	Native Born	Economic Migrants		Refugees
		English-speaking countries	Other countries	
Partial effect on earnings of:				
Schooling	1	2	3	4
Labor market experience in country of origin (T)	1	2	3	4
Years since migration (YSM) (T constant)	—	3	2	1
Parameter				
YSM at which earnings of migrants and native born are equal	—	1		2

NOTE: 1=highest or earliest; 4=lowest or latest.

bility in the United States. These hypotheses are summarized in the second row of Table 2.

The weaker the transferability of skills, the lower the earnings and the greater the probability of unemployment for the immigrant when he first arrives. With the passage of time in the United States the immigrant acquires knowledge, habits, and skills that increase his productivity on the job and reduce the incidence and duration of unemployment. This may occur through an informal learning-by-living adjustment process, by a more formal job training (or retraining) program, or by formal schooling. The Cuban emigree lawyers and doctors who found dishwashing their best job opportunity when they first arrived have, over time, either acquired new skills or gradually acquired American licenses.

The effect on earnings of years since migration is expected to be inversely related to the extent to which country-of-origin skills are transferable to the U.S. labor market. In the extreme case, if skills are perfectly transferable across countries, time in the place of destination would have no effect on earnings over and above the effect of total labor market experience.[7] Thus, for the same schooling and age, the number of years an immigrant has been in the United States is likely to be least important as a determinant of earnings for economic migrants from English-speaking countries and most important for non-English-speaking refugees. This hypothesis is summarized in the third row of Table 2 and is shown schematically by the slopes of the earnings profiles in Figure 1.

Self-Selection of Immigrants. There is substantial support for the hypothesis that immigrants tend to have a higher level of innate ability and work motivation than their fellow countrymen with similar characteristics who remain at home. In his study of immigration to the United States in the century before World War I, Marcus Lee Hansen wrote: "Countries of origin were dismayed by their loss when they saw their ports thronged with the sturdiest of their peasantry. Efforts to stem the movement were attempted." [8] More recently, theoretical and empirical studies suggest a higher propensity to migrate among those who are more able, are more achievement motivated, or have a higher level of schooling.[9]

The extent of the self-selection of migrants in favor of the more able will vary across countries. The self-selection would be more pronounced the larger the costs of migration, including the costs of the subsequent adjustment in the new environment. The smaller costs of migration for economic migrants from English-speaking countries

---

[7] Time in the United States could even have a negative effect on earnings. Bartel and Borjas found that among adult men who engage in voluntary job change in the United States, earnings are initially higher than would be predicted on the basis of their demographic and skill characteristics, but that with the passage of time their earnings regress toward the predicted value. See Ann P. Bartel and George Borjas, "Middle-Age Job Mobility: Its Determinants and Consequences," in Seymour Wolfbein, ed., *Men in Pre-Retirement Years* (Philadelphia: Temple University Press, 1977).

[8] Marcus Lee Hansen, *The Immigrant in American History*, Arthur M. Schlesinger, ed. (Cambridge, Mass.: Harvard University Press, 1940), p. 212.

[9] For a theoretical exposition of why migration rates would be higher for those with greater earnings potential, see Barry R. Chiswick, "The Effect of Americanization on the Earnings of Foreign-Born Men," *Journal of Political Economy*, October 1978, p. 900. For some empirical studies, see June A. O'Neill, "The Effect of Income and Education on Inter-Regional Migration," Ph.D. dissertation, Columbia University, 1970; Aba Schwartz, "Migration, Age and Education," *Journal of Political Economy*, August 1976, pp. 701-19; Kathryn Tidwick, "Need for Achievement, Social Class, and Intention to Emigrate in Jamaican Students," *Social and Economic Studies*, March 1976, pp. 52-60; Anthony M. J. Yezer and Lawrence Thurston, "Migration Patterns and Income Change: Implications for the Human Capital Approach to Migration," *Southern Economic Journal*, vol. 42 (April 1976), pp. 693-702. See also, Schultz, "Value of Ability."

FIGURE 1

SCHEMATIC REPRESENTATION OF EARNINGS PROFILE
BY YEARS SINCE MIGRATION

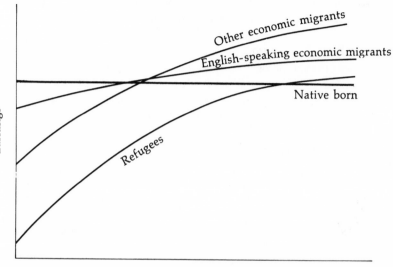

Years since migration

implies that the favorable self-selection will be less intense, which at
least partially offsets the greater transferability of their skills. In comparison with economic migrants, refugees are less likely to be self-
selected on the basis of high labor market ability and work motivation,
because factors other than labor market success are important determinants of their migration. This is shown schematically in Figure 1
by the lower earnings profile for refugees than for economic migrants.

If the distribution of innate ability and motivation is similar
across countries, the average level of ability and motivation would be
higher for the immigrants (particularly economic migrants) than for
the native born in a population. Then the question arises: Are the
advantages of greater ability sufficient to offset the disadvantages of
the less than perfect international transferability of knowledge and
skills so that the earnings of immigrants eventually equal that of the
native born? The years since migration at which this earnings crossover occurs, if it does occur, is a parameter of considerable interest
that will be estimated. Because of the less favorable self-selection of

369

refugees, the earnings crossover will occur later for them than for economic migrants, if it occurs at all. This hypothesis is summarized in the fourth row of Table 2. The schematic earnings profiles in Figure 1 are drawn under the assumption that the earnings crossover occurs sooner for economic migrants than for refugees.

There is likely to be a regression toward the mean in the distribution of ability from one generation to the next. That is, the children of high (low) ability parents have an average level of ability less (greater) than that of their parents, but greater (less) than the average level of ability in the population. This would arise if some aspects of ability are transmitted from one generation to the next through genetic or environmental factors.[10] In this case, the earnings of the children of immigrants would exceed those of the children of native-born parents to the extent that their greater level of innate ability and motivation outweighs disadvantages from having parents with a foreign origin. If the favorable self-selection of immigrants is less intense for refugees than for economic migrants, the earnings advantage of the children of refugees would be smaller than that of the children of economic migrants. This issue will be examined through a comparison of the earnings of the native born on the basis of their parents' place of birth.

Statistical Framework. The statistical framework for analyzing the earnings of immigrants and testing the hypotheses has been developed elsewhere and will be described only briefly here.[11] By the use of the so-called human capital earnings function, annual earnings (in natural logarithms) are expressed as a function of a set of explanatory variables, which include years of formal schooling, years of labor market experience (measured by the number of years since age five that the person was not in school), weeks worked, marital status, area of

---

[10] If the children of high (low) ability parents had higher (lower) ability than their parents, the variance of ability would increase from one generation to the next. Intuitively, this seems unlikely. For some recent evidence on the well-established principle of regression to the mean in standard measures of ability from one generation to the next, see Lloyd G. Humphrey, "To Understand Regression from Parent to Offspring, Think Statistically," *Psychological Bulletin*, vol. 85 (1978), pp. 1317-22.

[11] See Chiswick, "Americanization," pp. 897-921; and Barry R. Chiswick, "Sons of Immigrants: Are They at an Earnings Disadvantage?" *American Economic Review*, February 1977, pp. 376-80. For an analysis of occupational change, see Barry R. Chiswick, "A Longitudinal Analysis of the Occupational Mobility of Immigrants," in Barbara Dennis, ed., *Proceedings of the 30th Annual Winter Meeting, Industrial Relations Research Association* (Madison: University of Wisconsin Press, 1978).

residence, whether the person is foreign born, and, if foreign born, the number of years since migrating to the United States. Earnings include wage, salary, and self-employment income.

The training variables of interest are years of schooling, years of labor market experience, and years since migrating to the United States. Preliminary analyses indicated that the effect of schooling on earnings for the foreign born is the same whether the schooling is acquired in the United States or in the country of origin. For this reason, the analysis below will not distinguish where the schooling was acquired.[12]

In a cohort of immigrants, among those with the same number of years of schooling, those who are older have had more work experience in their country of origin. On the other hand, for those with the same amount of schooling and total labor market experience, having been in the United States longer means less training in the country of origin and more of it here. The effect on earnings of years since migration, when total labor market experience is held constant, measures the differential effect of U.S. over country-of-origin experience.

Two demographic variables, marital status and area of residence, are included to control statistically for characteristics that affect earnings and may vary systematically with nativity, but that may not be related to differences in productivity.[13] Ignoring these variables can provide misleading interpretations. For example, a very high proportion (68 percent) of black male immigrants live in metropolitan areas in New York State, compared with 10 percent of native-born blacks. On the other hand, 8 percent of the foreign-born and 44 percent of the native-born black men live in the urban South. Wages tend to be high in metropolitan areas in New York State and low in the southern states for all workers. If region of residence is ignored, black immigrants would appear to be much more productive than native-born blacks, not because of greater skills or work motivation, but because they are more likely to live in a high-wage area.

---

[12] Although the effect of schooling on earnings is smaller for immigrants than for the native born (with the exception of black immigrants), the effect of schooling is similar for the sons of immigrants and the sons of native-born parents. This suggests that the smaller effect on earnings of U.S. schooling for immigrants may arise from their previous schooling having been acquired in another country, rather than from having parents with foreign schooling.

[13] The area control variables used in the analysis are generally urban/rural and South/non-South residence, but this varies somewhat by racial-ethnic group.

The Contemporary United States

Having developed the hypotheses to be tested and having set out the statistical framework, we can now proceed to the analysis of the economic progress of male immigrants and sons of immigrants in the contemporary United States.[14] The data are from the *1970 Census of Population*. The analyses are performed separately for seven racial-ethnic groups: whites, two Hispanic subsets of whites (Cubans and Mexicans), blacks, and three groups of East Asian origin (Chinese, Japanese, and Filipinos).

The intragroup procedure adopted here permits an analysis of earnings among immigrant generations without confounding the findings with differences in the racial-ethnic mix of first-, second-, and higher-generation Americans. The procedure tests the proposition that the substantial differences in the immigration histories of the seven groups do not call for separate stories or hypotheses to explain the relative progress of the foreign born in each group. Rather, the findings indicate that a single, relatively simple model can explain the economic progress of immigrants regardless of their racial-ethnic group. This proposition is further tested in the next section when the progress of immigrants in four other settings is examined.

White Immigrants.[15] Among adult men in the United States in 1970, 5 percent were foreign born, and of these, 91 percent were white. The white immigrants earned slightly less than the native born in 1969, about 1 percent less when measured by mean earnings and 3 percent less when measured by the mean natural logarithm of earnings (the logarithm of the geometric mean). The white immigrants had about a year less schooling than the native born, were three years older, and were more likely to live in an urban area outside the South. They have been in the United States on average for about twenty-two years (see Table 3).

If other variables are held constant, the white immigrants earned 3 percent more than the native born. However, white immigrants who have been in the United States for ten years earned about 3 percent less than the native born, while those in the United States twenty years earned about 6 percent more than the native born. The earnings crossover occurred at thirteen years of residence in the United States.

---

[14] For the purpose of this analysis, persons born abroad of American parents are excluded from the data. Few people are in this category. If one parent is a U.S. citizen, the children are entitled to U.S. citizenship.

[15] This discussion is based on Chiswick, "Americanization."

TABLE 3

COMPARISON OF EARNINGS FOR NATIVE- AND FOREIGN-BORN ADULT MEN IN THE UNITED STATES, BY RACIAL-ETHNIC GROUP, 1970

Racial-Ethnic Group and Nativity[a]	Means				Relative Difference in Earnings[b]			
	Annual earnings (dollars)	Schooling (years)	Age (years)	Years since migration (YSM)		Other variables held constant[c]		Years since Migration at Earnings Crossover[d]
					Overall	YSM=10	YSM=20	
White								
Native	9,738	11.9	42.8	—	−0.03	−0.03	+0.06	13
Foreign	9,662	10.8	45.6	21.7				
Cuban								
Native	10,341	12.3	43.6	—	−0.44	−0.16	+0.03	18
Foreign	6,857	10.8	42.2	7.2				
Mexican								
Native	6,523	8.9	39.6	—	−0.21	−0.05	+0.04	15
Foreign	5,474	6.1	41.9	18.0				
Black								
Native	6,138	9.9	41.8	—	+0.05	−0.02	+0.10	11
Foreign	6,585	11.0	40.4	11.3				
Asian								
Japanese								
Native	10,389	12.6	43.6	—	−0.14	−0.12	+0.03	18
Foreign	9,191	14.3	38.4	10.9				

(Table 3 continues on the next page.)

373

TABLE 3 (Continued)

Racial-Ethnic Group and Nativity[a]	Means				Relative Difference in Earnings[b]			Years since Migration at Earnings Crossover[d]
	Annual earnings (dollars)	Schooling (years)	Age (years)	Years since migration (YSM)	Overall	Other variables held constant[c]		
						YSM=10	YSM=20	
Chinese								
Native	10,745	12.7	41.8	—	−0.35	−0.26	−0.08	—[e]
Foreign	8,019	11.9	42.8	16.8				
Filipino								
Native	7,010	11.1	36.8	—	−0.08	−0.06	+0.11	13
Foreign	7,086	11.0	44.6	18.9				

NOTE: The table refers to men aged twenty-five to sixty-four years in 1970 who worked and had nonzero earnings in 1969 and, for the analyses for black and Asian immigrants, were not enrolled in school in 1970.

[a] Racial-ethnic identity is defined by the questions on race and Spanish origin. White men are used as the native-born comparison group in the Cuban analysis. The Mexican analysis is for the five southwestern states. The Cuban and black analyses are for urban areas.

[b] The difference in the means of the natural logarithm of earnings. A negative coefficient indicates lower earnings for the foreign born. For small differences, when multiplied by 100, the parameter is the percentage difference in earnings.

[c] Other variables are years of schooling, labor market experience and its square, the logarithm of weeks worked, marital status, and geographic distribution. The variable for years since migration and its square are evaluated at YSM=10 and YSM=20.

[d] The number of years in the United States at which the earnings of the foreign born equal the earnings of the native born, when other variables (note c) are held constant.

[e] The earnings of Chinese immigrants approach but do not equal the earnings of native-born Chinese-Americans.

SOURCE: 1970 Census of Population, Public Use Sample, 5 percent questionnaire, 1/100 sample except for a 1/1,000 sample for the white analysis.

TABLE 4

PARTIAL EFFECTS ON EARNINGS OF SCHOOLING, LABOR MARKET
EXPERIENCE IN COUNTRY OF ORIGIN, AND YEARS SINCE MIGRATION FOR
ADULT MEN IN THE UNITED STATES, 1970
(percent)

Racial-Ethnic Group	Schooling		Labor Market Experience in the Country of Origin[a]		Years since Migration to the United States[b]
	Native born	Foreign born	Native born	Foreign born	
White	7.2	5.7	2.13	1.41	1.12
Cuban (urban)	7.3	3.1	2.22	0.33	2.37
Mexican (Southwest)	5.2	3.9	1.80	1.67	1.34
Black (urban)	4.6	3.3	0.78	1.18	1.60
Asian					
Japanese	6.3	5.9	1.73	1.52	2.38
Chinese	6.7	4.8	2.73	-0.60[c]	2.70
Filipino	5.8	6.4	1.30	1.46	1.94

NOTE: The foreign born are compared with native-born men of the same racial-ethnic group, except for the Cubans where the comparison is with native-born urban white men. Unless noted otherwise, the data are for men aged twenty-five to sixty-four years in 1970 who worked at least one week and had nonzero earnings (wage, salary, and self-employment income) in 1969. The analyses for black and Asian men exclude persons enrolled in school in 1970. The parameters are estimated from a linear regression of the natural logarithm of earnings on schooling, labor market experience and its square, the logarithm of weeks worked, marital status, and geographic area, and, for the foreign born, years since migration and its square.

[a] The quadratic experience variable (T, T^2) is evaluated at T=10.

[b] The quadratic years since migration variable (YSM, YSM^2) is evaluated at YSM=10.

[c] Set of country-of-origin experience variables (T,T^2) has no significant effect on earnings.

SOURCE: 1970 Census of Population, Public Use Sample, 5 percent questionnaire, 1/100 sample, except for a 1/1,000 sample for the white analysis.

Schooling has a smaller effect on earnings in the United States for the foreign born than for the native born (see Table 4). Earnings rise by 5.7 percent per year of schooling for the foreign born and by 7.2 percent for the native born. Among the foreign born, however, the effect of schooling on earnings is larger for men from the English-speaking developed countries than for other white immigrants, 6.6 percent compared with 5.2 percent.

The effect on earnings in the United States of labor market experience acquired in the country of birth is also smaller for the foreign born than the native born. Living in the United States an extra year, however, raises earnings by more for the foreign than the native born. The differential effect on earnings of job training in the United States as compared with training in the country of origin is small for immigrants from the English-speaking developed countries, but larger for those from other countries. After ten years in the United States, the partial effects are 0.35 percent for the former and 1.40 percent for the latter.

Among the native-born adult white men, one-fifth have a foreign-born parent. Parentage makes virtually no difference in the level of schooling, but those with a foreign-born parent are more likely to live in urban areas outside the South. The 12 percent difference in earnings in favor of those with foreign-born parents is reduced to 5 percent when training and demographic variables are held constant (Table 5).

These findings for white men are consistent with the hypotheses developed above. A country-of-origin analysis for white men indicates that those born in Cuba and Mexico have earnings that are substantially lower than those of other white immigrants. Among the second-generation white men, earnings are substantially lower for those of Mexican parentage and are substantially higher for Jews.[16] The earnings of white men born in Cuba and Mexico are studied before proceeding to the analysis for black and Asian immigrants.

Cuban immigrants. Unlike the other major immigrant groups in the United States Cuban immigrants came recently and migrated at

---

[16] The country-of-origin analysis is based on a one-in-a-hundred sample of the population. Approximately 98 percent of men of Cuban and Mexican origin in the 1970 census are classified as white in the question on race. Parents' country of birth is the father's if he was foreign born, otherwise it is the mother's. There are too few adult second-generation Cuban-Americans for a separate country variable.

Religion is not asked in the census. The Jewish variable is for a subset of Jews, those raised in a home in which Yiddish, Hebrew, or Ladino (Judeo-Spanish) was spoken either in addition to or instead of English. Although in general having a non-English mother tongue is associated with 2 percent lower earnings for second-generation Americans, if other variables are held constant, a Jewish mother tongue is associated with 15 percent higher earnings. Because the information on mother tongue does not exist in the data set with year of immigration for the foreign born, no separate analysis of the earnings of immigrants can be made for Jews.

TABLE 5

DIFFERENCE IN EARNINGS BETWEEN FOREIGN PARENTAGE AND
NATIVE PARENTAGE ADULT MEN BORN IN THE UNITED STATES, 1970
(percent)

Racial-Ethnic Group	Relative Difference[a]
White	4.9
Mexican[b]	5.1
	8.6[c]
Black (urban)	
All states	8.4[c]
New York State	10.7[c]
Asian	
Japanese	5.2[c,d]
Chinese	4.3[c,d]
Filipino	9.0[c,d]

NOTE: Earnings in 1969 for native-born men aged twenty-five to sixty-four years in 1970 who worked and had nonzero earnings in 1969.

[a] The parameter is 100 times the coefficient of a foreign parentage dichotomous variable when the natural logarithm of earnings is regressed on schooling, experience, marital status, the log of weeks worked, geographic area, nativity of parents, and, in some equations, mother tongue. For small values the parameter is the percentage difference in earnings. A positive value indicates higher earnings for those with foreign-born parents.

[b] Men with Spanish surnames living in the five southwestern states.

[c] Mother tongue is held constant. Evaluated for a Spanish mother tongue in the Mexican analysis and an English mother tongue in the black analysis.

[d] Coefficient is not significantly different from zero. The sample size is small for native-born men with native-born parents.

SOURCE: 1970 Census of Population, Public Use Sample, 15 percent questionnaire, 1/1,000 sample for white men, and 1/100 sample for other groups.

an older age. Nearly half the Cuban immigrants live in urban Florida and another one-fifth live in urban areas in New York State. The analysis for Cubans provides a means of studying the experience in the United States of a refugee population. Their migration was stimulated by Castro's accession to power in 1959 and the subsequent social, political, and economic changes that were a consequence of converting Cuba into a Marxist-Leninist state.[17] Seventy-eight percent of adult Cuban-born men in the United States in 1970 were in the country for ten or fewer years. Among adult foreign-born men in 1970, the

---

[17] See Brody, *Cubans in Exile.*

average number of years since migrating was seven for the Cubans, as compared with eighteen for the Mexicans and twenty-two for all white immigrants. Since there are very few native-born men with Cuban-born parents, the benchmark for comparison with the native born is all white men living in urban areas.

Cuban-born men had very low earnings in 1969, $6,857 compared with $10,341 for native-born white men (Table 3). Some of this earnings differential is attributable to their lower level of schooling (one and a half fewer years of schooling) and the greater proportion living in a low-wage state, Florida. Adjusting for differences in schooling, age, place of residence, and other demographic factors substantially reduces the earnings disadvantage of the Cuban born (the difference in the mean logarithm of earnings is reduced from 0.44 to 0.24).

The key factors for understanding the lower earnings of the Cuban refugees are the small effect on earnings of training received in Cuba and the short time they have lived in the United States. The effect of an additional year of schooling on earnings in the United States is 3.1 percent for the Cubans (Table 4). This can be compared with 7.3 percent for native-born urban white men, 5.2 percent for white immigrants from all non-English-speaking countries, and 3.9 percent for Mexican immigrants. Years of labor market experience in Cuba have virtually no effect on earnings in the United States. Labor market experience in the United States, on the other hand, has a substantial effect on earnings.

The earnings of Cuban immigrants do eventually reach parity with native-born white men. For those in the United States ten years, earnings are lower by about 16 percent, while earnings are higher by 3 percent for those in the United States for twenty years. Earnings equality is reached at about eighteen years in the United States (immigrated in 1951), that is, for the small cohort of immigrants who came to the United States before Castro came to power. It remains to be seen in the *1980 Census of Population* whether the Cuban refugees who arrived in the United States between 1960 and 1964 will attain earnings parity with the native born.

The earnings pattern for the Cuban immigrants is consistent with our expectations for a refugee population. Schooling and labor market experience acquired in Cuba have a small effect on earnings in the United States, whereas U.S. labor market experience has a large effect on earnings. Other things the same, the Cuban immigrants who came here after Castro came to power have lower earnings than other white immigrants and the native born. The earnings gap is narrower, however, the longer the refugees have been in the United States. The Cubans who came here in the early 1950s did have the same earnings in 1969 as the native born.

Mexican immigrants. The Mexican-American population includes some of the "oldest" and some of the most recent immigrants to the United States. About one-quarter of Mexican-origin adult men were born in Mexico, and of the three-quarters born in the United States half have a foreign-born parent. Among those with native-born parents, many can trace their ancestry to migrations from Mexico in the seventeenth century to what is now the southwestern region of the United States.

Mexican-Americans earn less than other white men of the same immigrant generation. Other things the same, first-, second-, and later-generation Mexican-Americans earn about 15 to 25 percent less than Anglos, and the difference does not appear to diminish between successive generations. Although the earnings of Mexican immigrants do not catch up to the earnings of native-born whites, the patterns found among successive generations for whites as a group also appear among successive generations for Mexican-Americans.

Compared with native-born Mexican-Americans, Mexican immigrants have low earnings ($5,474 as compared with $6,523 in 1969) and nearly two years less schooling (Table 3).[18] When other variables are held constant, however, the earnings disadvantage of Mexican immigrants narrows sharply to 5 percent. Compared with native-born Mexican-origin men, the immigrants who have been in the United States ten years have 5 percent lower earnings while those in the United States twenty years have 3.4 percent higher earnings. After about fifteen years in the United States the earnings of Mexican immigrants equal that of native-born Mexican-origin men.

Mexican immigrants are disadvantaged not only by a low level of schooling, but also by a small effect of schooling on earnings (3.9 percent compared with 5.2 percent for native-born Mexican-origin men) and a smaller effect on earnings of labor market experience in the country of origin (Table 4). Labor market experience acquired in the United States, however, has a substantial favorable effect on the earnings of Mexican immigrants.

Many of the earnings-related characteristics of native-born men with parents born in Mexico are very similar to those of Mexican-

---

[18] This section reports findings for the 86 percent of Mexican-origin men living in the five southwestern states. Similar conclusions emerge if the analysis is performed for all states.

origin men with both parents born in the United States. They have about the same level of schooling and are about the same age. The latter are, however, more likely to live in rural areas. Among native-born men of Mexican origin, nearly all (98 percent) of those with native-born parents were raised in a home in which Spanish was spoken, either exclusively or together with English.

Overall, second-generation Mexican-Americans earned 9 percent more than those with parents born in the United States. Even when the training and demographic variables are held constant their earnings advantage ranges from 5 to 9 percent (Table 5). The sons of Mexican immigrants have a clear earnings advantage over the sons of native-born parents of Mexican origin.

Penalosa arrives at a similar conclusion in his analysis of the family income of native-born Mexican-Americans using data from the *1960 Census of Population*.[19] He attributed this finding to self-selection in migration when he wrote:

> Until fairly recently both Hispanos and Californios [descendents of 17th century settlers from Mexico] were largely located in their ancestral rural areas, and attended isolated and largely *de facto* segregated schools. . . . Immigration in itself ordinarily implies some desire for change, a desire not necessarily shared by a conquered people. It would appear that foreign immigrants and their families have been acculturating more rapidly to dominant Anglo society than the native-born members of ethnic enclaves of centuries standing.

Black Immigrants. From the end of the period of the legal importation of slaves in 1808 until recently there was little immigration by blacks into the United States. In the post–World War II period, and particularly since the mid-1960s, the immigration of blacks has increased sharply, although blacks are still a small proportion of the nation's 400,000 immigrants per year. In 1976, for example, only 40,000 persons, or 10 percent of the immigrants, were from the predominantly black countries of the Caribbean and sub-Saharan Africa.[20] As a result, in 1970 only 1.1 percent of the blacks in the country were foreign born and another 1.1 percent (disproportionately children) were native born with a foreign-born parent.[21] It is likely, however,

---

[19] See Fernando Penalosa, "Education Income Discrepancies Between Second and Later Generation Mexican-Americans in the Southwest," *Sociology and Social Research*, July 1969, pp. 448-54.

[20] U.S. Department of Justice, Immigration and Naturalization Service, *1976 Annual Report* (Washington, D.C., 1978), table 14.

[21] U.S. Bureau of the Census, *1970 Census of Population*, Subject Report no. PC(2)-1A, "National Origin and Language" (Washington, D.C., 1973), table 1.

that black immigrants and their children will become an increasing proportion of the population in the coming decades.

Black immigrants are primarily from the Caribbean area. Forty percent were born in the English-speaking West Indies (present and former dependencies of Britain) while 50 percent were born in non-English-speaking countries in the Caribbean basin, including Cuba. Less than one-tenth were born in Africa or the Atlantic islands. Among native-born blacks with a foreign-born parent there is a less intense concentration of parent's country of birth in the Caribbean area (about 60 percent), with a larger proportion from Africa and other parts of the Eastern Hemisphere.

On average, foreign-born black men had substantially higher earnings than native-born black men in 1969, $6,585 compared with $6,138 (Table 3). This arises from several advantages in earnings-related characteristics. Foreign-born black men have more schooling (by one year) and are more likely to live in urban areas in the Northeast. Nearly all foreign-born blacks, as compared with four-fifths of the native-born blacks, live in urban areas. Two-thirds of the foreign born live in New York State (8 percent of the blacks in the state) compared with one-tenth for native-born blacks. Because earnings are higher in urban New York than in urban areas of other non-southern states, the analysis is computed for all states and for New York State to test the sensitivity of our findings to the different geographic distribution of native- and foreign-born blacks.

Compared with native-born black men with similar earnings-related characteristics, foreign-born urban black men earned 2 percent less if they were in the United States for ten years, but 10 percent more if they had lived here for twenty years. Among those blacks living in metropolitan areas in New York State, the earnings of the foreign born were 5 percent lower at ten years since migration and 6 percent higher at twenty years. The earnings crossover occurs at eleven years since migration in an all-state analysis and at thirteen years among persons living in metropolitan areas of New York State.

The effect of schooling on earnings is larger for black immigrants from the English-speaking West Indies than it is for other black immigrants, as predicted by the hypothesis that there is a greater transferability to the United States of the skills acquired in English-speaking, British-oriented school systems.[22] Among black immigrants

---

[22] The partial effects for schooling are 5.4 percent for English-speaking immigrants and 3.0 percent for other immigrants. Moreover, the effect of schooling on earnings is greater among blacks from the English-speaking West Indies than for native-born blacks. This may reflect the poor quality of schooling received by native-born blacks when the 1970 cohort of adults were youths.

an extra year of labor market experience in the country of origin has a larger effect on U.S. earnings for those from the English-speaking West Indies. The differential effect on earnings of living in this country an extra year is smaller for the English-speaking immigrants. That is, U.S. labor market experience is more productive relative to a similar exposure in the country of origin the less similar are the two countries.[23]

Second-generation black Americans earn 26 percent more than urban blacks whose parents were born in the United States, $7,719 compared with $6,110. This arises in part because of the former's higher level of schooling (by two years) and greater tendency to live in a high-wage region of the country. Other things the same, for those raised in a home in which English was the only language spoken, second-generation black Americans earned 8 percent more than those with native-born parents, and the differential is 11 percent if the data are limited to metropolitan areas in New York State (Table 5).

The earnings pattern among blacks of different immigrant generations is very similar to the pattern that was hypothesized on the basis of the international transferability of skills and the favorable self-selection of immigrants.

East Asian Immigrants. Nearly 1.4 million persons in the United States in 1970 were racially of East Asian origin, primarily Chinese, Japanese, Filipino, or Korean.[24] The timing of immigration to the United States has been influenced not only by economic circumstances here but also by war and the economic and political circumstances in the countries of origin.

The migration of East Asians to the United States began with the movement of Chinese laborers to California as part of the Gold Rush of 1849. Chinese immigration reached a peak in the 1870s (123,000 immigrants) and then declined as restrictive legislation was enacted. Contracts to supply unskilled ("coolie") labor were prohibited by

---

[23] Evaluated at ten years after migration, the partial effects are 1.0 percent for blacks from the English-speaking West Indies and 1.8 percent for other black immigrants. The very weak effect on earnings of labor market experience for U.S. blacks when measured by cross-sectional data has been attributed to the sharply improved economic prospects of younger cohorts of blacks.

[24] The question on race in the *1970 Census of Population* elicited that there were about 590,000 Japanese, 435,000 Chinese, 340,000 Filipinos, and 70,000 Koreans in the United States. (U.S. Bureau of the Census, *1970 Census of Population*, Subject Report, "Japanese, Chinese, and Filipinos in the United States," 1973, table 1, p. x). Since then, in addition to substantial immigration from China, the Philippines, and Korea, nearly 200,000 Indochinese refugees have been admitted to this country.

legislation in 1875. The Chinese Exclusion Act of 1882 and its subsequent amendments barred the immigration of Chinese laborers, and as a result immigration from China declined sharply. The annexation of Hawaii in 1898 ended large-scale Chinese immigration to these islands. It was not until World War II (December 1943) that the Chinese Exclusion Act and its amendments were repealed, China was given a small quota (105 per year), and foreign-born Chinese were made eligible for citizenship. Immigration from China (including Taiwan and Hong Kong) increased as a result of the end of the national origins quota system with the 1965 amendments and special refugee relief programs since 1949 (Table 1).

There was little immigration from Japan to the United States until the 1890s (1891–1900, 26,000), and this immigration reached a peak at the turn of the century (1901–1910, 130,000 immigrants). Starting with the "Gentlemen's Agreement" of 1907 between the government of Japan and the executive branch of the U.S. government, with few exceptions Japanese laborers were barred from migrating to the United States.[25] The exclusion was set into law with the 1917 immigration amendments and remained in effect until Japan was given the minimum quota of 100 in 1952. The end of the national origins quota system with the 1965 amendments had relatively little effect on immigration from Japan, presumably because the country had already attained a high level, and a high rate of increase, of income.

Following the annexation of the Philippines as a result of the Spanish-American War (1898) and until 1935, Filipinos were nationals of the United States and were not subject to immigration restrictions. Filipino migration to Hawaiian sugar and pineapple plantations increased as they were substituted for the restricted Chinese and Japanese laborers. The migration of Filipinos to the mainland increased in the 1920s from Hawaii and the Philippines. With independence, the Philippines was given a small quota, although immigration was facilitated by special provisions for joining the armed forces. The 1965 immigration amendments, however, have resulted in substantially increased Filipino immigration (see Table 1).

The historical pattern of immigration from East Asia has determined the distribution of Asian-Americans by immigrant generation. Among adult men, the Japanese are predominantly second-generation

---

[25] The annexation of Hawaii in 1898 had less of an effect on Japanese migration to these islands because it was two decades before formal legal restrictions were imposed and the Gentlemen's Agreements were less stringently enforced with regard to the Hawaiian Islands.

TABLE 6

DISTRIBUTION OF JAPANESE, CHINESE, AND FILIPINO MEN AGED
TWENTY-FIVE TO SIXTY-FOUR YEARS, BY IMMIGRANT GENERATION, 1970
(percent)

	Foreign Born	Native Born with a Foreign-Born Parent	Native Born, Both Parents Native Born	Total
Japanese	12.8	68.8	18.3	100.0
Chinese	64.8	23.9	11.3	100.0
Filipino	73.0	21.4	5.6	100.0

SOURCE: *1970 Census of Population,* 5 percent and 15 percent questionnaires,
1/100 sample.

Americans, while the Chinese and Filipinos are predominantly foreign
born (see Table 6).

Adult Chinese and Japanese men born in the United States earned
more than native-born white men in 1969, in part because of the
former's higher level of schooling and tendency to live in high-wage
states, California and Hawaii (Table 3). Other things the same, there
is little difference in earnings among native-born whites, Chinese, and
Japanese. Foreign-born Chinese and Japanese men, however, earned
less than foreign-born white men, despite advantages of schooling
and geographic location.[26] They are, however, at an earnings disadvantage in having been in the United States for fewer years. Other
things the same, including time in this country, Japanese immigrants
earn about the same as white immigrants, but the Chinese immigrants
earn less. Filipino men, whether native or foreign born, have much
lower earnings than white men or other men of Asian origin, both
overall and when other variables are held constant. The reasons for
the very low earnings of Filipino men are as yet unclear.

Years of schooling and years of labor market experience in the
country of origin have a smaller effect on U.S. earnings for the foreign
born than the native born among the Japanese and Chinese, although
not among the Filipinos (Table 4). Among foreign-born Asian men,

---

[26] Foreign-born Chinese and Filipino men have an exceptionally large inequality
of years of schooling, with unusually high proportions of men having high and
very low levels of education.

schooling and labor market experience in the country of origin has the smallest effect on earnings for the Chinese. Indeed, among Chinese immigrants work experience in the country of origin (primarily China) has no effect on earnings, while that acquired in the United States has the largest differential impact. These patterns are consistent with the Chinese having the largest proportion of refugees.

Do the earnings of the foreign-born Asian men ever reach or exceed the earnings of native-born men with similar demographic and geographic characteristics? For Japanese immigrants the earnings crossover occurs at eighteen years in the United States, after which the foreign born have higher earnings (Table 3). Among the Filipinos the earnings crossover occurs at thirteen years. Only among the Chinese do the earnings of the foreign born never equal that of the native born, although the difference becomes quite small.

When the data are limited to native-born men it is possible to analyze whether it matters where one's parents were born. Other things the same, Asian-Americans with a foreign-born parent earn 4 to 9 percent more than those of the same race with native-born parents (Table 5). This is essentially the same finding as for the other racial-ethnic groups.

Because of this earnings advantage of second-generation Americans and the very high proportion of native-born Asian-Americans who are second generation in comparison with the white population, the earnings crossover between the foreign and native born comes later for the Asian-Americans. That is, if the relative weight of second-generation Americans among the native born were the same as for the white population, the earnings crossover for the Asian foreign born would come sooner. The rankings among the three Asian groups would not change. The Filipinos would be at the lower end and the Japanese at the upper end of the eleven- to fifteen-year interval found for other racial-ethnic groups. For the Chinese, the earnings crossover would not occur until somewhat more than twenty years after migration. That is, it occurs for those who came to the United States before the Communist takeover of China in 1949.

The most recent group of East Asian immigrants are the refugees from Indochina. Since the fall of Saigon in April 1975 nearly 200,000 Indochinese refugees, of whom about 90 percent are Vietnamese, have entered the United States. Many of these refugees acquired skills in their home country that are not readily transferable to the United States. At present there is little systematic data on the economic progress of these refugees. A panel survey of over 400 Vietnamese refugee families conducted in August/September 1975 and in July/

August 1976 suggests that they are making substantial progress.[27] The proportion of men aged sixteen years and over who were employed increased from 67 to 86 percent. Of the employed household heads, the proportion in white-collar and craft jobs increased from 35 to 71 percent. The proportion of employed household heads with monthly earnings exceeding $600 increased from 19 to 41 percent. It is still too early, however, to determine their ultimate economic success in the United States.

The findings of the comparative analysis of earnings for the three largest groups of East Asian origin are consistent with the hypotheses developed above. Skills acquired prior to immigration are less productive in the United States than the skills of the native born. This is shown among the Chinese and Japanese by the smaller effect on earnings of schooling and experience acquired in the country of origin for the foreign than the native born. These training variables have a particularly small effect for Chinese immigrants, among whom are a disproportionate number of refugees.[28] For all three East Asian immigrant groups, and particularly for the Chinese, labor market experience in the United States has a larger effect on earnings than experience prior to migration.

The implications for earnings of the favorable self-selection of immigrants, particularly economic migrants, emerge from the data. The earnings of the foreign born eventually equal and then exceed those of the native born for the Japanese and Filipinos in roughly the same length of time as for the non-Asian immigrants that were studied. Among the cohort of Chinese immigrants, which is expected to have a less intensely favorable self-selection because of the high proportion of refugees, the crossover either does not occur or occurs much later (that is, for those who came to the United States before 1949). The favorable self-selection of immigrants apparently affects the second generation. Within each of the three East Asian groups the sons of immigrants earn more than the sons of native-born parents.

Other Times, Other Places

The previous section examined in detail the economic progress of foreign-born men in the contemporary United States. Stable patterns

---

[27] Opportunity Systems, Inc., *Third Wave Report: Vietnam Resettlement Operational Feedback*, prepared for HEW Refugee Task Force (Washington, D.C., September 1976), tables 33, 35, and 36.

[28] The patterns for the Filipinos differ and are similar to those found in the comparison of native-born blacks and blacks from the English-speaking West Indies.

consistent with the previously developed hypotheses were observed across racial-ethnic groups regarding the effect on earnings of time in the United States, language and skills acquired in the country of origin, and type of immigration. This section extends the analysis to see if these hypotheses are supported by data from other times and from other places. To do this, the earnings of immigrants in four different settings are studied. These are the United States at the turn of the century, and contemporary Canada, Great Britain, and Israel.

United States at the Turn of the Century. Starting in the 1870s and accelerating in the next two decades, the number of immigrants to the United States increased sharply, with an increasing proportion coming from southern and eastern Europe. These developments heightened concern as to the effect of immigration on the country and led to the establishment of the U.S. Immigration Commission to study the progress and impact of immigrants and issue policy recommendations. The commission conducted a survey in 1909 of over a half million wage and salary workers in mining and manufacturing, primarily in the Northeast and North Central states. Sixty percent of the sample were foreign born.

The commission's report, issued in 1911, was one of the bases for the literacy requirements in the 1917 amendments and the quota systems introduced in the 1920s. Although it has been alleged that the commission's interpretations of the data, and hence their policy recommendations, were based on prejudice against the "new immigrants" from southern and eastern Europe, it has also been alleged that the data themselves are untainted by this prejudice.[29] In recent years, modern statistical techniques have been applied to the detailed cross-tabulations published by the commission, even though the randomness of the sample has not been established. Francine Blau's study, the most recent, uses a methodology closest to the one used above for the analysis of the contemporary United States.[30]

Blau was concerned, in part, with earnings differences among four groups of men, the native born with a native-born father, the native born with a foreign-born father, immigrants from "advantaged countries" (Group 1 immigrants, from English-speaking Canada and

---

[29] For a sense of some of the emotions surrounding the debate in the professional literature, see Douglas, "New Immigration."

[30] See Francine D. Blau, "Immigration and Labor Earnings in Early Twentieth Century America," in Julian L. Simon and Julie da Vanzo, eds., *Research in Population Economics*, vol. 2 (Greenwich, Conn.: JAI Press, 1979), and the references therein.

northern and western Europe, excluding Ireland), and immigrants likely to be subject to discrimination (Group 2 immigrants, from southern and eastern Europe, Ireland, and French-speaking Canada). Several variables that determine earnings were held constant. These include the proportions that were literate, English-speaking, married, and living in the Central states, as well as the average age and industry characteristics.

Blau found that, other things the same, the wages of the foreign born in 1909 were higher by 1.1 percent for each extra year of residence in the United States. A similar value is obtained for white foreign-born men in the contemporary United States ten years after migration (Table 3).

Blau estimated the number of years in the United States that it takes for the wages of the foreign born to equal (and then surpass) the wages of the native born. It was eleven years for Group 1 immigrants (northern and western Europe) and sixteen years for Group 2 immigrants. These are the end points of the interval found in the analysis for the contemporary foreign-born population of the United States.

In the comparison between the native born with a native-born father and those with a foreign-born father Blau found that, other things the same, the earnings of the latter were higher by 2.4 percent, although the difference is not statistically significant. For the contemporary population, native-born adult white men with a foreign-born parent have a 5 percent earnings advantage, which is not significantly different from Blau's 2.4 percent.

The earnings patterns for the foreign born relative to the native born in the United States at the turn of the century appear to be consistent with our expectations and are very similar to the patterns found for the contemporary United States.

Canada. For an examination of the economic progress of immigrants in other places, it is useful to study a country with a socioeconomic structure and recent immigration experience similar to those of the United States. Over the past few decades, Canadian and U.S. immigration policies have been similar in several respects.[31] In the decades prior to the 1960s Canadian policy was based on country of origin and

---

[31] The discussion of Canadian policy is based on John Hucker, "A Synopsis of Canadian Immigration Law," *Syracuse Journal of International Law and Commerce*, vol. 3, no. 1 (Spring 1975), pp. 47-76; Canadian Department of Employment and Immigration, *Twenty Questions about Canada's New Immigration Act*, 1979, and *New Directions: A Look at Canada's Immigration Act and Regulations*, 1978.

was not very different from the U.S. national origins quota system. During the 1960s both countries abandoned their ethnocentric policies. Although the United States maintained hemisphere and country quotas for the Eastern Hemisphere and extended them to the Western Hemisphere, Canada did not adopt formal limits on the number of persons who may enter. As a result, in the past twenty-five years annual immigration has ranged from a peak of 282,000 in 1957 to a low of about 70,000 in the early 1960s, with immigration being higher during periods of economic expansion.

In the postwar period, until 1962, the primary criteria for immigration into Canada were the person's nationality, country of birth, and kinship ties with a Canadian citizen or permanent resident. Citizens of the English-speaking white countries and France experienced little difficulty entering Canada. Immigration from other European countries by persons without a Canadian sponsor was generally tied to the business cycle, with more visas issued in periods of economic expansion and fewer in recessions. By special agreements with the newly independent South Asian and later also the West Indian governments (former British colonies) a small number of immigrants could enter without sponsors if they met certain occupational requirements. There were racial differences in the extent to which Canadian citizens and permanent residents could sponsor the immigration of close relatives.

As a result of these policies, the foreign born who arrived in Canada prior to the 1960s were predominantly white and of U.S., British, Irish, or other European origin. This situation was not unlike that in this country, except that the United States had a large proportion of Mexican immigrants in the Southwest because of the common border.

Canadian immigration policy changed sharply in the 1960s. Legislation in 1962 and 1967 ended the emphasis on country of origin and the racial discrimination in the requirements for sponsored immigrants (close relatives). For persons other than sponsored immigrants, selection criteria were based primarily on the applicant's personal characteristics and were weighted toward the person's productivity and likely success in adjusting to Canada. Persons scoring above a certain number of points are granted immigration visas. In recent years between one-fifth and two-fifths of the immigrants have been without a Canadian relative and were thus admitted under the point system, as were another quarter with only distant relatives.[32]

---

[32] Canadian Department of Employment and Immigration, *Annual Report to Parliament on Immigration Levels*, 1978, pp. 20 and 22.

The change in immigration policies in the 1960s, together with factors external to Canada, altered the distribution of immigrants by country of origin and skill level.[33] The proportion of immigrants from Asia, Africa, and the West Indies increased from 4 percent in 1951–1960 to 11 percent in 1961–1966, to 26 percent in 1967–1973. An increased proportion of immigrant workers are professional or technical workers, from less than 10 percent during the 1950s to 20 to 30 percent in the 1960s and 1970s. It is too early to determine, however, whether immigrants entering under the new program will be more successful in Canada than earlier cohorts of immigrants.

Fortunately, there is a recent study by B. B. Tandon of the earnings of foreign-born males in Toronto, Canada, using data from the 1971 census of Canada and methodology similar to the one applied to the United States. Toronto is an important immigrant-receiving metropolitan area. Of the immigrants arriving in Canada in 1971, 30 percent settled in Toronto, and half the adult population of the metropolitan area is foreign born.[34]

Tandon analyzed the average hourly earnings in 1970 of Canadian and foreign-born males who were full-time members of the civilian labor force (that is, aged sixteen to sixty-four years and not enrolled in school or in the military). Using separate equations for the native and foreign born he regressed the logarithm of hourly earnings on years of schooling, years of total labor market experience, and, for the foreign born, years living in Canada. He found that a year of schooling had a larger effect on earnings in Canada for the native than the foreign born, 7.1 percent compared with 3.4 percent. The effect on earnings in Canada of an extra year of labor market experience in the country of origin is also larger for the native born, 3.5 percent compared with 1.1 percent when evaluated at ten years of experience. Among the foreign born with the same amount of schooling and labor market experience, earnings are higher the longer the period of residence in Canada, although additional years have a decreasing marginal effect on earnings (2.1 percent when evaluated at ten years since migration).

The earnings difference between native- and foreign-born Canadians can be related to the latter's duration of residence in Canada. With ten years of schooling (the mean schooling level for the foreign

---

[33] Louis Parai, "Canada's Immigration Policy: 1962-1974," *International Migration Review*, Winter 1975, pp. 470-71.

[34] B. B. Tandon, "Earnings Differentials among Native Born and Foreign Born Residents of Toronto," *International Migration Review*, vol. 12, no. 3 (Fall 1978), pp. 406-10.

born) and twenty years of postschool labor market experience, the foreign born in Canada for ten years earned 10 percent less than the native born, while those in Canada twenty years had 4 percent higher earnings. The earnings crossover, the number of years in Canada at which the earnings of the native and foreign born are equal, occurs at sixteen years. This is not very different from the earnings crossover at thirteen years estimated for white immigrants in the United States. A somewhat later earnings crossover may not be unexpected, however, if the subsequent migration of the foreign born in Toronto (an important first stop for immigrants) to other parts of Canada and to the United States is self-selected in favor of those who have made the best adjustments to North American labor markets.

The earnings of the foreign born in Canada in comparison with the native born are as predicted by the hypotheses developed above. The parallels between the immigration policies and the economic progress of the foreign born in Canada and the United States are striking. It cannot be determined at this time how the recent divergence in immigration criteria—whereby the Canadian emphasis is more on productivity and that of the United States more on kinship ties—will affect the economic progress and impact of immigrants.

Great Britain. Although often thought of as a country of emigration, Great Britain is currently and historically also a recipient of immigrants from outside the British Isles.[35] Toward the end of the nineteenth century and in the early twentieth century many immigrants came from southern and eastern Europe, some to stay permanently, and others for a brief spell as they continued on to North America or to British colonies. In subsequent decades, although migration from the European continent continued, immigration increased from what is now referred to as the New Commonwealth countries of Asia, Africa, and the Caribbean. In the 1950s and 1960s the New Commonwealth countries became the major source of immigration.

According to the *1971 Census of Britain*, 4.5 percent of all males were born outside the British Isles, a proportion not very different from the 5 percent foreign born in the United States. About half the foreign-born men in Britain were born in the New Commonwealth countries, three-tenths were born in Europe (non-Commonwealth), and one-tenth were born in the Old Commonwealth countries (Canada, Australia, and New Zealand) or the United States. Although race is

---

[35] This section is based on Barry R. Chiswick, "The Earnings of White and Coloured Immigrants in Britain," *Economica*, August 1979, using data from the *1972 General Household Survey*. For the purpose of this discussion, immigrants from Ireland are included in the native-born population of Great Britain.

not asked in the British census, survey data indicate that about a third of the foreign-born men were classified by the interviewer as coloured, that is, black or of South or East Asian origin. Hence, many of the immigrants born in the New Commonwealth are white, presumably descendants of Europeans returning to Britain.

To what extent are the earnings of immigrants in Britain relative to the native born consistent with our hypotheses as to the economic progress of immigrants? According to the *1972 General Household Survey* adult (aged twenty-five to sixty-four) foreign-born white men earned 6 percent more than adult native-born white men, but this difference disappears when other things, such as schooling (the white foreign born have a half year more schooling) and demographic variables, are held constant. The coloured foreign born earn about 19 percent less than the white native born, and this increases to about 24 percent when other factors (including the higher level of schooling of the coloured immigrants) are held constant. The earnings disadvantage of the coloured is smaller (about 4 percent) when the small sample of native-born coloured men, who are primarily the sons of immigrants, is compared with the white native-born men, whose ancestors have lived in Britain for generations.

The effect of schooling on earnings is larger in Britain for the native born than for the foreign born—7.5 percent for the native born, 6.9 percent for the white foreign born, and about 4 percent for the coloured foreign born. The racial difference may reflect a lower quality of schooling or a weaker transferability to Great Britain of the skills acquired in school. An extra year of British labor market experience also has a larger effect on earnings for the native than the foreign born.[36]

There appears to be little differential effect on earnings, for either the white or coloured foreign born, of labor market experience acquired in the country of birth rather than in Great Britain. This implies that most immigrants, particularly in the last two decades, were well Anglicized before they came. Indeed, according to the *1971 Census of Britain* two-thirds of the foreign-born males were born in the New or Old Commonwealth, the Republic of South Africa, or the United States, and nearly four-fifths of those living in Great Britain for twenty or fewer years were born in these countries.[37] Most of the

---

[36] After ten years of work experience in the country of origin, an extra year of labor market experience raises earnings by 2.2 percent for the native born and by 1.5 percent for the foreign born.

[37] *Census, 1971, Great Britain, Country of Birth Tables* (London: Her Majesty's Stationery Office, 1974), table 4.

immigrants from non-English-speaking countries (primarily the non-Commonwealth countries of Europe) have lived in Britain for more than twenty years. Beyond two decades, an extra year of labor market experience in the country of destination has little additional effect on earnings compared with an extra year of experience in the country of origin.

The earnings patterns for male immigrants in Great Britain are consistent with the hypotheses and with the patterns observed for foreign-born white and black men in the United States from English-speaking countries.

Israel.[38] The Jewish population of Israel is primarily foreign born or native born with a foreign-born parent. It has been estimated that in 1975, 49 percent of the Jewish population were foreign born, 41 percent were native born with a foreign-born father, and 10 percent (disproportionately youths) were third- or higher-generation residents of the area. Just over half the Jewish population is of Asian-African origin: 47 percent of the foreign born, 58 percent of the second generation, and 30 percent of the third-generation Israelis.[39]

A model of conventional economic migration, of persons moving from one country to another in response to an earnings differential, would be of limited value for explaining migration to Israel. The large-scale emigration of Jews from eastern Europe from the 1880s to World War I resulted primarily in migration to North America. The few who went to Palestine, at that time a poverty-stricken corner of the Ottoman Empire, were almost certainly not motivated by economic considerations. After World War I the territory became a British Mandate. Immigration increased in response to the promise of a Jewish homeland, tighter U.S. immigration restrictions, and the spread of active anti-Semitism in Europe, although from 1930 until independence in May 1948 the British attempted to limit sharply Jewish immigration. During the period of the British Mandate the proportion of refugees among the immigrants increased.

Israeli government policy, as expressed in the Declaration of Independence (1948) and the Law of Return (1950), has been to pro-

---

[38] The analysis for Israel is limited to the Jewish population. Jewish immigrants in Israel are often classified by their continent of origin, that is, Europe and America (primarily Europe) or from Asia and Africa (primarily North Africa and the Middle East). The demographic data on immigration are from Roberto Bachi, *The Population of Israel* (Jerusalem: Hebrew University, 1977), particularly chapters 8, 9, and 14. The analysis of earnings is based on a collaborative effort with Itzhak Goldberg. The data are from the *1976 Income Survey* and were provided by the Central Bureau of Statistics, Jerusalem, Israel.

[39] Bachi, *Population*, pp. 264-66.

vide all Jews the right to immigrate and become citizens, with minor reservations to protect the health and safety of the population. This objective was promoted by subsidizing migration and through intergovernmental negotiations. As a result, the proportion of refugees among the immigrants was quite high. Many of the European immigrants in the immediate postindependence period were displaced persons and former concentration camp inmates. During the three-year period from May 1948 to 1951, 18 percent of the Jews in Asia (including nearly the entire Jewish communities in Yemen and Iraq), 20 percent of the Jews in the Balkans, and 12 percent of the Jews in eastern Europe (excluding the U.S.S.R.) migrated to Israel. Primarily as a result of the migration of Jews from Moslem countries to Israel, the Jewish population of Asia and Africa (outside of Israel) declined from 1.3 million persons in 1945 to 0.3 million by 1975.[40]

Reemigration, that is, migration out of Palestine and Israel has also been characteristic of the Jewish population since Ottoman times. The proportion of the foreign born among emigrants is large and exceeds their proportion in the Jewish population. During the 1948–1969 period, the foreign born were 75 percent of the emigrants but only 63 percent of the population. The rate of reemigration is highest among American and western European immigrants and very low among immigrants from the Arab countries of the Middle East. The rate of emigration among the foreign born declines with the length of time spent in the country. Among the immigrants who arrived in 1962–1969, for example, the emigration rate (that is, the number emigrating as a proportion of those still in the country) within one year of arrival was 2.7 percent; between one and two years, 3.7 percent; between two and three years, 2.1 percent; between three and four years, 1.6 percent; between four and five years, 1.4 percent.

Although the subsequent emigration of immigrants is in part a consequence of the inability of some to adjust to a new environment, Bachi writes that "emigration movements have a prevalently economic motivation."[41] Within country-of-origin categories the reemigration rates are higher among the young adults, the single, the more educated, and the less religious, and among those for whom "Jewish motivation" was a weaker factor in the original migration. The destinations of emigrants have been primarily high-income areas. Among the emigrants (native and foreign born) in the 1948–1972 period, 43 percent went to North America, 37 percent went to western Europe, and 10 percent to Australia, New Zealand, and other parts of the Americas.

---

[40] Ibid., pp. 75 and 84.

[41] Ibid., p. 126; see also pp. 120-26.

These data suggest that migration to Israel is less likely to have been self-selected in favor of persons with high labor market ability and economic motivation in comparison with migration to the United States and Canada. Even if the emigration from the country of origin were favorably self-selected, the possibility of more favorable self-selection among those going to high-income countries rather than to Israel cannot be dismissed. Emigration out of Israel appears to have a more economic basis and is more likely to be self-selected in favor of those with ability and motivation to generate high earnings.

The foregoing has implications for our comparative analysis of the earnings of immigrants and natives in the place of destination. A migration stream composed primarily of refugees (whether Cuban refugees in the United States or Jewish refugees in Israel) in which the favorable self-selection is less intense implies a relatively lower earnings profile for the immigrants and an earnings crossover with the native born at a later time, if it occurs at all. The subsequent emigration of the more able among the immigrants also suggests a smaller effect on earnings of time in the country and a later earnings crossover when cross-sectional data are used. Finally, any earnings advantage of the native born with foreign-born parents would be weaker if the favorable self-selection among immigrants is less intense, or is even reversed.

The analysis of earnings is for data from a 1976 household survey for Israel and replicates the methodology applied to the United States. The data are for Jewish men aged twenty-five to sixty-four years in 1976 who were not enrolled in school and who worked and had positive earnings in 1975. The data permit the identification of the person's ethnic origin (European-American or Asian-African) on the basis of his country of birth or his father's country of birth if he is native born.[42] The ethnic origin distinction is useful because the skills acquired in Europe or the United States may be more readily transferable to Israel than the skills acquired in North Africa and the Middle East.

Overall, the foreign born earned 18 percent less than the native born (Table 7). Although the foreign born have two and a half fewer years of schooling, they have more labor market experience. Other things the same (schooling, age, marital status, weeks worked, and ethnic origin), the foreign born earned 17 percent less than the native born if they were in Israel for ten years and 9 percent less if they had

---

[42] Among the small sample of third- and higher-generation Israeli Jews it is not possible to identify ethnic origin. Because of intermarriage among Jews, by the third generation continent of origin has less meaning.

TABLE 7

Analysis of Earnings for Native- and Foreign-Born Jewish Men in Israel, 1976

Nativity	Sample size	Means of Variables				Partial Effects of Variables[a] (percent)			Relative Difference in Earnings[b]	
		Earnings (Israeli pounds)	Schooling (years)	Age (years)	Years since migration (YSM)	Schooling	Experience in country of origin	Years since migration	YSM=10	YSM=20
Total	3,228	33,072	9.6	42.3	—	—	—	—	—	—
Native born	681	38,446	11.5	35.3	—	5.2	2.9	—	—	—
Foreign born	2,546	31,641	9.0	44.2	22.7	3.6	1.2	0.9	-0.17	-0.09

NOTE: The table refers to the earnings in 1975 of Jewish men aged twenty-five to sixty-four years in 1976 who worked, had positive earnings in 1975, and were not enrolled in school.

[a] The partial effects were computed from separate regressions for the native and foreign born. The natural logarithm of earnings was regressed on schooling, experience (years since age five not in school), experience squared, log of weeks worked, marital status, Asian-African origin, and, for the foreign born, years since migration (YSM) and its square. The effects of experience and years since migration are evaluated at ten years.

[b] The parameter is the difference in the natural logarithm of earnings from a pooled regression including the same variables as in note a, evaluated at ten and twenty years since immigration. For small values, when multiplied by 100 the parameter is the percentage difference in earnings. A negative coefficient indicates lower earnings for the foreign born.

SOURCE: Israel Central Bureau of Statistics, 1976 Income Survey.

lived in Israel for twenty years. The earnings crossover occurs very late, between thirty-five and forty years in the country. Immigrants of Asian-African origin earned 12 percent less than those of European-American origin, other things the same.

Schooling has a smaller effect on earnings for the foreign born. Earnings rise by 3.6 percent for an extra year of schooling for the foreign born and by 5.2 percent for the native born (Table 7). Experience (years) in the country of origin also has a smaller effect on earnings in Israel for the foreign born. The relative difference between the foreign born and natives in the effects on earnings of schooling and labor market experience in the country of origin is larger in Israel than it is for the racial-ethnic groups in the United States or Canada, with the exception of the Cubans and Chinese in the United States (compare Tables 4 and 7). That is, the parameters for Israel are comparable to the relationships found for refugee groups in the United States.

Time in the country of destination has a somewhat smaller effect on earnings for the foreign-born in Israel (0.9 percent per year when evaluated at YSM = 10) than in the United States (Table 4), other things the same. This finding in cross-sectional data may arise from the reemigration of the more able, more economically motivated immigrants. And the reemigration of the more able immigrants appears to be a relatively more important characteristic of Israel than of the United States.

Among the native born, the earnings of second-generation Israelis (father foreign born) can be compared with those with a native-born father. The earnings advantage of the second generation found in the U.S. data and attributed to the favorable self-selection of immigrants is apparently not found in the Israeli data. For the same schooling and demographic characteristics, men with an Asian or African father have lower earnings (by 16 percent) than men with a native-born father, while men with a European or American father have the same earnings (lower by 1 percent, but the t-ratio is only 0.3) as those with a native-born father.

The earnings pattern for the foreign born as compared with the native born in Israel is consistent with our expectations for an immigration that is primarily not based on conventional economic factors. Israeli immigration has, in fact, been primarily of ideologically motivated individuals or the consequence of large-scale migrations of nearly entire communities as a result of political factors. The favorable self-selection of Jewish migrants to high-income third countries and the reemigration of immigrants has also been an important factor. As with refugees in the United States, it takes much longer for the earnings of the foreign born to catch up to the earnings of the native born.

Policy Implications

This study has been concerned with the economic progress of immigrant groups in the United States and elsewhere. Although the background and historical experiences of these groups vary, certain persistent patterns emerge, apparently from differences in the international transferability of the skills acquired in the country of origin and from the self-selection of immigrants in favor of those with more innate ability and economic motivation.

The analysis indicates substantial, perhaps impressive, economic progress of immigrants. The earnings disadvantage of male economic migrants when they first arrive is relatively short-lived. They catch up to the native born with similar demographic characteristics by the time they have been in the country eleven to sixteen years, and thereafter the immigrants have higher earnings. Their native-born sons earn 5 to 10 percent more than the sons of native-born parents, other things being equal. Among refugees, however, because of the weaker transferability of their skills and the less intensely favorable self-selection, earnings are lower. It takes several decades for their earnings to catch up with those of the native born, if it occurs at all.

There are clear patterns of racial-ethnic group differences in economic success, even though there is substantial variation in the earnings of individuals within each group. Among the U.S. immigrant groups (first- and second-generation Americans) studied here, non-Hispanic whites, Japanese, and second-generation Chinese have been the most successful, then blacks, and among the least successful are the Mexicans and Filipinos. An understanding of these differences may be important for domestic social policy as well as for immigration policy and are an important subject for future research.

In the empirical analysis it was not possible to distinguish immigrants who would be admitted under a kinship criterion, currently the primary basis for rationing immigration visas to the United States, from those who would be admitted under a productivity criterion.[43]

---

[43] Of the nearly 400,000 immigrants to the United States each year in the past decade, excluding those admitted under the special Cuban and Vietnamese refugee programs, nearly three-quarters have come under kinship criteria. The two "occupational preferences," in principle designed to facilitate the immigration of skilled workers and professionals, provide a maximum of 54,000 visas each year

There is a presumption, however, that a properly functioning productivity criterion would be more successful than a kinship criterion in identifying those who would have greater skills, with greater transferability to the United States, and more innate ability and work motivation relevant for this country.

Economic migrants selected under a productivity criterion are likely to have the highest earnings and easiest adjustment to U.S. labor markets—the immigrants would have highly transferable skills and would be very favorably self-selected. Their impact on the overall economic well-being of the native population is likely to be more favorable than an equal number of refugees or immigrants admitted under a kinship criterion. Immigrants admitted under a kinship criterion may have a more successful economic adjustment than refugees with the same demographic characteristics, because economic factors are likely to be more important in their migration decision and their U.S. relatives may ease the adjustment. Admitting refugees and those with relatives in the United States does satisfy other important social objectives, in particular, humanitarian considerations and, for refugees, U.S. foreign policy concerns. The current emphasis on kinship, however, makes those citizens and resident aliens with relatives in other countries, whether immediate or more remote, the greatest beneficiaries of U.S. immigration policy.

U.S. immigration policy can be expected to be based on a balancing of productivity and humanitarian considerations. The number of immigrants and the relative emphasis of these broad criteria will be determined through the political process. This should be done, however, with a more complete knowledge of the costs and benefits of the alternatives. This study has been one step in this direction.

---

for qualifying workers and their immediate family members. Under current regulations, however, except for those in preferred occupations (dieticians and physical therapists with college degrees), a cumbersome and costly administrative procedure must be followed, which requires considerable effort by a prospective employer. Since workers cannot be compelled to remain with their employer-sponsor, personal ties or whether the person is currently working for the employer (legally or not) may be important in encouraging an employer to help a worker obtain a labor certificate. For the current regulations on occupational preferences, see "Employment of Aliens in the United States: Labor Certification Program," *Federal Register*, January 19, 1977, pt. IV, pp. 3440-50.

The Forty-Second Anniversary of the Leading Indicators

Geoffrey H. Moore

Summary

Forty-two years ago Wesley Mitchell and Arthur Burns completed a brief research report that identified types of economic indicators that "have been tolerably consistent in their timing in relation to business cycle revivals and that at the same time are of sufficiently general interest to warrant some attention by students of current economic conditions." [1] *This study fathered a long series of investigations devoted to extending the system of indicators, testing its performance, explaining the interrelationships among the indicators, and putting the system into practicable form for current use. Since the leading indicators receive much public attention nowadays, their reliability is a matter of some importance.*

One way to assess reliability is to examine the subsequent performance of an early version of the system. For this purpose we have used the list and classification of indicators established in 1950 and compared their performance before World War II with their performance since 1948. The pre-1938 information was used in developing the 1950 list and classification; the post-1948 information of course was not.

The results demonstrate that taken as a whole the 1950 version of the indicator system lived up to its promise. The leading indicators continued to lead and the laggers to lag at each succeeding turn in the business cycle. The degree of consistency in performance after 1948 was not very different from what it was before 1938. The relation-

---

[1] Wesley C. Mitchell and Arthur F. Burns, *Statistical Indicators of Cyclical Revivals*, Bulletin 69 (New York: National Bureau of Economic Research, 1938).

ships exhibited in earlier cycles resembled those that appeared in sub-sequent cycles.

Nonetheless, changes did occur. Certain indicators that appeared to lag in earlier cycles moved more promptly in later ones. Some indicators, especially those expressed in current prices, failed to conform to recent business cycles. These and other changes, particularly the availability of new statistical information, have produced many modifications in the system of indicators that promise to enhance its usefulness and reduce its limitations as a guide to the future.

Origin of the NBER Leading Indicators

For four years the U.S. economy had been recovering from a depression. Nearly as many people were then employed as had been at the peak prior to the slump, but unemployment was still high, and the price level was rising again. In an effort to keep up with rising government spending, social security taxes were raised. Concerned about inflation, the Federal Reserve raised reserve requirements sharply. Interest rates shot up. By May the recovery had stopped dead in its tracks and one of the steepest recessions in history began, erasing much of the gain of the four-year recovery.

Let me hasten to note that the period just described, despite a superficial resemblance, is not 1979. It was 1937. The recovery was from the Great Depression, and it lasted from March 1933 until May 1937. By coincidence, the most recent recovery also began in March, that is, in March 1975, although the recession that preceded it was brief and mild by comparison with the 1929–1933 decline. Whether the recovery stops in 1979, as it did in 1937, we are far better equipped today to detect a recession in its early stages, to measure its extent and consequences, and hence to take steps promptly to deal with it.

This is partly because of what happened in 1937. In the late summer Secretary of the Treasury Henry Morgenthau, Jr., asked the National Bureau of Economic Research (NBER), a private organization devoted to objective studies of business cycles and other economic problems, to draw up a list of statistical series that would best indicate when the recession would come to an end. Wesley C. Mitchell, then the NBER's director of research and a renowned student of business cycles, enlisted the help of Arthur F. Burns, who later headed the NBER and still later became chairman of the Federal Reserve. In six weeks the job was done. The report that was presented to the secretary set forth a list of the most reliable indicators of cyclical revivals, explained how they were selected, and included a record of their past performance. It was published in May 1938.[2]

Thus was born the first set of leading, coincident, and lagging indicators that are now widely used to forecast, detect, measure, and appraise recessions and recoveries. In the summer of 1938 they were put to their first test. The recovery began in June, and the first signs of its appearance were registered in the leading indicators that Mitchell and Burns had identified.

Mitchell and Burns drew on an encyclopedic knowledge of the history and theory of business cycles as well as on an enormous stock of empirical information that had been assembled since the 1920s at the NBER. It was a resource that could be called upon as needed, as Secretary Morgenthau recognized. During the next four decades the continuing studies of business cycles at the NBER, in the U.S. Department of Commerce, and elsewhere in this country and abroad led to many improvements in the system of indicators. They were subjected to a series of tests of performance as new business cycles came upon the scene and as new techniques for managing the economy were applied.

Subsequent Performance of the 1950 List of Indicators

The degree of confidence that any method of analysis attains, and deserves, depends upon its performance after it has been developed. It must be subjected to trial with new data, not used at the time the method was devised and preferably not even available at that time. This kind of test of the leading indicators has indeed been made more than once. In 1950 I examined the performance of the Mitchell-Burns list of indicators at the 1937 peak and 1938 trough of the business cycle, since the data they had used in their analysis ended with the 1933 trough. The test broadly supported their results, but many new series had become available, new findings from research suggested additional materials, and the analysis needed to be extended to cover downturns as well as upturns. Hence a new list and classification of indicators, based on records available through 1938, was published in 1950.[3]

Ten years later, in 1960, another review was undertaken, and in 1966 still another, both under the auspices of the NBER.[4] In 1972 the

---

[2] Ibid.

[3] Geoffrey H. Moore, *Statistical Indicators of Cyclical Revivals and Recessions,* Occasional Paper 31 (New York: National Bureau of Economic Research, 1950).

[4] Geoffrey H. Moore, ed., *Business Cycle Indicators* (New York: National Bureau

Department of Commerce initiated an extensive review, publishing the results in 1975.[5] Some of the indicators originally selected by Mitchell and Burns have survived all these tests of performance. The length of the average workweek in manufacturing establishments and the index of common stock prices are examples. Others have been dropped altogether or replaced by similar series, and new series have been added. It is of some interest, however, to take a long look back to see how the initial system behaved in subsequent business cycles up to the present. For this purpose it will be more productive to concentrate on the 1950 list and classification of indicators rather than the 1938 list of Mitchell and Burns. The 1950 study, as already noted, covered both peaks and troughs, and the classification system bears a closer resemblance to the system now used. Furthermore, current data for each of the series in the 1950 list, or close equivalents, are published in the Commerce Department's monthly *Business Conditions Digest* and hence are conveniently available. The data record employed in the 1950 study ended with the 1938 business cycle trough. The test will pertain to the period from 1948 to 1975, during which time six business cycles occurred, with peaks in 1948, 1953, 1957, 1960, 1969, and 1973 and troughs in 1949, 1954, 1958, 1961, 1970, and 1975.

The principal question to be examined is whether, at these twelve turning points in the economy, the indicators selected and classified in 1950 lived up to the performance suggested by their record prior to 1938. Did the leading indicators lead and the lagging indicators lag? Was their behavior as consistent as their previous record would lead one to expect? What deficiencies became evident and why? The answers can tell something about the effectiveness of the method used to develop the information, as well as the degree of historical continuity in the economic processes that give rise to business cycles.

In 1950, when I began this research, business cycles had been puzzling scholars for more than a century, and efforts to prevent panics, crises, and depressions had long engaged the attention of lawmakers and government officials. Mitchell and others had studied a large number of hypotheses, theories, or models of how business cycles came about. No single theory had proved adequate for all time or all countries, and the evidence bearing upon the phenomenon was

of Economic Research, 1961); and Geoffrey H. Moore and Julius Shiskin, *Indicators of Business Expansions and Contractions*, Occasional Paper 103 (New York: National Bureau of Economic Research, 1967).

[5] Victor Zarnowitz and Charlotte Boschan, "Cyclical Indicators: An Evaluation and New Leading Indicators," *Business Conditions Digest* (U.S. Department of Commerce), May 1975; and "New Composite Indexes of Coincident and Lagging Indicators," ibid., November 1975.

scattered and lacked uniform treatment. Mitchell had come to believe that the most promising line of attack was to organize systematically and comprehensively the statistical evidence for a long period of time and for several countries, and then to use these data to develop an accurate description of business cycle phenomena as well as to test various hypotheses and suggest new ones.

As a result, the NBER in 1950 had a large collection of economic time series in monthly, quarterly, or annual form extending back in time as far as each series could be compiled and pertaining to the types of economic process that previous investigators believed relevant to the generation of business cycles. The series had been classified into economic groups deemed most useful in explaining differences in cyclical behavior or in accounting for the influence of one economic variable on another. Finally, a standard set of measures of cyclical behavior had been calculated for each series for the period it covered. The measures showed how consistently the series conformed to business cycles, whether they led or lagged and by how much, what rate of change and pattern of movement they exhibited in successive cycles and on the average, and so on. From these measures one could trace the relationships among numerous economic processes during the periods of prosperity and depression that the data covered, examine what changes had occurred in these relationships, and develop a systematic, reasoned account of past business cycles.

By summarizing a portion of this information I was able to identify, among these relevant types of economic process, those that had shown highly consistent conformity to business cycles and dominant tendencies either to lead, coincide with, or lag behind the turns in the economy as a whole. I used statistical significance tests as a way of reducing the likelihood that a certain record had been achieved by chance. It became clear that there were systematic sequences in the movements of different economic variables, such as orders, production, employment, inventories, prices, interest rates, and so on, and that these sequences had persisted over many business cycles during the past half century or more. It was also clear that some changes had occurred in the way the economy worked, and that they had affected and doubtless would continue to affect the observed sequences. Many of the sequences and the changes in them could be readily explained or at least rationalized, but many were of a complex nature that defied simple explanation. The riddle of the business cycle had not been solved. As a result, although the persuasiveness of the explanation and the statistical evidence offered grounds for some confidence that the sequences would persist in the future, how much and exactly what would persist and what would disappear, and when, were the great unknowns.

The types of economic process identified and classified in this way and the particular time series selected to represent them are shown in Table 1. In virtually every instance several indicators were available to represent a given type of process. For example, for employment the most comprehensive available series was (and still is) total civilian employment, based upon data from the household survey. But estimates of nonfarm employment are also compiled from reports by establishments. They cover a much larger sample of employees and are documented by payroll records. Hence the latter series is generally superior in its performance as an economic indicator and was selected to represent the employment process.

Fifteen of the twenty-one series selected as indicators in 1950 are still carried in *Business Conditions Digest*. More or less close relatives of the remaining six series can also be found in *BCD*, as Table 1 shows. Because these series represent the same types of process and are readily available in a computer data bank I have used them in testing the subsequent performance of the 1950 list.

Table 2 summarizes the lead-lag performance at each business cycle peak and trough since 1948 of the groups of leading, coincident, and lagging indicators selected in 1950. The twenty-one series were classified in the three groups according to their performance prior to 1938. The leading group (eight series) shows a mean lead at each business cycle turn except the last trough (March 1975). The lagging group (five series) shows a mean lag at each turn except the initial trough (October 1949). The coincident group (eight series) shows some tendency to lead at peaks but is virtually coincident at troughs. Since several of the coincident series were used, along with others, to determine the business cycle peak and trough dates, it is not surprising that they should roughly coincide with these dates. But the *sequence* of the turns in the three groups is not determined by the business cycle dates, and the sequence is in the expected direction for all but one of the twelve dates, the one exception being the March 1975 trough, where the averages for the leading and the coincident groups coincide.

Table 2 also shows that the proportions of timing comparisons that are in the appropriate class in 1948–1975 are not very different from the proportions in the period prior to 1938. At peaks, for example, 89 percent of the timing comparisons in the leading group during 1948–1975 were leads, as compared with 80 percent for the same group prior to 1938. At troughs, the 1948–1975 percentage of

TABLE 1

THE 1950 LIST OF LEADING, COINCIDENT, AND LAGGING
INDICATORS AND THEIR CURRENT EQUIVALENTS

No.	Original Series in 1950 List	BCD No.	Corresponding Series Currently in Business Conditions Digest
	Leading group		
1.	Liabilities of business failures	14.	Same
2.	Dow-Jones index of industrial common stock prices	19.	Standard and Poor's index of 500 common stock prices
3.	New orders, durable goods, value	6.	Same
4.	Residential building contracts, floor space	29.	New building permits, private housing units, number
5.	Commercial and industrial building contracts, floor space	9.	Same
6.	Average workweek, manufacturing	1.	Same
7.	New incorporations, number	13.	Same
8.	Wholesale price index, 28 basic commodities	23.	Industrial materials price index, 13 commodities
	Roughly coincident group		
9.	Employment in nonagricultural establishments	41.	Same
10.	Unemployment	37.	Same
11.	Corporate profits after taxes	16.	Same
12.	Bank debits outside New York	56.	Manufacturing and trade sales, value
13.	Freight carloadings	49.	Value of goods output in 1972 dollars
14.	Industrial production index	47.	Same
15.	Gross national product, value	200.	Same
16.	Wholesale price index, industrial commodities	335.	Same
	Lagging group		
17.	Personal income, value	223.	Same
18.	Sales by retail stores, value	54.	Same
19.	Consumer installment debt, value	66.	Same
20.	Bank rates on business loans	67.	Same
21.	Manufacturers' inventories, book value	71.	Manufacturing and trade inventories, book value

TABLE 2

SUBSEQUENT PERFORMANCE OF THREE GROUPS OF INDICATORS
SELECTED AND CLASSIFIED IN 1950

| Business Cycle | | Average Lead (−) or Lag (+), in Months | | | | | |
| | | At peaks | | | At troughs | | |
Peak (1)	Trough (2)	Leading group (3)	Roughly coincident group (4)	Lagging group (5)	Leading group (6)	Roughly coincident group (7)	Lagging group (8)
November 1948	October 1949	−15	−3	+2	−6	−1	0
July 1953	May 1954	−13	−2	+2	−4	+1	+2
August 1957	April 1958	−21	−6	+2	−2	0	+2
April 1960	February 1961	−9	−4	+2	−1	+3	+4
December 1969	November 1970	−8	−5	+2	−2	0	+15
November 1973	March 1975	−6	+6	+11	0	0	+9
Average 1948–1975		−12	−2	+3	−2	+1	+4
Expected value, based on prior record (through 1938)		−6	0	+5	−5	−2	+3

Timing comparisons, 1948–1975
(number)

Leads	40	28	4	32	13	6
Rough coincidences	6	26	10	28	36	11
Lags	5	6	15	5	13	16
Total[a]	45	43	22	45	43	22
Percentage of timing comparisons in appropriate class, 1948–1975	89	60	68	71	84	73
Expected percentage, based on record to 1938	80	72	88	81	67	72

NOTE: The indicators were selected and classified into leading, roughly coincident, and lagging groups (eight series, eight series, and five series, respectively) in Geoffrey H. Moore, *Statistical Indicators of Cyclical Revivals and Recessions*, Occasional Paper 31 (New York: National Bureau of Economic Research, 1950). The prior performance of these indicators or substantially equivalent series during business cycles through 1938 is shown ibid., pp. 64-65. The record for 1948-1975 is based on the same or substantially equivalent series, all of which are shown currently in *Business Conditions Digest*, a monthly publication of the U.S. Department of Commerce (see Table 1).

[a] Total is the sum of the leads, *exact* coincidences (not shown), and lags. Rough coincidences include leads or lags of three months or less, as well as exact coincidences; hence the sum of the three classes exceeds the total.

SOURCE: National Bureau of Economic Research, January 1979.

leads was 71, compared with 81 percent for the pre-1938 period. For all three groups of series together, at both peaks and troughs, the percentage of timing comparisons that turned out to be in the appropriate class was almost exactly the same after 1948 (75 percent) as before 1938 (77 percent).

Another aspect of the record that is important to the user of indicators is the likelihood that the indicator will not register a turning point in the vicinity of the business cycle turn, or that it will register a turning point when no business cycle turn occurs. The record of the 1950 list of indicators with respect to the first of these contingencies is shown in Table 3.

The record, both before and after 1938, reflects the relative sensitivity of the series, with the leading series being most sensitive and hence skipping few cycles, while the lagging series are the least sensitive and skip more cycles. In the leading and coincident groups there was little change in performance between the two periods, but in the lagging group more than twice as large a percentage of turns were skipped in the recent period. One of the reasons is that business cycles have been milder in the period since 1948 than before. Another is that four of the five lagging series are expressed in current dollars, and inflation has pulled such series upward even during recessions.

For the second contingency, the problem of false signals, a similar record is more difficult to obtain. The term "false signal" is not easy to define, and the 1950 study did not contain this information. Later work has shown, however, that the leading indicators are more subject to extra cycles that do not match the business cycle chronology, while the lagging indicators, again reflecting their relative insensitivity, seldom exhibit extra cycles.[6] This difference continued to prevail after 1948, as the following materials demonstrate.

Figures 1–3 present another form of summary of the performance of the 1950 list of indicators during 1948–1975. Here the three groups of indicators are combined into indexes by the method the Department of Commerce currently uses to construct its leading, coincident, and lagging indexes.[7] The indexes move down during each recession, up

---

[6] Moore, *Business Cycle Indicators*, pp. 52-53.

[7] The most nearly comparable set of indexes for the pre-1938 period is in Julius Shiskin, *Signals of Recession and Recovery*, Occasional Paper 77 (New York: National Bureau of Economic Research, 1961), pp. 50, 54. The leading and coincident indexes cover 1919–1940, the lagging index 1929–1949. However, the components do not precisely match the 1950 list of indicators. Another compilation, covering the eight leading and eight roughly coincident series in the 1950 list, 1919–1954, is in the form of diffusion indexes (percent of series rising). See Moore, *Business Cycle Indicators*, pp. 270, 272.

TABLE 3

PERCENTAGE OF BUSINESS CYCLE TURNS SKIPPED: 1950 LIST OF INDICATORS

Business Cycle Peaks and Troughs	Leading Group (8 series)	Coincident Group (8 series)	Lagging Group (5 series)
Number covered			
Before 1938	200	100	39
1948–1975	96	96	60
Percentage skipped			
Before 1938	6	8	13
1948–1975	6	10	27

during each expansion. The sequences among their turning points, identified by the use of a computer program, are with rare exceptions in accordance with the patterns expected when the selection of indicators was made in 1950 (see Table 4).[8]

In addition to the six recessions identified in the charts, three periods when the indexes declined are not recognized as recessions, namely 1951–1952, 1962–1963, and 1966–1967. The usual sequences are observed at these turns also (except that the lagging index did not decline in 1951–1952 or 1962–1963). Each of these periods has been identified as a period of slowdown in a chronology of growth cycles, although some of the sensitive leading indicators experienced declines as large as those during the business cycle recessions (see the section following).

During a period as long as 1948–1975, some tendency for the "quality" of the indicators to deteriorate might be expected. Among particular indicators there have been many instances of such deterioration, or at least changes in behavior. Railroad freight carloadings, for example, have not kept up with the trend of the economy, partly because of the increasing share of freight hauled by trucks, partly because the production of goods has grown more slowly than services. Inner tube production, one of the indicators in the Mitchell-Burns list, used to be an interesting indicator because of its sensitivity to the new car market and the tire repair business. The advent of the tubeless tire has made the inner tube almost a collector's item, found

---

[8] The exceptions are at the December 1969 peak, where the coincident index has a longer lead than the leading index, and the November 1973 peak, where the coincident and lagging indexes lag by the same number of months.

FIGURE 1

COMPOSITE LEADING INDEX, EIGHT SERIES, 1950 LIST OF INDICATORS

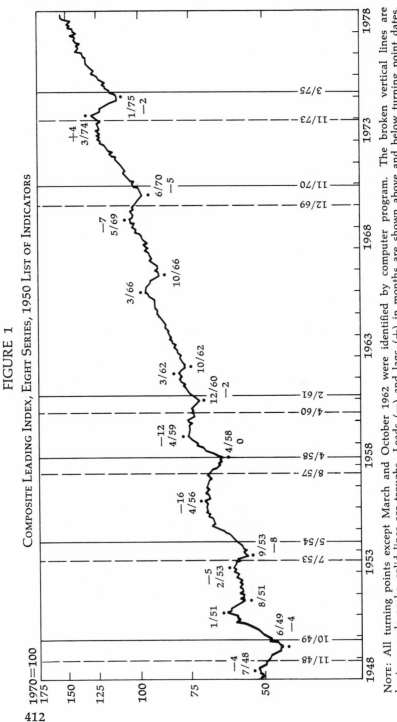

NOTE: All turning points except March and October 1962 were identified by computer program. The broken vertical lines are business cycle peaks, solid lines are troughs. Leads (−) and lags (+) in months are shown above and below turning point dates.

412

FIGURE 2

COMPOSITE COINCIDENT INDEX, EIGHT SERIES, 1950 LIST OF INDICATORS

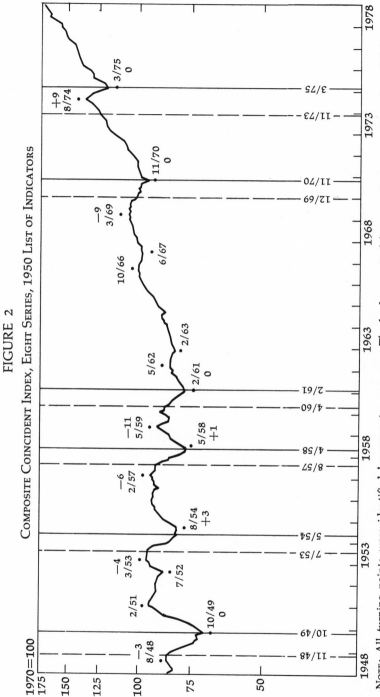

NOTE: All turning points were identified by computer program. The broken vertical lines are business cycle peaks, solid lines are troughs. Leads (—) and lags (+) in months are shown above and below turning point dates.

413

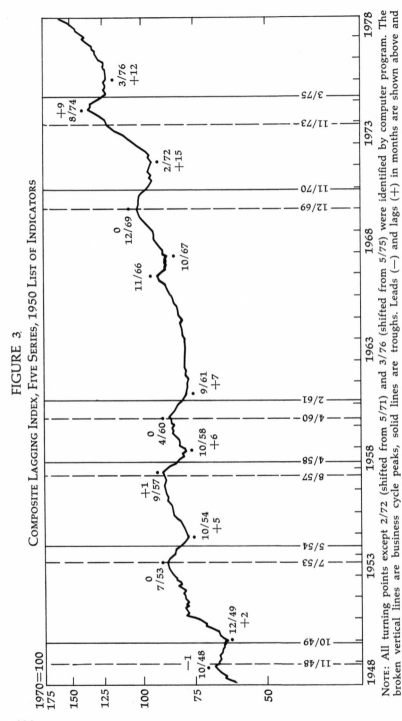

FIGURE 3

COMPOSITE LAGGING INDEX, FIVE SERIES, 1950 LIST OF INDICATORS

NOTE: All turning points except 2/72 (shifted from 5/71) and 3/76 (shifted from 5/75) were identified by computer program. The broken vertical lines are business cycle peaks, solid lines are troughs. Leads (−) and lags (+) in months are shown above and below turning point dates.

414

TABLE 4
LEADS AND LAGS AT BUSINESS CYCLE PEAKS AND TROUGHS: TWO SETS OF COMPOSITE INDEXES, 1948–1975

Lead (−) or Lag (+), in Months

Business Cycle		Indexes based on 1950 list						Indexes based on 1975 list					
		Leading		Coincident		Lagging		Leading		Coincident		Lagging	
Peak (1)	Trough (2)	P (3)	T (4)	P (5)	T (6)	P (7)	T (8)	P (9)	T (10)	P (11)	T (12)	P (13)	T (14)
November 1948	October 1949	−4	−4	−3	0	−1	+2	−10	−4	−1	0	+3	+5
July 1953	May 1954	−5	−8	−4	+3	0	+5	−4	−6	−2	+2	+2	+5
August 1957	April 1958	−16	0	−6	+1	+1	+6	−23	−3	−6	+2	+1	+4
April 1960	February 1961	−12	−2	−11	+1	0	+7	−11	−2	−3	0	+2	+9
December 1969	November 1970	−7	−5	−9	0	0	+15	−11	−8	−2	0	+2	+15
November 1973	March 1975	+4	−2	+9	0	+9	+12	−5	−1	0	0	**+10**	**+13**

(*Table 4 continues on the next page.*)

TABLE 4 (continued)

Lead (−) or Lag (+), in Months

Business Cycle		Indexes based on 1950 list						Indexes based on 1975 list					
		Leading		Coincident		Lagging		Leading		Coincident		Lagging	
Peak (1)	Trough (2)	P (3)	T (4)	P (5)	T (6)	P (7)	T (8)	P (9)	T (10)	P (11)	T (12)	P (13)	T (14)
Average		−7	−4	−4	+1	+2	+8	−11	−4	−2	0	+3	+8
Standard deviation		7	3	7	1	4	5	7	3	2	1	3	5
Peaks and troughs													
Average		−5		−2		+5		−7		−1		+6	
Standard deviation		5		5		5		6		2		5	
Correlation coefficient[a]		+0.80		+0.69		+0.95							

[a] With the corresponding leads and lags in cols. 9 to 14.

Sources: Cols. 1 to 8, National Bureau of Economic Research; cols. 9 to 14, *Business Conditions Digest*, various issues, p. 10.

mostly around swimming holes. There is a possibility, also, of selection bias and regression toward the mean. The top performers selected on the basis of a sample of information covering a certain period are not all likely to remain at the top in a second sample covering a different period. Some were at the top by chance in the first sample and are unlikely to remain there in the next. One can guard against this by making the first sample as large as possible, by applying significance tests in identifying the top performers, and by using other information that explains why they were at the top or supports the choice indirectly. These safeguards were employed in all the indicator studies, but the possibility of regression bias still remains, as well as deterioration because of economic change.

The lead-lag entries in Table 2 give some support to the hypothesis of deterioration. In particular, the average leads of the leading group of indicators have diminished at both peaks and troughs. But this is not decisive, for several reasons. One is that the corresponding entries in Table 4, columns 3 and 4, for the composite leading index based on the 1950 list, do not show as clear a trend. A stronger test, however, can be made by using the entries for the composite leading index based on the 1975 list, also in Table 4. Because the 1975 list was selected toward the end of the period, one would not expect a trend toward deterioration in these observations, and because they are correlated with the entries for the 1950 list (see the correlation coefficients in Table 4), they provide a means for allowing for some of the cycle-to-cycle variation in the leads and lags of the 1950 list. A simple way to do this is to subtract the entries in columns 9 and 10 from those in columns 3 and 4, which is equivalent to measuring the leads and lags of the 1950 list against the 1975 list. On this basis the entries in Table 4 give some support to the hypothesis of deterioration in the 1950 list, in terms of a trend toward shorter leads or longer lags than in its 1975 counterpart.[9] The entries in Table 2, adjusted in a similar manner, give stronger support.[10]

A further consideration with respect to deterioration is that the lags of the lagging group appear to have a tendency to lengthen,

---

[9] The correlation coefficient between time and the adjusted leads at peaks (col. 3 minus col. 9) is $+0.28$; at troughs (col. 4 minus col. 10), $+0.18$; and at peaks and troughs together, $+0.13$. Hence the trend accounts for a very small, statistically insignificant portion of the variation. Nevertheless, the coefficients have the expected positive sign.

[10] The correlation coefficients between time and the adjusted leads at peaks (Table 2, col. 3 minus Table 4, col. 9) is $+0.73$; at troughs, $+0.56$; at peaks and troughs together, $+0.64$.

especially at troughs. Coupled with the shortening leads of the leading group this means that the interval between the turns in the leaders and those in the laggers has not diminished. More generally, the sequences among the turns in the three groups of indicators do not reveal strong evidence of deterioration, although at troughs the intervals between the turns in the leading and the coincident groups may have shortened and those between the coincident and the lagging groups may have lengthened.

Table 5 summarizes the pre-1938 and post-1948 performance of each of the twenty-one indicators selected in 1950. About two-thirds of the series behaved in substantially the same way in the later period as in the earlier one. That is, the later information supports the earlier classification. Seven of the eight leading indicators are currently classified in *Business Conditions Digest* as leading at both peaks and troughs. The one exception, contracts for commercial and industrial building, is now considered leading at peaks and coincident at troughs. Corporate profits, in the coincident group in 1950, is now classified as a leading indicator. Even in the pre-1938 period, however, profits exhibited some tendency to lead by short intervals (note the average lead of two months at both peaks and troughs). Unemployment is no longer considered a coincident indicator because of its tendency to lead at peaks and lag at troughs. Personal income and retail sales, originally classified in the lagging group because they exhibited short lags in the pre-1938 period, have rarely done so since 1948. In addition, inflation has prevented these series from declining in some of the milder recent recessions. For the same reason, the wholesale price index for industrial commodities has not performed as a useful coincident indicator since 1960.

Additional Tests of the Indicator System

Clearly, the 1950 list and classification of indicators has continued to exhibit most of the properties it had when it was established. To users of this system of analysis this result will come as no surprise. As already noted, several reviews of this sort have been made, although none of them tested the 1950 list for the entire 1948–1975 period. Moreover, other kinds of tests have been made. One examines the behavior of the same data in other countries. Investigators in Canada, Japan, Italy, the United Kingdom, Australia, and New Zealand have done this, and within the past few years Philip Klein and I have compiled and analyzed comparable sets of indicators for six countries other than the United States. For this purpose we used

TABLE 5

PRE-1938 AND POST-1948 RECORD OF TWENTY-ONE INDICATORS SELECTED IN 1950

| | Mean Lead (−) or Lag (+), in Months | | | | Percentage of Timing Comparisons in Appropriate Class | | | |
| | At business cycle peaks | | At business cycle troughs | | At business cycle peaks | | At business cycle troughs | |
Series (1)	Through 1938 (2)	1948–1975 (3)	Through 1938 (4)	1948–1975 (5)	Through 1938 (6)	1948–1975 (7)	Through 1938 (8)	1948–1975 (9)
Leading group								
1. Liabilities of business failures	−10	−21	−8	−3	85	100	93	80
2. Common stock price index	−6	−9	−7	−5	80	100	80	100
3. New orders, durable goods	−7	−7	−5	−2	88	83	83	67
4. Residential building contracts	−6	−15	−4	−5	80	100	83	83
5. Commercial and industrial building contracts	−5	−10	−2	+1	80	60	67	20
6. Average workweek, manufacturing	−4	−11	−3	−2	75	100	60	67
7. New incorporations	−2	−14	−4	−5	71	100	79	100
8. Wholesale price index, basic commodities	−3	−10	−3	0	78	67	80	50
Average, eight series	−6	−12	−5	−2	80	89	81	71

(*Table 5 continues on the next page.*)

TABLE 5 (continued)

| No. (1) | Series (1) | Mean Lead (−) or Lag (+), in Months | | | | Percentage of Timing Comparisons in Appropriate Class | | | |
| | | At business cycle peaks | | At business cycle troughs | | At business cycle peaks | | At business cycle troughs | |
		Through 1938 (2)	1948–1975 (3)	Through 1938 (4)	1948–1975 (5)	Through 1938 (6)	1948–1975 (7)	Through 1938 (8)	1948–1975 (9)
	Roughly coincident group								
9.	Employment in nonfarm establishments	0	+1	−3	+1	58	67	58	100
10.	Unemployment	N.A.	−7	N.A.	+4	N.A.	33	N.A.	67
11.	Corporate profits after taxes	−2	−7	−2	−2	75	17	80	67
12.	Bank debits outside New York	+2	−1	−4	−1	69	67	60	83
13.	Freight carloadings	0	−1	−1	0	83	83	83	100
14.	Industrial production index	+1	−1	−2	0	100	50	83	100
15.	Gross national product	N.A.	−1	N.A.	−1	N.A.	100	N.A.	100
16.	Wholesale price index, industrial commodities	−4	−1	+4	+9	67	100	60	33
	Average, eight series	0	−2	−2	+1	72	60	67	84
	Lagging group								
17.	Personal income	+4	+1	0	−2	100	33	25	0
18.	Sales by retail stores	+4	−2	+2	−2	80	0	60	25
19.	Consumer installment debt	+5	+8	+4	+3	100	100	100	100

20. Bank rates on business loans	+6	+3	+5	+10	75	83	100	100
21. Manufacturers' inventories	+6	+5	+8	+4	100	100	100	100
Average, five series	+5	+3	+3	+4	88	68	72	73

N.A.: Not available. For series 10 and 15 no record of timing prior to 1938 is shown in the source; the selection of these series was based on other related series.

NOTE: See note to Table 2. The percentage of timing comparisons in appropriate class (cols. 6 to 9) means, for the leading group, the percentage that are leads; for the coincident group, the percentage that are rough coincidences (exact coincidences and leads or lags of three months or less); for the lagging group, the percentage that are lags.

SOURCE: National Bureau of Economic Research, January 1979.

the 1966 list rather than the 1950 list of indicators, but many of the same or similar series are in both lists.[11]

Another kind of test uses the same data but in a manner different from that originally contemplated. The use of the leading indicators to forecast the magnitude of change in economic activity is an example, since information on magnitude of change was not used in the 1950 study of indicators. I began carrying out one test of this sort during the recession of 1953–1954 and followed it up again in 1957–1958 and subsequent recessions. The idea was to compare the severity of the current recession shortly after it began with that of preceding recessions, using the initial changes in the leading and coincident indicators. The leading indicators generally gave earlier indications of the relative severity of the recession than the coincident indicators did.[12] Another test of this sort uses the changes in the leading indicators in a regression model to forecast subsequent changes in the coincident indicators. In these models the leading indicators have exhibited some ability to forecast the magnitude of change in GNP, industrial production, or foreign trade one or two quarters ahead.[13]

Yet another way to test the data is to compare the turning points in the lagging series with the opposite turns in the leading series. The logic of this comparison was recognized in the 1950 study (as well as in the Mitchell-Burns study that preceded it), but the information was not used in selecting the lagging or leading indicators. Briefly, the logic is that many of the lagging indicators represent costs of production (labor costs, interest rates) or factors bearing upon costs (inventories) and that their movements can have an inverse impact upon the leading indicators (new orders, housing starts, construction contracts). This potential inverse effect leads one to expect that upturns in the lagging indicators will precede downturns in the leading indicators, and downturns in the lagging indicators will precede upturns in the leading indicators. Moreover, if

---

[11] Geoffrey H. Moore, "The Current State of the International Business Cycle: A New Measurement System," in William Fellner, ed., *Contemporary Economic Problems 1978* (Washington, D.C.: American Enterprise Institute, 1978).

[12] Geoffrey H. Moore, "Economic Indicator Analysis during 1969–1972," in *Nations and Households in Economic Growth*, Paul David and Melvin Reder, eds. (New York: Academic Press, 1974); and Geoffrey H. Moore, "Slowdowns, Recessions and Inflation," *Explorations in Economic Research*, vol. 2, no. 2 (Spring 1975).

[13] Victor Zarnowitz and Beatrice Vaccara, "How Good Are the Leading Indicators?" *1977 Proceedings of the Business and Economic Statistics Section* (American Statistical Association, 1977); and Moore, "Current State of the International Business Cycle."

the connection is sufficiently close it should help account for the variation from cycle to cycle in the length of leads of the leading indicators.

Although the twenty-one indicators in the 1950 list were not specifically examined for this property at the time they were selected, the larger list of indicators studied at that time (seventy-five leading, twenty-nine coincident, and thirty lagging) did exhibit the relationship. Whether the subsequent behavior of the 1950 list conformed to the earlier behavior of this larger list can therefore be determined (see Table 6).[14] At all but two of the forty-one turning points since 1885 the upturns in the lagging indicators have preceded the downturns in the leading indicators, and the downturns in the lagging indicators have preceded the upturns in the leading indicators. The two exceptions occurred in 1904 and 1908, when the lagging group reached its peak in the same month that the leading group reached its trough. For nearly seventy years, in other words, there has been no exception to the rule.

Table 6 also shows that some of the leads in the inverted lagging series are exceptionally long, and in those instances a close connection with the leads in the leading series is not plausible. At the December 1969 business cycle peak, for example, the upturn in the lagging group that occurred ninety months before the peak could have little bearing on the downturn in the leading group that occurred nearly seven years later, ten months before the peak. Yet it is fair to say, on the basis of the entire record covering a ninety-year span, that these instances are exceptions, and that by and large the variability of the intervals between the opposite turns in the leading and lagging groups is not very different from that between the similar turns (see the note to Table 6). In this respect the record since 1948 resembles the record prior to 1938.

One factor that helps to account for the variability in the intervals just described is the influence of long-run growth or the occurrence of some extraneous event such as a war on the length of leads and lags. The upward trend in the economy affects both leading and lagging indicators and makes for long expansions and short contractions. When both the leading and lagging series are treated positively, the trend has a similar effect on both, tending to delay peaks and advance troughs. But when the lagging series are treated invertedly, the trend is inverted also. This tends to increase the intervals be-

---

[14] For additional references, see Geoffrey H. Moore, "When Lagging Indicators Lead: The History of an Idea," *NBER Reporter*, Winter 1978.

TABLE 6

CYCLICAL TIMING OF LEADING AND LAGGING INDICATORS, 1885–1975
(number of months)

Business Cycle Peak (1)	Lead(−) or Lag(+) at Business Cycle Peaks			Business Cycle Trough (5)	Lead(−) or Lag(+) at Business Cycle Troughs			Interval from			
	Median trough, lagging group (2)	Median peak, leading group (3)	Median peak, lagging group (4)		Median peak, lagging group (6)	Median trough, leading group (7)	Median trough, lagging group (8)	Trough, lagging, to peak, leading (9)	Peak, leading, to peak, lagging (10)	Peak, lagging, to trough, leading (11)	Trough, leading, to trough, lagging (12)
Mar. 1887	−20	−3	+6	May 1885	N.A.	−6	+2	N.A.	N.A.	N.A.	8
July 1890	−14	−5	+5	Apr. 1888	−7	−2	+13	17	9	5	15
Jan. 1893	−8	−5	+6	May 1891	−5	−4	+12	9	10	1	16
Dec. 1895	−14	−5	+5	June 1894	−11	−4	+4	3	11	7	8
June 1899	−6	−1	+10	June 1897	−13	−9	+18	9	10	4	27
Sep. 1902	−15	−4	+14	Dec. 1900	−8	−5	+6	5	11	3	11
May 1907	−27	−16	+6	Aug. 1904	−9	−9	+6	11	18	0	15
Jan. 1910	−11	−4	+7	June 1908	−6	−6	+8	11	22	0	14
Jan. 1913	−14	−3	+8	Jan. 1912	−17	−13	−2	7	11	4	11
Aug. 1918	−34	−20	+1	Dec. 1914	−14	−1	+10	11	11	13	11
Jan. 1920	−9	−2	+6	Apr. 1919	−7	−3	0	14	21	4	3
May 1923	−13	−4	+4	July 1921	−12	−5	+9	7	8	7	14
Oct. 1926	−24	−11	−1	July 1924	−10	−6	+3	9	8	4	9
June 1929	−15	−5	+2	Nov. 1927	−14	−4	+4	13	10	10	8
				Mar. 1933	−43	−5	0	10	7	38*	5

May 1937	−50	−2	+3	June 1938	−10	−4	+10	48*	5	6	14
Feb. 1945	N.A.	N.A.	N.A.	Oct. 1945	N.A.	N.A.	N.A.	N.A.	N.A.	N.A.	N.A.
Nov. 1948	N.A.	−11	+2	Oct. 1949	−9	−5	0	N.A.	13	4	5
July 1953	−45	−8	+3	May 1954	−7	−2	+1	37*	11	5	3
Aug. 1957	−38	−20	+2	Apr. 1958	−6	−1	+1	18	22	5	2
Apr. 1960	−23	−11	+2	Feb. 1961	−8	−2	+4	12	13	6	6
Dec. 1969	−90	−10	+2	Nov. 1970	−9	−2	+15	80*	12	7	17
Nov. 1973	−21	−8	+11	Mar. 1975	−5	0	+4	13	19	5	4
Average											
1885–1938	−18	−6	+5		−12	−5	+6	12	11	7	12
1948–1975	−43	−11	+4		−7	−2	+4	32	15	5	6
Standard deviation											
1885–1938	12	5	4		9	3	5	10	5	9	6
1948–1975	28	4	4		2	2	6	29	4	1	5

N.A.: Not available.

NOTE: If the four extreme items identified by asterisks (*) are excluded, the averages and standard deviations are:

	Column			
	(9)	(10)	(11)	(12)
Average				
1885–1938	10	11	5	12
1948–1975	14	15	5	6
Standard deviation				
1885–1938	4	5	4	6
1948–1975	3	4	1	5

SOURCES: 1885–1938: Geoffrey H. Moore, *Statistical Indicators of Cyclical Revivals and Recessions*, Occasional Paper 31 (New York: National Bureau of Economic Research, 1950), table 11, based on seventy-five leading and thirty lagging indicators. 1948–1975: Based on eight leading and five lagging indicators, 1950 list.

tween the troughs in the lagging series and the subsequent peaks in the leading series, and to reduce the intervals between peaks in the laggers and the subsequent troughs in the leaders. The effect is exaggerated whenever the trend has a dominant effect relative to the cyclical movement of the series.

By adjusting the series for the long-run trend this effect can be eliminated. In recent years this method of cyclical analysis has come to be known, here and abroad, as the growth cycle approach. The 1950 list of indicators can also be analyzed in this manner by trend-adjusting the composite indexes constructed from them. The trend-adjusted indexes (Figure 4) conform closely to the NBER chronology of growth cycles, and the timing sequences follow the expected pattern (Table 7).

The trend-adjusted coincident index based on the 1950 list displays the rare property of coinciding precisely at every one of the nine growth cycle troughs since 1949 (see col. 8). It deviates more from the peaks, especially in 1960, where the peak prior to the 1959 steel strike was higher than the peak that followed the strike, and in 1973, where the inclusion of aggregates expressed in current dollars, together with rapid inflation, delayed the peak in the composite index until August 1974. The trend-adjusted leading index led all but three of the growth cycle turns, and the lagging index lagged all but three. When the lagging index is treated invertedly, however, it leads at every turn, and by intervals that exceed the leads in the leading index at every turn but one. The variability of the leads in the inverted lagging index, as measured by the standard deviation, is no greater than the variability of the lags in the same index treated positively, or of the leads in the leading index. Moreover, the leads in the inverted lagging index are correlated with those in the leading index, supporting the hypothesis that rapid increases in the lagging indicators have deterrent effects on the leading indicators, while slow increases or declines have stimulating effects.

The behavior of the trend-adjusted indexes based on the 1975 list of indicators, which is also recorded in Table 7, supports the same inference. Indeed, the correlation just referred to is stronger in the leads based on the 1975 list. Furthermore, there is a high correlation between the timing observations based on the 1975 list and those based on the 1950 list. There is also little evidence of the possible deterioration in the timing behavior of the 1950 list when judged by comparison with the 1975 list, a matter that was explored above in terms of data unadjusted for long-term trends. The growth cycle performance of both sets of indexes is extraordinarily similar.

FIGURE 4

Three Trend-Adjusted Composite Indexes, 1950 List of Indicators

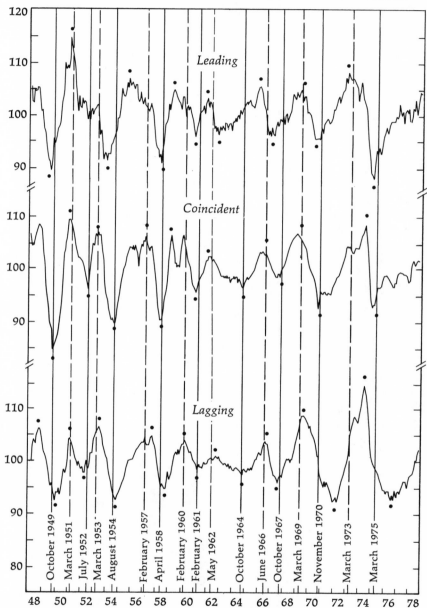

NOTE: The broken vertical lines are peaks and the solid lines are troughs in NBER growth cycle chronology

TABLE 7

Leads and Lags at Growth Cycle Peaks and Troughs, Two Sets of Trend-Adjusted Composite Indexes, 1948–1975

Lead (−) or Lag (+), in months

| Growth Cycle | | Indexes based on 1950 list | | | | | | | | Indexes based on 1975 list | | | | | | | |
Peak (1)	Trough (2)	Lagging inverted P (3)	T (4)	Leading P (5)	T (6)	Coincident P (7)	T (8)	Lagging P (9)	T (10)	Lagging inverted P (11)	T (12)	Leading P (13)	T (14)	Coincident P (15)	T (16)	Lagging P (17)	T (18)
July 1948	Oct. 1949	—[b]	−14	−6[a]	−4	+1	0	+1	+2	—[b]	−14	−6[a]	−4	−1	0	+1	+5
Mar. 1951	July 1952	−15	−17	−2	—[b]	−2	0	−1	−4	−12	—[b]	−7	−8	−2	0	—[b]	—[b]
Mar. 1953	Aug. 1954	−12	−14	—[b]	−8	+2	0	+3	+2	—[b]	−11	0	−7	0	0	+6	+8
Feb. 1957	Apr. 1958	−28	−7	−17	0	0	0	+7	+5	−22	−7	−17	−3	−14	+1	+7	+7
Feb. 1960	Feb. 1961	−17	−10	−10	−2	−9	0	+2	+2	−15	−8	−10	−2	−8	0	+4	+10
May 1962	Oct. 1964	−13	−24	−5	−24	−3	0	+5	+1	−5	—[b]	−3	−28	—[b]	—[b]	—[b]	—[b]
June 1966	Oct. 1967	−19	−13	−5	−10	0	0	+3	0	—[b]	−9	−3	−8	+4	−3	+7	0

Mar. 1969	−17	+2	0	+5	−17	−2	+7	+7						
Nov. 1970	−15	−2	0	+19	−13	0	0	+15						
Mar. 1973	−9	−1	+17	+17	−13	−1	+8	+18						
Mar. 1975	−7	0	0	+20	−6	−1	0	+21						
Mean	−16	−13	−6	+1	0	+5	−14	−10	−5	−7	−1	0	+7	+7	+9
Standard Deviation	6	5	6	8	7	0	5	8	6	3	5	8	7	1	5

NOTE: The 1950 list indexes were trend-adjusted by the phase-average method. The 1975 list indexes were trend-adjusted by eliminating the "target trend," 0.282 percent per month.

a Measured from highest value in available data, which begin in January 1948.

b No corresponding cyclical turn.

Changes in the Indicator System since 1950

Strictly speaking, only three of the twenty-one indicators selected by
the NBER in 1950 are among the twenty-two indicators selected by
the Commerce Department in 1975. They are the average workweek
in manufacturing, which is a leading indicator in both lists, and nonfarm employment and industrial production, which are coincident
indicators in both lists (see Table 8). Many of the remaining series
in the two lists, however, are substantially equivalent in terms of the
concept represented. Indeed, by the criterion of substantial equivalence, all of the leading indicators in the 1950 list are represented in
the 1975 list. In the coincident and lagging groups there is more
variation between the two lists.

The principal changes in the 1975 list are:

1. Most of the series in the 1975 list are in deflated form. Although there are occasions or purposes for which current dollar value
series are important, in times of rapid inflation it is useful to distinguish physical from nominal changes. This was not done systematically when the 1950 list was constructed.

2. The series on new orders and contracts for plant and equipment, constructed initially by Victor Zarnowitz,[15] is an improvement
over the two series in the 1950 list that overlap it in content: new
orders for durable goods and contracts for commercial and industrial
construction. The new series can be better matched conceptually with
plant and equipment investment expenditures. The idea for such a
series, however, was put forward in the report on indicators by
Mitchell and Burns in 1938.

3. The series on net business formation, which takes into account
both the formation of new firms and the discontinuance of existing
firms, improves upon the two series in the 1950 list that are related to
it: new incorporations and liabilities of business failures. The failure
series, however, possesses some value in its own right because of its
bearing on profits, which are not represented at all in the 1975 list
(see below).

4. Personal income and retail sales, both of which were used in
current value form in the 1950 list and classified as lagging indicators,
are deflated and otherwise modified in the 1975 list and classified as
coincident. Transfer payments such as social security and unemployment benefits are omitted from personal income in the 1975 series.
Since some types of transfer payments move in a countercyclical man-

---

[15] Victor Zarnowitz, *Orders, Production, and Investment: A Cyclical and Structural Analysis* (New York: National Bureau of Economic Research, 1973).

TABLE 8

Comparison of the 1950 and 1975 Lists of
Leading, Coincident, and Lagging Indicators

BCD No.	Original Series in 1950 List	BCD No.	Corresponding or New Series in 1975 List
	Leading group		
1.	Average workweek, manufacturing	1.	Same
	* * *	3.	Layoff rate, manufacturing
6.	New orders, durable goods, value	8.	New orders for consumer goods and materials, in 1972 dollars
	* * *	32.	Vendor performance
13.	New incorporations, number	12.	Net business formation
9.	Commercial and industrial building contracts, floor space	20.	Contracts and orders for plant and equipment, in 1972 dollars
N.A.	Residential building contracts, floor space	29.	New building permits, private housing units, number
	* * *	36.	Net change in inventories on hand and on order, in 1972 dollars.
N.A.	Wholesale price index, twenty-eight basic commodities	92.	Change in sensitive prices
N.A.	Dow-Jones index of industrial common stock prices	19.	Standard and Poor's index of 500 common stock prices
14.	Liabilities of business failures		* * *
	* * *	104.	Percent change in liquid assets
	* * *	105.	Money supply (M_1), in 1972 dollars
	Roughly coincident group		
41.	Employment in nonagricultural establishments	41.	Same
37.	Unemployment, number of persons		* * *
16.	Corporate profits after taxes		* * *
N.A.	Bank debits outside New York	57.	Manufacturing and trade sales, in 1972 dollars
47.	Industrial production index	47.	Same
200.	Gross national product		* * *

(Table 8 continues on the next page.)

431

TABLE 8 (continued)

BCD No.	Original Series in 1950 List	BCD No.	Corresponding or New Series in 1975 List
335.	Wholesale price index, industrial commodities		* * *
	* * *	51.	Personal income less transfer payments, in 1972 dollars
	Lagging group		
223.	Personal income, value		* * *
54.	Retail sales, value		* * *
66.	Consumer installment debt, value	95.	Ratio, consumer installment debt to personal income
	* * *	72.	Commercial and industrial loans outstanding
67.	Bank rates on business loans	109.	Prime rate charged by banks
N.A.	Manufacturers' inventories, book value	70.	Manufacturing and trade inventories, in 1972 dollars
	* * *	91.	Average duration of unemployment
	* * *	62.	Labor cost per unit of output, manufacturing

N.A.: Not available.

ner and the total has been growing rapidly, personal income exclusive of transfer payments has wider cyclical movements and closer conformity to the business cycle. This treatment, of course, does not mean that the broader concept of income is not useful, or indeed more relevant in analyzing income-consumption relationships. Retail sales are combined with manufacturers' and wholesalers' sales in a comprehensive series on the physical volume of trade in the 1975 list. This aggregate had not been constructed in 1950, although the series on bank debits was often used to represent the total volume of trade.

5. The 1975 list contains only monthly series, whereas the 1950 list included three quarterly series: corporate profits, gross national product, and bank rates on business loans (the bank rate series became available monthly only in 1977). The omission of quarterly series is both an advantage and a disadvantage. As a component of a monthly composite index, a quarterly series must be interpolated to be included, and as a rule the figures will not be as up to date as the monthly series. Hence the index will be subject to revision when the quarterly

figures become available, and in any case the interpolation is an arbitrary procedure. On the other hand, the exclusion of quarterly series may mean the omission of a significant economic variable. Probably the most serious omission in the 1975 list is profits. GNP is partly represented by other series in the coincident group, and bank rates are reflected in the prime rate, which is the monthly series included in the 1975 list.

6. No series on inventory change was included in the 1950 list of leading indicators, whereas the 1975 list includes the change in inventories on hand and on order. In view of the importance of inventory change as a factor in business cycles, this is clearly a major improvement. Of note, also, is the inclusion of the change in the volume of goods on order, following the work of Ruth Mack and others.[16] From the buyer's point of view, outstanding orders must be considered part of the available inventory and subject to close control through the placement or cancellation of orders. Another series in the 1975 list that adds to the information on ease or tightness of market conditions is vendor performance, an indicator pertinent to the speed with which orders are being filled.

7. The 1975 list contains two series on the volume of means of payment: the money supply expressed in constant prices and the rate of change in liquid assets. Concepts of this sort have long had a place in business cycle theory, and interest in them has broadened since 1950. The deflated money supply (M_1) has fallen victim to obsolescence since 1975, however, as ways of economizing on the use of money have had substantial effects on its behavior. Hence the inclusion of this indicator in the 1975 list has been a mixed blessing, and in 1979 it was replaced by a broader concept of money, M_2.

In addition to the improvements in the list of indicators available to analysts during the past quarter century, many new devices to aid the analyst have been developed. Seasonal adjustment is now routinely accomplished, thanks largely to the development by Julius Shiskin of a computer program for this purpose. Shiskin was also responsible for the development of the composite index as a method of summarizing the behavior of a group of indicators that are homogeneous with respect to cyclical behavior but heterogeneous with respect to unit of measurement.[17] Charlotte Boschan was largely responsible for devising computer programs that identify cyclical peaks and

---

[16] Ruth P. Mack, *Information, Expectations, and Inventory Fluctuation: A Study of Materials Stock on Hand and on Order* (New York: National Bureau of Economic Research, 1967).

[17] Shiskin, *Signals of Recession and Recovery.*

troughs in time series, that construct patterns of change in time series during successive periods of recession or of recovery, and that measure long-run trends and growth cycles.[18] These aids to analysis have been of enormous value in providing prompt, relevant, comparable, and readily understood measures of economic performance. Without these aids the various publications that present current information on the state of the business cycle, such as *Business Conditions Digest* in the United States, *Japanese Economic Indicators* in Japan, and *Economic Trends* in the United Kingdom, would be far less instructive than they are.

Future Developments in Indicator Analysis

Public attention to economic indicators and their analysis in the United States as well as in other countries is widespread and growing. Part of the credit for this belongs to the government publications just mentioned, as well as to the news columns, magazine articles, TV coverage, and numerous private reports on the business outlook. Part belongs to the improvements in the quality, relevance, coverage, and timeliness of statistics pertaining to the economy. Credit must also be given to the continuing research effort devoted to the analysis of economic indicators. Without such research any system of indicators would soon become obsolete and fall into disrepute.

But the fundamental fact, which both justifies and sustains the public attention to economic indicator analysis, is the continuity in the cyclical behavior and interrelationships of economic variables. We can learn and have learned from the past. The business cycle experience of the United States before World War II has proved a useful guide to business cycles since then. It is this historical continuity that underlies the basic and persistent consistency in the behavior of a set of indicators during the twenty-five years since they were selected. No one could be certain of this behavior in 1950. Only by looking back is it easy to see both the continuity and the significant changes.

Today we can no more foresee the future of economic indicator analysis than we could in 1950. We can, however, confidently predict that it will be useful to keep abreast of changes in economic behavior and to keep devising and testing new methods of analysis. Research along these lines has paid good dividends in the past and probably will do so in the future. As new ideas and new findings are generated

---

[18] Gerhard Bry and Charlotte Boschan, *Cyclical Analysis of Time Series: Selected Procedures and Computer Programs* (New York: National Bureau of Economic Research, 1971).

by research, they can be applied to the current scene, spurring interest and broadening understanding.

Two relatively recent developments suggest some directions that this research might take. One is the application of indicators on a global scale. Researchers in many countries are pursuing active research programs that apply the techniques of indicator analysis to data for their own country. Application to the analysis of foreign trade flows is in its infancy, but the infant shows promise. Application to the analysis of the external markets of the developing nations, as well as to internal aspects of their economies, is also in its infancy, but the infant is alive and well. Two international agencies, the Organization for Economic Cooperation and Development in Paris and the European Economic Community in Brussels, are starting to develop expertise in indicator analysis, and this may encourage a wider research effort among their member countries.

The second recent development is the application of indicator analysis to the subject of inflation. Swings in the rate of inflation have not attracted the sustained attention of researchers to the same extent that business cycles have. The interest has been more episodic, associated with periods of wartime inflation, hyperinflation, crisis, and panic. Perhaps the present period of inflation is merely another episode, but even if it proves to be such, the application of indicator analysis to the process of inflation will add to public understanding of it.

Chronologies of the rate of inflation, constructed for different countries by methods similar to those used in constructing business cycle chronologies, have much to teach about where and when inflation is subsiding or accelerating. One of the lessons, for example, is that none of the major industrial countries of the West has experienced a decline in its rate of inflation without also undergoing, at about the same time, a slowdown or recession in real economic growth. Studies of the types of prices, costs, or other factors that are most sensitive to or influential in the process of inflation may yield leading indicators of inflation analogous to the leading indicators of business cycles. One of the more obvious bits of evidence attesting to the need for a wider appreciation of such inflation indicators is simply this: the record of economic forecasts of inflation reveals a distinct lag in the forecasts relative to the actual rate of inflation.[19] In part, at least, this lag may be attributable to the fact that forecasters have concen-

---

[19] Geoffrey H. Moore, "Lessons of the 1973-1976 Recession and Recovery," in William Fellner, ed., *Contemporary Economic Problems 1977* (Washington, D.C.: American Enterprise Institute, 1977).

trated too much of their attention upon variables, such as capacity utilization rates, that do not have a good record in leading or anticipating the rate of inflation. There seems to be no inherent reason why price forecasts should be more susceptible to lags than, say, output forecasts. Yet, they have been. The construction of a system of inflation indicators, similar to the system that already exists for output, may help to improve the record of inflation forecasts.

Extension of the indicator approach on a global scale and its extension to the problem of inflation are but two of the directions requiring research effort. Many other problems, small and large, demand attention. A fully "deflated" set of indicators has not been developed; a satisfactory monthly price/cost ratio is needed; a comprehensive monthly series on credit extensions is not available; measures of the money supply have been suffering from obsolescence; and so on. New methods of seasonal adjustment requiring less revision when additional data become available must be tested. "Index models" and "stage of process models" that combine the indicator and econometric approaches may make both more fruitful. If these and other researches prosper, there may be less resemblance between the indicator system forty years hence and the present system than there is between the present system and the one devised when Mitchell and Burns began their work forty-two years ago.